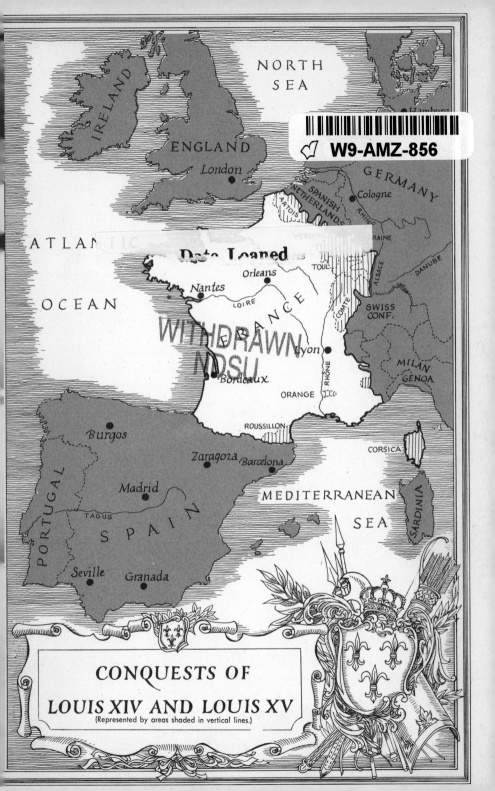

IRELAND

ENGLAND
London

NORTH
SEA

Hamburg

GERMANY
Cologne

SPANISH NETHERLANDS
ARTOIS
RHINE
LORRAINE
VERDUN
TOUL
Paris
ALSACE
COMTE

ATLANTIC

OCEAN

Nantes
Orleans
LOIRE
FRANCE
Bordeaux
Lyon
ORANGE
RHONE
ROUSSILLON

DANUBE

SWISS
CONF.

MILAN
GENOA

CORSICA

Burgos
Zaragoza
Barcelona
Madrid
PORTUGAL
TAGUS
SPAIN
Seville
Granada

MEDITERRANEAN

SEA

SARDINIA

CONQUESTS OF
LOUIS XIV AND LOUIS XV
(Represented by areas shaded in vertical lines.)

THE PILGRIMAGE OF WESTERN MAN

By the same author

MAZZINI

STRINGFELLOW BARR

THE PILGRIMAGE
OF
WESTERN MAN

Harcourt, Brace and Company

NEW YORK

D
16.8
B315

*To the memory of my father and mother
who taught me to love the great tradition
which every generation must learn and change*

AUTHOR'S NOTE
AND ACKNOWLEDGMENTS

EVERY generation is compelled by its own experience to ask itself new questions about what preceding generations have done and suffered, and to answer those questions by rewriting history. Our generation has undergone two world wars, which have shaken civilization to its base. Now a third world war threatens to shatter what is left. By early 1939 it tardily dawned on me that the system of sovereign nation-states was dead but not yet buried. It had taken a ghastly World War, an unstable peace, and the obvious approach of World War Two to teach me that no existing government could any longer hope to protect adequately the lives and property of its citizens, much less guarantee them a reasonable degree of justice or freedom. That fact caused me to think through again my understanding of European history, and to ask of history those questions which it seemed to me timely for my generation to ask.

The answers I thought I heard are this book. If I am accused of distorting "the facts of history" to propagandize for world government, I invite my reader to entertain an equally plausible hypothesis: that thirty years of historical study caused me to see modern history as I have tried to tell it in this book; and that seeing it that way, I wrote this book. I invite the reader to consider also a more general proposition: that from every intelligible narrative of past events there emerges, either implicit or explicit, a program of action for the future. For Man remembers and reflects.

This book was begun in the Library of Harvard University, in 1936, and continued at intervals in the libraries of Dartmouth College, the University of Chicago, New York University (both at University Heights and Washington Square), and the University Club of New York. To the Librarians of those institutions and to the members of their staffs I owe warm thanks for their hospitable courtesy and their expert help.

For help of various kinds I owe thanks also to Gladys Baldwin Barr, Stephen Benedict, Scott Buchanan, Lambert Davis, and Robert Giroux; and to others too numerous to list here. I owe especial thanks to Joseph Reither, who in 1936 helped me plan this book, particularly the earlier chapters. All of these persons gave me valuable advice. If I did not always follow it, that fact may now exonerate them from any responsibility for the defects the final draft exhibits. Finally, the generosity of Marshall Field III, and the co-operation of the Educational Fund of Chicago, secured me the leisure to complete my task.

STRINGFELLOW BARR

February, 1949
New York City

CONTENTS

PROLOGUE

IF the generation that lived in the relative peace and golden prosperity of the period between 1870 and 1914 had looked backward across six centuries, over the weary way, the bloody path, which Western Man had trod, it might have noted the extraordinary succession of visions that had guided his pilgrimage. There had been that early vision of the City of God, a vision first reported by St. Augustine almost fifteen centuries before, a vision of a Christian Society, a "Pilgrim City," moving through a pagan world as the children of Israel moved through the desert toward a Promised Land that would indeed be home. St. Thomas Aquinas had philosophized about that City; the Gothic cathedral had shown it forth in "visible speech"; its greatest poet, Dante, had observed its stragglers in purgatory and its enemies in hell, and had ascended into heaven to seek the source of its hope, of its faith, and its charity. But the Middle Ages waned, the hope and faith weakened, the Dance of Death haunted men's minds, and the Pilgrim City lost heart.

Then, almost suddenly, the humanists and scientists and artists of the Renaissance showed men the glory of this world; its merchants showed them its luxury, its discoverers led them to El Dorado, with both sword and cross held high. Its Reformers denounced the corruption of the Church and urged them to look inward for God's guidance. Imperceptibly, and with no intent to deny Augustine's vision, men discovered their own enormous powers — above all, their power of reason, which seemed able to conquer mysterious Nature herself, by understanding her immutable laws. They discovered the power of monarchy and Roman law, which could impose peace on the City, a peace that seemed to bring plenty in its train. They agreed with Francis Bacon that by systematically studying Nature, Man might "in some part" recapture Eden, where by his fall he had lost "his dominion over creation."

He might at least build a City of Man. Should he not do so? Had not reason been given him by God? Were not the laws of Nature, the laws of Newton's mechanical universe, laid down by God Himself? The extraordinary success of that Baconian step brought material prizes that had been unimaginable; brought a sense of pride beyond what Western Man had ever felt; and, in the fullness of time, brought the Machine. And although the Machine threatened at first to wreck the City of Man, it also promised abundance for all mankind. Meanwhile, monarchy had outlived man's need for protection against a turbulent nobility, and repressed rather than released man's growing energies. Monarchy was overthrown. It was overthrown because it seemed against reason and against Nature. And a new vision of the City of Man appeared, a vision of a free and humane City, governing itself by its own will and its own common sense, a City in which men would be equal sons of God, if indeed there was a God; a City, certainly, in which men would be brothers and would co-operate to their mutual advantage, whatever their particular views about God might be. As the City of God faded slowly and became blurred in outline, the brave new City of Man grew in brilliance; and men exchanged a fading memory for a burning hope. Or, stated in more traditional terms, there seemed at last a fair chance of making God's kingdom come, of His will being done, on earth as it is in heaven. Bacon had won the argument: Knowledge was indeed Power. From Robert Owen's cornucopia, the new Machine, poured the goods man needed or desired. And Science promised to increase them. Men turned to the Machine.

Its moral authority secure, the Machine whirred on; and had shortly constructed a world community. Or at least a world market, a world economy, that made mankind one neighborhood. But that neighborhood contained scores of sovereign, armed nation-states and profound antagonisms, fears, and hates: the fear and hatred each armed nation inspired in its neighbor; the hatred of a propertyless class for those who owned the Machine and profited by it, of exploited colored colonials for their white European masters. And in 1914, in the heart of Europe, now lifted by Science into a comfortable, prosperous, middle-class heaven, hell itself broke loose. The homeland of the first civilization that ever dominated the whole world was suddenly plunged into the inferno of World War One.

When that paroxysm of violence had passed, the nation-states struggled to recapture their lost economic paradise. But the armed nation-states were still there, grouped now in a League, but sovereign still; mass unemployment remained, and clogged the very Machine itself; no common government had been agreed on; at last, a tyrant-state tried by force of arms to impose order, and World War Two devastated Europe.

The men of Europe staggered to their feet, recognized that, for weal or woe, they now dwelt in a world which the Machine had made one neighborhood; " united " their separate armed states in a second league of sovereign governments; and began at last to speak of a common federal government for mankind. The task was terrifyingly difficult. But what was the alternative? World War Three? With jet planes at supersonic speeds? With atomic bombs and bacterial weapons? It was now Armistice Two, and the United States and the Soviet Union were proceeding with the greatest armament race in history.

This is the story told in the following pages. It is a true story, but it is only one of many true stories that could be told of the Pilgrimage of Western Man, of his long and painful odyssey, of his search for unity, for freedom, and for justice under law. The reason for telling this story rather than one of the others is simply that always, in his pilgrimage, he must review his acts and memories, if he would find his bearings in the strange new countryside; if he would know in the face of new perils and new challenges which of his memories are most relevant and revealing; if he would continue his pilgrimage with faith, with high heart, and with deepened understanding. " In my beginning is my end."

THE PILGRIMAGE OF WESTERN MAN

I.

THE CITY OF GOD

By the year 1500 Western civilization was already adapting or trying to scrap its medieval heritage, and it is not easy to make sense
of the world of Columbus, of Martin Luther, of Erasmus unless we
grasp the force and form of the European tradition which had come
down to them. Now it happens that in the thirteenth century that
tradition was understood and expressed with such remarkable clarity that many historians have characterized the thirteenth century by
the term, "the medieval synthesis." What do they mean? And did
such a synthesis, or pervasive ordering of human activities, ever take
place?

If it did, the term still involves a paradox that has led to endless
wrangling. On the one hand, our thirteenth-century European ancestors appear to have been far more certain than we are that they
knew what life was about. They exhibited a sense of direction that is
strangely unfamiliar to our modern temper, and their sense of direction is reflected in the ideas that they discussed and in the art forms
they created. On the other hand, their lives were full of war, famine,
disease, poverty, filth, discomfort, violence, oppression. Those historians who look at their art — and fortunately much of it remains to be
looked at — are struck by its unearthly atmosphere of beauty, of se-
renity, of inward spiritual order and force. The others examine the

3

political, economic, or military history of the period, and report to us that the thirteenth century is nothing we need feel homesick for. This apparent contradiction between the world that medieval man felt in his soul and the world he lived in can be understood if we realize that medieval man was in some ways more realistic than we are. He was not the reformer that modern man is, and he assumed that things like poverty, disease, crime, and war cannot be eliminated from life here on earth. But he considered human existence as a very imperfect copy of a divine order toward which it is man's duty, and man's highest privilege as a man, to aspire. This ideal world appeared to him more real than the mad whirl of luck and accident in which he passed his daily life. Therefore he found his satisfactions within himself more largely than modern man does, and he put up with a physical environment that now strikes the modern as unbearable.

The basis of this inner vision by which medieval man lived, and which enabled him to find earthly existence tolerable and even to create here things of imperishable beauty, was the Christian faith of his ancestors, which was taught him by the Catholic, or universal, Church. The doctrine of that Church commanded man to love God with his whole soul and his whole mind, and to love his neighbor as himself. It taught man that the only permanent happiness, either in this life or after it, was in serving God and in doing his duty to his neighbor; and it held that his duty to his neighbor could be defined only in terms of his duty to God.

How such a doctrine applied in detail to this confused human world was the special business of the Church, which had been founded for the purpose of preaching Christ's message to men. But the Church tried to achieve this purpose not only through words but through a system of ritualistic and symbolic ceremonies, which it claimed it had received from Christ. It was through these holy rites, the seven sacraments, that the Christian received grace to live the difficult life his religion held up before him as a constant goal. These sacraments were fitted to every major crisis in the individual's life. He was born into the world, as animals are born. But he was born into the Church through Baptism, and was thereby made a child of God. He reached an age at which he could use his powers of reason, and he was confirmed and strengthened in his determination to live a Christian life, by the rite of Confirmation. Throughout his life, he participated in the rite of the Holy Eucharist, or Holy Communion, at which he received the body and blood of Jesus Christ through the mystery of the commemorative bread and wine. Being human, he would continually fall short of the Christian goal: the sacrament of Penance was offered him. To accept it, he must examine his conscience, feel contrition that he had sinned, resolve to sin no more, confess to a priest of the Church what his sins were, and do " penance " — that is, perform some disciplinary task, named by his confessor. When he grew up and came to marry, his marriage was hallowed and made permanent by the Church. Or, if he chose to forego home and family in order to enter the Church's service, through the sacrament of Holy Orders he received from a bishop of the Church the power and grace to perform his sacred duties. And at last, when he came to die, a priest of the Church with holy oil administered Extreme Unction. All of these sacraments were commonly performed by priests or bishops of the Church, and some of them could be performed only by them. It was essential therefore that the Church enroll a numerous body of officials to minister to mankind. Moreover, since the Church's labors covered Western and Central Europe, and since extensive gifts from the faithful had made it Europe's principal landholder, the wise administration of this wealth, in the interest of the poor, the sick, and the helpless, called for an administrative organization. Finally, since even among Church officials some men had deeper understanding of religious truths than others, it was essential that there be officers and subordinates in the ecclesiastical administration. And indeed, an elaborate army of officials developed, from the Bishop of Rome who was Pope and head of the Church on earth, down to the parish priest.

In addition to the sacraments, the inhabitant of Christendom was daily reminded of his membership in that spiritual body, by sacramentals — that is, holy customs of the Church. When he was in danger, he was likely to make the sign of the cross. As he entered his church, he might cross himself with water that had been blessed. And within, candles, palms, ashes, images of the saints, and the crucifix were his constant reminders of man's dependence on God. He was taught to pray, to ask blessing on his food before he ate, and on every side art and custom united to insist that man is something more than an unusually intelligent animal. For was he not the in-habitant of what St. Augustine long before had called the " City of God," the communion of all those who lived, with no matter how many human lapses into sin, according to God's will rather than according to man's natural inclination? It was the Church's task to hold constantly before the inhabitants of the City of God the divine will and purpose, to bridge the awful gap between the vision of the City of God and the actual, wretched conditions of human existence. And it succeeded at least to this extent — that medieval institutions, whether economic, political, or social, reflect to an amazing degree the principles of Christian doctrine.

According to this doctrine, economic activity is never more than a subordinate function of society. The first concern of a Christian society is the increase of spiritual grace in its members. And though man must eat to live, while still on this earth, his economic habits and arrangements should conform to his final purpose. Agriculture was considered the most praiseworthy of economic activities. In-dustry, while less necessary in its specialized form than agriculture, was nevertheless justified. Commerce, on the other hand, was looked on with doubt and disfavor. For the exchange of goods is rarely as necessary as the production of food and the making of clothes and shelter. And most exchange of goods is carried on by men who seek profit rather than the mere satisfaction of our material necessities. Actually, the earlier Middle Ages had tended to confirm this reason-ing through experience. Christendom had then lived on the basis of subsistence agriculture; industry tended to be carried on by the peasants of each separate estate, for use and not for profit; and ex-change, or trade, was a rare phenomenon. But by the thirteenth cen-tury agriculture, industry, and commerce were all recognized as as-pects of economic activity.

Even by the thirteenth century Europe was by modern standards an almost townless countryside. The overwhelming proportion of its population lived on manorial estates. The labor of farming the estate was carried on by serfs — peasants legally bound never to leave the estate, but also legally entitled never to be discharged or sent off. Farming methods were crude, farm tools were crude, the cattle were not scientifically bred for quality but were poor and runty, and in constant danger from wolves. The peasant lived in a wattled cottage, with straw-thatched roof, without windows, and with a hole in the roof for chimney. In the wet weather his earth floor was slimy. In addition to trying to support himself under such conditions, he was legally obliged to work from one to three days each week for the lord of the estate, and frequently to pay him in farm produce for the use of the manorial mill or the common baking oven, or even the village well. He was in constant danger from some marauding nobleman, warring against the peasant's lord. Even after the rise of towns in the eleventh and twelfth centuries, the estate did not produce much surplus. Since highways were incredibly bad, and trade feeble, crop failure was likely to spell stark famine.

Yet for a hardy, industrious peasant, life on this earth was not wholly grim. Unlike the slave (and there were sometimes slaves on the estate), he could not be sold or driven from his land. And he had lots of company. For he was a member of a community much more powerful than we moderns can readily imagine. He lived where his father and grandfather had lived before him. His world was small, but it was intense, and it was shared. He and his neighbors usually shared a common pasture, a common woodland, a common meadow, and a common wasteland. Though they worked hard, they enjoyed more holidays than the modern worker. In addition to Sundays, there might be as many as forty church holidays a year. Then the peasant could dance, sing the ballads his parents had taught him, and play games. Or he might go to one of the local fairs, where much of the trade was carried on. Or perhaps wandering conjurers or acrobats or mountebanks with trained bears arrived, and there would be a performance at the manor house or even in the village church! There are no statistics by which this peasant's joys and sorrows may be measured today, but since he was taught not to overvalue earthly existence, and since his experience in a world of almost unchanging custom prevented his thinking constantly of ways to improve his personal lot, and since above all there were people of his own kind around him bearing the same burdens he bore, it would take a bold modern to assume that the typical peasant was an unhappy or discontented man.

Nor should we be surprised that the Church should have accepted so willingly such " labor conditions " as these. Actually, the Church establishments, monasteries, abbeys, and the like, had serfs of their own, and the human beings who ruled them would not likely be critical of the system that made their property valuable, and useful to society as a whole. Moreover, it would have been hard to see what else in medieval society a serf would have been good for, except being a serf. Finally, the Church was by its own doctrines more interested in teaching the nobles to care properly for their serfs, and in protecting them from aggression, than in changing the social function of any individual.

But turn away from the estate, and the human life on it, to the towns which, now by the thirteenth century, have developed a new and special kind of human pattern. As the serf is the labor basis of the manorial estate, so is the artisan the basis of the town. This artisan may himself have been a serf once. Perhaps he was freed by his lord, as a special boon for faithful service rendered. Perhaps he was discontented and ran away to town, where by a law widely in use he could not be recaptured after he had been a townsman for a year and a day. If he found work here, he most likely found it in a " craft guild," one of the groups into which medieval industry was early organized. He will not feel lost, as so many country people do on coming to a great modern city with its impersonal freedom. Where before he belonged to the manorial village, now he works for the master of a guild. His guild has special religious rites, and a strong sense of comradeship. Tanners, weavers, drapers, fullers, vintners, goldsmiths, butchers, all are organized in their respective guilds. The guild has strict regulations, made necessary by the conceptions of medieval economics. It is composed of masters, each a trained worker in his own particular industry. The masters take under their protection a certain number of boys as apprentices, or learners, who are boarded and lodged but not paid. After the masters have taught them the complicated technique of the industry, the apprentices are promoted to be journeymen, and may work for wages. If they become sufficiently expert, they may hope to be accepted as masters in the guild. This careful schooling makes for good work, and for pride in good work. The guild regulates such matters as hours, wages, conditions of labor, and standards of craftsmanship.

By doing these things the craft guild has solved for the townsman the problem, so important to medieval Christendom, " Who is my neighbor? " The proper obligations of neighborliness, responsibility to one's fellow-craftsmen and to the consumer, have been recognized. The guild has grown up beside the manorial village, a new type of neighborhood, a miniature of the City of God.

Even before the craft guild of the industrial worker had been developed, the trade guilds of the merchants were dominating the towns. Frequently the merchant guild bought freedom from the lord on whose estate the town had grown up. Sometimes the merchant guild fought for that freedom. In either case, it was likely to form a " commune," which it governed, with or without the aid of the craft guilds. It looked out for the joint interests of its members, tried to keep open the channels of trade, guaranteed the food supply of the town, and the supply of raw materials. As commerce grew, it was apparent that trade was redefining the functions that agriculture and industry were to discharge. With the development of currencies, the lord of the manor, and the peasants too, found a readier market for surplus produce and were able to buy with the receipts things they could not produce on the manor. Meanwhile, industry, having migrated from the manor to the craft guild of the town, gained a larger market.

It was universally assumed that in commerce every article had a " just price " that could be estimated. The craft guild faced a moral obligation to see that that price was maintained. The article should fetch the cost of the raw materials that went into processing it, plus the cost of the processing. The processing cost was estimated by awarding to the workman a wage that would keep him according to the accepted standard of living for his class. In other words, the worker in a craft guild had a right to a living. If he earned more, he was gouging somebody.

This rule was pretty easily applied to the problem of the craft guild; but the merchant was a more complicated phenomenon than the craftsman. According to medieval thinking he was really less necessary. Still, even a relatively self-subsistent manor needed some things from other places, which it could get only from merchants: iron perhaps, for farm tools, a millstone, salt, and spices as food preservatives, not to mention a few innocent luxuries like pepper and silk for the lord. What should the merchant charge?

The clearest answer that the Middle Ages could give was that he might accept a moderate gain, provided his purpose was to make a living and not to get rich. But obviously the just price was harder to estimate in the case of a merchant trading over large areas than in the case of the cobbler at his bench. The theory of the just price was an application of absolute justice to the actual fact of monopoly. But even the greatest thinkers admitted the difficulty, in practice, of stating the just price for the merchant.

The entire economic system of the Middle Ages was conceived of as merely supplying the animal basis for the Christian life. For, as St. Thomas Aquinas observed, man inclines, in addition to following animal appetites, " to know the truth about God and to live in communities." Medieval man, whether in manorial village, guild, or commune, thought of himself as a member of a community united to all other members by a common faith. But since man is imperfect, and since injustice menaces every human community, some political system was imperative. In the Middle Ages this system was feudalism. Under it, a ruling class, the nobility, lived on the labor of the serf. The " body politic," like the human body, had various parts to serve various functions. There were the priests who ministered, the nobles who ruled, and the serfs whose labor supported the whole. The control of the land, the administration of justice, the making of law, and the protection of the people were all in the same hands. The nobles, wrote John Wyclif, were supposed " to defend God's law by power of the world." The manor was held — rather than owned outright — from a superior lord, who in turn held land from another lord, and so on in theory to the Emperor. He who held land owed his lord part of the produce, military aid in war, and attendance at the lord's court. By the thirteenth century, the Church had softened and rationalized the brutal fact of a warrior caste living on the labor of a servile population. It attempted, by the " Truce of God," to " close " certain days of the week and certain seasons of the year to the private warfare the nobles enjoyed waging against each other. It had stated the responsibilities of the nobility to the community: to furnish good law and good government and not to oppress the people unjustly. It had tried to give a religious character to the whole feudal system by intervening in the initiation of knights, and by insisting that a knight must love God, be steadfast in faith, uphold the Church, be true to his liege lord and his word, and protect and succor the weak and oppressed. The ideal of knightly behavior which the Middle Ages held up to the noble as his obligation was exemplified in the romances of King Arthur and his Round Table. In short, the noble had great power, but Church and community sentiment demanded of him a high standard of performance.

Inside the towns, the structure of society was changing, as commerce multiplied wealth and comfort, and as individuals achieved promotion in the different grades of the guilds. But beyond the town walls, out in the open countryside, the old social cleavages remained. There was an almost mystical distinction between gentle blood and servile blood. And indeed the difference must have been superficially apparent. For generations the peasant had been bred for toil. For generations the noble had been bred for fighting and commanding. A different costume, different habits, a different set of special virtues appropriate to a special function in society, fixed a great gulf. The gulf was conceived as having been set by God. And cut off from noble and serf alike, by costume, occupation, and sacred vows, was still another type: the priest.

> God hath shapen lives three;
> Boor and knight and priest they be.

The modern is inclined to wonder why the serf population put up with such hardships. But the serf was not eager to take over the government of Europe any more than a well-disciplined child is eager to take charge of his family's household. He looked for guidance to his lord. He doubtless hoped his lord would be just, but his lord was not answerable to his serfs for injustice, but to God Almighty. The serf was answerable to the same God for his faithfulness to the lord. If he failed in his responsibilities to his lord and his fellow-serfs, it was possible to force him to leave the manor and to become a wanderer, a man without a lord, which in that dangerous and hard-riding society might easily mean capture by slave-traders. No, his task as he saw it, was to render faithful service. Given this fixed and mutual relationship, there were immense possibilities of kindness and of devotion. It was possible for a medieval lord to mention in his will, a serf " and his whole litter," as one would mention an animal and its young; but how deep must have been the attachment between many a lord and his "people"!

From this brief glimpse into the medieval world, it is possible to make certain judgments. Its people were intricately classified according to the community function their particular class discharged. All activities were pointed up to man's duty to God and his duty to his neighbor. The Church kept him in communion with God. The noble supplied government and defense. The serf produced food for all. The artisan supplied Christendom's simple needs for industrial goods. The merchant carried on the exchange of commodities from place to place. But we should not expect the human institutions of that world, whether manor, craft guild, or merchant guild, to reflect the will of God or to mirror the order of heaven except with the distortions produced by human vice and human weakness. If we are not yet convinced that this order was at least what medieval man consistently aspired to, we should turn to his intellectual statement of the purpose of life. Obviously, the ideal unity of Christendom can be more clearly expressed in writing than in the harsh practical arrangements of politics and economics.

Fortunately for us, medieval man made some remarkably clear intellectual statements of his faith in God and in the purpose of human life. These statements were made under the auspices of the Church. For not only did the Church pray for the noble, the serf, and the artisan; it thought for them as well. Not only were hospitals, hostels, asylums, and almshouses the business of the Church; so also were libraries, schools, and universities. The university assumed, along with the rest of society, that all things were God's. Theology, the study of God, was therefore the "queen of the sciences." All other subjects needed to be related to it if conclusions about them were to be valid.

This ordering of man's chief interests in relation to his duty to God was undertaken by more than one medieval professor, or "schoolman"; and the so-called scholastic philosophy, attempting to harmonize what has been revealed to us through God's Word and what we can know through human reason, often took the form of great "summaries" or *summas*. A *summa* was not supposed to serve the purpose of a modern encyclopedia, to give all the "facts."

It was concerned with placing in their proper order the basic principles of human life. If successful, it furnished, not information, but a better understanding of human existence. Of all the *summas* of medieval times, perhaps the most famous today was the *Summa Theologica* of St. Thomas Aquinas. He also wrote a *Summa Contra Gentiles* to answer the objections which Jews, Mohammedans, and other unbelievers were making to Christian doctrine. It undertook to show that though that doctrine included revealed truths which human reason alone could not have discovered, yet there was no conflict between these truths and those which reason did discover. And holding that the objections of unbelievers to Christian doctrine sprang not from any conflict between doctrine and reason, but from faulty reasoning, St. Thomas attempted to answer their objections reasonably.

In the *Summa Theologica,* St. Thomas inevitably has to discuss political and economic institutions, since these are important expressions of man's duty to his fellows. St. Thomas has been accused by moderns of working out a defense for the brutal injustices and inequalities of medieval society. But those who accuse him quite misunderstand his purpose. What he was concerned with doing was to say how medieval institutions could be judged, to define their ideal functions. He was well aware that these institutions, being operated by human beings, discharged their respective functions imperfectly. Unlike most moderns, he was not romantic enough to assume that you could reform society and get human institutions that would be perfect.

The amazing thing about this *Summa* is not that it was well done, but that it should have been attempted at all. To St. Thomas and to his generation it seemed both desirable and possible to state coherently all the essential principles a man needed in order to understand his world and in order to understand the nature of another and a more important world so far as God had revealed it to men. If we would understand our thirteenth century, we must recognize this confidence that in the light of theology the basic principles of all human experience can be brought into order. In the light of that confidence, St. Thomas could discuss the angels as well as economic problems here on earth, man's happiness, the human will, and the passions of love and hate. And the sublimity of his style is inherent in his declaration that " they are called wise who put things in their right order."

In the English translation, the *Summa Theologica* runs to twenty-one volumes. It is not widely read today. On the one hand, its principles are not those of most moderns; on the other, its reasoning is too close and compact for them to follow. But the thirteenth century, happily, has left us another testimonial of its extraordinary sense of the unity of life, which speaks to more people than St. Thomas now can, and which speaks, not in Latin as he did, but in stone and glass. This second testimonial is, of course, the medieval cathedral.

Our civilization has not produced a greater miracle than the Gothic cathedral. As the solution of a problem in engineering, it is as ingenious, as natural, and as homemade, as the feudal system was in the field of politics. In France, where it first arose, and whence it spread to England, Spain, Germany, and Northern Italy, the master masons faced difficult fact. The Romanesque churches, which they had inherited from an earlier time, were built with heavy walls and domed roof. The windows could not be large, and the thickness of the walls they were set in diminished the light they brought through. This was not so bad in the sunny glare of South European towns; in Northern France, where dull, gray skies are so often the rule, bigger windows must be devised. The masons met the problem by making the roof of the cathedral an intricate system of pointed arches, resting on columns. Once the wall was no longer needed to support the roof, but was used only to shut out the out-of-doors, large windows could be safely introduced, with brilliant stained glass for the light to filter through. The effect inside was indescribably brilliant: the forest of slender stone columns branching like trees and meeting in arches overhead (at Cologne there were more than a hundred columns); the blazing blues and greens and reds of the stained glass, in which the artist had told some Bible story or pictured the lives of the saints and martyrs. But since the exterior columns of those that support the roof are not joined by arches to other columns in eight different directions — as all the interior columns are — they will tend to buckle outward. Particularly at the four corners of the cathedral, the thrust of vaulted masonry becomes a problem. The master masons thereupon adopted a solution that was completely naïve, that should have been ugly, and that is actually one of the cathedral's greatest glories. They threw great stone buttresses against the walls outside, to keep their church from caving in. The final result vaguely suggests a great ship with oars, presumably being rowed to heaven; and the buttresses are handled with such sure taste that they greatly add to the meaning of the structure.

But the cathedral had to do more than house the faithful. It was built around the central fact of the Holy Eucharist, the miracle the priest performed, the miracle through which the consecrated bread and wine were changed into the body and blood of Jesus Christ. Every art that man practiced was therefore recruited to perfect the cathedral and to glorify God. Every legitimate activity of man, arranged in its proper relation to other activities — as, indeed, in the *Summas* of St. Thomas — ought to be treated here by the artist. The cathedral must be an open book, to tell Christ's message of hope to that overwhelming part of the community that could not read real books. It should be filled with sermons in stone. It should be adorned with sculpture — " visible speech," as the poet Dante called it.

So the clergy called in the artists. But they did not call them in " to express themselves," as a modern would say. They gave the artists explicit directions as to the theological truths that were to be embodied in sculptured stone, in stained glass, in carven wood. An elaborate and intricate order of symbols was worked out, and it was within this stringent discipline that the artist created beauty, that beauty which St. Augustine had defined as " the splendor of order " and St. Thomas Aquinas as " that which, being known, gives joy." This artist would probably have been drawn to his art originally by natural gift. But he had had to add, along with the shoemaker and the weaver, a long apprenticeship, years of careful instruction in the " customs " of the guild, under the personal direction of a master. And he had had to create something himself of sufficient beauty to earn him the title of " master " from his peers.

The sculptor might work out a complicated Biblical allegory in stone. The painter might be charged to do an altarpiece. The copyist and the illuminator worked to make books worthy of use in the divine service. The musicians set to appropriate music the words of the Mass. Magnificent costumes were designed, for the use of the clergy participating in the dramatic ritual. Occasionally, religious plays were given in the cathedral, and the first beginnings of modern drama were worked out. In the exuberance of this magnificent unison of praise to Almighty God, the artist was not prevented from creating in stone or other medium grotesque or humorous fantasies like the famous gargoyles and chimeras of Notre Dame in Paris. For these humorous, satirical comments are part of human life, and in the cathedral all human life is to be offered up to God.

Just as the idea of propping a church up from the outside should have produced an ugly church, but did not, so the combination of all these moods in one building — contemplation, aspiration, tranquillity, gaiety, mischievous satire — should have produced confusion, but it did not. For the relations of all the parts to the whole are so exquisitely ordered, the rows of ecclesiastics according to rank, of angels according to their orders, the constant reiteration of powerful traditions in the arrangement of certain holy personages — all this served to create a style and a form so powerful that the minor vagaries of the artist merely increase one's awareness of the splendor of order, which is beauty.

Even in St. Thomas Aquinas' day, not many were expected to understand his *Summas*. The medieval man never assumed that all men were equal in understanding. But for those whose understanding must be guided through the forms which art alone can create, there was this powerful language of stone, speaking of Christendom, uniting its millions of voices in praise of God; of the nine orders of angels praising His Holy Name; and even — for the Middle Ages were not squeamish about such things — the damned crying out their eternal remorse in Hell. Nowhere so clearly or so movingly as in the cathedral did medieval man state his belief in the ultimate unity of all Christendom, of all classes, of all nations, in a social pattern revealed to Christians by God. And from the squalor, the plague, the famine, from the perpetual tragedy of all human life, he turned to the cathedral to renew his faith in the ultimate purpose of human life.

II.

THE CITY OF GOD
IS BREACHED

THE weak spot in the medieval synthesis would naturally be found at the point of maximum change. This point was commerce. We have already observed that the feudal order of medieval Christendom had a certain fixity in its institutions, and in its social relationships. Socially, men belonged either to the First Estate, or clergy, responsible for the religious and intellectual life of the community; or they belonged to the Second Estate, the nobility, and were responsible for political direction and military security; or they belonged to the Third Estate, which was responsible for the economic subsistence of all. This nice division of mutual responsibility between all Christians was the institutional reflection of the same vision that produced the great *Summas* of St. Thomas, in the intellectual sphere, and that created the Gothic cathedral in the artistic. But, with the growth of towns, and of commerce, dislocation threatened the whole pattern. The task of the merchant, considered in relation to society as a whole, was to distribute the goods of serf and craftsman alike. But the merchant was also importing goods from the Orient which were greatly in demand and for which, therefore,

the European customer would pay fat prices. Fat prices meant fat
profits, and immediately the merchant collided with the medieval
theory of the just price, a price fixed by labor value and not by what
the traffic would bear.

Here again we may get light from St. Thomas. According to him,
the merchant might lawfully charge more for an article than he had
paid for it, either because he had improved it, or because of a change
in price due to place or time, or because of danger incurred in trans-
ferring the article from place to place. But in general the Church
distrusted the motives of the merchant. Instead of earning a living
through furnishing society with the economic service of distribution,
the merchant always risked forgetting his social function and turning to money-making as an end in itself. Church writers continued
to wrestle with the subject of profit. Moreover, questions of commercial morality were handled in Church courts, along with certain
other types of cases touching wills and marriages which were later
taken over by the "lay" courts of the state. Again, when monasteries
undertook to sell industrial products which the monks had made, a
special officer was appointed to supervise this business, and his methods were carefully watched, in order that the idea of the just price
should prevail, and not the modern idea of maximum profit.

The Church's distrust of the merchant appeared justified in the
sequel. For, as the merchant began in the course of business to acquire sums of money, and as money was still scarce and much in
demand, other people began offering to pay him for the use of it,
as they were already paying Jews. Such "usury"—the word still
covered the taking of any interest on loans—the Church flatly condemned, and so did Christendom at large. It was good to produce
food by toil in the fields. It was reasonable to devote all one's time
and one's special aptitudes to a handicraft, counting on a reward for
one's labor that would buy food which others had grown. It was
risky to earn a living by merely exchanging goods for profit, for
this "satisfies the greed for gain which knows no limit and tends to
infinity." But the most fatal occupation of all for a Christian, and
the least neighborly, was to exact money from others simply for the
use of money. And although, as commerce and finance grew in the
fourteenth and fifteenth centuries, the Church gradually modified
its position in detail, the man who made money by the manipula-

tion of money was never satisfactorily fitted in with the picture men had formed of the City of God.

The Church had developed its theories of economic morality in a period when neither commerce nor money had much importance. Most loans were made to people in distress: they were "consumption" loans. Europe was not yet familiar with loans to capitalize production and thereby to increase the sum total of wealth. Churchmen and laymen alike inclined therefore to view the charging of interest, or "usury," as merely exacting toll from the misery or misfortune of one's neighbor. Even today many men would shrink from asking interest on a loan to an intimate friend. The manor comprised an intimacy of human relationships it would be hard to duplicate today. It is easy to see why medieval man felt that the taking of interest on money was an antisocial act, a loathsome act for any member of the Christian community, and therefore one properly relegated to Jews, who were not members of that community.

Again, Christians had for centuries made gifts of land to the Church, and the Church was consequently Europe's greatest landholder. The officials of the Church, being human, reacted to money wealth as any heavily vested interest would react. They had every reason to fear that the influence the Church exerted for the good, in an agricultural society, would rapidly diminish under the competition of another influence, the influence of money power.

The position the Church adopted was not a satisfactory one. While continuing to object to the new merchant-princes and usurers of the towns, the Church itself tended more and more to make use of the money economy for its own ends. In the old days many of its monasteries had been agricultural colonies opening up new lands; and these monasteries, to secure the means of carrying on their good works, marketed their surplus products. Sometimes they engaged in handicrafts — in wood, leather, textiles, or metal — and these they sold also. And then, finding themselves with surplus money on their hands, they did precisely what the merchant would do later: they turned to banking. As handlers of mortgages and loans, they were indeed Europe's earliest banking houses. The Cistercians, for example, were the chief traders, shipowners, and moneylenders of Scotland in the twelfth and thirteenth centuries. Toward the end of the thirteenth century, these same Cistercians, this time in Flanders, converted their great estates into capitalistic enterprises and fed the new towns. Serfdom being decadent, they let their lands to share-croppers.

Meanwhile, the Papacy, the central government of the entire Church, became the greatest banker in Christendom, with Lombards and men of Cahors for its fiscal agents. These agents, "the Pope's merchants," as they were called, not always of too high a character, undertook to squeeze out of the people new Church taxes, in an effort to replace the gifts the Church had received in earlier and less worldly days.

The First Estate, or clergy, then, distrusted the new merchant and banking class, even while becoming entangled in the money economy which the merchant and the banker best knew how to manipulate. But the nobility also had many reasons to dislike the moneyed townsman, or "burgher." In the first place, where the clergy gave intellectual reasons for considering money-making dangerous, the noble despised gain as unworthy. The noble had never shrunk from force, from the display of physical courage under danger, but the patient scheming of the merchant was a game he had little chance of understanding. Moreover, though in theory his was a Second Estate, ranking below that of the clergy, in the things of this world it was his to command. How could he "defend God's law by power of the world" if usurers were to hold more power than he?

Yet the noble, accustomed to the best, was finding that the new "best" was more expensive than the old. The old best could be required of his peasants; the new came from the East and must be bought from the merchant. The merchant, incidentally, was normally sprung of servile blood. What could be simpler and more justifiable for the noble than to fall on this insolent new class of commoners and take his share? Traditionally, the noble was responsible for the maintenance of highways adjacent to his estate. Traditionally, he might secure help toward maintenance by imposing tolls on those who used the highway — pilgrims, for instance, or messengers, or merchants. It was a short step from there to becoming a highway robber, seizing for his own use a share of whatever came past his castle. It might involve artificially detouring traffic, and even stretching ropes across rivers, to create toll obstacles, but it was worth it.

The merchant, in order to defend himself from these feudal nobles turned robber, lent financial aid to the king; for what the merchant needed, if he were to do business, was the "King's Peace," which forbade private wars between nobles. The king was thereby freed from depending on his nobles for an army. He now hired an army of mercenaries, of professional soldiers; and medieval warfare became less a dangerous sport for nobles, like hunting, and more a business, the business of kings. Under the old feudal system, before money taxes became important, a king went to war by calling on his dukes for the military aid they owed him in return for the land they held from him. By the same token, the dukes would call on the barons, the barons on the knights. When the whole "levy" was assembled, the attack might begin. But each fighter was responsible to his *immediate* superior, not to the king. And if a duke concluded that his king was fighting an unjust war, and that he the duke was therefore morally freed from following him any longer, he might pass the word down the line through count, baron, and knight — and a whole division of the king's army would withdraw. If, on the other hand, the opposing king had been able to raise money from the trading population of his towns, and had entered this war with an army of hired soldiers, he would enjoy a decisive advantage. His mercenaries would not go home while the wages held out, whether the war was just or unjust, pleasing to God or unpleasing. War as a sporting duel in which God would arm the just side with greater courage became at this point somewhat meaningless. The king had ruined the sport of nobles by hiring "ringers." Small wonder that the coalition between the king and his merchant towns angered and frightened the noble. Small wonder that he resented the King's Peace. In so far as the king had taken over the military defense of society, the noble was more and more robbed of his function, of his meaning, and therefore of the respect of other classes.

Struggling to maintain his standing, at least in physical things, in a rising money economy with a rising standard of living, the noble only too often oppressed the peasant and tried to squeeze new taxes out of him. And the serf replied with such frightful uprisings in the fourteenth century as the Jacquerie in France and the Peasants' Revolt in England. The feudal relationship was giving way before the rise of absolute monarchs. Disapproved of by the Church and hated by the jealous nobility, the merchant nevertheless went on piling up profits, lending his money for interest, and accumulating a revolutionary new form of power, capital. He took his place alongside the Jew as the scapegoat of Christendom. For like the Jew before him, he was performing an economic function which Europe in a confused sort of way desired to have performed. And it is an ironical fact that one of the most definite results of forbidding usury was to force up the rate of interest. Apparently the merchant felt that if he were going to hell for accepting interest, he might as well go comfortably.

It is true that his social function satisfied "the greed for gain which knows no limit and tends to infinity." But it should be said for the merchant that he was facing uncharted seas, both literally and figuratively. He was finding that the price offered in a given market often bore little relation to labor-value but was derived from unpredictable shifts in public taste. Besides, could he base his prices on labor-value unless other merchants did the same thing? Also, since his occupation was a hazardous one, and since his losses, from shipwreck, pirates, robber-barons, and bad transportation generally, were considerable, he required a backlog of capital, equivalent to the backlog of grain a manorial village might store in its barns against famine. But money backlogs can be loaned out more readily than grain backlogs, and it seemed a pity to waste opportunities that were literally golden. Meanwhile, with the comforts and luxuries he brought in, he taught Europe how to lay up treasures on earth, and steadily weaned the European away from his old dream of the City of God and invited him to the pleasures and excitements of the City of Man.

In the towns of Italy and the Netherlands the merchant was creating little islands of a new type of civilization, a civilization in which hard common sense was replacing mystical intuition, in which education was beginning to escape Church control, in which the joys of life hereafter paled before the immediate joys of this world. The merchant continued, of course, to practice Christianity, but his feeling against the Church often grew strong. And in his guilds he organized mutual-benefit societies which took over some of the traditional functions of the Church, like the care of the sick and the poor.

Luxury, commerce, profits, and interest entered the agrarian City of God largely through the Italian city-states. Ironically, they entered the City when the City used military force on those outside its walls — the Moslems. In the "Dark Ages," when the culture of Western Christendom was still in embryo, when agriculture was on a subsistence basis and when commerce was practically nonexistent, Western Christendom had had little intercourse with the Orthodox world to the east or the Moslem world to the south. But in the twelfth and thirteenth centuries the West had launched a series of extraordinary military crusades into the Near East, for the purpose of rescuing Christ's sepulcher from the Moslem infidels. Although the Crusades failed to secure Christ's tomb more than temporarily, they did weaken Moslem power in the eastern Mediterranean and acquaint the crusaders of feudal Europe with the luxuries and comforts of a more sophisticated civilization than their own. During the period of the Crusades a group of towns in Italy were able to develop increasing commerce with the Near East — the Levant. Genoa traded with Constantinople and along the shores of the Black Sea. Venice played an even greater role in the trade of the eastern Mediterranean, its coasts and islands. From the Levant Venetian merchants brought back products which Moslem middlemen secured from India, the East Indies, China, and even Japan. They brought the spices which the Western European had learned to crave, partly to make a monotonous diet more interesting, and partly to help him swallow meat which, given the lack of refrigeration, needed spices to disguise its true condition. Pepper was wanted in vast quantities, cinnamon, ginger, nutmegs, cloves, all-spice. Moreover, kings and barons, back from the Crusades, were eager to buy diamonds, rubies, and pearls like those they had admired on the persons of their late enemies, the Moslems. The Italian merchants had brought back also camphor and cubeb for medical use; musk, cane sugar, indigo, sandalwood, aloewood, alum. They brought back the luxurious household furnishings of the Levant: porcelain, glass, rugs, tapestries, metalwork. They brought the silk and satin which both the nobility and wealthy town merchants were beginning to use in costume. And back to the Levant they carried such simple, and for the most part unprocessed, goods as arsenic, antimony, quicksilver, tin, copper, lead, coral, and woolen cloth from the Netherlands.

Of all the towns that grew and waxed fat on this new Eastern commerce, Venice was perhaps the most brilliant example. Strategically located at the head of the Adriatic, Venice became the natural middleman between Northern Europe and the Levant. While England, France, and Germany were still governed by a feudal nobility, the Venetian had become probably the most perfect commercial type in Europe. He participated in the Crusades by transporting feudal armies to the East — and the price he charged was the cession of a Venetian Quarter in the Moslem cities which the crusaders conquered. He was not even above deflecting one of the crusades to conquer the Christian city of Zara, which competed with the Venetian commerce. His long acquaintance with the Moslem East gave him the easy tolerance of the trader and a skepticism about everything except cash. His intercourse with Constantinople had given him St. Mark's Cathedral, a fine example of Byzantine architecture.

To protect her commerce, Venice developed a powerful navy and gradually built an imposing commercial empire. She acquired the Dalmatian coast and control of the Adriatic. She acquired commercial rights in Sidon, Tyre, Acre, and other cities of the Levant. As her share of the Fourth Crusade, she took, not the Holy Sepulcher, but the islands in the Aegean. And in 1380 she overthrew her chief rival, Genoa. With a population of some 800,000 she was the most imposing and the most " modern " city in Christendom. Her merchants had adopted a republican form of government, dominated by wealthy men. Her political institutions were designed to make of her a huge joint-stock company to exploit the East, a company whose directors were few, rich, but politically wise. Her diplomacy was the most renowned in Europe. For her military protection and the better to feed her population, she had conquered a considerable area of mainland at her back. The landed nobility had been absorbed into her republican government, helped to direct Venetian politics, served Venetian interests as diplomats, engaged in overseas commerce, and fought in the Venetian army and navy.

On the sea the Venetian Republic had placed six fleets of merchant ships, built by the city and let to the highest bidder. One fleet plied to the Black Sea, a second to Greece and Constantinople, a third to the wealthy ports of Syria, a fourth to Egypt to pick up goods from the Orient, a fifth to the North African coast. The sixth fleet habitually sailed past Gibraltar, touched at Lisbon, and pushed on to Eng-

land and to Flanders, to distribute Eastern goods and to collect commodities for the East. Throughout the Mediterranean empire of
Venice, her consuls stood ready to aid her merchants, to protect her
diplomatic interests, and to refit her ships. For the enterprising Republic had standardized the ships it constructed in order that each
consul might keep in stock spare parts for replacement. Christian
ships were also constructed for quick conversion to fighting craft if
war broke out.

Although Venice was, in the late Middle Ages, Christendom's
most perfect example of a society built by merchants less for the
glory of God than for the pursuit of gold, Venice by no means stood
alone. The Republic of Genoa, the Republic of Florence, and the
Republic of Milan were similar commercial communities. Sometimes
these Italian republics, dominating the surrounding countryside like
the city-states of ancient Greece, were ruled by an oppressive oligarchy of rich merchants and bankers. Sometimes the oligarchy
would be overthrown by one of their own number, acting in the
name of the oppressed, and the government would become a tyranny. But whatever outer form the government might take, no political arrangement could survive in these rich city-states unless it
was built on money and unless it fostered the making of money.
While the feudal nobility of France were still engaging in private
wars that resembled glorified duels and that were concerned with
such chivalrous concepts as honor and fidelity — along with pillage
and plunder — the city-states of Italy were coolly conducting commercial wars and were hiring professional soldiers for the purpose.

The Italian city-state did business with a group of cities in the
Netherlands: Ghent, Bruges, Antwerp, Brussels, Liége, Utrecht,
Delft, and Rotterdam. Here the dominant economic activity was the
manufacture and sale of cloth. Beyond the Netherlands lay another
group of powerful trading cities: Lübeck, Hamburg, Bremen, Dan-
zig, Königsberg, and farther south, Cologne. These cities had early
organized a naval league, for mutual protection, known as the
Hansa. The power of the Hanseatic League came to rest largely on
the herring fisheries of the Baltic, for herring was one of the principal food staples of medieval Europe. But by 1500 the Hansa's power
had declined.

Something has already been said of the way in which the kings of

Christendom combined forces with the new merchant class and overthrew the great nobles who contested their political power. By 1500 this process had been followed with particular success in the cases of England, France, Spain, and Portugal. Other kings had followed the pattern, but rarely with such success. The King of Scotland was still checked by a powerful feudal nobility. The King of Denmark had consolidated a monarchy that ruled over both Denmark and Norway. But efforts to construct powerful centralized monarchies in Central and Eastern Europe had been largely frustrated.

If Christendom had ever realized perfectly the political ideal of the feudal system, every king in Western Europe would have owed allegiance to the head of the " Holy Roman Empire," that ghost of ancient Rome which Charlemagne had raised, and which by 1500 had continued to exist with ups and downs for seven hundred years. Actually, the monarchs of England, France, Spain, and Portugal continued to assert their independence. Even within the German-speaking countries of Central Europe and the states of Northern Italy the Emperor exerted very limited real authority. By 1500, the Holy Roman Empire consisted of a heterogeneous collection of some three hundred states practically restricted to " the Germanies." In the fifteenth century, European kings were making themselves independent of their Emperor, yet they were at the same time subjecting more completely to their wills their own feudal nobility. They did it by supporting, and taxing, the merchant.

This natural community of interest between king and merchant will explain why Charles VII of France was able to secure from Jacques Cœur, the merchant prince of Montpellier, money advances with which to recover Normandy, Gascony, and Guienne from the English. It will explain why Louis XI selected his counsellors largely from the merchant class. Everywhere the king was concerned with raising money. Henry III of England fostered the sale of wine from the royal vineyards in Gascony, and in the next century the Black Prince was profiting from tin and was shipping salt fish for sale at Bordeaux. Merchants were making loans to the crown in return for trading privileges and mining concessions. Kings were mortgaging their domain lands, pledging their future revenues, and selling to merchant-princes the privilege of collecting their taxes —

at a handsome profit. Towns were being induced to make "forced loans," which they often recognized would never be repaid and were a kind of tax. For it was not till the late Middle Ages that taxes came to be more and more often "expressly granted" by the king's subjects. As the king built up his machinery of government, there were more and more officials whom he wished to pay in money. Often enough, some of this money was raised by selling new and lucrative offices in the royal government. Consequently, the king's constant need of money and the king's growing governmental establishment, designed to carry out policies that would bring in more money, tended to accelerate each other. For the day of the chivalrous medieval monarch had passed; the new royal type was no longer the lion, but the fox — or even the spider. It was not through gallantry that great kingdoms were to be built, but through marrying the heiresses of desirable provinces, through permitting usurers to soak up money from the king's subjects until the king found the sponge worth squeezing, and through carefully satisfying the commercial needs of the towns.

Sometimes, it is true, the king showed little understanding of this strange new sort of political power. He debased his coinage to get more wealth for himself — and the towns replied by instituting their own coinage. On first coming to the throne, he might refuse to take over his predecessor's debts — and he discovered that repudiation is bad for credit. But through his association with his royal merchants he was eventually to learn the responsibilities of his position — the protection of the new moneyed class.

In the Middle Ages, his power had been severely limited by public opinion. It depended on the loyalty of his subordinates, and this loyalty had to be earned. When medieval writers dealt with politics, they dealt with it as a branch of ethics. It was held in feudal law that a noble had the right to make war on his overlord, even the king, if justice were denied him. As late as the sixteenth century Vittoria, perhaps the greatest of Spanish jurists, wrote: "If a subject is convinced of the injustice of a war, he ought not to serve in it, even on the command of his prince." But with the new, impersonal power which money brought, the king could buy the obedience of his subjects, or at least buy mercenary soldiers who could impose obedience. In the twelfth century John of Salisbury wrote a famous political treatise, *Policraticus,* in which kingly power was still treated as a moral problem. But by the early sixteenth century a Florentine historian had written another and more famous political treatise, *The Prince,* which treated the problem of sovereignty as a purely practical matter unconnected either with religion or morals. Machiavelli has been criticized ever since for furnishing to the monarchs of Europe the recipe for immoral political success. But the fact is, the monarchs of Europe already knew the recipe, instinctively if not intellectually. Machiavelli, who as a government official in the Republic of Florence had had unusual opportunity to see how things actually got done, was analyzing the ways by which kings and princes might rise to power and might hold power when they had risen. It was his observation that Christian behavior in international affairs never worked, certainly not in Italy. " Everyone," he writes calmly, " understands how praiseworthy it is in a prince to keep faith, and to live uprightly and not craftily. Nevertheless we see, from what has taken place in our own days, that princes who have set little store by their word, but have known how to overreach men by their cunning, have accomplished great things, and in the end got the better of those who trusted to honest dealing." A monarch should know how to lie, cheat, steal, murder, and at the same time pretend to do none of these things. In the hands of Machiavelli, the theory of politics was freed from ethical considerations and therefore from religion.

Politics had, indeed, been a restless subdivision of religion, even in less sophisticated parts of Europe than the Italian city-state. Commerce was not the only sphere of human action to escape from the directive influence of the Church and thus from the European's ordered scheme of human values. The fact that lay courts, operated by a feudal nobility, had meted out justice alongside of ecclesiastical courts, had led to overlapping jurisdictions and disputes as to what was God's and what was Caesar's. The struggle between the Holy Roman Empire and the Papacy had raised the same problem, in the famous disputes over " investitures." A bishop was obviously, in terms of his religious function, a subordinate of the Pope; but a bishopric rich in land and fighting men might also be an essential fraction of the Emperor's economic and military power. The right to choose and install, or " invest," this subordinate was therefore a

vital right. Thus the landed Church collided with the landed rulers
— not only with the Emperor of the vast, ramshackle Holy Roman
Empire, whom it worsted, but with the new, self-assertive kings,
who were often more difficult to deal with.

Indeed, the medieval system was slipping. In agriculture, under
the impact of money, the manorial community began to disintegrate.
Common land was divided up, because it could be worked more intensively that way. The lord frequently moved to the town and became an absentee owner. The old relationship between the lord as
protector and the serf as faithful follower began to crumble. The
lord sometimes became merely the taxer, and the serf the rebel. In
industry, the craft guilds, with their ancient wisdom in techniques
and their apprenticeship system for handing that wisdom on, were
giving way before industrialists who bought raw materials and " put
out " the materials to workers, who lived in their homes and were
paid on a piecework basis. The long and intimate association of master and apprentice had become the impersonal and temporary one of
enterpriser and laborer. And it is commerce that more and more
dominates industry instead of being subordinate to it, as it had been
in medieval economic thought. And commerce will dominate agriculture too, for with the break-up of the feudal system, a central government based on the support of the towns will take over political
power. In this same period of disintegration, the art of the cathedral
becomes less sure of itself and therefore more ornamental, flamboy-
ant, and irrelevant. And there is a melancholy note in painting, a
morbid interest in death. " The Dance of Death " becomes fashionable in art: skeletons call for their human victims. The inevitable
end is looked on now with a sort of despairing resignation, not as
the door to paradise. Christendom has lost its confidence in the promise of the cathedral and the *summas*.

The failure of the Church to retain effective leadership and to embrace all the activities of European man produced a vicious situation. Since, more and more, apparently harmless human activities
were carried on without being related to the Church's teachings, it
began to seem as if those teachings were not a liberating discipline
but an artificial and deadening restriction.

The failure of the Church to embrace successfully, and to infuse
with the Christian tradition, all the activities of men led men also to

be more critical of the human frailty of the Church's priests. The failure of the Church to convince men that she held the secret to the riddle of man's tragic fate on earth led men to seek the solution of that riddle elsewhere. As a result, the spread of heresy became a new danger.

Heresy, the holding of incorrect opinions about the truths the Christian faith involved, is a subject that most moderns dislike and scorn. Yet it is essential, if we are to comprehend the behavior of our ancestors, to realize what heresy meant for them. Heresy has been cynically defined as the theological opinion of those who lost out. This is a wisecrack that unfortunately misses the point, by implying that it never mattered which side did win out, or in other words, that nothing genuine was under discussion. But for men like St. Thomas, who thought God did matter and who believed, in addition, that it was possible to think reasonably and logically about the truths revealed to man by Him, it was important that such thinking be done competently, consistently, and correctly. The word heresy is derived from a Greek word meaning " choice," and the heretic is one who arbitrarily chooses out one aspect of an intellectual system and makes it serve purposes it cannot logically serve. In short, every system of thought, whether theological, scientific, or economic, has premises, conclusions, and chains of reasoning that are in some definite relation to one another. To change that relationship is to destroy order and produce confusion.

Ever since there had been a Church, there had been heresies. This was natural and indeed desirable, for Christian theology took shape and clarified itself in the process of combating heretical teachings. But now in the last centuries of the Middle Ages heresy was peculiarly dangerous to society as a whole, because the Church, after permeating every activity of Christendom, had begun to lose its guidance over some of those activities. Heresy was therefore no longer a quarrel among a small sect of fanatical believers, as in the early Church. It was a threat to confuse the principles on which society as a whole had been organized. It was therefore considered a political and economic danger, as well as a religious one.

The Church, its prestige in decline, fought a rearguard action. As early as the mid-thirteenth century, it had organized the Inquisition, a formal court to hunt out heretics. The Inquisition flourished chiefly in Southern and Central Europe but there were attempts to introduce it throughout Europe. Horrible as its tortures and burnings were, it offered at least the advantage of taking to a court matters which had often been settled by lynch law. For general opinion was overwhelmingly in favor of burning heretics. You tortured a heretic, not to punish him, but as a " third degree " to get information about himself or other suspects. But you burned him as an hygienic measure, to prevent the spread of infection — in this case an infection which the medieval mind considered vastly more dangerous than physical disease. Men really thought theology mattered. Men really thought that the vast intellectual labors of men like St. Thomas had ordered that knowledge of God and His ways which they possessed. Men really thought that to confuse that knowledge was to inflict on society a mortal wound. And men accepted torture and burning as part of the judicial process. No wonder that the Church, faced with a decline in Christian faith, took over formally the task of fumigation.

But the Inquisition was used for so many other purposes and with so much clumsy cruelty that it could hardly hope to repair the breaches in the walls of the City of God. In some places, under the guise of religious regulation, it was actually used to strengthen the monarchy against its enemies. In France, it helped the king to bring into completer subjection the Albigensians, a group of heretics in Southern France, puritanical and anticlerical, against whom the Pope and the king launched a religious and military crusade. The Church not only branded as heresy misstatements about religion; she inclined to smell heresy behind any economic or political teaching that was at variance with the material interests of the Church. Thus peasants who protested against paying the tithe, a Church tax, might be doing so for reasons of heresy. So might towns which levied taxes on Church property.

Finally, the activities of the Inquisition led to all the bitterly humorous aspects of a spy system. When the Inquisition summoned at Toulouse a man suspected of the Albigensian heresy, he vigorously protested that he had a wife and children, ate meat, lied and swore, and was a faithful Christian. The unwary non-heretic might be much more likely to get into trouble with the Inquisition than the tricky heretic. Bernard Gui, one of the most active of the inquisitors, complained that if you asked the suspect what he believed, he would reply, "I believe all that a good Christian should believe." If you tried to discover what he thought a good Christian was, he would say, "He who believes as the holy Church teaches and believes." If you then asked him what he called the holy Church, he would counter with: "What, master, do you believe and hold to be the holy Church?" And when you had told him, he would say, "And I also believe so." But the harassed and disillusioned inquisitor adds that what he really means is that he, the suspect, "believes that I truly believe that to be the holy Church which I state to believe so."

In so far as the history of Europe since 1500 may be considered "modern" and in so far as the word "modern" implies a protest against medievalism, moderns will revolt against the confusions and obstinacies and obscurantism of the fourteenth and fifteenth centuries rather than against that curious harmony of the thirteenth, which has left such clear evidences of its existence in the sedate Latin rhythms of the *Summas* and in the marvelous intricacies of the Gothic cathedral. For Christendom was never offered, at any time, a clear, clean choice between the clarity and vigor of the thirteenth century and the excitements of the sixteenth. The choice offered it was between the confusions of the fifteenth — of medievalism in full decline — and the new freedoms of the sixteenth.

III.

THE RELIGIOUS REVOLUTION

As the religious fervor of the Middle Ages waned, new monastic foundations and other pious gifts became more and more rare. Yet, as Europe grew richer, the papal government found ever greater need for money. It was therefore constantly tempted to multiply taxation. Priests demanded fees for performing the sacraments of the Church. Monastic foundations, finding their agricultural wealth inadequate to compete with the rising tide of trade, and frequently facing a labor shortage, stepped up their feudal dues. In some ways the mood of the people was peculiarly propitious to exploitation by a corrupt priesthood. There are signs that a sort of perverted piety afflicted the late Middle Ages. People confused the seven sacraments of the Church with a multitude of unimportant sacramentals. Pierre d'Ailly objected to the ever increasing number of churches, to the ever increasing number of festivals, saints, holy days, images, paintings, new hymns, vigils, fasts. By making all things holy, all things were being made common and familiar. As Europe's religious feeling declined, her religious customs tended to multiply mechanically. The Gothic cathedral had been the expression of a profound and exquisite sense of form; now this form was giving way to mere formalism, and in this thicket growth of genuine Christian doctrine and mere folklore, confusion was setting in. St. Roch would intercede with God to cure the plague for you. Or he would cure it himself. Or he would give it to you! And St. Roch was not the only saint who had by this process become, not a member of the heavenly choir, a link between human need and divine aid, but a demon to be appeased. At most he might be one of the innumerable gods from whom one might secure an increase in worldly goods. Pilgrimages, too, were multiplying in number. Many such pilgrimages were made to churches which contained the relics of beloved or famous saints. The Elector Frederick the Wise of Saxony, for instance, had collected relics in a big way, with a catalogue illustrated by the famous painter Lucas Cranach. Frederick had a lock of St. Elizabeth's hair, a portion of St. Euphemia's head, two fingers and a hand of the Holy Innocents, one of St. Beatrice's teeth, and a piece of St. Juliana's leg. Such collections not only gratified the owner: they brought countless pilgrimages, and pilgrims spent money. And it is clear that the relics of saints were no longer merely affectionate reminders of those who had gone before and who had loved God more than all else. In the eyes of at least many of the poorer people, there was a magic in such things. Similarly, the images of saints which were the artistic glories of the medieval churches had for many persons ceased to be symbols and had become genuine idols.

All too often, the Church exploited the superstitions which had grown up around even its most beautiful practices. This exploitation took the form of a number of financial abuses. The "benefices," or endowments which attached to certain Church offices, were often enjoyed by men who made no attempt to discharge the duties of office. Giovanni de' Medici, for instance, received the tonsure when he was seven years old and was immediately showered with benefices. At fourteen, he was a cardinal. But this son of Lorenzo the Magnificent was destined for even higher things. When Pope Julius II died in February, 1513, the young cardinal was picked to succeed him. On March 15th he had been ordained a priest; on the 17th he had become bishop; on the 19th he became Pope Leo X. This was the Leo who proposed to "enjoy the Papacy."

Benefices often meant large private incomes, and for such incomes the new appointee was prepared to pay to his superior — to his bishop or to the Pope — an "annate," or portion of his first year's revenues. The same man might hold many benefices and make no pretense of discharging the duties for which these endowments were originally set up. Large fees were often charged by the papal government for dispensations to infringe certain rules of the Church, and for the conduct of trials appealed to Rome.

But of the numerous financial abuses which marked the Church's failure to solve the problems of a money economy, one of the most glaring was the practice of selling "indulgences." The origin of the practice is perfectly understandable. In the sacrament of penance, God's forgiveness was transmitted by the priest as His representative, but only if the sinner was genuinely sorry for his sins and resolved to sin no more. In addition, as a disciplinary device, and to help the contrite sinner to remember and avoid his sin, the priest imposed a "penance." He might direct the forgiven man to say a certain number of prayers, or to make a pilgrimage to some spot made holy by the life of a saint, or to perform some service for his Christian neighbors, like repairing a road or building a bridge. During the Crusades, the Pope announced that those who "took the cross" and fought the infidel, would thereby earn an "indulgence." This indulgence would free them, not from guilt — only sorrow for the sin committed and priestly absolution could accomplish that — but from some of the punishment they would suffer in purgatory. But persons who, for reasons of health or family responsibility, could not join a crusade, might secure an indulgence by contributing money to fit out a crusader. Gradually, as the Church's need for money grew, the Pope more and more frequently offered indulgence for a money payment. Then the practice grew up of securing through money payment an indulgence, not to secure the donor himself from the pangs of purgatory, but to rescue some other person. It was announced that the Church possessed, as a result of the good lives led by its saints and the good deeds done by many of the faithful, a "treasury of merit," which the Church might draw on in favor of its weaker sons and daughters. The treasury of merit was based on a very essential quality in medieval faith, its powerful sense of community, of the community between all those on earth or in heaven who adored God. But by the early sixteenth century, the common practice of the granting of indulgences had degenerated into what was often a matter of bookkeeping; and certainly in the eyes of many an ordinary Christian, anybody with the cash could buy a pardon for the sins he had committed.

Although these financial abuses of the Church caused many ecclesiastics grave misgivings, they were more unpopular among the Germans than in Italy. Compared with the Germans, the Italians were a highly civilized and highly sophisticated people. The Renaissance cult of beauty was more alive in Italy than in Germany. The artist was held more in honor there. And the Italian was more inclined than the German to overlook the frailties of individual human beings as well as the injustices connected with any great human institution. Where the German was shocked by a loose-living priest, the Italian was inclined to be merely scornful. " If you want to go to hell," ran a popular saying in Lombardy, " become a priest." Even the Pope might come in for very free abuse. In his great poem, *The Divine Comedy,* Dante had exhibited several popes in hell, but it would never have occurred to him to abolish the Papacy.

There were, of course, reformers in Italy also. A book dedicated to Pope Julius III, entitled *Anatomy of Vice,* demanded:

How many of you priests keep concubines and are simoniacs full of worldly ambitions? How many of you carry arms as if you were soldiers? How many come to the altar of Christ with bastard sons by your sides? How many celebrate Mass with the poison of hate in your heart? How many of you loan money at usury and trade in cattle and horses? How many of you sell the rites of burial, the tolling of the bell, the carrying of the cross? How many are unbridled liars?

But this passage was written in the middle of the sixteenth century. More characteristic of that century's early years is the disgust expressed by the Florentine historian Guicciardini in his memoirs:

I know none more disgusted than myself by the ambition, the avarice, and the effeminacy of the priests; each of these vices is odious, and ill-fitting those who profess the life which depends on God.... Yet my relations with the Popes have compelled me to love their grandeur *per il particulare mio* — for the sake of my own interest — and if it were not for this I should have loved Martin Luther as myself, not for freeing me from the laws of the Christian religion as it is universally interpreted and understood, but to see this troop of scoundrels put in their right place, where they should remain either without vices or without authority.

But in general the sophisticated Italian was inclined to put up with the abuses in Church administration. He approved of the patronage the Pope extended to the arts. He might easily approve even of the magnificence the Renaissance Popes displayed in their living. He inclined to take pride in the fact that nearly all the Popes and a large proportion of the higher officials of the Church were Italians: in that sense Italy ruled Europe. He was humorously pleased that uncouth people like the Germans could be persuaded to send their hard-earned money in the name of religion to increase the magnificence of Rome and of Italy. He sometimes resented the Pope's political activities but, if he belonged to a powerful family, he frequently shared in the wealth and privileges which a Pope's election might bring to all the new Pope's friends and connections. In the ordinary Italian, familiarity with the capital of Christendom had bred contempt, but it had also bred an easy tolerance.

The most effective protests against the increasing wealth and worldliness of the Papacy were voiced in northern Europe. In the fourteenth century John Wyclif was a teacher of theology at Oxford who late in life became a reformer. Wyclif was shocked by the various abuses in the Church, saw the degradation of the Church during the period when the Popes lived at Avignon under the thumb of French kings, and witnessed the struggle of rival Popes which finally resulted from the "Avignon captivity." In his native England, he observed that preaching had reached a low level. Either the priests of the Church were repeating half-understood statements from the scholastic philosophers, or preaching friars were regaling their listeners with dubious incidents from the lives of saints, incidents which were either pure folklore or were borrowed from classical mythology.

Wyclif attended a conference at Bruges to negotiate with a papal ambassador a reform of the English Church. But he accomplished nothing, and came to the conclusion that nothing could be accomplished through the corrupt clergy of his day. A devout Christian himself and a moving preacher, he declared to his fellow-Englishmen that the priest can hold his office from God only through righteousness and its works. Wyclif doubted whether a priest living in mortal sin could transmit Christian grace through the sacramental system, and this led him to doubt whether auricular confession could be really necessary.

He taught that the Church has no concern with temporal power. Christ and his apostles possessed no property. It followed for Wyclif that indulgences, which had already grown to be one of the important sources of the Church's revenue, were a cursed robbery. For all these reasons he instituted a " simple priesthood " to go about England preaching his doctrine. But his movement was persecuted, and his priests suffered violent deaths.

Most of Wyclif's writing is devoted to the criticism of clerical corruption. He commonly refers to the Pope himself as anti-Christ. Except for the doctrine of transubstantiation — that in the Eucharist the bread and wine are actually changed by a holy miracle into the body and blood of Christ — Wyclif was not much concerned with matters of doctrine. It was the administration and personnel of the Church that he was attacking. Given his desire to reach the common people with Christ's gospel, and given his feeling that this could not be effectively done through a corrupt clergy, it was natural that, with the help of a group of friends, he should translate the Bible into English, and that, in the matter of salvation, he should place increasing emphasis on Holy Scripture and decreasing emphasis on the sacramental system. Given his disapproval of the treasure the Church was laying up on earth, it was natural that he should advocate that lay rulers take over the temporal goods of the Church and administer them for the good of the communities which God had designated them to rule. Since much of the scandal attaching to the clergy arose from sexual irregularity, he urged that the Church should not require its priests to remain celibate but should permit them to take wives.

Wyclif was not only immensely popular with the people. His belief that Church property should be taken over by lay governments endeared him to the English Parliament. In 1377, when Wyclif was under accusation of heresy, Parliament consulted him as to whether it should allow certain treasures collected by the Church to be sent out of the country to Rome. Wyclif declared Parliament might prohibit the export of this treasure. His popularity was such that, despite papal bulls and denunciations, he died a natural death at the age of sixty.

An early Church reformer in another part of Northern Europe was less fortunate. John Hus was a lecturer at the University of Prague in Bohemia and, like Wyclif, had an immense following among his students. He served as rector of his university. Hus came under the influence of Wyclif's writings and began to preach reform. Like so many Northern Europeans, he was profoundly shocked by the easy morals of Italian prelates and Italian popes. To many Bohemians, Italy must have seemed a cesspool of immorality: was not the street in Prague, where the houses of prostitution stood, called " Little Venice "?

In general, Hus carried on the Wyclif tradition in preaching. He made use of some of the English reformer's ideas and sometimes of his phrases, but in certain directions his claims went even further. For instance, he held that to sell an indulgence was an act of simony — the term applied to members of the clergy who sold Church office, as Simon the Magician would have had the apostles sell him the ability to perform miracles. He defined the Church as a body of persons predestined to heaven by God's will, and hence in no need of indulgences. In general, Hus' teaching, like Wyclif's, tended to make the clergy less necessary to Christian believers.

When the strain between Hus and the local clergy resulted in disorders, the city council of Prague tried to suppress his preaching by force, but Hus' congregation rose in arms in his defense. Prague, as the focus of heresy, was threatened with a papal interdict: and at the request of the King, Hus withdrew to voluntary exile. He left behind him an open letter of appeal to the " curia," the papal court in Rome, and this letter attracted such attention that the Emperor Sigismund offered him a safe-conduct to the Council of Constance and urged him to appear before the Council and defend his conduct. He did so, but his uncompromising attitude won only his condemnation. He even alarmed the Emperor by declaring that neither priest nor king living in mortal sin had a right to exercise his office. The safe-conduct which the Emperor had given him was violated; and Hus, refusing to recant, went to the stake.

Just as Wyclif's preaching had stimulated English antagonism to a corrupt Church controlled from Italy, so Hus' preaching stimulated Bohemian patriotism against Rome. Like Wyclif, he believed the corrupt clergy of his day were unfitted to perform holy offices. But also like Wyclif, he was led by his arguments still further. From demanding a reform in the Church, both men came to question whether the offices themselves were essential.

Wyclif's " simple priests " had been hounded down and done to death as heretics, and John Hus of Bohemia had paid at the stake for his heresy. But at the opening of the sixteenth century there still remained, not only in England and Bohemia but throughout Europe, Christian priests and Christian laymen who agreed substantially with Wyclif's and Hus' criticisms. And it was in the early years of the sixteenth century that a German leader was to launch much the same heresy as theirs and was to shatter permanently the unity of the Catholic Church in Europe.

In the early years of the century a German monk in the Augustinian monastery of Erfurt was wrestling with his soul. The mental and spiritual tortures he went through sprang from his profound conviction that nothing could bridge the terrible gap between God's infinite goodness and the essential sinfulness of human beings like himself. In his agony of spirit he felt that God was angry with him, to which his old confessor retorted: " You are a fool. God is not angry with you; it is you who are angry with God." But this monk, Martin Luther, with his terrible longing for salvation, was to look back years later on his suffering and say: " I know a man who has often, though only for brief periods, suffered the pains of hell such as no tongue or pen could describe and no one could believe, if he had not himself felt them. If they had lasted for a half or even a tenth part of an hour, he would have perished altogether and his bones would have crumbled to ashes."

From the agony of introspection to which he subjected himself in his monastery, he finally emerged to a new confidence, and to a belief that although man was helpless to effect his own salvation, even through the disciplinary " good works " which the Church enjoined, yet by throwing himself on Christ's mercy he could be saved by faith alone. His return to equilibrium was aided also by his appointment to active work as professor of Aristotelian logic and ethics in the new University of Wittenberg which that inveterate relic-hunter, Elector Frederick the Wise of Saxony, had recently founded.

Wittenberg was to give full attention to the "New Learning," and an able humanist, Philip Melancthon, was brought there to teach Greek.

Luther was also sent to Rome on an administrative mission from his order. Rome overwhelmed him with its sacred tradition, its countless relics, and even the remains of its ancient history. The new Renaissance art did not interest him. And, like many a German visitor of the day, he was frankly appalled by the elegance and luxury and vice in which the Italian clergy lived. But he hunted out relics and made a general confession of all the sins of his past life. He wished his parents were dead in order that he might rescue them from purgatory by doing penance in Holy Rome.

Back in Wittenberg again, he undertook lectures on the Bible and soon became one of the university's most popular lecturers. He was not interested in speculative philosophy; he was after practical morality. Although he did not know very well the writings of St. Thomas Aquinas, he condemned the schoolmen. As for Aristotle, whom St. Thomas had revered as "The Philosopher," Luther considered him inferior as a philosopher to Cicero. In short, he was already proving himself what he was later so clearly to be: vigorous, daring, essentially unintellectual. His old university of Erfurt thought him presumptuous. In any case, with his tremendous vitality, and with his enormous confidence in his own instincts and intuitions, he was bound sooner or later to collide with a Church which was in so many respects decadent.

When the collision came, it was characteristic of the times that it should have involved the House of Fugger. Like so many of the new capitalists, Jacob Fugger of Augsburg was of humble extraction. His grandfather had come to Augsburg as a weaver, but the family fortunes had steadily risen and by 1487 Jacob was lending money to the Archduke of Tyrol, on the security of his Tyrolese silver mines. Next year another loan placed in his acquisitive hands the entire silver production of the Schwartz. By shrewd marriages, a favorite device of the monarchs whom Fugger was to back, and through the formation of syndicates, the Fugger family got control of considerable copper production also. In 1490 the Archduke of Tyrol handed over his government to Maximilian I of Austria. In 1507 Maximilian faced the fact that if the Swiss mercenary troops he proposed to hire could not be paid, they would go over to his enemy, the King of France. But this time there were no more mines. So Fugger took a mortgage on certain of the Emperor's crown lands. The serfs on these lands had for centuries paid feudal dues to a nobility which protected and governed them. They now paid dues to an Augsburg banker — one of the usurers they had been taught to despise — whose responsibility was neither government nor military protection but the acquisition of economic power over other men.

To silver, copper, and the produce of Crown lands, the Fuggers added valuable holdings in the production of salt, one of the community's most vital needs, and in the collection of customs duties. By 1508 their banking houses had ramified throughout Europe. When the League of Cambrai was organized against Venice in that year, it raised for the Emperor subsidies of 170,000 ducats. It was necessary to transfer payments, by bills of credit, from Rome, Florence, and Antwerp. Fugger prestige grew throughout Europe when the transfers had been effected in less than six weeks.

But practice had made the Fuggers perfect. They had been accustomed to handle the transfer of Church taxes from Northern Europe, through their Rome branch. The Pope was one of their large depositors. It was now the Fuggers who undertook the Church's delicate financial transactions in the Archbishopric of Mainz. When Albert of Brandenburg was consecrated Archbishop, and thereby became one of the seven Electors of the Holy Roman Empire, he had agreed to pay an " annate " of 30,000 ducats to the Pope. Since the election of a new emperor would involve heavy bribes to the electors, Albert had doubtless done a good piece of business. But meanwhile, he had had to borrow 21,000 ducats from the Fuggers, and the archiepiscopal revenues now proved to be insufficient to pay off the debt. With the help of the Fuggers he thereupon secured from the Pope an appointment as General Commissioner for Saxony and other parts of Germany, to manage the Jubilee Indulgence just declared by the Pope. In 1517 John Tetzel, a whirlwind preacher and seller of indulgences, began his operations. Wherever he went, he was accompanied by an agent of the Fuggers; and when the money of the faithful had filled his chests, it was the Fuggers' agent who took charge of the receipts and remitted them to Leipzig. From that city, one half of the profits went to Rome; the other, to the Fuggers in settlement of the Archbishop's indebtedness.

"Do you not hear," John Tetzel cried in one of his sermons, "do you not hear your dead parents crying out 'Have mercy upon us? We are in sore pain and you can set us free for a mere pittance. We have borne you, we have trained and educated you, we have left you all our property, and you are so hard-hearted and cruel, that you leave us to roast in the flames when you could so easily release us!'" According to Luther, Tetzel also promised that even though a man had committed the impossible sin of "violating the Mother of God," an indulgence would save him from punishment.

Tetzel did a tremendous business, although there was complaint that some of the faithful passed off bad coin on him. The Fuggers' agent stood beside him to supervise a campaign in which his master was as directly interested as the dead parents. The chronicle of a Saxon town tells of a man who met Tetzel's whirlwind campaign more than halfway. For the sum of thirty sous, so runs the chronicle, he bought from Tetzel pardon for a sin he was about to commit, and Tetzel did not take the time to find out what the sin was going to be. When Tetzel closed business for the day and left with his chest of money, this man fell on him in a wood and stole all his funds. He was of course brought to trial; but he produced the pardon he had bought from Tetzel in advance, to excuse the assault he already planned to make on Tetzel, and the Duke absolved him from punishment.

Meanwhile, members of Luther's congregation were rushing off to buy John Tetzel's pardons; and when they confessed their sins to Luther, they offered these pardons in lieu of penance. Luther declined to honor Tetzel's pardons and Tetzel naturally accused him of heresy. Luther thereupon took a step which certainly did not appear to him as the dramatic act it has looked like to later generations. He posted on his church door in Wittenberg ninety-five theses, or statements of his position, which he was prepared to defend in public disputation. The theses were written in Latin, and the presumption was that a scholar was inviting other scholars to debate with him certain points of theology which Tetzel's sale of pardons had raised. The offering of such theses was a perfectly customary act. The famous Italian humanist, Pico della Mirandola, once issued a broad-side challenge by drawing up nine hundred theses and offering to defend them all. But for several reasons the manner of Luther's act was unusual. In the first place, though written in Latin, the theses were couched in Luther's provocative style. Since they were immediately translated into German and widely circulated, the matter of style was important. Moreover, Luther not only attacked the methods by which Tetzel and others were preying on the superstitions of the people; he attacked the theory of indulgence itself. Leo X saw Luther's theses. "A drunken German wrote them," was his very Italian comment. "When he is sober he will think differently."

Even had Leo been correct, the damage had been done: Tetzel's sales dropped off sharply. Tetzel had in effect drawn checks on the treasury in heaven, and Luther had declined to honor them. In terms of the complicated spiritual bookkeeping which the Tetzel type of indulgence involved, something very like a credit panic had ensued. Incidentally, it was a credit panic which affected the House of Fugger. There was nothing for it but Tetzel must issue countertheses: these the Wittenberg students loyally and publicly burned. Leo was still inclined to look on the whole business as a monk's quarrel.

In 1519 Charles V, with the aid of the Fuggers, was elected Emperor of the Holy Roman Empire. In that same year Luther was drawn into a debate with another theologian named John Eck, at Leipzig. Impulsive, excitable, and not always aware of the full implications of what he was saying, he was no match for his antagonist. Luther claimed that the Papacy was an institution of purely human origin, and that if the Pope were wrong it might be necessary to appeal to a general council of the Church. But, crowded to the wall, he admitted that he thought that a general council might be wrong too. He was now thrown back on Holy Scripture, and was faced with the difficult fact that different people had construed Holy Scripture in different ways. Finally, Eck led him to state that it was necessary to discriminate even in Holy Scripture, since some parts of the Bible did not teach Christian truth. Eck announced that Luther was a Hussite. Luther went home, read Hus more carefully than he ever had before, and concluded: "We are all Hussites without knowing it."

He now embarked on a life of fierce polemic, in sermons, letters, and pamphlets. He claimed he kept three presses going. For journalistic polemic he was ideally suited. He was a master of the new language which had bubbled up from the common life of the people while the scholastics were still thinking and writing in medieval Latin. It had long been used in the oral folklore of the people, though before the introduction of printing it had seldom been written down. In this vigorous and popular tongue the denunciatory monk flung his invectives at his enemy. " Never have I seen a more ignorant ass than you," he rejoined to an assailant. His billingsgate, once he had split definitely with the Pope and had undertaken seriously the job of denouncing " Papists," has a fine rhythm:

This shall by my glory and honor, and I will have it so, that henceforth they will say of me that I am full of bad words, of scolding and cursing against the Papists. I have often humbled myself for more than ten years, and used the very best language, but have only increased their wrath, and the peasants have been the more puffed up by my supplications. Now, however, because they are obdurate and have determined to do nothing good, but only evil, so that there is no longer any hope, I will hereafter heap curses and maledictions upon the villains until I go to my grave, and no good word shall they hear from me again. I will toll them to their tombs with my thunder and lightning. For I cannot pray without at the same time cursing. If I say, " Hallowed be Thy name," I have to add, " Cursed, damned, reviled be the name of the Papists and all who blaspheme Thy name." If I say, " Thy kingdom come," I have to add, " Cursed, damned, and destroyed be the Papacy, together with all the kingdoms of the earth which oppose Thy kingdom." If I say, " Thy will be done," I have to add, " Cursed, damned, reviled, and destroyed be all the thoughts and plans of the Papists and of everyone who strives against Thy will and counsel." Thus I pray aloud every day and inwardly without ceasing, and with me all that believe in Christ. And I feel sure that my prayer will be heard. Nevertheless I have a kind, friendly, peaceable, and Christian heart toward everyone, as even my worst enemies know.

But although abuse and invective were his forte, he could say of one of his works later in life: " I have read my book over again, and wonder how it happened that I was so moderate. I ascribe it to the state of my head, which was such that my mind was prevented from working more freely and actively." Usually, his head was in good condition and his mind was free and active. No wonder his enemies quailed.

In 1520 Luther fell in with a famous German nationalist, Ulrich von Hutten, and with Hutten's protector, the knight Franz von Sickingen. Luther had always been passionately devoted to his German land and to his somewhat uncouth German people. But in that year, with his growing dislike of the corrupt and oppressive Italian Papacy, he launched his *Address to the German Nobility*. This pamphlet, which was written in German, urged the princes to reform the German Church. In the eyes of many of his compatriots, he had stripped the Pope of his authority; but he instinctively knew that there had to be some authority somewhere and he called on the princes of Germany to exercise that authority in reforming the states over which they ruled. He denounced the orders of begging friars, thought there should be fewer festivals and holidays, urged marriage and family life for the clergy, and pled for the improvement of education. It will be recognized that in all these steps he was sketching a secular society. Finally, he denounced the Fuggers: " I do not understand how a hundred gulden can gain twenty in a year or how one can gain another, and that not from the soil or cattle where success depends not on the wit of men but on the blessing of God." This almost medieval preference for agriculture and landed property over commerce and usury was music to the nobility's ears. In the same year he published a Latin pamphlet on *The Babylonian Captivity of the Church*. It can scarcely have been a surprise, since he had ended his *Address to the German Nobility* with the threat: " I know still another song concerning Rome. If they wish to hear it I will sing it and pitch it high. Do you understand, dear Rome, what I mean? " He did pitch it high. He attacked the whole sacramental system as being unnecessary to the salvation of a Christian, if that Christian had faith alone. Now, whether the Catholic Church could or could not rightly claim that all seven sacraments had been ordained by Christ, it is certain that these sacraments had been the consolation of generations of Christians before Luther, and the symbols through which they achieved communion with God. But from the point of view of practical Church organization, the sacramental system was imperative. Most of the sacraments could be administered only by the clergy and it was therefore the sacraments which made the Church a necessity to every citizen of Christendom. By asserting that the Christian could achieve salvation without the mediation of the Church, Luther was robbing it of its function; and by robbing it of its function, he inevitably made the Church appear an expensive and useless luxury. A third pamphlet, published in that same year, 1520, *The Freedom of a Christian Man,* declared that it was more important that the Christian should serve his neighbor than that he should renounce the world and embrace the ascetic life of a monk. Evidently Luther wanted to drive home his point that the workaday life of a good and pious citizen was as good as the life of self-denial and withdrawal which the great teachers of the Church had embraced.

On June 15th of the year in which these three pamphlets were published, a papal bull was issued, giving Luther sixty days in which to recant his heresies, and the alternative of excommunication. Excommunication involved, of course, shutting him entirely out from the life of Christendom. But in November he publicly burned the bull of excommunication along with the canon law of the Church. The following year the Emperor Charles V summoned him before the diet of the Holy Roman Empire and tried to get him to recant. He refused, and was promptly banned — that is, outlawed throughout the Empire.

To protect Luther until things had blown over a bit, the Elector Frederick the Wise had him kidnapped and placed him in one of his strongholds, the Wartburg. There Luther spent almost a year, during which he wrote a German translation of the Greek New Testament and of the Hebrew Old Testament, and though Luther's Bible was far from being the first to be published in German his command of racy idiom made his work a classic. More than that, it made the speech of the Saxon chancellery, already the common diplomatic language of the various German states, the tongue of all the Germans. To that extent, Martin Luther created a nation.

While Luther unwillingly remained in the Wartburg, a group of strange prophets — the Anabaptists — had come to Wittenberg. They had come from the Saxon town of Zwickau, not far from the Bohemian border. Luther's insistence that both Pope and general Church council might alike err and that even some parts of Holy Scripture were superior to others, and that the only court of last appeal for re-

ligious truth was the individual conscience, had been taken at
Zwickau for what it was worth. Thomas Münzer, of Zwickau, had
led the Anabaptists, men who disapproved of infant baptism and
who therefore insisted on rebaptizing. Should these people be allowed to preach their false doctrines? Luther thought not. By 1526
he was writing:

They are not obliged to believe; only open scandal is forbidden them. . . .
In their chambers they may worship when they wish and as many gods
as they please, but publicly they shall not so blaspheme the true God and
lead people astray.

And again in 1529:

Although no one is to be compelled to believe, no one, on the other hand,
is to be permitted to blaspheme the doctrine, but he must give his reasons
and listen to argument. If his grounds stand the test, well and good. If
not, he must keep his mouth shut and believe in private what he pleases.
So it is done in Nuremberg and here in Wittenberg. For, when it is possible, opposing doctrines are not to be tolerated under one government,
that trouble may be avoided.

The Zwickau prophets claimed divine illumination and urged the
overthrow of all existing institutions. They came so close to convincing some of Luther's followers that all social distinctions should
be done away with, that manual labor was alone legitimate, and
that divine revelation from God was the ultimate guide, that Wittenberg was in turmoil. Back came Luther from the Wartburg, exclaim-
ing: " As for your prophetic spirit, I smash it on the snout."

But a much more serious outcome of Luther's attack on the Papacy was the Peasant's War of 1525. By attacking the one authority
which men everywhere agreed was at least theoretically the highest
authority under God, Christ's vicar on earth, the Pope of Rome, Luther had inevitably weakened respect for every other sort of authority. As a result, the German peasantry rose and drew up a list of economic grievances. Like Luther himself, the revolutionaries cited
Holy Scripture and announced that they were willing to forego any
of the reforms they urged, provided they could be shown to be in
conflict with the Bible. But Luther drew a sharp distinction between
the spiritual freedom which he claimed as the common right of all
and the political, economic, and social freedom the peasants were

now after. When things came to a showdown, he denounced the peasants bitterly and urged the princes to suppress them without mercy: " Whoever can should smite, strangle, or stab, secretly or publicly! "

In that same year of 1525, when he was forty-two years old, Luther took a step that amazed and distressed many of his admirers: he deliberately married an ex-nun. He and Catherine von Bora appear not to have been in love. But he was hunting husbands for Catherine and for two other nuns who at his instigation had given up the ascetic life, and he had been allowed to understand that Catherine would be willing to marry him. Somewhat suddenly he accepted the advice he had already given in an open letter to the Archbishop of Mainz. Luther's marriage naturally raised a tremendous hue and cry. His enemies were quick to assume — what was wholly false — that Luther's break with the Church sprang from the determination of a monk to marry a nun.

But Luther's practical demonstration that he disapproved of clerical celibacy came, after all, late in the game. Not only had both Wyclif and Hus in the preceding century urged the marriage of the clergy, Luther's friend and colleague, Carlstadt, had already married, and the even more influential reforming priest, Huldreich Zwingli, of Switzerland, had taken a wife. Zwingli was a far more radical reformer than Luther: he succeeded in abolishing Church images and the ceremony of the Mass, Church processions, organ music in churches, and the sacraments of Confirmation and Extreme Unction. It is typical of the hesitancy which Christians felt in abolishing the sacraments of the Church that a large number of persons hastened to have Extreme Unction administered to them before its final abolition.

To Luther, Zwingli's assertion that the Eucharist was merely a symbolic commemoration of Christ's last supper with his apostles and that the bread and wine only symbolized Christ's body and blood, was anathema. To Luther, the words " This is My Body " meant but one thing, that Christ's body was actually present in the bread as his blood was in the wine.

The Zwinglians, then, did not join the Lutheran movement, and five years after Zwingli's death, in 1536, a more remarkable man than Zwingli came out of France to lead them. This leader was John

Calvin, who had set out to be a priest but had decided on law instead. Although he studied law, his interest in religion continued. Among his early friends was his relative Olivétan, who made the first French translation of the Bible. And it was Calvin's own reading and his own effort to interpret the Bible for himself that led him to disagree with the teachings of the Catholic Church. He turned to Greek and studied the New Testament in the original. It was, then, half as a humanist that Calvin went to Paris and came into contact with the New Learning. But he came also into contact with the growing sentiment for Church reform and he himself subscribed to the Lutheran teaching of justification by faith alone. In 1534 he came to an important decision. He resigned his Church benefices and felt free to preach actively the new doctrine. He became a leader of the religious reformers in France.

Francis I, who was eager not to offend the German Protestant princes with whom he had allied himself against the Emperor Charles V, declared publicly that he was not attempting to suppress Protestantism in France but that he was merely trying to destroy the Anabaptists. But Calvin wished to make it clear that he and his followers were in no sense Anabaptists, and he therefore composed his *Institutes of the Christian Religion*. This book, which Calvin wrote in Latin in order that he might gain a hearing from the learned of all countries, and which he dedicated to the King, is a long treatise which fills three or four volumes of argument. Ranging from a chapter "Upon the Knowledge of God, considered as the Creator and Sovereign Monarch of the World" to a final chapter "Upon Political Administration and Civil Government," Calvin wrote what the medieval world would have called a *summa*.

This clear-headed, legal-minded, logical Frenchman, not content with the freedom Luther had won from the restraints and restrictions of the organized Catholic Church, attempted to set up on different assumptions a new Church for the moral government of mankind. In 1536 Calvin went to Geneva, where he found a highly confused condition of affairs. Many of the Genevans had renounced obedience to Rome, largely as a political revolt against the Duke of Savoy. Now they were being preached to and harried by fanatical teachers who foregathered wherever Protestant sentiment arose. Into this excited and distraught atmosphere Calvin stepped, and immediately imposed order. He drew up twenty-one articles as a basis for the unity of the congregation and then invited its members in groups of ten each to sign his articles. He established schools in which the children would be taught his catechism. He and his immediate followers exercised a fairly effective control over the government of Geneva, and caused that government to legislate rigorously in favor of the godly life. The clergy of the city met under Calvin's direction as the " Congregation," a " venerable company " that discussed and prepared legislation for the consideration of a " Consistory." This Consistory was in turn composed of members of the clergy and of twelve laymen or elders. State and Church were completely identified. It was the obligation of the Consistory " to keep watch on the life of everyone." There was no Catholic confessional, but a spy system took its place. A joke or a mere gesture might bring a man under suspicion. Adultery, blasphemy, witchcraft, and heresy were capital crimes. In the years from 1542 to 1546, when Geneva had a population of about 16,000, this godly government executed fifty-eight persons and banished seventy-six. People were punished for taking too much wine, whether or not they became intoxicated. The color and quality of clothing were governed by law. Citizens were punished for using such expressions as " by the body," " 'sblood," " zounds." In the public inns nobody might sit up after nine o'clock except spies. The proprietor of an inn was required to see that all his guests asked a blessing before eating or drinking, and said grace afterward. Calvin himself often selected the women he thought suitable as wives for his acquaintances. When James Gruet fell under suspicion, and when a search of his house disclosed that he had scribbled on the margin of one of Calvin's tracts " All rubbish," he was put to the torture every day for a month, in order to force him to betray other sinners. He himself was sentenced to death for " disparaging authors like Moses, who by the Spirit of God wrote the divine law." It is no wonder that, when John Knox of Scotland visited Geneva in 1556, he should describe it as " the most perfect school of Christ that ever was on earth since the days of the apostles."

Although Luther had been excommunicated as a heretic, and although Zwingli and his successor Calvin departed even further than Luther from the traditional teachings of the Church. each of these reformers had secured support from men who were less interested in doctrine than in freeing their country from the control of a Pope whom they were coming to regard as an Italian prince. In the case of England, Wyclif had given his blessing to the English Parliament's ban on exporting English money to pay the Pope's taxes. This feeling of the English that the Bishop of Rome had usurped an authority over the nations of Christendom which was not his by virtue of Christian doctrine, set the stage for a break between the English Church and the Papacy in 1534. In that year Parliament declared the king the " only supreme head in earth of the Church of England." That the reigning King of England, Henry VIII, who had himself written an attack on Lutheran teachings under the title *The Defence of the Seven Sacraments,* should have become the leader of this separatist movement was facilitated by highly personal considerations. Henry VIII was married to Catherine, the aunt of the Emperor Charles V. Having no male heir by her, he wished to secure an annulment of his marriage from the Pope and to marry one of her maids in waiting, Anne Boleyn. The Emperor Charles V objected to the annulment. The Pope complained that he was between the anvil and the hammer. And Henry VIII obtained his annulment from the Archbishop of Canterbury. The breach between the Pope and the English King had resulted in the establishment of a separate Church of England which remained, for the time being, Catholic in doctrine but which insisted that the Pope had usurped authority not traditionally his.

When Luther came to die in 1546, it was already obvious that the religious problem of Christendom was not as simple as he had at first supposed. His denunciation of certain gross financial abuses in Church administration, abuses which Christians throughout Europe wished to abolish, had led him to attack a minor doctrine of his Church, the doctrine of indulgences. His debate with Eck had surprised him into attacking the authority of the Pope and even of a general council of the Church, and had led him to declare that ultimately the individual conscience is man's only religious guide. The tremendous acclaim which his statements won throughout Germany surprised even him and sufficed to show what powerful forces in Christendom were prepared to revolt against the Church. German nationalists like von Hutten had rallied around him. In his enthusiasm he had attacked the whole sacramental system. Excommuni-

cated by the Pope and banned by the Empire, he had insisted that
he was bound by his conscience to go ahead with his reforms. But
he thought of himself as merely reforming the traditional Catholic
Church in Germany and as putting the Pope in his place. However,
if private conscience was to be man's ultimate religious and moral
guide, a good deal would depend on the number and quality of private consciences in Europe. Wild-eyed prophets had swarmed into
his beloved Wittenberg from Zwickau and had preached a topsy-
turvy social order. Luther had attacked doctrines because the Papacy
could point to no authority for them in Holy Scripture; and the
peasants of Germany, failing to find scriptural authority for the
feudal dues they were paying, rose in bloody revolt. Luther denounced them for misreading the Scripture. But the peasants, particularly in South Germany, felt that the reformer had betrayed them
and many of them returned to the Catholic fold. The nobility, again
in South Germany especially, felt that Luther's doctrines had proven
fatal to social order, and returned to Catholicism.

Luther had freed his "Christian Man," and Christian Man was
completely demoralized. In 1529 Luther complained:

Everywhere the condition of the churches is most miserable. The peasants learn nothing, know nothing, and do nothing except abuse their
liberty. They do not pray at all, nor do they go to confession or communion. They act as if they were wholly free from religion. As they neglected their own papal usages, they now despise ours.

But he characteristically knew where to place the blame, and
added: "Dreadful it is to contemplate the administration of the Roman bishops."

Those German princes who had adopted Luther's reforms were
threatened by the Imperial Diet of 1529, and their " protests " against
the Diet's terms had added the term " Protestant " to the Church vocabulary of Europe. To consolidate their forces, Philip of Hesse persuaded Luther to confer with the Swiss reformer Zwingli in 1529,
eleven years after Luther's debate with Eck. Luther was not hopeful.
He declared that one could "expect nothing good from the devil."
They agreed that each would go on teaching his own opinion " without invective." Zwingli and his followers, Luther wrote, " are not
only liars, but falsehood, deceit and hypocrisy itself " and he despised

" their pestilential books." One of the last books he wrote was on the Eucharist, and in it he bitterly denounced Zwingli and his followers. Already, therefore, not counting the poor Anabaptists and other wild men, there were two large Protestant sects. Luther's adored Philip Melancthon, the Wittenberg humanist, had drawn up a very mild statement of the Lutheran faith and had presented this Confession to an Imperial Diet at Augsburg in 1530. But the Catholics would have none of it. At Luther's death Southern Germany had remained almost wholly Catholic. The North was already Lutheran. By then also, Christian III, King of Denmark and Norway, had introduced Lutheranism in his realms. So had the King of Sweden. Was Luther aware to what extent these Kings, as well as many of the " reformed " German princes, had turned against Catholicism in order to confiscate for the benefit of the ruler the wealthy lands of the Church?

Calvin had ruled his " most perfect school of Christ " at Geneva for a decade. And Calvin, like Zwingli, was guilty of denying the presence of Christ in the bread and wine. In 1546, the very year of Luther's death, Calvinist nobles in Scotland — where John Knox was spreading the " true doctrine " of Geneva — murdered the Catholic primate of Scotland, Cardinal Beaton. Henry VIII of England was still alive and outlived Luther by another year. He had freed his kingdom from the Pope's control, but he was burning every Protestant he could catch, whereas he only beheaded those who claimed the Pope was lawful ruler of the Church of England. It was ten years now since John of Leiden, an enthusiastic Anabaptist, had seized the city of Münster and set up a wild New Jerusalem. His followers had run through the streets crying, " Out you godless, God will awake and punish you! " They had smashed their way into houses and chased from the city all who would not accept rebaptism. They had celebrated a burlesque Mass in the Cathedral, at which the King's fool officiated and the people had brought as offerings " cats, dogs, rats, mice, bats, and bones " while the crowd roared with laughter. But the very year that Calvin took charge of Geneva, John of Leiden's Münster fell. That was an important year. In it also Menno Simons, a Netherlander and a Catholic priest, became an Anabaptist, and now the Mennonite movement was spreading apace. It was from out of this confusion that Martin Luther cried in his later years: " If the Devil catches me idle, he insinuates conscientious fears lest I have taught falsely, rent asunder the Church, resting so fine, still, and peaceful under the Papacy.... Truly I can't deny that the consequences often make me anxious and uneasy."

IV.

EUROPE CROSSES THE SEAS

BY 1500 the growth of commerce had revolutionized the way of life and the customs which Christendom had evolved in the time of the cathedrals. Moreover, this growing commerce was steadily expanding the geographical extent of Christendom itself. It is not easy to draw on a map for any given century the exact boundaries of this Christendom. For Christendom was a human culture, a complex of ideas, and a way of looking at life, and at no time were all the people who accepted this culture cut off from the rest of the world by neat political boundaries. There is strong evidence that the focus of this culture in the thirteenth century was in Northern France and that from Northern France it radiated through Western Europe, growing more and more dilute as it reached the less "civilized" peoples of Central Europe.

Despite the difficulty of defining Christendom as a geographical area, its character is discernible in certain definite traits. Throughout its extent men considered themselves members of the Catholic Church, governed by the Bishop of Rome, or Pope, through a huge personnel of subordinate Church officials. In the great architectural period of the twelfth and thirteenth centuries, the Gothic cathedral tended to spread from northern France and to express the spiritual yearnings of every Catholic community. The Holy Eucharist and the other sacraments of the Church, around which medieval art had been built and toward which each art had so richly contributed, were administered in the Latin tongue, which had become not only the holy language of Europe, the language men spoke to their God, but the vehicle also for Europe's intellectual life. This common religious government, then, this common art form, and this common language of God and man defined the society which we have been terming "Christendom." By the tenth century Christendom had expanded on its eastern frontier through the conversion of the Poles. In the next century the Magyars and the Scandinavians had been won. By the twelfth century missionaries were active among the Pomeranians, the Estonians, and the Finns. Throughout all these centuries, in short, the missionary spirit of the Church and the land hunger of the West European population combined in an expansive movement. The thirteenth century had closed before the Christian peoples of Northern Europe had occupied agriculturally the territory that was to be theirs. The pressure of population in Germany, for instance, had been pushing her frontier steadily eastward.

Beyond the bounds of Western Christendom lay the Eastern Roman, or Byzantine, Empire with its thousand-year-old capital at Constantinople. Although it too was Christian, its church language was Greek, its art and architecture wholly different in spirit from the Gothic, and it did not recognize the claim of the Pope to govern all Christians everywhere. In the eleventh century its missionaries had carried "Eastern Orthodox" Christianity and Byzantine art and culture to the barbarous Russians in the North, whom tenth-century invaders from Scandinavia had organized into a Russian state. By the thirteenth century another invasion, this time of Tartars from the Mongolian East, had profoundly affected the Russians' culture. South of Western Christendom lay the Moslems, or Mohammedans who had swept out of Arabia in the seventh century, had conquered Egypt, all North Africa, and most of Spain. By 1500, also, those other Moslems, the Ottoman Turks, had swallowed up what was left of the Byzantine Empire in Southeastern Europe.

In the fifteenth century, the urge for Eastern trade and the desire to spread the Christian religion drove Western Christendom to seek ocean routes to the Orient. National monarchs like the King of Portugal resented the Italian middleman. The spice trade of the Orient was still in the hands of the Italian city-states, particularly Venice. It was assumed by geographers that although, so far as anybody knew, no human being had ever reached India by sailing down the Atlantic coast of Africa, such a feat was possible. If the Portuguese monarch could find a sea route around Africa, his merchants could get at the fabulous wealth of the Indies without paying the tolls which Europe now had to pay to Moslem and Italian traders alike. It is estimated that the products of Cathay — or China — increased in cost five times before they reached Europe. The Sultan of Egypt was cashing in handsomely through the tolls he levied on Eastern goods bound for Europe.

It was the life dream of Prince Henry " the Navigator," a member of the royal house of Portugal, to find a route around Africa for the double purpose of Christianizing Asia and of breaking the Moslem-Italian monopoly on Oriental wares. This dream was not his alone. Venice's " Flanders fleet," which touched regularly at Lisbon on its way to England and the Low Countries, spoke far more eloquently to the Portuguese than any book could have done, of the riches that awaited the discovery of a sea route to India. But if the heavily laden Venetian fleet had not opened the eyes of the Portuguese, there were famous books to do so. Among the most widely read of these was a remarkable travel book by a thirteenth-century Venetian merchant, Marco Polo, who had spent many years at the Chinese Emperor's court, who described glamorously the vast wealth of Cathay, and reported that the Great Khan would welcome the Christianization of the Chinese people. Prince Henry founded a school of navigation, collected experienced Italian sailors, and gathered the most learned geographers he could find. But although he devoted the decades from 1415 until his death in 1460 to the enterprise, he did not succeed in opening up more than half the Atlantic coast of Africa. Even this sufficed to bring the Portuguese a valuable trade in gold and in Negro slaves. In 1488 Bartholomew Diaz reached the Cape of Good Hope, and nine years later another Portuguese, Vasco da Gama, rounded the Cape and made India. Da Gama returned to Lisbon next year with a cargo of goods that paid the cost of his expedition sixty times over.

The new ocean route spelled the doom of Venetian supremacy,

and Venice realized it. It is said that when news of Da Gama's exploit reached Venice the women and even the little children wept in the streets. The spices, the silks, and the precious stones of the East poured into Lisbon. And out from Lisbon poured the merchants and missionaries of Portugal. They entered Cathay in 1517 and Cipango — Japan — twenty-five years later. From their headquarters at Goa, in India, Portuguese viceroys ruled a mighty commercial empire.

The Portuguese have been criticized for never building up a settled colonial empire. But Da Gama did not round the Cape in search of land or even of political power. He sailed to the East to Christianize Asia and to do business with it. He would take Christ to the heathen and bring back gold. He sailed, that Portuguese viceroys might build mints and construct churches. And he succeeded so admirably that a nation of three millions dominated Europe's trade for decades. That mints and churches had to be supplemented with fortresses sprang from the fact that, if the Portuguese entered India, the Moslem monopoly perished. It was for that same reason that an army of 40,000 men protected Portugal's outposts in the East. But, even with that force under arms, the Portuguese hugged the coasts. " The Portuguese," remarked a Chinese observer, " are like fish: remove them from the water and they straightway die."

Portgual had set out to win a purely commercial empire in the East, and she had won it. But the only colonial empire she won, she blew into by accident. In 1500, three years after Da Gama discovered the Cape route, Pedro Cabral, who was following it, was driven too far to the west by winds and currents and unexpectedly ran into Brazil. Populous Asia has never invited European land-settlement, but Brazil was destined to support a large European population.

But Portugal was fated to undergo severe competition overseas. Among the many Europeans who read with eagerness Marco Polo's amazing account of his travels in Asia and of court life under the Great Khan of Cathay was a Genoese sailor named Cristoforo Colombo. He read also whatever he could find on the sciences of geography and of navigation. He studied the Old Testament. And, combining all these interests, he reached a mystical belief that he was predestined to carry Christianity to Cathay and the Indies by sailing west from Europe. The project was not wildly impracticable.

He had navigated the Mediterranean, was familiar with the waters around the British Isles, and had taken part, as captain of a ship, in one of Henry the Navigator's thrusts down the African coast. Geographers of his day were aware that the earth was round, and fortunately for his cherished dream they believed its circumference was much smaller than it actually is: it should not therefore be an impossibly long voyage to reach Cathay by a western route. But Columbus wanted not merely the honor and glory of carrying the Cross to Asia; he wanted royalties on the profits that a new trade route of this sort would bring. It would therefore be useless to open a new western route, unless he opened it in the name of someone powerful enough to enforce a valid claim to it. That meant but one thing: a monarch.

He took his idea to the King of Portugal. A royal commission sat on the plan; and although Columbus quoted passages of the Old Testament as well as more recent writings, the commission judged the idea impracticable. He went to Spain; and, in the very year that Ferdinand and Isabella succeeded in overthrowing the last vestige of Moorish power in the Peninsula, he convinced Isabella that the Spanish Crown should back his project. An agreement was drawn up, guaranteeing Columbus' future financial rights in the discoveries of the new route to Cathay. On August 3, 1492, he sailed from the little Spanish port of Palos with three small ships. The largest, his own, was a ship of 100 tons, about ninety feet long, and carried a crew of fifty-two men. The crew were hardly a picked group. Whatever scientists might say, the average sailor had his own ideas about the dangers of the Western Ocean; and at the last minute it had been necessary to recruit jailbirds from Spanish prisons. They took along an assayer, to test the gold they would find, an interpreter who knew Hebrew and Chaldean, and a letter of introduction to the Great Khan of Cathay. By the time they reached the Canaries the crew were already grumbling, and when, in September, the Canaries finally dropped out of sight behind the eastern horizon the crew wept with fright and begged to be taken home. Columbus had to keep two ship's logs, one true log for his private use, and one false log in which he underestimated distances for the benefit of his frightened men. Every strange fish or bird they saw he used as proof that they were nearing the shores of Asia. But as no shores appeared, the crew grew mutinous. Columbus cajoled them, "laughing with them," says an early Spanish biographer, "while he was weeping at heart!" On the night of October 11th a light was sighted, and next morning Columbus landed on an island in the Bahamas, which he christened Holy Saviour.

In the reports which he drew up for the Spanish monarchs, he smelt gold everywhere, he was sure they were near Cipango, the natives were gentle and could be readily Christianized. So he rushed back to Spain with his reports, to receive the congratulations of the Crown and the plaudits of Europe. He had won his coveted title, "The High Admiral of the Ocean-Sea and Viceroy and Governor-General of the Islands and Mainland of Asia and the Indies." At Barcelona he appeared before Ferdinand and Isabella and paraded in the streets his exhibits of parrots, native fruits, vegetables, strange stuffed animals, and — since he was sure he had reached the East Indies — natives whom he designated as Indians.

The faith that he would one day bear Christ's doctrine to Cathay now seemed justified, and remembering that his patron saint, Christopher, had borne the Christ-child across the flood, he took to signing his letters with a curious Greco-Roman combination: *Xpo Ferens,* "Christ-bearer." In public, he ceased to be known by his Genoese name, Cristoforo Colombo, and became Don Cristóbal Colón.

Columbus had left a small Spanish settlement on the island of Haiti and now prepared to fit out a second expedition and to take to his colony the equipment of a permanent Spanish post. One of those who assisted in provisioning this second expedition was Amerigo Vespucci, a Florentine pork-butcher and financial agent. It was this Amerigo who later explored several hundred miles of the mainland of South America and wrote a book about that continent. By then the world knew what Columbus never did know, that it was not Asia but a new continent that he had reached. Since Amerigo's book was signed by his Latin name, Americus, the new continent came to be called, not Columbia, but America.

Back to the West Indies went Columbus in September, 1493, with sugar cane, rice, vines, horses, cows, sheep, goats, pigs, and agricultural tools. He also took plenty of soldiers. But meanwhile it was gold, and not promises, that the Spanish Crown was after. And for gold Columbus hunted. During his absence in Spain his Spanish colony had got into trouble with the natives over gold and women, and had been wiped out. He rebuilt the settlement and set about exploring the West Indies. Island after island he came upon. In his anxiety to identify the Chinese mainland, he insisted that Cuba was Cathay, and forced his crew to sign an affidavit that it was not merely another island. He finally located the Biblical " gold of Ophir " in Haiti and immediately rushed back to Spain, not with the gold, but with the news. More parades. Spain was disappointed. But Columbus asked for six more ships.

There was no rush of recruits for the third voyage, and again he enlisted jailbirds. He planned now to spend his future profits on an expedition to recapture the Holy Sepulcher as a thank-offering for his success, and he dedicated his third voyage to the Holy Trinity. Sure enough, the first land he saw was crowned with three mountains and he named it Trinity. In the straits between Trinidad and the mainland he struck fresh water from the Orinoco and identified it as one of the rivers from the Garden of Eden. But despite these successes his colony had become so disorderly that the Viceroy was recalled to Spain in chains.

He made one last voyage, this time with four small ships. He scouted the eastern coast of Central America and was shipwrecked on the island of Jamaica. While he sent for help from his colony in Haiti, he and his crew depended on the natives of Jamaica for their food supply. But the supply service grew less dependable and Columbus was forced to collect the natives one night and threaten to darken the moon. As he had already calculated on an eclipse, the miracle worked and the supply of food increased. One of Columbus' most faithful followers took a canoe and a handful of men, paddled 150 miles across the Gulf of Mexico to Haiti, and finally sent a rescue party.

He never found the great supplies of gold that he had hoped for. He never delivered his letter of introduction to the Great Khan of Cathay. But he still believed that both gold and Khan were there, and Heaven and Cathay remained inextricably mixed in his mind. He sought to bear forth Christ — and bring back gold. " Gold," he wrote to Isabella after his last voyage, " is the most estimable of all materials. With it one may establish a fortune and obtain everything desirable in the world of wishes. One can with it even get his soul into paradise." Ferdinand and Isabella had been inclined to agree with him. Precisely because he had brought shiploads of promises back to Spain, parrots and Indians and stuffed animals, but very little gold; precisely because, though an extraordinary leader at sea, he had failed utterly to rule his colony of jailbirds and adventurers, all his plans had gone awry. Other colonial administrators had been appointed in his place. And he complained that other fortune-hunters were allowed to poach on his preserves. The last years of his life he passed largely in composing complaints to the Crown, and he died, ill and broken, in 1506, at Valladolid.

Spanish soldiers lost no time in exploiting and rifling the new world Columbus had opened up; and Spanish priests lost no time in Christianizing the natives. That it was a completely new world was proven by 1522. In September of that year the remains of a Spanish expedition, led out by a Portuguese captain, Ferdinand Magellan, returned to Seville. Only one of Magellan's five vessels ever reached port, and Magellan himself had been killed by natives in the Philippine Islands. But the handful of men who returned could report that they had done what Columbus had wanted to do: sail west to Asia. They had passed south of the American continent, crossed the enormous expanse of the Pacific Ocean, and returned from the East Indies by the Portuguese route around Africa. After which, thirteen of them marched barefoot through the streets of Seville to do penance: somehow, in circling the world westward they had mysteriously lost a day and they had consequently kept their feasts and fasts just one day wrong, for many months!

Both Portugal and Spain now possessed empires outside Europe. What if they were to collide? The question was submitted, by mutual agreement, to the one authority in Christendom higher than a king, and the Pope's arbitration resulted in a treaty, dividing the extra-European world into two hemispheres, Portugal receiving the eastern half and Spain the western, with the division so arranged as to leave Brazil in Portuguese hands. But whereas Portugal's empire remained an affair largely of trading posts and missions, the Spaniards had accidentally fallen upon a wealthy and underpopulated continent. Where Portgual had at her feet the spices and silks and gems of Cathay and the Indies, America offered to Spain, not the luxuries of an ancient civilization to be gained by trade, but gold and silver bullion to be seized from helpless natives.

It is true that when Cortez entered Mexico with six or seven hundred Spanish soldiers, he overthrew an Aztec Empire that was far from uncivilized. He overthrew it because he possessed horses and gunpowder, where the Aztecs possessed neither; and because the Aztecs had long been as certain that a white god would come out of the East as Columbus was sure that he was predestined to bear Christ to the West. Another adventurer, Pizarro, needed but one hundred and eighty men to overthrow the Inca Empire in Peru. From both Mexico and Peru there poured back enormous quantities of gold and silver that dazzled and intoxicated Europe. Even before Peru fell, Albrecht Dürer, the German artist, had seen " the things brought the King from the new golden land " at Brussels in 1520. " And all my life I have never seen anything that so rejoiced my heart as did these things."

But the Golden Land, El Dorado, was more than a place from which they brought things to the king, even gold and silver things that rejoiced Dürer's heart. It was — or should have been — India; it was Cathay, it was Cipango. The gold of Ophir was there. So were the rivers which flowed out of the Garden of Eden. Ponce de León sought there the Fountain of Youth. It was a place men longed to bear Christ to. It was not an asset to be developed, burgher-fashion. It was not taken by burghers, but by conquistadors, who fought for Christ and gold. The Conquista was fierce, harsh, and holy, a terrible and tragic experience for conquered and conqueror alike. The natives were massacred by thousands, their children worked to death in the mines. The Indian population bade fair to die out, and Negro slaves were imported, from Africa and from the Spanish peninsula. But not only did the natives die. Spanish priests died there, preaching the message of Christianity. They built cathedrals, founded universities, studied the Indian dialects, described and classified the strange new flora and fauna. And when the first wild decades of the Conquista had ended, Spain had built an empire in her own image: an empire of military crusaders who had fought the Moors for centuries before they had sacked Mexico, who had lived on the stark Spanish plateau before they had penetrated the stark deserts and overgrown jungles of "New Spain." There had been nothing in Spanish history to produce the commercial virtues and thrifty habits of a Netherlands burgher. It was a history that had produced instead the virtues and vices of Europe's feudal nobility: pride, courage, and an unquenchable desire to find the Holy Grail, even through pillage and bloodshed and lust — to bear forth Christ and bring back gold.

V.

THE PARAGON OF ANIMALS

IN the fourteenth and fifteenth centuries, as Christendom's affirmation of heaven weakened, and as its vision of another world became blurred, the Church's denial of "this world" grew more and more difficult to live with. The powerful discipline expressed in St. Thomas' *Summas,* and even the powerful discipline under which the artist and master craftsman constructed Europe's cathedrals, ceased to provide a common language of liberating symbols and came to be regarded as tyrannical and oppressive. But when St. Thomas' account of the universe ceased to make sense, men lowered their eyes from his "theological virtues" and from the soaring pinnacles of the very cathedrals they had but recently built, and looked about them with a fresh curiosity. Consequently, at first in Italy, where the commercial city-states had early broken up the medieval synthesis, but by the sixteenth century throughout Western Europe, men tried to slough off the theological heritage of the Middle Ages, and felt an immense sense of release from an authority which had decayed, which had become unintelligible, and therefore purely restrictive. They looked at earthly, and even at earthy, things with a new pleasure and reflected that after all God had created this earth and had considered it good. Should not men enjoy it? Should not they examine it, and understand it better? If God had clothed men's souls in flesh, why should the flesh be denied?

But the thirteenth century would never have denied that God's world was good. It had only insisted that the goodness and utility of this world must be judged by purposes which the human senses alone could not discover. This world was good precisely in so far as it took its imprint from that other world to which the medieval soul had constantly aspired. It was in this spirit that that most lovable of medieval saints, Francis of Assisi, had preached to the birds, had talked to animals, and had lifted his heart in praise:

> Praise to you, my Lord, and to all your creatures,
> First, for our brother Master Sun,
> Who makes the day, and who lights it for us,
> Who is graciously shining,
> And with splendor bears witness of you from the sky.
>
> And praised be my Lord for Sister Moon,
> And for the Stars, because they are brilliant
> And precious and fair.
>
> Praised be my Lord for Brother Wind,
> For Air and for Cloud,
> For Weather, gentle or otherwise,
> Through whom your creatures are nourished.
>
> Praised be my Lord for Sister Water,
> Who is useful and humble, cherished and chaste.
>
> Praised be my Lord for Brother Fire,
> Who helps us to see in the night,
> Who is fine and merry, hearty and strong.
>
> Praised be my Lord for Mother Earth,
> Because she nurses and rules us,
> Bearing her varied fruits,
> Her flowers of many hues, and her kindly herbs.

St. Francis was here praising the world which God had created, but to a considerable extent the European of the sixteenth century had himself created a new world. His geographical explorations had not only brought him nearer to the all but heavenly delights of India and Cathay. They had brought before his amazed eyes the "New World," of which the Middle Ages had told him nothing. As the sixteenth century wore on, these same eyes of his were to explore the Milky Way and the moons of Jupiter. They were also to peer more deeply into mankind's own past on this earth. It is therefore not hard to see why Europeans became dazzled by the revelations of Nature, or why their interests became less and less religious.

Already in the great days of the Republic of Venice, economic life had ceased to be the subordinate activity of feudal serfs, and had become a dazzling career that led to adventure and to money power. In fact, Cathay with its fabulous wealth had almost become a new heaven toward which the medieval merchant aspired. Vasco da Gama had, to that extent, found a shorter route to heaven. Columbus and the Spanish explorers who opened the New World faced the open seas and the American wilderness with a faith in something more than economics. Jacob Fugger and the bankers of Antwerp placed no limit on their enterprise: economic activity was not subordinate; it had become, from the medieval point of view, insubordinate. So had Machiavelli's politics.

But not only had the economic and political functions of society freed themselves largely from ethical control. The same thing was happening in the arts, in literature, and in science. By the sixteenth century all these activities were freeing themselves from their religious implications and were becoming "secular." Now the word secular is ordinarily used as a synonym for nonreligious. It is derived from the Latin word *saeculum,* meaning "century," that is, time as distinguished from eternity. The medieval Church had taught that eternal things were more important and more essential to man than things in time, things belonging to the present century, secular things. The most striking thing about the slow transition from the medieval world of the cathedral to the fifteenth and sixteenth centuries is that in the fields of economics, politics, art, literature, and science, European civilization became secularized. In this process of losing its religious interests and insights, it discarded the art forms which it had developed through a period of powerful religious faith, and it rediscovered and copied the art forms of the Romans and Greeks. It likewise rediscovered Latin and Greek literature and grew enthusiastic over the scientific interests of Greek philosophy. Because Greek and Latin civilization appeared, quite inaccurately, to have been reborn, Europe's new interest in that civilization earned the name of "Renaissance," or Rebirth. The name is unfortunate. The profoundly interesting thing about the "Renaissance" period is not that men turned to the classical art and the classical literature, but that in dissatisfaction with the forms which they themselves had created, they were willing to turn away to something else.

By the fourteenth century men's heightened interest in the things of this world was already leading them to discard scholastic philosophy, that is, the philosophy and theology of the great schoolmen like St. Thomas Aquinas. For this scholasticism seemed to them, in their impatience, irrelevant to the brave new world they saw about them. It so happened that Italian merchants were not only bringing from the East the luxuries which made the brave new world so brave; they were also creating intercourse between the Greeks of the Byzantine Empire and the men who lived in such towns as Florence, Milan, and Venice. By 1400, Greek scholars had fled before the steady encroachments of the Ottoman Turks to settle in Italy, to lecture and to teach. When Constantinople fell before the Turks in 1453, the influx of educated Greeks into Italy merely accentuated a process that was already old. Already Italians like Petrarch had begun to collect long neglected Latin manuscripts, and now the manuscript-lovers of Italy began to study Greek too. The medieval world was by no means wholly ignorant of Greek and Latin literature. It had read Vergil, Cicero, Caesar; and scholastic philosophy had adapted the ideas of Aristotle to the needs of Christian doctrine. Indeed, when the medieval reader turned to Latin authors it was to find out in what ways they had prefigured Christian doctrine and the Christian Church. But Petrarch and the other admirers of the "New Learning" were reading the classics purely as human documents, because they were interesting, thoughtful, expressed with great beauty, and because they were completely free from the theological presuppositions of the Church, and completely free from its asceticism and humility. The ornate and sonorous Latin of Cicero supplied the enthusiasts of the New Learning with what was in effect a new language and a new vocabulary, fundamentally different from the ecclesiastical Latin of the schoolmen. Scholars like Petrarch, therefore, who could no longer adjust themselves psychologically to the world as pictured by the schoolmen, and who yet felt the fundamental human need of a coherent picture of this world in which we live, found a habitation in the statements, the assumptions, and the implications of Greek and Latin classics. These were the " humane letters " or " humanities "; and those who studied them were " humanists." No longer was Latin, ecclesiastical Latin, to be merely the convenient common medium of European thought; now classical Latin was to be taught in universities, many of them founded for the purpose of spreading the New Learning, in order that the student might converse spiritually with the great heroes of the pagan world. The University of Paris might carry on a rearguard action in defense of medieval scholasticism, but Louvain in the Netherlands; Freiburg, Tübingen, and Wittenberg in Germany; St. Andrew's in Scotland; and Upsala in Sweden would teach the classic spirit, which was self-confident, self-reliant, self-assertive, and secular.

As the Italian Renaissance continued, Popes like Nicholas V patronized more and more both the Latin and Hellenic studies on the one hand and the new art on the other. Nicholas himself unquestionably felt that theology must absorb the new classical studies or else see the powerful new scholarship lined up against theology. He was therefore capable of giving Lorenzo Valla 500 ducats for his translation of the Greek historian Thucydides, and he opened to scholars his own collection of some 5,000 manuscripts, the best library this side of Constantinople. Papal Rome became also the geographical center of the new art. It was Pope Julius II who requested Michelangelo to build a church for him, worthy of a pontiff who would surpass all his predecessors in glory. When Michelangelo's design turned out too monumental to apply to any existing church in Rome, Pope Julius ordered the Renaissance architect Bramante to tear down the Basilica of Constantine, the Basilica in which Charlemagne had been crowned emperor in the year 800 and which was then already old in Christian tradition, and to build in its place a new and magnificent St. Peter's, larger, more beautiful, and more impressive than any church in Christendom. The tearing down of that ancient church and the building of the new St. Peter's in Renaissance style completely symbolizes the Church's absorption of the new and secular spirit of the age. It was a Pope's printer who published Machiavelli's treatise, *The Prince*. It was a cardinal of the Church who shrank from reading St. Paul, for fear of spoiling his style. Pius II, who had, under his classical pen name, "Aeneus Sylvius," become himself a famous humanist, believed that the Roman Empire had fallen because the scholars had deserted paganism for the Papacy. When Platina wrote a vindictive history of the Popes and presented it to Pope Sixtus IV, Sixtus made him librarian of the Vatican. In short, the Papacy was such a center of the New Learning that when Erasmus visited Rome in 1515, he could extol the light and liberty he found there. Lorenzo Valla, perhaps the ablest of the Italian humanists of his generation, wrote a critical essay on the New Testament which was later published by Erasmus. He also exposed as historically false the Emperor Constantine's "Donation" of temporal sovereignty to the Pope in a tract which Ulrich von Hutten was to print later in Germany. But he was an official in the Pope's household and, when he had exposed the Donation of Constantine, Pope Leo X merely remarked: "What profit has not that fable of Christ brought us!" For nowhere in Europe had the delirious joy in living, which the Renaissance released, more fully taken possession of Christendom, than here in Christendom's spiritual capital, Rome.

Starting in Italy, the secular or humanist spirit spread to the other countries of Europe. In Germany, John Reuchlin became an accomplished Greek scholar and a pioneer in Hebrew grammar and philology. Philip Melancthon taught Greek at the new University of Wittenberg. The Dane Povl Helgesen was a professor at Copenhagen, an historian, a grammarian. The French humanist William Budé helped Francis I to establish the Collège de France — a seminary of the New Learning; and wrote excellent Greek and Latin. In England John Colet, Dean of St. Paul's cathedral, was proficient in Greek and Latin; and Thomas More, an even better known humanist, found his spiritual world not only in the classics but in a heaven of his own creation, which he pictured in his *Utopia*. That the humanists were seeking a habitation of the soul, to take the place of the heaven the schoolmen had described, will appear symbolically from the fact that, just as the Venetian shipper substituted Cathay for the Christian heaven as the world a man would best devote his life to, and just as the America of Columbus and Amerigo Vespucci became another heaven of infinite possibilities for man, so More modeled his Utopia, a country that existed only in his humanist's imagination, on Vespucci's account of America. For Utopia was a land that possessed all the things which Thomas More's England lacked.

The most influential humanist in Europe was Desiderius Erasmus. Erasmus was born at Rotterdam in 1486, the illegitimate son of a priest. He himself entered a monastery at an early age, though rather to obtain conditions for study than from any religious motive. As a student, he came under the influence of Lorenzo Valla, a Biblical scholar who did much to undermine the historical claims of the Church. Erasmus served as secretary to the Bishop of Cambrai and later entered the University of Paris to study theology. He turned passionately against the decadent scholastic philosophy of Paris. Completely uninterested in the science, the geographical discoveries, or the art of his day, he wanted to become elegant and witty and a man of the world and a classical scholar. He lived a nomadic existence, now in Venice, now at Oxford, now in Rome with the Pope, now with the King of England or the King of France. Everywhere, he studied, wrote, edited the classics. He held the chair of divinity in Cambridge University. He drew a pension from the Church in England. He knew Thomas More and John Colet and spent happy hours conversing with them or writing them affectionate and interminable letters, loaded with classical quotations. He enjoyed enormous prestige with the advocates of the New Learning throughout all Europe. The development of printing, which had spread through Europe in Erasmus' youth, gave him a tremendous power that a hundred years earlier he could not have secured. In one year some 24,000 copies of one of his works was struck off by one printing press alone. Books were no longer expensively copied by hand; and a reading public was growing by leaps and bounds, particularly among the new middle class.

Although Erasmus made important contributions to the study of the Greek New Testament, and although he engaged in such philosophical controversies as an argument with Luther over the freedom of the human will, he is best known by his brilliant satires. In his *Praise of Folly* he described sarcastically the theologians and monks of his period and denounced their exploitation of pilgrimages and relics. He published a volume of *Adages* and one of *Collo-*

quies, both works in the form of satirical dialogue. In his colloquies
he denounced war and the absurdities of grammarians. He argued
for the education of women. On a multitude of subjects, in easy conversational form, that every intelligent reader could grasp, he dis-
coursed on the weaknesses and absurdities of human life. He did
not even spare his fellow-humanists. Though he himself both studied and loved Greek and Latin literature, though his books were
written in Latin, and though he even wrote on such subjects as the
pronunciation of the classical tongues, yet his sense of humor could
not stomach humanists who in their enthusiasm for the classics
called Christ " Jupiter optimus maximus " and alluded to the apostles as " the conscript fathers." It was these people who looked on
the " middle ages," the period between the great days of the Greeks
and Romans and the great days of the humanists themselves, as
" dark," and their horror of " monkish " Latin knew no bounds. But
Erasmus' contribution was never immoderate denunciation but gay
and mocking laughter at the things that he disliked. He was urbane,
insinuating, and therefore immensely effective in undermining the
crumbling edifice of medieval culture. His tolerance extended even
to the greatest of the scholastics, St. Thomas Aquinas, although gentle John Colet, who had been schooled in the writings of the Church
fathers could demand of Erasmus impatiently: " Why do you praise
to me a man who, had he not had so much arrogance, would never
have defined all things in such a rash and supercilious way? " Erasmus claimed and perhaps did possess a faith in Christianity; but
there was hardly an aspect of Christianity as it was practiced in his
day that he did not laugh out of court. Apparently, it was only toward the end of his life that he realized the full effects of his laughter. For his real interests were not focused on God but on man, and
the aspects of Christianity which he championed were those which
he thought would make for kindlier, more tolerant, and perhaps
more comfortable, living in sixteenth-century Europe.

The humanists had turned away from scholastic thought because
it failed to confirm or explain the new and joyous vision of a secular world. Because the great creative artists of Greek and Latin literature had found in life precisely the human interest that European
civilization was now beginning to feel, the humanists turned to the
classics, reveled in their literary beauties, and aped their forms. But

if scholastic philosophy attempted to justify the heavenly vision which Europeans no longer saw, Gothic art *was* that vision. Because Gothic art had developed a precise language for the purpose of saying things which men no longer wanted to say, and also because Gothic art had itself largely degenerated, had ceased to liberate, and had therefore begun to confine, Renaissance artists turned to the art forms of the Greek and Roman world for a language of symbols suited to their new needs. The pathos, and at its worst the morbidity, of late medieval art began to give way to a sense of power, of joy, and of self-confidence. Artists began to despise the work of their medieval ancestors and to christen it " Gothic " as if it had really been created by the Gothic barbarians who overran and destroyed Roman civilization. Particularly in Italy, where the ruins of Roman civilization had always given men a feeling for classical art, the new artists of the Renaissance looked on Gothic as something that had flowed into Italy from barbarous Germany. When Michelangelo wished to deride San Gallo's plan for a new St. Peter's — a plan for which his own was later substituted — according to Vasari he " would often publicly declare ... that with its innumerable projections, pinnacles, and divisions of members, it was more like the work of the Teutons than of the good antique manner, or of the cheerful and beautiful modern style."

It was Italy, then, that first felt a joyous sense of release that the artist was no longer obligated to represent the human in its relation to the divine, but might direct his attention to the purely human. It was as if a great load had fallen from the artist's shoulders, and this more than anything else explains the boiling energy, the tireless activity, and the incredible productivity of Renaissance artists. It was Italy, therefore, that first renounced the ascetic qualities of Gothic for a riot of cupids, nymphs, and Roman triumphs. Fra Angelico, one of the foremost religious painters of medieval times, had once observed: " Art demands much quietness and to paint the things of Christ you must abide in Christ." This would have seemed obvious, to saint and sinner alike, in his age. But the Renaissance artist, flushed with the sensuous pleasure he had discovered in human beauty, would undertake to paint Christ himself as a superb Greek athlete, or as the " Jupiter optimus maximus " of the humanists! And the faces of Christ's apostles became under his brush, not luminous with spiritual suffering and understanding, but proud and noble like those of the Roman conscript fathers. From the work of Giotto to the work of Andrea del Sarto is merely a matter of two centuries, but it is also the whole distance from the representation of divine things to the representation of human things. Doubtless del Sarto found Giotto's work childlike and naïve; but it is certain that Giotto would have found del Sarto, in his appeal to the senses, merely weak. It was inevitable that when the artist turned from the divine to the human, in the same way he would turn from the eternal, the timeless, to a concern with time. When a medieval Italian artist pictured Christ and the apostles, he placed them in an Italian landscape and dressed them in the costumes that the artist himself and his contemporaries were wearing. Details of time and place did not present themselves as problems to an artist who was attempting to represent eternal values. Even the Italian *quattrocento* — the 1400's — which already delighted in Roman ornament, still dressed its gods and goddesses, its saints and martyrs, in contemporary clothing; but it was followed by an age in which the artist turned archaeologist and tried to represent accurately both time and place. For the artist's increased liking for the here and now naturally forced on his attention the fact that there had once been a there and then.

Again, since the medieval artist was primarily concerned with the eternal values that the Church attempted to teach humanity as a whole, his own personal individuality was not of consequence and we can rarely discover who created a particular work of art. But with the Renaissance, the artist became self-conscious, developed a more highly individual style, and took to signing his work.

Among the brilliant and versatile artists of the Italian Renaissance, perhaps none was more brilliant and certainly none was more versatile than Leonardo da Vinci. Leonardo was a painter, sculptor, architect, writer, musician, mechanic, civil and military engineer, anatomist, and natural philosopher; and in each of these capacities he showed a soaring genius. He started life as the illegitimate son of a Florentine lawyer and a woman of humble origin. His father acknowledged him, brought him up with his family, and apprenticed him to Andrea del Verrocchio, a goldsmith, sculptor, and painter. For Leonardo had already shown a consuming interest in drawing, in modeling, and in music. In 1477, his work found favor with Lo-

taken him some ten years to complete, was being riddled by the French King's Gascon archers.

His first handicap, then, was that his lust for scientific experiment prevented much of the work he left from surviving in its complete form. But a second handicap was that the same intense scientific curiosity led his sensitive and rapid mind from object to object, and from study to study, so that his attention was constantly dispersed, his work interrupted or unduly prolonged, and the visible record of his genius left fragmentary and incomplete. He was not only the inheritor and perfecter of a magnificent artistic tradition; he was at the same time a lonely pioneer in the field of scientific investigation. It was this passion for investigation that made it quite impossible for Leonardo to take over classical art uncritically as a substitute for declining medievalism. His inquiring mind was seeking answers to questions which neither Greek nor Roman posed. Freed from the assumptions alike of medieval schoolmen and ancient philosophers, he turned to the observation of Nature and he concluded that " Nature is constrained by the order of her own law, which lives and works within her." Again, " To know God and to know the truth the way is simple. Observe Nature, discover her laws. And the language of those laws is, of course, mathematics." It is jottings like these, from Leonardo's notebooks, that explain why his penetrating eye, the eye of a scientist as well as of an artist, looked through the draped garments to the human form beneath, recognized in the draperies themselves laws of structure which made wool hang differently from silk and which made each reflect light in its own way. Into the human body itself that sharp eye penetrated, to the layers of muscle beneath the surface, and on to the delicate articulations of the human skeleton. But even while he observed, he stood aside mentally and watched himself observe in order to see what prejudices might be blurring his vision. It was his deep scientific interest that led him to construct fortifications, design canals, project flying machines, and invent extraordinary mechanical devices. But his inward necessity to account for everything, to bring artistic creation and scientific inquiry under one discipline, put a heavy strain even on a Leonardo. And perhaps this is why one of the most characteristic expressions of his peculiar genius is to be found in the vagrant jottings of his famous notebooks. Open these notes and you read:

"Necessity is the mistress and guide of Nature..." or again, "There is no certainty where one can neither apply any of the mathematical sciences nor any of those which are based on the mathematical sciences." "Experience is never at fault; it is only your judgment that is in error in promising itself such results from experience as are not caused by our experiments."

Actually, the most vivid reflection that remains of the spirit of Renaissance man is not in the genius of Leonardo but in the amazing autobiography of a far less important artist, Benvenuto Cellini. Cellini's varied career exhibits every facet of the Renaissance character. For the asceticism of an earlier age, one gets vigorous animal enjoyment. For the strongly marked social castes, one gets an adventurer-artist at home with men and women of every station. For Christian humility, one gets the most unbridled egotism. For the powerful ideal of what is lawful and of who should administer the law, one gets the swaggering, dueling, murdering Benvenuto. For the art that " demands much quietness," one gets the tumultuous energy of Cellini, an energy which displays itself in higher form in the Titans which Michelangelo painted on the ceiling of the Sistine Chapel disguised as Hebrew prophets. We get the tremendous interest in classical sculpture — practically no classical painting had survived — and this leads Cellini to hunt old coins and cameos and busts, and to adapt them to his own needs. One gets finally the Renaissance's immense versatility. Cellini was no thinker like Leonardo, no scientist. Not even in the fields which he did exploit did he seriously rival giants like Leonardo and Michelangelo, though he evidently believed he did. But he was a goldsmith, a sculptor, a soldier, a bravado, a competent musician, a master craftsman capable of seeing his sculpture straight through the foundry, and a lover — by his own account — of the stamp of Casanova. He was petted by kings; he could bicker and wrangle with the Pope himself; and he displayed to a high degree the hysterical excitement which his generation felt at the new worlds that they were conquering.

When the scholars of the Renaissance turned to Latin and Greek manuscripts, they found not only a finished literary excellence that intoxicated them with admiration; they found also some few remains of Greek scientific inquiry. Among other things, they discovered that, although Ptolemy had indeed taught the still prevalent

dinal Bellarmine stating that no abjuration had been required of Galileo, nor any penance imposed. For some time he refrained from publicizing his researches. But in 1618 the appearance of three comets precipitated a discussion. In reply to the work of a Jesuit astronomer, he published his polemical treatise, *The Assayer*. As a matter of fact, the views which Galileo set forth in this work were by no means all correct. He then reprinted his treatise in Rome in 1623 and dedicated it to Pope Urban VIII, although the work implied a defense of the Copernican system. During his visit to Rome he was received many times by the Pope who had been an old friend of his, and who discussed Galileo's theories with him at length. He wrote a long letter to Galileo's patron, the Grand Duke of Tuscany, praising the distinguished learning and commending the exemplary piety of the Grand Duke's "philosopher and mathematician extraordinary." He granted a pension to Galileo's illegitimate son Vincenzo, and afterward transferred it to Galileo himself for the rest of his lifetime. But the Pope balked at repealing the censure of 1616.

In 1630 Galileo published his *Dialogue on the Two Great Systems of the World*. Like Erasmus, Galileo excelled at witty dialogue, and his new book, with its ironical introduction "to the Discreet Reader," pitted a conservative philosopher, whom the author appropriately christened Simplicius, against a Copernican, whom he christened Salviati and whom he evidently identified with himself. In fact Simplicius was made to rebuke Salviati in the very words of the Pope's earlier official admonition to Galileo.

Galileo was called to Rome, to face the Inquisition. He was now seventy years old. He was lodged in the best apartments of the palace of the Inquisition. On June 21, 1633, he was examined. In his defense he claimed that he had never since 1616 "held" the condemned theory. But he was convicted as "vehemently suspected of heresy" and was forced to recant. By way of punishment, he was, first, to recite once a week for three years the Seven Penitential Psalms (although later he was permitted to let his daughter say them in his stead) and, secondly, to remain under incarceration at the pleasure of the tribunal. This "imprisonment" he spent in the palace of the Inquisition from June 21 to June 24; and then proceeded to the Villa Medici. On July 6 he went to Siena, where he visited for several months his old and trusted friend, the Archbishop Piccolomini. In December he was permitted to return to Florence on condition that he retire to his villa. For the remaining eight years of his life he pursued his scientific studies, visited by such men as Milton and Grotius.

Galileo's clash with the Church passed into European legend as the classic struggle between the freedom of the mind and the obscurantism of a powerful but dying institution. For this reason, although it was Copernicus and not Galileo who was the pioneer of modern astronomy, Galileo has a special importance which Copernicus lacks: he precipitated a struggle between the theology of the Church and the secular studies of the scientist. The issue, as Cardinal Bellarmine recognized, was at best confused. The Church's interest was less in what Galileo saw through his telescope than in the fact that Galileo was apparently trying to discredit the Church's teaching. For this reason his friends in the Church urged the necessity of tact. In addition, the Church of the late sixteenth and early seventeenth centuries was not the Church of the great schoolmen. In so far as it had allowed the leadership of European thought to slip from its hands into the hands of humanists like Erasmus and of scientists like Galileo, it had lost somewhat the habit of discussion and, like most large institutions, disliked having things disturbed.

Late as Galileo lived, in comparison with Leonardo or even Erasmus, he also was a true son of the secular Renaissance. He was a son of the Renaissance in his self-assertion, in his egotism, in his curiosity, in his confidence in Nature. Not only in the field of the new astronomy, but in the field of physics and other natural sciences, Galileo took an active part. Progress had already been rapid in mathematics, in metallurgy, and the field of mining. A Netherlander named Vesalius, who was a professor at the University of Padua, published a famous treatise on anatomy in the same year in which Copernicus' work on astronomy appeared. And in 1628 William Harvey, an English physician who had also studied in Padua, announced his discovery of the circulation of the blood.

The secular spirit which expressed itself in humanism, in Renaissance art, and in scientific speculation and discovery found another and powerful vehicle in the "vernacular" literatures which were now developing. During the centuries which followed the fifth-century barbarian invasions of the Roman Empire, and during a long period when commerce and communication all but ceased, each little district of Italy, France, or Spain developed its own special variety of spoken Latin. Europe, consequently, possessed thousands of spoken languages, each of them valid for only a small territory. In England the Anglo-Saxon invasions wiped out the Latin tongue, but the Norman Conquest was eventually to introduce into English one of the innumerable variants of spoken Latin: Norman French. As centralized states began to develop in the late Middle Ages, the language of the king's capital became more and more the standard tongue throughout all his possessions. Originally, the "French" spoken in the district around Paris had been on an equal footing with Norman, Picard, Walloon, Burgundian, or Angevin. But with the rise of the French monarchy, with its capital at Paris, French became the language of the upper classes; and its competitors sank to the level of "dialects." Even then, Latin continued to be the universal language of Europe. Moreover, it was the language in which scholars wrote and had to write, because it alone possessed a vocabulary capable of expressing scholarly thinking. But as Parisian French developed, along with Castilian Spanish, and the Italian of Florence and Tuscany, poets and prose writers began to produce in them works which the merchant class, not always familiar with Latin, could read and enjoy. Already by the thirteenth century the friars, or traveling preachers, had written hymns in these vernaculars and had adapted airs to them. By that same thirteenth century, Castilian was supreme in Spain and during the fifteenth and sixteenth centuries it developed a literature which relegated the other languages of Spain, like Catalan and Andalusian, to the position of local dialects. Also in the thirteenth century Dante, who wrote his serious political works in Latin, had neverthelesss written his *Divine Comedy* in the speech of his native Florence, and in no small measure it was the strength and beauty of the *Divine Comedy* that made Florentine into standard Italian. Petrarch also had prized his Latin writings, in which he aped Cicero; but he is remembered by his Italian sonnets. And Boccaccio's popular book of stories, *The Decameron,* likewise helped to make of Italian a literary medium. The languages of Lombardy, Venice, Genoa, and Sicily were thrust aside. Although for a brief period in the fifteenth century the excitement of the humanists over Latin manuscripts threatened to eliminate

Italian as a literary language, the effort of humanist pedants to " purify " medieval Latin and to revive the more elaborate construction of Cicero merely deadened Latin for the ordinary writer and drove him to express himself in the new Italian. Germany, too, spoke a multitude of similar languages, one of which — the German dialect of the Netherlands — was to develop separately as modern Dutch. Just as Martin Luther's popular German translation of the Bible did much to standardize a literary German, so Cranmer's *Book of Common Prayer* did much to standardize literary English. The English translation of Thomas More's *Utopia,* a book originally written in Latin, contributed its share to the formation of literary English. Machiavelli's *Prince,* his *Florentine History,* and Guicciardini's *History of Florence,* and Vasari's *Lives of Italian Artists* helped to strengthen the young Italian language. Spanish was being enriched by Bartolomé de las Casas' *History of the Indies* and by Cervantes' *Don Quixote.* In Portugal Camoëns' epic on Da Gama's discovery, the *Lusiads,* popularized modern Portuguese.

It would be hard to overestimate the importance of the growth of these relatively few standard languages, which now largely usurped the intellectual kingdom in which Latin had once reigned alone. Latin had been and in 1500 still was the Church language, the holy language, of Europe, the language Christians used when they prayed in their cathedrals. But it had also been the language of philosophy, of science, of diplomacy, even of business. This made for a certain unity in European thought. But as the new languages developed, each one tended to develop along its own special line and therefore to express a different spiritual unity, a " nationalism." It was the rise of these nationalisms that greatly aided the national monarchs of England and France and Spain and Portugal to seize power. In the political sphere, the king overthrew the local noble: in the sphere of literature and thought, the national language overthrew the dialect. Sometimes, as in the case of the Albigensian " crusade," an exquisite local language like Provençal might be all but eliminated under the onslaught of " Frenchmen " from the North.

What one of these new national tongues could be made to do in the hands of a master was nowhere better shown than in England. The somewhat clumsy tongue from which Chaucer had created the exquisite poetry of his *Canterbury Tales* and in which Wyclif had berated the abuses of the Church became in the late sixteenth century, in the reign of Elizabeth, the vehicle of an incredible outburst of great drama. In the tragedies of writers like Webster and Marlowe there appear the overweening pride, the tremendous contradictions, and the terrible inward confusions of the Renaissance. There is the relative absence of religious devotion and the fascinated analysis of the human passions. All these things and more achieve immortal expression in the tragedies of William Shakespeare. Shakespeare could turn from the writing of comedies in a flexible tumultuous idiom that in many ways resembled the powerful French of Rabelais, and could explore each tragic emotion of the human heart. He could exult, as the Renaissance did constantly exult, in the strength and self-sufficiency of man, through the mouth of Hamlet: "What a piece of work is man! how noble in reason! how infinite in faculty! in form and moving how express and admirable! in action how like an angel! in apprehension how like a god! the beauty of the world! the paragon of animals!"

But instantly, with the disillusionment which is quite as characteristic of the Renaissance as is its pride, Hamlet cries: "And yet, to me, what is this quintessence of dust? man delights not me." And Macbeth, the tyrant king of Scotland, after selling his soul to the forces of evil personified in the three witches, after violating the laws of hospitality to murder his king, after murdering his most loyal friend, all to secure the material power which Machiavelli urged princes relentlessly toward — when this Macbeth hears of his wife's death and faces his own overthrow, it is these words of disillusionment that Shakespeare, the tragic poet of the Renaissance, puts into his mouth:

> To-morrow, and to-morrow, and to-morrow,
> Creeps in this petty pace from day to day,
> To the last syllable of recorded time;
> And all our yesterdays have lighted fools
> The way to dusty death. Out, out, brief candle!
> Life's but a walking shadow: a poor player,
> That struts and frets his hour upon the stage,
> And then is heard no more: it is a tale
> Told by an idiot, full of sound and fury,
> Signifying nothing.

VI.

THE TRAGEDY OF PHILIP II

"Because of us the tempest and the thunderbolts have come." This remark was made by a French cardinal at the General Church Council which the Pope had convened at Trent in 1545. The cardinal's diagnosis of the Protestant Reformation was the diagnosis of most thoughtful Catholics. They knew, long before Luther pointed it out, that the administration of the Church was riddled with abuses. Reform had been repeatedly urged. But nothing substantial had been accomplished, until now a large part of Northern Christendom had seceded from the Catholic, or universal, Church. Not the least of Luther's accomplishments was to force the Papacy to recognize that reform from within the Catholic Church must be seriously undertaken. Throughout the early years of the sixteenth century the Popes had been worldly, urbane, art-loving, and patrons of the new learning. But beginning with 1534, a series of unusually earnest and high-minded men were elected to the papal throne, and it was under their guidance that a general council was called at Trent, on the border between the Popes' native Italy and Martin Luther's Germany. The difficulties of convening the Council had been tremendous. The papal government had traditionally opposed the convocation of general councils, which might put an effective check on the increasingly monarchical power of the Popes. More than once in the preceding century efforts to reform the Church through general councils had foundered on papal opposition. The problem was now complicated by the existence of the new churches of Protestants, who it was vainly hoped might be yet brought back to the faith of their fathers. But even within the traditional Catholic Church, the growth of national feeling was creating new and unaccustomed strains. The German Catholics and the Italian Catholics were at loggerheads. Finally, the two most powerful Catholic monarchs of Europe, the King of France and the King of Spain, were almost constantly at war.

But the Council was convened and Protestant delegates were invited. It was to no avail. By the time the Protestant theologians had appeared, the Council had already fixed its opinion, and the Protestants felt they were losing time by staying. The Catholics thereupon undertook, not a discussion with the new heretics, but a consolidation of the Catholic position that they hoped might yet win some Protestants back. They devoted their time to two main problems: to a clear definition of the dogmas and beliefs of the Catholic Church, and to a reform of Church administration. On the matter of dogma, they offered no compromise to the " Protestant heresy." On the matter of reform, they carefully eliminated the very abuses which had brought down upon them " the tempest and the thunderbolts " of Martin Luther.

Luther had objected to certain Catholic doctrines on the ground that they were not derived from Holy Scripture. The Catholics now affirmed that the historic Church was the medium of a continuous revelation and a continuous interpretation. Therefore the traditions of the Church supplemented Holy Scripture as a basis for Christian doctrine. The Protestants had generally shown a desire to have the Church become its primitive self again, but the Catholics were unwilling to renounce the spiritual growth and institutional experience of fifteen centuries. The Protestants had also differed with the traditional Church and among themselves on the number of sacraments. The theologians at Trent reaffirmed that all seven sacraments were indispensable. Protestants like Zwingli and Calvin had substituted for the Mass — in which the bread and wine were miraculously transformed into the body and blood of Christ — a purely commemorative ceremony, in which ordinary bread and ordinary wine were shared by the faithful in memory of the bread and wine which Christ and his apostles had shared at the Last Supper. The Protestants, after first objecting to an idolatrous worship of holy images, had tended not only to abolish the images themselves but to forbid the " invocation of saints," in which the Christian prayed a saint of the Church to intercede with Christ on his behalf. Trent reaffirmed the invocation of saints and the veneration of images. It recognized also the veneration of holy relics, which most Protestants had turned against. The crisis between Martin Luther and the Papacy had come over the sale of indulgences, which shortened the period during which a departed soul needed to be purged of its sin before entering paradise. The whole theory of purgatory had been discarded by Protestants. Trent reaffirmed both the existence of purgatory and the right of the Church to issue indulgences. Finally, the chaos which Protestantism had frequently brought in its train derived from its denial of any authority except the individual conscience. In the name of his conscience, Luther had denied the authority of the Pope, had broken his vow of celibacy and had taken a wife. But in the name of *his* conscience, John of Leiden had denied the authority of Luther and had taken four wives. Wherever Protestantism flourished, the problem of authority had become acute. Luther forbade the Anabaptists to worship in public. Luther denounced Zwingli for heretical beliefs. Calvin was burning and torturing Christians who did not find in their consciences what he found in his. And everywhere individuals were claiming direct communication with God, Who, it must be confessed, apparently directed them to do some quite remarkable things. Facing this problem of authority, the Council of Trent declared the Pope the supreme interpreter of Church canons.

In the field of reform, the Council took strict measures against simony, or the sale of church offices. It insisted that bishops and prelates should actually fulfill in residence the obligations of their offices. It took steps to improve the education of priests. It retained Latin as the language of Church liturgy, but urged frequent sermons in vernacular. Although it had defended the theory of indulgences, it forbade the sale of indulgences for money. It strictly forbade a priest to charge money for administering the sacraments. Facing the fact that Biblical criticism in the hands of men like Valla and Erasmus had pointed out errors of translation in the Vulgate, or official Latin version of the Bible, the Council undertook a revision of the Vulgate. The rise of printing had made it possible for irresponsible or ignorant writers to disseminate widely any ideas that might come into their heads. Both the universities and the monarchs had recognized this fact and had taken steps to control the output of printed matter. One of the favorite devices of censorship was to publish lists of prohibited books. The Council of Trent provided that such an " Index of Prohibited Books " should be issued by papal authority. As a further check on heresy, and on the intellectual, political, and social confusion which tended everywhere to follow in its wake, the Council reorganized and strengthened the Inquisition.

In general, the practical effects of the " Catholic Reformation " undertaken at Trent were to render the intellectual position of the Church more rigid. Gone were the days when scholastic philosophy speculated imaginatively within the wide framework of the Catholic faith. To the sixteenth century it looked as if speculation had been far too free and had led to endless quarrels and disorders. Perhaps it was only that the sixteenth century was less sure of the framework and could therefore not achieve free movement within it. However that may be, the temper of the Catholic Reformation, of those who spoke at Trent, and of those who approved what was said there, was against free discussion and speculation, and in favor of accentuating the basic fixity of Church doctrine. In addition, although it no longer seemed possible to preserve the high degree of spiritual unity which the Catholic Church had once expressed, it appeared for that very reason doubly desirable that the Pope, as visible head of the Church, should secure the unquestioned loyalty of at least the clergy.

Both in the matter of a more rigid statement of doctrine and in the matter of securing completer obedience to the Papacy, a new monastic order, the Society of Jesus, was to make a fundamental contribution. The founder of this order, Ignatius Loyola, was a Spaniard, an aristocrat, and a soldier; and this threefold character of his was to stamp itself indelibly on the Society which he founded, and was indeed characteristic of the Catholic Reformation itself. Loyola was painfully wounded in a battle with the French and during his convalescence this soldier, whose principal reading had been the chivalrous romances of war and love, read a life of Jesus Christ. The religious conversion which followed led him to dedicate his soldier's heart to a new form of military service, the battle for Jesus Christ against the forces of the Devil. After a pilgrimage to Jerusalem, Loyola studied at Barcelona, Alcalá, and Salamanca; and began teaching a few followers the comfort he had found in his new form of military service. He was arrested by the Inquisition, and forbidden to discuss certain topics until he had become better educated. He thereupon studied for seven years at Paris, where he took his M.A. degree. In Paris he gathered about him six other students, and in 1534 the little group took a common oath to devote their lives to saving souls for Christ. Loyola returned to Spain with the intention of joining his group later in Italy and of establishing a mission in Palestine for the conversion of the Mohammedans. Repeatedly hauled before the Inquisition, he nevertheless successfully introduced reforms in his native town. For Loyola was always intensely interested in practical morality. He put a check on gambling, he stimulated Church worship, and he introduced an efficient poor law, which he probably borrowed from the Netherlands.

The rising power of the Turk made it impracticable for the little group to go to Palestine, and in 1538 by the Pope's consent the Society of Jesus was founded at Rome. Its organization was that of a military company, and obedience to the "General" was to be absolute. The company as a whole was responsible only to the Pope and dedicated itself to strengthening his authority. Moreover, although in the early days of his conversion Loyola had practiced a severe asceticism, his "warriors of God" were to wear no monk's costume, were not to lead the ascetic life of the monastery, and for chanting God's praise they were to substitute care of the sick, aid to the poor, and preaching. From the organization of the company until Loyola's death fifteen years later he served as General.

Loyola chose his warriors with the greatest care, and their activity and courage were incredible. They established schools, in which incidentally the dangerous New Learning was faced and dealt with. To avoid the scandals that had too frequently arisen from having convents of nuns placed under the supervision of monastic orders, Loyola secured papal exemption from this responsibility. In their zeal as reformers, they compared favorably with the later Puritans. They opposed certain demoralizing sports like bull-fighting. They attempted to check the ostentatious use of jewelry, too much reading of the books of chivalry which the General had once reveled in, the use of cosmetics; and they even substituted for ordinary playing cards special cards containing moral teachings. They exercised themselves in healing blood feuds between families; and they established homes for reformed harlots.

The warriors of God faced some difficult problems. Their company inevitably aroused the jealousy of older monastic orders; and in recruiting new members it was accused of stealing boys from their parents. But it played a conspicuous part in guiding the Council of Trent into decisions favorable to the Pope; and it secured through its patience, its tact, and its skillful political maneuvering the support of crowned heads and wealthy nobles alike. Perhaps its most brilliant success was the missionary work it undertook in Portugal's Eastern empire, where Francis Xavier tempered the brutalities of colonial administration, converted thousands of Hindus and Japanese to Christianity, and finally died on the China coast. The Jesuits, as they came to be called, went also as missionaries to Brazil; and they even made an unsuccessful effort to extend the Roman Catholic Church in Ethiopia. Years after Loyola's death, they were to flock as missionaries to North America.

Loyola was a soldier and a moralist, never an intellectual. But even a soldier must have his articles of war; and Loyola supplied for the basic spiritual discipline of his warriors a remarkable book, his *Spiritual Exercises*. This book is no *summa*, nor does it compete with Calvin's great treatise. It is a manual of great psychological penetration, providing a technique for intense self-examination and for acquiring a rich imaginative realization of the personality of Jesus Christ. It was intended to stimulate in the believer not only an intellectual, but a sensory, perception. It directed his mind and his senses to the story of Christ's life on earth and to a vivid picture of the torments of hell. Its direct and powerful appeal to the sensuous imagination rather than to speculative intellect is as characteristic of Loyola's Spanish blood as it is of his military background. It was designed to raise the morale of the warrior of God, and to strengthen his endurance under no matter what trials, and to give him the soldierly virtue of obedience. " We should always be disposed," wrote its author, " to believe that what appears to us white is black, if the hierarchy of the Church so decides." For Loyola, Christianity was not an affair of scholastic speculation but of soldierly obedience to the head of Christ's army on earth, the Pope.

The wound which led to Loyola's fruitful convalescence and to his vow to fight for Christ, he had acquired serving the Emperor Charles V against the French. That monarch had mounted the throne of Spain on the death of his grandfather Ferdinand of Aragon, when he was only sixteen, as Charles I of Spain. When he was nineteen the death of his other grandfather, Maximilian, placed in his hands the lands of the Hapsburgs; and when with Jacob Fugger's aid he won the election to the Imperial crown, the Emperor Charles V ruled over more people and more land than any prince of Christendom had ever governed. His possessions in his native Netherlands, in Bohemia, a part of Hungary, Austria, the southern half of the Italian peninsula, and Spain, encircled France like a vise; and his inheritance of the far-flung Spanish Empire guaranteed him enormous resources. The French King, Francis I, who had competed with him in the Imperial election, was his constant enemy; and Francis' son and successor, Henry II, continued the struggle with Spain. From 1522 until his abdication in 1556 Charles V carried on a series of intermittent wars with Francis and Henry. The net result of these confused struggles, in which now the Emperor and now the French king was temporarily successful, was that France left Spain supreme in the Italian peninsula — the chief theater of the wars — while extending her own frontier eastward at the expense of the Holy Roman Empire.

But the French fear of Hapsburg encirclement and the French monarch's claims to Italian territories had not been Charles V's only concerns. From 1526 to 1547 he was involved with the efforts of his brother Ferdinand of Hapsburg in defending Hungary from the advance of the Moslem Turks. This Turkish problem he bequeathed to his son Philip II. Finally, Charles V had banned the heretic Martin Luther and had attempted to put down Protestantism in the Empire. His efforts aroused the antagonism of those German princes who had accepted Lutheranism and who had thereby been enabled to confiscate the wealth of the Church within their dominions. The

Catholic-Protestant quarrel in Germany therefore took on the color of a struggle between an Emperor anxious to centralize his authority, as the kings of England and France had done, and a group of princes and great nobles determined to prevent centralization. The Catholic Emperor failed to solve his German problem and in 1555 signed with his rebellious Protestant princes the Peace of Augsburg. The Peace of Augsburg meant in terms of religion that each prince was free to decide whether his state was to be Catholic or Lutheran. On the political side, it meant that the Holy Roman Empire was to retain a degenerate form of feudalism and could not be centralized into a German national state. A year after the Peace of Augsburg, Charles abdicated.

The son who succeeded him on the Spanish throne as Philip II so completely dominated European history in the second half of the sixteenth century that the confused and apparently disconnected episodes of those years can be seen perhaps more clearly through his eyes than from any other point of view. From earliest infancy Philip II was constantly reminded of the special role which he would be called upon to play and which set him apart from other human beings. The circumstances of his birth itself indicate with what feelings Spain welcomed him into the world. While his mother was still in the pains of childbirth she was profoundly impressed with the great destiny that awaited her offspring; and she was determined that no outcry of hers, no manifestation of either pain or weakness, should detract from the dignity to which kings are born. One of her Portuguese ladies in waiting feared that this effort of self-control would add to the sufferings of the Empress and begged her to give natural vent to her feelings. " Silence! " said the Empress. " Die I may, but wail I will not."

Philip's father, the Emperor Charles V, gave personal attention to the boy's education and training. Philip was impressed from the start with the seriousness of his position. His intellectual precocity, particularly his aptitude for mathematics, delighted his father. He was given not only the best teaching that could be found, but the strictest. And even then, his father wrote him concerning Philip's teacher: " Siliceo has certainly not been the most fitting teacher for you. He has been too desirous of pleasing you. I hope to God that it was not for his own ends."

When the serious little boy was twelve years old his mother died. The Emperor, weary of governing the most extensive empire in the world, and oppressed by the defeat of a great expedition he had sent against the Moors of Algiers, consoled himself with the supervision of his son's education, and devoted a portion of every day to his schooling. The little prince's gravity, his prudence, and his studiousness delighted Charles.

As far back as Philip could remember anything, one of the great facts of life had been the wars against the Protestants. Apparently this was the normal state of affairs; and apparently the suppression of heresy was the natural function of an Emperor who ruled the bulk of the Catholic world and who had been appointed by God to govern His people and to defend their faith. He himself was being sternly trained to play well the part of an absolute monarch who would not be subject to the influences of mistaken loyalties or affections. When he was sixteen his father had left the regency of Spain temporarily in his hands. He had left Philip also, as advisers, Tavara, Cardinal-Archbishop of Toledo, and De los Cobos, the Secretary of State. The Emperor had written to him, carefully explaining why these two advisers had been selected. They had been picked, he wrote, because they were the heads of political factions. The sixteen-year-old regent must not trust either one separately. Charles went on to point out the hypocrisy, the greed, and the frailties of character and conduct in each; and urged Philip to listen to the opinions of everyone, especially those who were his rivals for power, and then to decide for himself. And he took care to warn him against the greatest of all the Emperor's Spanish subjects, the Duke of Alba. "The Duke of Alba," the Emperor wrote his son, "would have liked to be affiliated with them [Tavara and Cobos] and I do not think he would have followed either party...." But "you must avoid placing him or other grandees very intimately in the home government, because he and others will exert every means to get in your good will, which will afterwards cost you dear. I believe he will not hesitate to endeavor to tempt you even by means of women, and I beg you most especially to avoid this. In foreign affairs and war make use of him, as he is in this the best man we now have in the kingdom." If Philip was later to exhibit a suspicious nature, it was not a merely temperamental defect. He had been schooled to it by a man who had learned the art of government in the harsh school of experience.

The vast empire which Charles V had inherited as a youth was largely the result of the genius which the Hapsburg family always exhibited for shrewd and profitable marriages. When little Prince Philip was only twelve, Charles tried to marry him to Jeanne d'Albret. Jeanne d'Albret would inherit the Kingdom of Navarre, which stretched on either side of the western Pyrenees. But Charles' great rival, Francis I, had his own ideas about Navarre, and thwarted the match. Now at the age of sixteen Philip married the Princess Maria of Portugal, his first cousin. Eleven months later the Princess Maria died, shortly after giving birth to a son. The boy-husband shut himself up in a monastery to give way to his grief; and the people of Spain, with whom he was already immensely popular, mourned his bereavement as a national affliction.

Charles V had originally planned that on his death Spain and her vast colonial empire would pass to Philip, and that the rest of his European possessions, including the ancient Hapsburg possession, Austria, would go to Charles' brother Ferdinand. This should guarantee Ferdinand his election as Emperor of the Holy Roman Empire. But Charles was now so impressed with Philip's developing abilities that he decided to leave Philip all his realm except Austria and its dependencies.

In 1548 the young Prince started on a tour of his future domains. He passed through Italy and then crossed Germany to visit his father's native land, the Netherlands. He met Charles in Brussels. The festivities which celebrated their presence lasted for days. Philip, who in his tastes and habits was Spanish to the fingertips, was disgusted at the rough horseplay and drunken orgies of the Germans and Flemings. He made little effort to hide his surprise and dislike. As part of the ceremonies, he must " break a lance " at one of the tourneys. He was a graceful rider but he was neither robust nor athletic, and he made a poor impression. Above all, he could speak neither German nor Flemish.

He remained with his father until 1551, learning the details of Imperial administration, and then returned to Spain. Meanwhile, Charles' subordination of the interests of the Holy Roman Empire to his Spanish policy had caused even the Catholic Maurice of Saxony to desert the Emperor and to aid the German Protestant princes against him. Henry II, who had succeeded his father Francis I as King of France, promptly lent support to Maurice in order further to embarrass the Hapsburg Emperor, and succeeded simultaneously in raising a storm against him in Italy. The French won victories in Piedmont and in Siena, and Charles' control of the Italian peninsula was threatened. In Germany, Maurice had captured the city of Emberg; but when Charles fled from Emberg, Anton Fugger, successor of the great Jacob, fled with him. In these desperate straits he succeeded in raising another 400,000 ducats from Anton. But with the French supporting his German enemies and crowding him in Italy, he needed more than Fugger's loan, if he was to maintain Hapsburg power.

He turned to England. Henry VIII had made himself head of the English Church in the place of a foreign Pope; had closed the monasteries and confiscated their wealth for himself and his powerful nobles; had burned all Protestant heretics; had married six wives in succession, two of whom he had beheaded; and had died in 1547. He was succeeded on the English throne by his son Edward VI, then still a boy of ten. Edward died six years later, but during his brief reign, both Lutherans and Calvinists were permitted to preach their doctrines freely. The Latin service books of the Catholic Church gave way to the English Book of Common Prayer, and the Anglican Church became increasingly Protestant.

But with the young King's death, the sickly daughter of Catherine of Aragon, Henry's first wife, mounted the English throne. This daughter, Mary Tudor, was a Catholic like her Spanish mother and like her first cousin, the Emperor Charles V, now hard pressed by the German Protestant princes. Charles determined to arrange a marriage between England's new Catholic Queen and his widowed son. For Philip, who had always disliked foreign marriages anyhow, the thing was a matter of duty. " I have no other will than that of your Majesty," he wrote to his father, " and whatever you desire, that I will do." Mary, on her side, gladly accepted the proposal as a means of rescuing her English subjects from the heresy they had learned during their six years under Edward VI.

Having accepted this newest responsibility which his position had brought him, Philip did things handsomely. He sent a special envoy to Mary with gifts of magnificent jewels. Then he set out himself, with a great train of Spanish nobles. The fleet which convoyed them to England comprised 100 vessels and was carrying 8,000 soldiers to reinforce the Emperor's army, which was attacking the French from the Netherlands. To avoid occasion for disagreeable incidents, Philip allowed not a man of the army to land in England; and the nobles who accompanied him, the proudest in Europe, were carefully instructed to give precedence to their English hosts.

Philip found Mary a faded little woman, eleven years older than himself, with red hair and no eyebrows, somewhat fanatical on the question of this marriage which would bring salvation to thousands of her subjects. To the reticent Spaniard, her endearments seemed embarrassingly frequent, but he played the role of lover as best he might, and never hinted to the Queen that after all this marriage was a political affair. He soon observed that he had not much to go on. The Londoners were declaring that " he had only come to beget an heir to the crown, and then he might go — the sooner the better." He observed also that the real ruler of England was not Mary but the Royal Council. He carefully refrained from interfering in the English government, and through his tact he gained some members of the Council to his side. As to the Protestant heretics, the spawn of Edward's reign, he advised moderation and urged persuasion rather than force. Charles was detaining Cardinal Pole, the papal legate to England, in the Netherlands until Philip could explore further the ticklish question of restoring the Church property which Mary's father, Henry VIII, had confiscated.

The news that Mary was with child and that England had an heir to the crown caused great rejoicing, and Philip discreetly seized this favorable opportunity to get it moved in Parliament that aid be sent to his father against the French. Meanwhile, Philip's counsel of moderation was lost on the Catholic churchmen of England; and, particularly after Philip had left the country, the holy persecution began. Protestants went to the stake throughout England; and the slaughter earned the Queen the unenviable title of " Bloody Mary." Both Philip and his Spanish churchmen disapproved of the persecution, but the holocaust could not be stopped. And the Emperor needed Philip in Flanders.

He left England on August 6, 1555. By then it was evident that the Queen was not pregnant, and this fact largely robbed Philip of what little popularity he had been able to earn in England. When he joined his father, he was King of Naples and Sicily, and Duke of Milan, as well as Consort to the Queen of England. But on October 25, at a touching ceremony in the great hall of the palace at Brussels, the Emperor Charles V abdicated to his son the sovereignty of his native land, the Netherlands. " Gentlemen," he remarked to the assembly, " you must not be astonished if, old and feeble as I am in all my members, and also from the love I bear you, I shed some tears." Philip answered him; but, unlike his father, he was no Netherlander, he could not speak Flemish, and he was forced to make use of an interpreter. In the next year Charles transferred to his son Spain, the Spanish Empire, and his Italian possessions; and to Charles' brother Ferdinand, Austria and the government of the Holy Roman Empire. Philip II was King of Spain, not Holy Roman Emperor; but he controlled the Empire to a considerable degree and in wealth and power he appeared indisputably Europe's foremost monarch. But his father, ill and worn out with the cares of government, had retired to a monastery to prepare himself for the next life; and in doing so, he had left Philip not only an empire but some extraordinarily complex problems. In a period when communications were still terribly slow, Philip's various domains were dangerously spread out. Everywhere except in Spain, the country of his birth, Philip was a foreigner to his subjects. He was not only a foreigner: his sensitiveness, his reticence, and his dignity made of him an aloof and unsympathetic figure. His melancholy mysticism gave him an expression which his enemies might find merely dour. The distrust of men which Charles had given him as part of the training of a prince, his abstemious habits, his instinctive dislike of frivolity, of vulgarity, of coarseness, his stringent self-discipline, and his deep belief that he had been divinely appointed to save Catholic Europe and its civilization from the religious and political chaos that menaced it — all these qualities unfitted him for the government of a polyglot empire. The various portions of that empire were united in his person, and in his person alone. Yet of all the peoples he governed, probably the Spanish alone understood him, and that because he was profoundly Spanish himself.

Even Spain was not a united nation but a combination of Crowns;

and Philip II, like every monarch of his century, contended with feudal, semi-independent nobles for the right to govern. Charles V, with an eye to subduing this nobility to his will, and with the hope of uprooting it locally and robbing it of its political function, had gathered the great nobles of Spain to his court, where he introduced the pompous and splendid etiquette of the House of Burgundy. The dangerous rulers of local princedoms were becoming chamberlains, equerries, and ushers to the King. Philip II, despite his own simple tastes, kept this social machinery going in the interests of royal power.

In addition to consolidating the position of the Crown in Spain, Philip accepted unquestioningly his obligation as Europe's leading monarch to tear up and burn out heresy wherever he found it. This does not mean that he placed himself at the disposal of the Pope. On the contrary, he saw no reason why the Pope should hold a temporal domain, and he used the Papacy in whatever way best suited his policy. The antagonism was mutual; and Pope Paul IV, a Neapolitan, who hated the power of Spain, had allied himself with Henry II of France and with the Turk, in order to drive Charles V from Naples. But Charles had succeeded before abdicating in arranging a five-year truce with Henry. The Pope was furious and set about inducing the French king to break his treaty.

Philip tried to secure the support of his English wife's subjects against the King of France. But what finally got that support was the action of the King of France himself. To offset Philip's influence in England, Henry allowed two ships of English Protestant refugees to launch an expedition from the French coast and to seize Scarborough Castle. But even after England's entry into the war, the English offered ineffective support. The net result for England was the loss of the French port Calais, the last tiny fragment of the wide French provinces which England had held for centuries. Shortly afterward Mary died, and was succeeded by her half-sister Elizabeth, daughter of Anne Boleyn. In 1559 the Peace of Cateau-Cambrésis was signed. It left Spain, France, and England with exhausted treasuries, but it securely re-established Philip's hold on the Italian peninsula.

In Philip's personal experience, nearly every brand of rebellion had

started with religious heresy. It was Lutheran princes who had prevented his father from giving the Holy Roman Empire a strong central government. It was English Protestants who had rendered
Mary's reign difficult. It was obviously his duty as the devout Catholic King of the most powerful Catholic state in Europe to destroy
those who were defying the Church and who would inevitably defy
their King. One of his first acts, therefore, on his return from the
French war in the autumn of 1559 was to attend a great " auto-da-
fé " in Valladolid, one of those public burnings of heretics which
the Spanish Inquisition was to organize throughout his reign. Under
his influence the Inquisition became quite as important a weapon of
a central government fighting its political enemies as of the Catholic
Church fighting heresy. In addition to turning loose the Inquisition
on those who contested royal authority, Philip undertook an elaborate reorganization of the vast administrative machinery through
which he governed the Netherlands, his Italian possessions, and the
Colonies. Because he held to his father's advice to play off his advisers against each other — with the exception of Ruy Gomez, a
friend of his boyhood whom he kept always near him — it was no
simple matter to delegate authority. The result was that all important matters passed through Philip's own hands, a system that
weighed heavily on the King himself and that frequently intruded
details between him and larger matters of policy.

Of these larger matters there was no lack. The Turks, who had
swallowed most of Hungary, now threatened through their fleets to
dominate the Mediterranean. Philip's administrative reorganization
of Spain and his extirpation of heresy clamored constantly for his attention. National feeling, which had grown so swiftly in Europe
during the sixteenth century, threatened to tear his extensive empire
into pieces. Finally his obligation to root out Protestantism in his
distant domains was as real in his own mind as the necessity to suppress heresy inside Spain. But the ancient rivalry between the Valois
dynasty of France and his own Hapsburg line meant that the Catholic kings of France were always prepared to join any of his enemies, whether German Protestant princes or Turkish infidels. And
since the death of his wife Mary, Elizabeth had a second time severed the English Church from the Papacy, and Protestant feeling in

England was constantly growing. Even at Rome there might always be a Pope, who, like Paul IV, would unite Frenchman and Turk against him.

For a brief moment after the French war had ended favorably for Philip in the treaty of Cateau-Cambrésis, the French problem bade fair to be solved. For the Peace was cemented by a marriage between Philip II and Henry II's daughter, Elizabeth of Valois. But, alas, just when things seemed brightest, Henry II died and was succeeded by three feeble sons, Francis II, Charles IX, and Henry III. All three of these kings were dominated by their Italian mother, Catherine de' Medici, tricky, ambitious, resourceful. During Henry II's latter years, although his father and he had pretty well burned out Lutheranism, the teachings of Calvin were gaining increased support from the French commercial classes and some of the French nobility. These Calvinists, or " Huguenots " as they were called, had formed a strong political party to fight for their right of worship; and to maintain her own power, Catherine de' Medici played the Catholics and Huguenots off against each other.

Unable to be sure of Catherine and of France, his treasury exhausted by the recent war, Philip was forced to face the Turkish peril again. A formidable Turkish fleet had scourged the coasts of his South Italian and Sicilian possessions and had attacked Nice. The Turks had then overrun Minorca, and had entrenched themselves in Tripoli where they had seized a fortress from the Knights of St. John of Malta. In Tripoli they were oppressing their fellow-Mohammedans, the Moors. The Master of the Knights of St. John insisted that if Spanish troops invaded Tripoli the Moors would help the Christians against the Turks. But if Spain were to succeed, the Turks must be surprised by a quick move. Philip's slow-moving and cumbersome administration got under way tardily and, when the expedition finally started, the Turks were ready for them. Philip lost sixty-five ships and 5,000 men. But harassed as he was on all sides, he was determined to protect Christendom and his own dominions from the Turks: a fresh fleet of seventy galleys was organized, and was destroyed by storm before it had even left Spain.

Meanwhile, his administration had come to grief in the Netherlands. Neither Philip nor his Spanish administrators had ever been liked there. Nor did Philip like his heavy-eating, deep-drinking, and rough-speaking Flemish subjects. When Philip attempted to reapportion the dioceses of the Church in the Netherlands, and when he left 4,000 Spanish troops in the Netherlands to reinforce the suppression of heresy, the States-General protested. But it was Philip's belief that the center of opposition was one of the principal noblemen of the Netherlands, the German William of Nassau, Prince of Orange. When William of Orange insisted to him on the eve of his departure for Spain in 1559 — never to return — that the opposition to Spanish policy lay in the States-General, Philip for a moment forgot his habitual reserve. " No," he replied, " not the States, but you! you! you! " Whether or not he exaggerated the enmity of William of Orange, it was a serious tactical error on his part to declare his antagonism and to leave the field of operation open to William.

Meanwhile, everything he attempted in the Netherlands bore evil fruit. He could not until 1561 remove the troops he had left there because he could not pay them off. When his French wife's dowry finally enabled him to pay them and withdraw them, the Netherlanders had already been permanently antagonized by their presence. The foreign bishop Granvella, whom he had put in charge of the Church in the Netherlands, antagonized the burghers by his luxurious habits. Protestantism was increasing, and Philip's efforts to extirpate heretics and protect the Catholic faith aroused hatred of everything Spanish. Granvella complained, " They want to reduce this country to a sort of republic, in which the King can do no more than they like." Protests were sent to Philip, but he seems not to have understood clearly what the real grievances of the Netherlanders were. Thousands of Flemings fled to England, thereby strengthening the woolen industry and the economic power of a country which was growing increasingly anti-Spanish.

In 1566 a group of noblemen and burghers petitioned Margaret of Parma, Philip's half-sister and regent of the Netherlands, to secure the abolition of the Inquisition, but one of her advisers exclaimed, " What, madam, is your Highness afraid of these beggars? " The petitioners promptly took the name of " Beggars," and they used as their insignia the wallet and the bowl of the common beggar. " You know how the Spanish Inquisition is hated here," wrote Margaret to Philip. " I have already told you that to suppress heresy here I am asked to cast into the flames 60,000 or 70,000 people, and the governors of the provinces will not allow it. They wish to resign, and I also shall be obliged to do so." Philip's reply was characteristic: "Why all these disquietudes? Are not my intentions understood? Is it believed that I have any intentions other than the service of God and the good of the state?" But he finally gave in and authorized Margaret to pardon the leaders and suppress the Inquisition. He even tried to win William of Orange to his side. But his deepest feelings he expressed to the Pope: "Before allowing any backsliding in religion, or in the service of God, I will lose all my dominions, and a hundred lives if I had them, for I will never be a ruler of heretics."

The suppression of the Inquisition came too late. Anti-Catholic rioters sacked churches, smashed images, and ruined the great cathedral at Antwerp. The Duke of Alba was storming for permission to take an army to the Netherlands and exterminate the rebels. In 1567 Philip sent him by sea with a large force. England, terrified at the approach of a great Spanish fleet through the Channel, began to fit out ships of her own. In the Netherlands, Alba introduced a tribunal known as the "Council of Blood," and for six years executed, despoiled, and frightened from the country thousands of Netherlanders. Lutherans in Germany, Huguenots in France, and Protestants in England prepared to meet this fresh manifestation of Catholic tyranny.

Meanwhile, the death of Philip's third wife, Elizabeth of Valois, brought upon Philip the realization that his alliance with France was definitely at an end and he must carry out his heresy-hunt alone. Mary Stuart, Queen of Scotland, the Catholic candidate for the English throne, whom Philip had helped with money, had been thrown into prison by Elizabeth. English and Dutch privateers scoured the seas for Spanish shipping. But Philip's hands were too full in the Netherlands to allow him to risk a war with England. At home he was struggling with the Moriscos, or Christianized Moors, who had been goaded into revolt by laws designed to make good Spaniards of them and who had called in Mohammedan Moors from Africa to aid them in their struggle. Philip suppressed them with frightful slaughter, but now the Turks had been encouraged in the Mediterranean by Catherine de' Medici and were growing active again.

English privateers like Hawkins and Drake were preying on the Spanish treasure ships which brought Philip the products of his

American mines. Elizabeth was underhandedly sharing in the profits of these piratical enterprises. Philip attempted to punish her with a trade war, but he had too many problems on his hands and eventually gave way. Meanwhile, Philip had sent the Duke of Alba money to pay his troops in the Netherlands, but a storm had forced the Spanish ships to take refuge in an English port and Elizabeth had confiscated Philip's treasure. Alba, hard pressed to find money to pay his troops, instituted a confiscatory system of taxes.

The resentment of the Netherlands was now complete, and even the Catholics of the south joined the northern Protestants under the leadership of William of Orange. While Alba was still soaking the Netherlands with blood, the Turks were threatening to drive the Venetians and other Christians from the Mediterranean and thereby to expose Philip's Italian domains to constant depredation. In 1571, therefore, Philip launched a naval crusade against the Turks, under the leadership of his illegitimate half-brother, Don Juan. Throughout Catholic Christendom prayers were offered in all the churches for the success of the crusade. In the fleet itself, the men fasted, confessed their sins, and received absolution. At daybreak of October 7, the Turks were sighted off Lepanto, and Don Juan exhorted his men: "You are come to fight the battle of the Cross, to conquer or to die.... Christ is your general!" Though badly outnumbered, Philip's crusaders won an overwhelming victory and for decades put an end to the Turkish peril in Europe.

In 1573 Philip replaced the bloody Duke of Alba with the more politic Requesens, but things went from bad to worse. A mutiny of the Spanish troops, who were without pay or food, became famous as the "Spanish Fury." Thereupon the seventeen provinces of the Netherlands concluded the Pacification of Ghent, promising to aid each other against the Spaniards until the Inquisition should be abolished and their customary rights should be restored. Fortunately for Philip, he sent to the Netherlands in 1578 Alexander Farnese, Duke of Parma, who by skillful diplomacy won back to Spain the ten Catholic provinces of the South. The Northern Provinces the following year formed the Union of Utrecht by which they agreed to maintain their rights as one province. The Northern Provinces were never rewon, but neither did Philip ever recognize their independence in his lifetime.

Much of Philip's failure in the Netherlands had been due to the opposition of Elizabeth. He had tried more than one method for solving the English problem. He had unsuccessfully proposed marriage to Elizabeth. He had subsidized the movement to overthrow her in favor of Mary Stuart, Queen of Scots. He now determined to try force. To defend his shipping, to protect his colonies from English privateers, and to force England to cease aiding his rebellious subjects, he fitted out in 1588 the most formidable fleet that Europeans had yet beheld: 130 ships, 8,000 seamen, and 19,000 soldiers. He counted on picking up Farnese with 33,000 veterans from the Netherlands, and he counted on a Catholic uprising against Elizabeth when Spanish priests entered England. It was a terrifying prospect for the English. Despite the defection in the Netherlands which had robbed Philip of some of his wealth and power, there had been ample compensation: eight years before he collected his " Invincible Armada," he had laid successful claim to the crown of Portugal and to the immense Portuguese empire in the Orient. But actually the Spanish Armada was ill equipped, its fighting skill was inferior to that of the English, it was badly provisioned, and some of its ships were in such poor condition that they had to take refuge in French ports and never reached the scene of action at all. Whereas Philip's ships had expected to grapple those of the English and thereby permit Spain's unrivaled infantry to bear the brunt of the combat, the smaller and more easily maneuvered English vessels held off and fought with artillery. English Catholics proved as loyal to Elizabeth as English Protestants, and what the English did not do to the Armada a terrific storm did. Of the 27,000 men who sailed from Spain, only 10,000 returned.

In 1585, three years before his Invincible Armada was destroyed by English weather and English seamanship, Philip's consistent intervention in French affairs took a new and decisive turn. For nearly a quarter of a century, under the weak reigns of Henry II's three sons, France had been torn with civil war. On the one side was the growing power of the Huguenots. On the other side, a group of Catholics, determined to exterminate the heretics, had formed a Holy League under the Duke of Guise. In the center, playing off Leaguers and Huguenots against each other, was the Queen Mother, Catherine de' Medici, who actually governed through her sons. If the Holy League should triumph in France, Philip would not only advance the cause of the thing he held dearest, the Catholic faith; he would secure at his flank a Catholic France that would counter-balance his rebellious Protestant subjects in the Netherlands and his implacable enemies, Elizabeth of England and her privateers. In 1585, therefore, he entered a compact with the Duke of Guise's Holy League, to guarantee that on the death of Henry III, the Huguenot leader, Henry of Navarre, should not succeed to the throne. This treaty resulted in the so-called "War of the Three Henrys"— Henry III of France; Henry of Navarre, heir to the French throne; and Henry, Duke of Guise, backed by Spanish money. Elizabeth naturally sent aid to the Huguenot leader, Henry of Navarre. The upshot of these confused struggles was unfavorable to Philip. Guise was assassinated in 1588, and King Henry III the next year. The Huguenot Henry of Navarre now claimed the throne as Henry IV.

Henry IV's solution of the religious problem was as characteristic of his temperament as Philip II's autos-da-fé were characteristic of his. The late King Henry III had felt the same obligation which Philip felt, to cleanse his kingdom of heresy; but the persecution of Huguenots had gone against his grain. He stated before the Parle-ment of Paris in 1586: "Against my conscience, but very willingly, I came here on a previous occasion to seek the relief of my people by the proclamation of that Edict of Toleration which I have now come to revoke, in accordance, it is true, with my conscience, but most unwillingly, since from this act will follow the ruin of my realm and of my people." But Henry IV, although he had been the leader of a religious minority that had suffered constant persecution from French Catholics and that had even in 1572 undergone the frightful massacre of the Night of St. Bartholomew, was fundamen-tally not interested in matters of religious faith. Consequently, while Philip II willingly risked the mightiest empire in Europe for his re-ligious convictions, Henry IV willingly risked his religious convic-tions — or preferences — to secure the French throne for himself and peace for his distraught subjects. His concern was not the spiritual welfare of his people, but their economic prosperity. Recognizing that France was overwhelmingly Catholic, and would always be gov-erned with difficulty by a Protestant king, Henry shrewdly em-braced Roman Catholicism. He thereby so strengthened his power that he was able to issue the Edict of Nantes, guaranteeing a reasonable toleration to his former co-religionists, the Huguenots. He refused to renounce in detail points of Protestant doctrine to which his Catholic bishops objected and stated tersely that he would not sign a confession containing puerilities that he was certain the bishops did not believe themselves. But he promised to be a Catholic and to " renounce all heresies." With this highly practical, though theologically vague statement, Henry IV heard Mass and France found peace.

Philip's efforts had therefore gone for nothing. His invasion of France in 1590 to help the Holy League to unseat the still unholy King had ended by merely diverting men and money from the Netherlands, and thereby helping the Dutch to secure their independence from Catholic Spain and the Spanish Inquisition. The Holy League's promises to Philip to cede French territory if he would but place their own extreme Catholic party in possession of the French throne, now went unhonored. The Pope praised the Holy League and claimed not to believe the Huguenot King's conversion to the true faith — but the wily Henry IV remained triumphantly on his throne. Many of his Huguenot subjects felt he had deserted true religion for Catholic superstition; and the Catholics saw in the Edict of Nantes and the toleration it extended to Huguenot worship, signs that the Pope's darkest suspicions were correct. But Henry IV, when the Catholics objected to his toleration of Huguenots, was both brief and eloquent: " I must insist upon being obeyed. It is time that we all, having had our fill of war, should learn wisdom by what we have suffered."

Philip II died on September 13, 1598. His life has been given here in some detail, because the confused political and military history of sixteenth-century Europe can be more clearly understood by watching it from Madrid than by taking a conducted tour. It would have been possible to give successively the main events of Spanish history during this period, then of French history, then of Dutch, and then of English. But the history of European civilization in the sixteenth century is the product, not the sum, of the histories of European nations. No other individual of Philip's generation had at his disposal such vast resources, but neither had any other individual with even half his power so deep an interest in the unity of Europe. His enemies might naturally object that he saw that unity through Spanish eyes. But because unity was his constant objective, the tangled events of his day can perhaps be best ordered in relation to his purposes.

His reign was an almost complete failure. He had backed the Council of Trent, which had met because Luther had split Christendom in two. But though the Council of Trent strengthened the organization of the Catholic Church, northern Protestant Europe remained outside the fold. He had tried to cleanse the Netherlands of heresy; and his ban of William of Orange in 1581 had merely brought on his head the Act of Abjuration, by which the Northern Provinces declared their independence. He had tried to secure the co-operation of England, and he had tried to aid Mary in bringing England back to Catholicism. His efforts had ended in a struggle with English privateers and pirates, secretly backed by Protestant Elizabeth; in the Invincible Armada, blessed by the Pope as a Catholic crusade; and in the triumph of English seapower, which now challenged his communications with his colonies. He had tried to save France from heresy, and his armed intervention had ended with the smiling and skeptical Henry IV on the French throne. Five months before Philip lay dying, the ex-Huguenot King had issued his Edict of Nantes, which guaranteed the rights of Calvinist heretics to worship on French soil.

His only major success in foreign affairs was his defense of Christendom against the Turks; and it is characteristic of his purposes and methods that the men who fought at Lepanto fought as crusaders against the infidel. Within the Spanish peninsula success and failure had been mixed. He had secured the crown of Portugal and had thereby combined under his control the Oriental trade empire of the Portuguese and the American colonial empire of Spain. But his Dutch seafaring subjects, in their rebellion against Philip, now had an excellent justification for preying on Portuguese trading posts. He had used the Inquisition to centralize the Spanish monarchy, and with excellent results. Spain was the first European power to accept the theory of absolute monarchy. But by persecuting the Moriscos he had injured perhaps the most industrious group of subjects in Spain; while by persecuting Dutch Calvinists he had merely driven them to Elizabeth's England to swell her economic power. He had tried to break England's economic power by cutting off English trade with Spain and Portugal, and he had merely succeeded in driving English shippers to open up routes to the Orient.

He had indeed failed. But the ordinary diagnosis of his failure does not help in understanding sixteenth-century Europe. The modern student of history is accustomed to measure a nation's achievements in terms of economic welfare. Philip, like other monarchs, wanted economic power, but he wanted it for a definite purpose. He sacrificed the blood and treasure of Spain to restore the unity of Catholic Christendom. If the unity of European civilization was not worth restoring, then obviously Philip " squandered his resources." But this talk of squandering will not help to understand Philip, who valued European unity, nor to understand the magnificent military achievements of his Spanish soldiery. And it will in no way help to understand the inner meaning of Spanish life in his reign.

For Spain was not merely the source of all oppression, as the Dutch, the English, and many of the French inevitably felt. Spain was the cultural center of Europe. Her language was the language of elegance throughout Christendom and was the court language of the Holy Roman Empire for at least a century. The Escorial, the great square granite palace which Philip's architect, Herrera, built some thirty miles from Madrid, symbolized the somber quality of Spanish culture, but it symbolized also its grandeur, and its fundamental purposes. For it was characteristic of Spain that the King's palace should be a cross between a monastery, a church, and a tomb. It was characteristic also that from the King's bedroom Philip could look through a window directly into the domed church inside the Escorial. The Escorial was enriched by such Italian artists as Titian, Tintoretto, and Cellini; and by the Spanish painter Velásquez and by the Greek painter who became a Spaniard, El Greco.

The sixteenth century saw in Spain not only the crusading religious zeal of Loyola and his Jesuits. It beheld the famous Spanish mystics St. Teresa and St. John of the Cross. Like the German mystics who preceded them, these Spaniards saw direct visions of Christ; but characteristically, their mysticism led, not to a break with the established Church, but to an enrichment of that Church's life and to some of Europe's greatest mystical literature. The expressions of Spanish culture in this century are extraordinarily homogeneous and brilliantly illuminate the aspirations of Philip himself. The reigns of

Philip II, Philip III, and Philip IV witnessed an amazing outburst in literature: Lope de Vega with his plays and poems, serving in the Invincible Armada, becoming a priest, scourging himself — so it was said — every Friday; Cervantes, novelist, playwright, poet, who was wounded fighting the Turks at Lepanto; Calderón, successor to De Vega's laurels in the drama, patronized by Philip IV, serving first in the army and then in the Church, and becoming Philip IV's honorary chaplain. It was the painter El Greco, who could still feel the medieval ascetic spirit when the rest of Europe had forgotten it, whom Philip II commissioned to execute an altarpiece for his church in the Escorial. There was Ribera, the painter who loved to do bloody martyrdoms and who spent most of his life at Naples when Naples was ruled from Spain. There was Zurbaran, like most Spanish painters deeply religious in his interests, who became town painter of Seville and finally " painter to the King." And there was Zurbaran's great friend Velásquez, who produced chiefly court portraits and who was pensioned by the King. There was Morales, whom Philip II summoned to help decorate the Escorial. And there was the religious painter Murillo, like his friend, the great Velásquez, born in Seville. In music there were Vittoria and Querro, the former a vice-master of the Royal Chapel in Madrid.

It is worth remarking how many of these writers and painters and artists were soldiers, or priests, or both. That Spanish culture under the Philips should have expressed itself through such men explains eloquently why the role of Spain under Philip II was that of a nation of medieval crusaders. It was Spain's tragedy, and Philip's, and for that matter Europe's, that the mightiest power in Christendom in the second half of the sixteenth century should have been belatedly medieval, a nation still dominated by priest, noble, and peasant; a nation that possessed the no longer popular virtues of an aristocracy, pride of bearing and unreasoning courage. Perhaps the key to a genuine understanding of the policy of Philip II lies not in Spain's religious painters, nor in the music of Vittoria, nor in the plays of De Vega, but in the one Spanish book whose title at least is still the best known outside Spain in the whole of Spanish literature: *Don Quixote,* by Miguel de Cervantes. Don Quixote was a knight, born not when knighthood was in flower but when it had run to seed, and Cervantes apparently offered him in good faith as a humorous anachronism. But although his level-headed servant Sancho Panza shared with Henry IV of France an understanding of what Europe's new and secular civilization was about, yet Don Quixote, tilting at windmills, is not merely humorous. He is heroic and tragic. So was Philip II.

VII.

THE TWO CHRISTENDOMS

W<small>HEN</small> Philip III succeeded his father on the Spanish throne in 1598, the Spanish Empire entered upon what might have been a period of economic recovery. The English problem, the French problem, and the old problem of the Calvinist Netherlands bade fair to settle themselves. The defeat of the Spanish Armada ten years before had rendered it unlikely that Protestant England could ever be brought back into the Catholic fold. Moreover, five years after Philip III came to the throne of Spain, the redoubtable Elizabeth died; and James VI of Scotland inherited her throne as James I of England. This union of England and Scotland, a union that was purely personal, not only strengthened England against possible attack. Actually, James I made peace with Philip the year after he assumed the English crown, restrained the freebooters and privateers whom Elizabeth had secretly encouraged to prey on Spanish treasure galleons and on Spanish colonies, and sent one of the most famous of Spain's tormentors, Sir Walter Raleigh, to the block. In France, on the other hand, the assassination of Henry IV by a Catholic fanatic in 1610, just as he was preparing to take up arms again against the Hapsburgs, placed France under the weak regency of his widow, Marie de' Medici, and made it unlikely that Spain would suffer an attack from that quarter. James I had tried to marry his son and heir to a Spanish princess; Marie de' Medici actually did marry off her son Louis XIII to Philip's daughter Anne. Meanwhile, Philip had secured a truce with the Calvinist Netherlands in 1609, which indeed did not permanently recognize Dutch independence but did protect Philip's Portuguese colonies in the Orient from further Dutch onslaughts. For nearly half a century the Dutch problem had weighed on Spain. Not only had Philip II felt compelled to pour men and money into the Netherlands itself. It had been a constant invitation to his French enemies to strike him while his hands were tied. It had furnished Elizabethan England with a constant means of weakening Spanish power without having to attempt an impossible frontal assault on Spain herself. Spain under Philip III now seemed prepared to surrender Philip II's dream of Catholic unity so far as England, France, and the Netherlands were concerned. England remained Anglican; the northern Netherlands remained Calvinist; and the French brand of Catholicism tolerated Huguenot heretics.

But in one part of Europe the Protestant heresy remained unfinished business and the dream of Catholic restoration a genuine possibility. That part was precisely the Holy Roman Empire, in which Martin Luther had permanently unleashed Protestant heresy, and for which members of Philip III's own Hapsburg family were responsible as Emperors. The Holy Roman Empire was Europe's greatest political expression of the medieval Catholic past which Philip II had given his life to recapture. Despite the fact that the Empire was overwhelmingly German in speech and in tradition, its Emperors had never succeeded in converting it into a national German monarchy. In England and in France king and merchant had combined against the great feudal lords and had broken their political power in favor of centralized monarchy. But the cities of Germany, despite their immense prosperity in the early sixteenth century, had never given the Emperor the support that would have enabled him to bring the German princes to heel; and by the opening of the seventeenth century a decline in German commerce in favor of the national states on the Atlantic seaboard had permitted the Holy Roman Empire to remain essentially medieval in its political and social organization. That meant in turn that the great medieval ideals had remained unchallenged by the new commercial nationalism, the ideals of a universal faith and of a universal Christian Empire.

These were the ideals which had led the Emperor Charles V to feel responsible for suppressing the Lutheran heresy. These were the ideals which his son Philip II had labored to maintain. Charles had bequeathed Spain, its colonies, the Netherlands, and his Italian possessions to Philip, and only his Austrian possessions to his brother, Ferdinand. Therefore, although Ferdinand became Holy Roman Emperor, it was Philip II on whom the responsibility fell for defending Europe's traditional civilization against such disruptive forces as the French kings with their Turkish allies, Dutch rebels with their Calvinistic heresies, and Protestant England with its piratical attacks on Spanish shipping, and its interventions in favor of Dutch heretics and French Huguenots. During the reign of Philip II, therefore, the treasure that poured annually from Mexican and Peruvian mines was used by his crusading subjects, not only to protect Christendom from the powerful onslaughts of the infidel Turk, but to underwrite the restoration of Catholic unity in Europe.

That effort had failed. And his son, Philip III, appeared at least temporarily willing to accept the failure. But in 1618 the revolt of Calvinist Bohemia against his Austrian cousin, the Emperor Matthias, posed the Protestant problem afresh. A band of armed Bohemian nobles burst into the castle at Prague, seized two emissaries of the Emperor Matthias and their secretary, and threw them out of a window into a ditch some seventy feet below. None of the three men was killed, the Protestants said because they had landed on a dunghill, and the Catholics said because Mary, the Mother of God, had saved them. The immediate reason for this act of insubordination against the Emperor Matthias, who was also King of Bohemia, was the expectation that he would shortly be succeeded by his brother, Ferdinand of Styria. Bohemia was nine-tenths Calvinist, while Ferdinand was a militant Catholic, educated by Jesuits, and had already shown by his persecution of Protestants in Styria, what Bohemian Calvinists might expect of him. When he did actually succeed to the throne, as the first Holy Roman Emperor to have been educated by Jesuits, the Bohemian revolt spread to Austria itself and took the form of a demand for a sort of aristocratic republic. When emissaries of the movement arrived at Ferdinand's palace he knelt before his crucifix. It was later rumored that the figure of Christ had bowed and had murmured: " Ferdinand, I will not forsake thee." The Bohemians had turned for aid, not certainly to a crucifix, but to the half-barbarian Bethlen Gabor, Protestant Prince of Transylvania and ally of the Turks. They were consequently accused of wishing to plant the Crescent on the ruins of Christendom. Ferdinand secured substantial financial aid from the Pope and sent an appeal to his cousin, Philip III of Spain.

Philip III was trying to rescue Spain from the bankruptcy which his father's long crusade for Catholicism had cost her. But Philip III was if anything more ecstatically devout than his father. It was Philip III who promised the Pope never to commit mortal sin again if the Pope would do four things for him. He asked that certain saintly Spaniards be recognized officially as saints by the Pope. He asked for the strict enforcement of the doctrine of Immaculate Conception. He begged for a gift of holy relics. And he asked that at his death — he was now thirty-four — every altar in the world that should say Mass for his soul might receive special privileges. And now Ferdinand II, his close cousin and the man responsible to God for the Holy Roman Empire, demanded his aid in putting down a Protestant rebellion. Khevenhüller, Ferdinand's ambassador, threatened Philip with the awful terrors of the Last Judgment should he permit the Bohemian rebels to conquer and should he thereby permit so many souls to fall into hell-fire.

The Bohemians now called a Diet which officially excluded Ferdinand from their throne, and elected in his place a Calvinist prince, the Elector Frederick of the Palatinate. They hoped that this would secure for them the aid of Frederick's father-in-law, James I of England, and of the other Protestant princes of the Empire. They were disappointed. James was pursuing a Spanish policy and limited his aid to good advice. The German Lutheran princes, on the other hand, had never lost any love on the Calvinists and now hoped, by remaining neutral, to secure better treatment from the new Catholic Emperor. Meanwhile, Frederick and his English wife showed a complete incapacity to govern Bohemia, and the Bohemians showed a complete unwillingness to tax themselves adequately enough to make Bohemian independence succeed.

The Battle of the White Hill, just outside Prague, took hardly more than an hour. Ferdinand's army was led by Count Tilly, a native of Brabant who had first studied to become a Jesuit and had then decided to become a soldier. He had served in the Spanish armies and later under Maximilian of Bavaria, the Emperor's most important Catholic prince. Tilly was himself a rabid Catholic of the proselytizing variety and had refused offers to enter Protestant service. At the White Hill his army's cry was " Holy Mary," and his soldiers were promised the intercession of the Mother of God by a monk who inspired them with fanatical courage. Frederick's army lacked morale, and a hopeless panic resulted. Prague fell, and the new monarch, whose reign the Jesuits had insisted would not out-last the winter, went down in history as " the Winter King."

Ferdinand's punishment of the Bohemian rebels was terrific. Lands were widely confiscated, ringleaders were executed, the popu-lation was starved and tortured, and Ferdinand's dragoons were quartered on the stubborn to bring them around to the true faith, and were thereby known as " angel-makers." The Lutherans were at first spared. The Lutheran clergy were even allowed to keep their wives, provided they would speak of them in public as their cooks. But when the Lutherans, too, refused to turn Catholic, they were banished. The population of Bohemia fell from 4,000,000 to 800,000.

Ferdinand's conquest of Bohemia looked like a complete triumph for Spanish and Austrian arms, for the Hapsburg family, for the restoration of Catholicism, and for Ferdinand's Jesuit advisers. Un-fortunately for Ferdinand, in order to secure the necessary aid of his principal Catholic vassal, Maximilian of Bavaria, he had prom-ised Maximilian as his reward of service the Elector Frederick's orig-inal possession, the Palatinate. The Palatinate was a Calvinist state, and now this new and militantly Catholic Emperor was proposing to turn it over to his most Catholic prince. Protestant opinion was outraged, and ever since 1608 Protestant opinion had been organized in a Union of German Protestant Princes. It was precisely because the Winter King had been the leader of this Union that the Bohe-mians had vainly imagined that the Union would back them in their rebellion. Catholic opinion likewise had been formally organ-ized in 1609, a year later than the Union, in a Catholic League. That the Union and the League should have been facing each other for a decade before the Bohemian revolt and less than six decades after the Peace of Augsburg was due to several factors. The Peace of Augsburg had stipulated that in the future Catholic ecclesiastics who turned Lutheran should not confiscate the Church lands which they had governed. This rule had not been observed. Moreover the Peace had dealt only with the Lutheran problem and had ignored the Calvinists. During the following half century Calvinists had increased in numbers and were clamoring for the protection which the Peace had secured to Lutherans. Finally, the reformation of the Catholic Church at the Council of Trent had led many Catholics in the Empire to hope for the religious reconquest of Protestant territory, and Loyola's Jesuits, who had done so much to make the Council of Trent a success, were constantly urging such reconquest.

The Protestant Union had done little to aid the Bohemians. But it was bitterly opposed to having the Calvinist Palatinate awarded to the Catholic Maximilian of Bavaria, and even some of the Catholic princes objected to this expansion of Maximilian's power. The Emperor publicly fell back on a compromise, awarding the Palatinate only temporarily to Maximilian. But the Emperor had been educated by Jesuits and accepted fully a doctrine widely held in Catholic lands, that promises and even oaths to heretics need not be kept. And he privately assured Maximilian that the Palatinate would be permanently his. In 1625, the Lutheran King of Denmark, Christian IV, decided to intervene on behalf of the German princes. He was backed by an English subsidy: the Emperor's treatment of James' son-in-law, the Winter King, James' failure to arrange a Spanish marriage for his son, and the steady growth of anti-Spanish feeling in England had swung James over to the cause of German Protestantism. Christian IV, on his part, King of Denmark and Norway, was anxious to dominate the north coast of Germany.

With only the army of Tilly to ward off Danish invasion, Ferdinand turned for help to a Bohemian noble, Wallenstein, who had become the richest man in Bohemia through buying up at depreciated prices the lands which Ferdinand had confiscated there. Wallenstein had begun life as a Protestant; had become a convert and pupil of the Jesuits; but had failed to become a fanatic. He agreed with Ferdinand to raise an army of 21,000 men and to serve the Emperor on a business basis with a handsome share of the booty guaranteed. But whereas Tilly fought for Catholicism and for Maximilian of

Bavaria, it became more and more obvious to the princes of Germany, whether Catholic or Protestant, that Wallenstein's huge private army was being used for the double purpose of enriching himself and of making Ferdinand an absolute monarch like the kings of France and England. With this end in view, Wallenstein recruited a motley army of Catholics and Protestants, from all over Europe, and he made efficient service, not religious creed, the only standard of promotion. He became " General of the Holy Imperial Armada and of the Baltic and the North Sea," and Duke of Friedland. Nevertheless, Ferdinand failed to trust completely this amazing leader who wished to make a modern monarch of him, this financial and military genius who was determined to convert a religious struggle into a war that would create a nation. For the pious Ferdinand, this war remained religious. Consequently, when Tilly and Wallenstein had overwhelmed Christian of Denmark in 1626, Ferdinand determined to recognize his responsibility as a Hapsburg defender of Catholic Europe. Without notifying his would-be kingmaker, Wallenstein, he signed, in the very year that peace was made with Denmark, the Edict of Restitution.

The Edict of Restitution declared that all ecclesiastical property which Protestants had taken over despite the Peace of Augsburg was to be reclaimed; and that in lands taken back by the Catholics, Protestants need not be tolerated. An immense number of churches and former monasteries were promptly seized; Jesuit colleges were built; and a Catholic University was established at Goslar to spread Catholic teaching in the land of the heretics. The Catholic League, which had persuaded Ferdinand to sign the Edict of Restitution, now persuaded him to get rid of the ambitious Wallenstein. It was at this moment, when the Protestant princes were in an uproar and when Ferdinand had dismissed his ablest military leader, that the Lutheran King of Sweden, Gustavus Adolphus, landed with an army in Germany.

Gustavus had planned for years to intervene on behalf of the Lutheran princes and it was James I's bad judgment that led him to back the swaggering Christian IV rather than his rival Gustavus. Gustavus wanted to extend the power of Sweden and he considered himself charged by God with the defense of the true Lutheran faith. He had already pushed Russia back from the Baltic and had defeated Poland. He was convinced that the Catholic Emperor Ferdinand II would dispute his expansion into North Germany; and he had secured substantial financial backing from Richelieu, now the first minister in France, who was willing to back this Lutheran Swede if he could thereby weaken the powerful German monarchy that Wallenstein had wished to make supreme. Gustavus landed in 1630 and in two years had overwhelmed Tilly and his Catholic army, and was sweeping toward the hereditary dominions of the Austrian Hapsburgs. In terror, Ferdinand recalled Wallenstein to power and tightened his alliance with Philip IV of Spain, who had succeeded his father in 1621. In 1632 Wallenstein and Gustavus Adolphus met at Lützen. Wallenstein was defeated, but Gustavus was killed. Wallenstein thereupon reorganized his army, defeated the Swedes at Nördlingen, and began to treat for peace independently of the Emperor. He intended a reorganization of the Empire on the basis of freedom of religious belief, the rescinding of everything done since the outbreak of the war in 1618 that contradicted this principle, and an indemnity to the Swedes to get them out of the Germanies. But the Spanish, the Bavarians, and the clergy bitterly opposed religious toleration and persuaded the Emperor that Wallenstein, with his independent policy, was usurping the Imperial power. Indeed, Wallenstein's movements at this time really were marked by intrigue. He was treating privately with the Emperor's enemies, probably because he felt strong enough to impose ultimately on the Emperor himself the peace of religious toleration which he felt the Empire must secure. In the circumstances it was easy to convince Ferdinand that Wallenstein was betraying him, and Ferdinand ordered his arrest. Some of Ferdinand's officers, convinced that Wallenstein was a traitor, in 1634 assassinated Wallenstein to the cry of: "Long live Emperor Ferdinand!" In the next year, since both sides were exhausted by the war, a treaty was signed at Prague between the Emperor and the principal Protestant leaders.

The Peace of Prague provided for the almost complete control of all troops by the Emperor, for the dissolution of the princely leagues, for the mutual restoration of captured territory, and for the division of ecclesiastical lands between Catholics and Protestants on the basis of ownership in 1627. It would probably have brought Europe's most terrible religious war to a permanent close had it not been for a factor in no sense related to religion. That factor was the determination of Richelieu to continue the struggle until France's traditional enemies, the Hapsburgs, had been more nearly eliminated, and until the disunity of the Empire had been guaranteed. Richelieu therefore no longer contented himself with subsidizing Swedish and German Protestants to fight the Emperor; he brought France herself into the war with the particular task of fighting Spain. The French period of the Thirty Years' War was to last from 1635 to 1648.

By 1635, when France openly entered the Thirty Years' War, the character of the struggle had definitely and finally changed. It had begun as a struggle between Catholic Germany and Protestant Germany. But from the first this simple alignment was complicated by a number of hard facts. The Emperor Ferdinand had been technically leader of Catholic Germany, but he had also tried from the start to centralize his control over the Empire. This, even the Catholic princes whom he led were determined to prevent. In the beginning his main dependence had been Spain and Maximilian of Bavaria, the leader of the Catholic League. His ablest general had been the Catholic Tilly, who was actually Maximilian's man, not his. Wallenstein had offered him a professional army that was adapted, not so much to the defense and the extension of Catholicism, as to strengthening Ferdinand's authority over the German princes, Catholic as well as Protestant. Ferdinand had allowed the Catholic League to secure from him the Edict of Restitution and had thereby reasserted the religious motive of the war. Thereby, also, he had repudiated Wallenstein's policy of a powerful monarchy based on religious toleration. Gustavus Adolphus had intervened on behalf of the Lutheran princes, now driven to desperation by the Edict of Restitution. Ferdinand's profound desire to save Catholic Europe from Protestant rebellion was matched by Gustavus' profound desire to save Protestant Europe from Catholic reaction. Ferdinand proposed to carry out his plan by strengthening the political power of the Emperor. Gustavus proposed to carry out his by building a mightier Sweden that would make the Baltic a Swedish lake, and that would be powerful enough to protect the Protestant states of North Germany against the Catholic South. But Gustavus had fallen in battle, and Wallenstein had been slain by Imperialist fanatics. Richelieu, whose subsidies had made it possible for Gustavus to enter the war in the first instance, had now thrown into the arena the armies of France to keep the Emperor from forming a compact German state on France's flank, and to extend French territory.

By 1635, when France entered the arena, the Thirty Years' War had raged for seventeen years. Every important country in Christendom had been involved in the struggle. At immense cost in blood and treasure, Europeans had discovered what the actual stakes were. The religious struggle had naturally been complicated from the very beginning by political ambition and territorial greed. But by 1635 it was evident that the dominant motives of the war were no longer religious at all. The Netherlands wanted to gain permanent independence from Spain. The Swiss wanted independence from Austria. The French wanted to break the Hapsburgs and expand their own frontiers. The Swedes wanted territorial compensation for the effort they had made. The various German princes had each his special ambition to satisfy: they were therefore constantly swapping allegiance and driving bargains of their own. Ferdinand III, who succeeded his father as Emperor in 1637, was driven to open negotiations for peace four years later, but the Peace of Westphalia was not finally signed until 1648, and even then the French continued to harass the Spanish for eleven years longer.

Before the French entered the war the Spanish had been able simultaneously to help the Austrian Hapsburgs and make one more attempt to destroy the independence of the Netherlands. But they were now driven to defend themselves against the French in the Southern (Spanish) Netherlands, in Franche-Comté, in Northern Italy, and even in Spain. For a while the veteran and renowned armies of Spain made such good headway that they were able to invade French territory both from the Spanish Netherlands and from Spain. But as the French developed experience, as the Dutch lent them their support, as Portugal rose in a war of independence against Spain, and as revolts broke out in Italy and in Spain itself, Philip IV began to give way. In 1643 Europe was amazed to learn that the French had routed Spanish infantry at Rocroi. It was nevertheless not until 1659 that Spain could bring herself by the Treaty of the Pyrenees to admit defeat. France received a strip of the Southern Netherlands and the province of Roussillon, which Spain had held north of the Pyrenees.

By the Peace of Westphalia also France had made important gains. She not only received Alsace, except for the free city of Strasbourg; her rights to the bishoprics of Metz, Toul, and Verdun were formally admitted. Sweden obtained part of Pomerania and the bishopric of Bremen. Both Switzerland and the United Provinces of the Netherlands were recognized as independent states. Most important of all, France saw to it that each of the German states, some three hundred in number, might make war and peace independently and coin its own money. What was left of the religious problem was settled along the lines of the Peace of Augsburg, signed nearly a century earlier: the head of each German state had the right to choose for his people between Catholicism, Lutheranism, and Calvinism. Church land was to be held by Catholics or by Protestants according to its status in 1624.

Europe had learned its lesson: its interests were no longer dominantly religious. The cost of the lesson, however, was a bit high. Thirty years of warfare, of burning, of pillaging, of forced contributions, and of murder had left the Germanies disorganized and prostrate. Criminals followed the various mercenary armies to clean up whatever the armies had not already wrecked. Indeed, the hordes of camp followers were as responsible as the soldiers for the general devastation. At a battle during the last year of the war the Emperor's army consisted of 34,000 combatants, and 127,000 women, children, and useless men. At the lowest estimate, a third of the population had disappeared, and the local Diet in Franconia bravely faced the problem of repeopling the countryside by decreeing that every man might have two wives and no man under sixty might become a monk. Commerce had gone to pieces, and there were industries which did not recover for a century. Germany was not only materially, but intellectually, a desert.

At the Peace of Westphalia the diplomats of Europe officially liquidated the medieval ideal of the religious unity of all Christendom. A generation had been disillusioned by the physical horrors and by the final moral bankruptcy of Christendom, and by the thirty-year death agony of its unity. The Holy Roman Empire, the most obvious political expression of the old ideal of unity, entered the war already weakened by religious discord, but it emerged thirty years later a complete wreck, nowhere near as strong as the compact monarchies of the West over which it had once exercised a shadowy claim to authority. In its place the Peace of Westphalia recognized once and for all that there were two German cultures, a Catholic and a Protestant. Implicitly, it also recognized that there were two Christendoms, a Catholic and a Protestant. Theoretically, these two Christendoms might have continued to exist side by side. In this fashion, in the days when Christendom was still one, it had existed side by side with Orthodox Russia and with Moslem Turkey. But there were many practical difficulties in such a solution. The tradition of the two Christendoms was so largely a common tradition that the secession of Protestant Christendom was hard to accept. Moreover, from the very decade of its birth, Protestant Christendom had tended to break into parts. It was not merely Catholic and Protestant that had fought religious wars. Lutheran and Calvinist had failed to live in peace together; and both had persecuted Anabaptists.

It was becoming terrifyingly obvious that the political and economic institutions of Europe had rested, and no longer rested, on a common faith in the same God. For those institutions had been evolved by people who believed that man's duty to his neighbor was defined by his duty to God. But Europeans no longer believed in the same God. There was now a Catholic God, a Lutheran God, a Calvinist God, an Anabaptist God, and a host of other deities less important historically. The duty a Calvinist owed to his God differed from the duty a Catholic owed to his: Catholic and Calvinist emphasized quite different virtues. Moreover, just as a Calvinist's duty to God differed from the Catholic's, so did his duty to his neighbor. Inevitably, the political and economic institutions which all Europeans had inherited from their common Catholic past failed to serve the needs of the new Protestant cultures which had sprung up in Northern Europe. It was because Catholic and Protestant alike had seen only too clearly the connection between their institutions and their profoundest religious beliefs, that Europe had been torn by religious wars for more than a century. Catholics like Philip II realized that they were fighting to preserve not only the Catholic faith which they had inherited, but its product, Catholic civilization, which they had inherited along with it. Calvinists at Geneva upheld not merely the doctrine expressed in Calvin's *Institutes of the Chris-*

tian Religion; they upheld also the godly way of life which en-
thused John Knox on his visit to Geneva. The modern student of
history frequently assumes that the religious wars were the struggles
of fanatics whose only point of difference lay in unprovable theological assumptions and that they were not fought about anything real
at all. Or he assumes, on the other hand, that they were purely the
product of Philip II's political ambition, of the land hunger of Lutheran princes, and of Dutch determination to steal Portugal's colonial empire. Either assumption betrays a lack of the historic sense.
Either assumption merely means that the modern has failed to grasp
a connection which the sixteenth century grasped with searing clarity, the connection between a religious faith which is deeply felt,
and the human institutions evolved by the men who hold it.

Two Christendoms faced each other, the Protestant North and the
Catholic South, and important cultural differences separated the two.
Luther had insisted that the peasant's labor was just as much a
" calling," a " vocation," as the monastic life. The Protestant world
extended that idea to cover business enterprise, in which the good
Calvinist made God his partner. Catholic Christendom still tended
to regard work as the curse God laid on Adam, as a necessary evil:
the economic process was merely a means to an end; it supported
a man's body while his soul sought spiritual good. Protestant Christendom, on the other hand, and particularly Calvinist Christendom,
glorified work as the ideal spiritual discipline. In Catholic countries
" Our Lady Poverty," beloved of St. Francis, continued in honor,
and beggary flourished. In Protestant countries, not only was labor
honored, but poverty came to be despised, as God's proper punishment for laziness and inefficiency. The moral virtues of diligence,
thrift, sobriety, and prudence governed the good Protestant, and
God prospered him. No wonder that it was the centers of commerce
particularly that were drawn to Protestantism as the natural expression of their religious life. Catholic Christendom, entrenched
particularly in the rural classes, was the stronghold of social con-
servatism; Protestant Christendom turned to strenuous enterprise.
Economic gain tended in Catholic peoples to take the medieval form
of seizing wealth to squander, as the Spaniard seized the gold and
silver of Mexico. Protestant peoples gave themselves more and more
to profitable business procedure, where the prize went not to the

brave and dashing but to the careful, the self-controlled, the hard-working. The Protestant found in gain, not a perpetual distraction from the spiritual life, but a means of measuring work, and in work he found the proper discipline for attaining to such life. For the Catholic asceticism of poverty, the Protestant substituted the asceti-cism of work: where the Catholic sacrificed worldly wealth for love of God, the Protestant sacrificed leisure and ease. In Catholic coun-tries the arts of painting and sculpture and architecture continued to symbolize the Christian way to the lowly worshiper. These " vani-ties " that rejoiced the eye were looked on by the Calvinist as idola-trous distractions. The Calvinist therefore suppressed the arts and worshiped God in an unadorned building. For the elaborate cere-monial of the Catholic Church, he substituted plain, honest dealing, even with God. For the " good works " of Catholicism — charitable gifts, penitential tasks — he substituted a constant worldly activity, dedicated to God and measured in terms of success. Where the Cath-olic turned to the Church for an interpretation of Scripture, particu-larly in the Christian revelation of the New Testament, the Protes-tant read the Bible for himself and showed a marked preference for the Old Testament, the story of God's chosen people, chosen like the " elect " of the Calvinist faith, and ruthless to the enemies of the Lord. For the confessional he substituted the individual's own con-science. Of all authority below God Himself he was suspicious, which meant inevitably in practice that each man tended to apply his own moral sanction or at best the moral sanction of the " elect," even against the King.

These are obviously generalizations. It would be easy to show ex-ceptions; but it would be equally easy to show that in general the two Christendoms which emerged from the hell of the Thirty Years' War themselves recognized these general differences. And these gen-eral differences meant in turn that a traditional, conservative, art-loving, authoritarian, unprogressive Catholic world faced a Protes-tant world to the north that was progressive, enterprising, restless, increasingly commercial, decreasingly artistic, resentful of authority, practical, thrifty, individualistic. Between those two worlds lay a gulf of misunderstanding, and a widening gulf of mutual hatred and suspicion.

The loss of Europe's religious unity, then, had shaken the very foundations of European civilization. It was no longer simple to define just dealings between men, since justice had always been stated in religious terms. What were now to be just dealings between ruler and subject? What would be just dealings between producer and consumer? What, in view of the unspeakable barbarities of the Thirty Years' War, fought under the opposing banners of a Protestant Jesus and a Catholic Mary, were to be just dealings between the separate states of Europe? Could there be any basis for just arbitration in international affairs, or must the Thirty Years' War continue until not only the Germanies, but the whole of Europe, were desert waste reverting to savagery?

Of the generation who saw the Thirty Years' War begin, no man faced these new and terrifying problems with more conspicuous success than Hugo de Groot, a Dutch humanist who wrote under the Latinized name Grotius. Grotius was born in Delft in 1583, two years after the Dutch Netherlands had by the Act of Abjuration declared their independence from Spain. His family were members of the powerful commercial aristocracy then developing in the Netherlands, and he was brought up in the Calvinist faith. He studied at the University of Leiden and his education was humanistic: chiefly the classical languages, with some Hebrew and Arabic. When he was only fifteen he secured his first practical experience of international affairs by accompanying a Dutch diplomatic mission to the courts of Henry IV of France and Elizabeth of England, whose aid the Dutch were constantly soliciting against Spain. He began to write early and voluminously: poetry, drama, theological discussions, and finally, for he became a lawyer, treatises on international law. His early recognition that European civilization had lost its way caused him to publish when he was only eighteen a tragedy in Latin on the subject of Adam as an exile from the Garden of Eden. Many years later, when he was in his fifties, a young English poet named John Milton saw him in Paris, and Milton was to write on a similar theme his famous *Paradise Lost*.

In 1606 Grotius finished, but never published, a Latin treatise on the right of seizing prizes at sea; for the young lawyer had been engaged by the recently organized Dutch East India Company to defend it for seizing a Portuguese vessel. Grotius next turned his attention to the chief concern of his life: the reorganization of European civilization. Recognizing the profound cleavage between Catholic and Protestant Europe, he wanted at least to preserve the unity of Protestant Christianity and of Protestant culture. How difficult even that would be he knew by painful experience, for Calvinist Holland was already torn by theological disputes, by a struggle for power between the executive and legislative branches of the government, and by a contest between the central government and the local governments of the seven provinces which had formed the Union of Utrecht. But the theological and political quarrels that were rending the Netherlands were merely the miniature replicas of the theological and political quarrels that rent Protestant Europe. Grotius made a voyage to England and tried to induce James I to call a general council of all Protestant churches, that would do for Protestantism what the Council of Trent had done for Catholic Europe. He believed that, if points of agreement could be drawn up, the points of disagreement would become less acute and Lutheran and Calvinist could no longer be played off against each other by the Catholics. But James could not be persuaded. On Grotius' return to the Netherlands, he unhappily became involved in a theological dispute and thence by stages in a defense of the rights of the province of Holland against the central government of the Netherlands. In 1618 the central government imprisoned Oldenbarneveldt and Grotius. Oldenbarneveldt was executed, but three years later Grotius escaped and went into exile. While Grotius had been reflecting in prison on the clash of religious opinion in little Holland, a clash which had led directly into a dispute over political authority, the drama of the Thirty Years' War had begun and was demonstrating a similar connection between religion and politics on a European scale. In 1634 Grotius assumed a responsible role in this greater struggle by becoming Sweden's ambassador at Paris. Eleven years later he was called to Sweden and died on his way there at the age of sixty-two.

But his fame does not rest on his services as intermediary between Sweden and her paymaster, Richelieu. It rests on a treatise on international law which he wrote at Paris after his escape from prison and which he published there in 1625 under the title, *On the Law of War and Peace*. Grotius was by no means the first European to recognize the necessity of evolving for Europe some principle of common authority to take the place of the Papacy, which the Protestant North no longer recognized, and the Holy Roman Empire, which had long been ineffectual and which was to be rendered completely impotent by the Peace of Westphalia. Pope Urban VIII, who had held from the start that the Thirty Years' War was not religious in essence, and had cited in proof Gustavus Adolphus' agreement with Richelieu to tolerate Catholics in conquered territories, offered in 1638 to mediate between the contestants, but Protestant Sweden would have none of it. Sweden's unwillingness to accept as mediator the religious head of Catholic Europe was vindicated after the Peace of Westphalia, when Urban's successor, Innocent X, horrified at the concessions made to Protestant heretics, declared the final settlement, the product of thirty years of European agony, " null and void, accursed and without any influence or result for the past, the present, or the future," and urged that Catholic princes should not keep the agreement even if they had sworn to it.

Since Protestant Europe could therefore hardly be expected to vest international authority in the Papacy, where was it to turn? Henry IV of France, the skeptical Huguenot prince who had officially accepted Catholicism to gain the French crown, and had placed royal authority behind an Edict of Toleration, might be expected to furnish an answer. As a matter of fact, Henry repeatedly discussed with his great Huguenot minister, Sully, their " Great Design " for Europe. Henry's plan was first to ruin the domination of the Hapsburgs, which had encouraged Catholic Europe to make perpetual assaults on the Protestant North, under the leadership of Philip II of Spain, and would later summon it to a new crusade under Ferdinand II, Emperor of the Holy Roman Empire. With Hapsburg predominance out of the way, and with the remaining great states of Europe on the basis of approximately equal power, a league of European nations would then be formed, in which the small states too would have their place. Europe would thereby be reunited into a sort of Christian Federated Republic. The plan was broached to Elizabeth of England, who professed to approve of the idea. But Henry IV was assassinated by a Catholic fanatic just as he was about to take the first and most important step toward realizing the Great Design — or, for that matter, toward strengthening the state he governed: another attack on the Hapsburg power.

There were other Europeans who saw the necessity of facing the problem of international relations in a Europe which had fallen into pieces religiously. But it was the achievement of Grotius, in his treatise *On the Law of War and Peace,* to order in one coherent whole the various theories of international law from classical times to his own day. Europe, still in the throes of the horrible struggle in the Germanies, gave Grotius a ready hearing, and his book was to exert enormous influence in the future. He furnished Protestant nations with a rational basis for international relations, apart from the traditional theology of the Catholic faith which they had abandoned. He thereby furnished the basis for the modern state system which emerged from the Peace of Westphalia and which has lasted to the present day. Seeking for an authority which all men would recognize, Grotius attempted to locate it in three forms of law: the law of Nature, which is implied by the fact that man is a social being and a rational being; the law of God, which should at least theoretically lead nations to follow Christ's teachings as far as possible; and the law of nations, which the Roman Empire had developed in its practical dealings with the customary rights of subject peoples.

It will be observed that Grotius' repeated attempts to form a new moral unity in Europe, based upon the beliefs which all Protestants held in common, has found a place in his final treatise as "the law of God." But it will also be observed that the law of God is no more than a Christian ideal to be aimed at by a civilization which was already laying less and less emphasis on religious ideals. Anyhow, who was now to define the law of God? Christendom had once possessed, in the universal Church, a sort of supreme court to define and interpret the law of God. But in the new civilization of the Protestant North, the law of God was defined by a national church normally under the authority of a national monarch. No wonder that, given this clash of jurisdictions, international relations would be governed more and more by the customary law of nations, and by the law of Nature. Grotius' law of Nature assumed that man was essentially, "by nature," social and rational.

If this was a hazardous assumption in the case of peacetime relations between states, it was doubly hazardous in time of war. Gustavus Adolphus is said to have kept a copy of *On the Law of War and Peace* under his pillow at night. In Grotius' introduction, Gustavus might read:

Holding it, for reasons which I have stated, to be most certain that there is amongst nations a common law, which is of force with regard to war and in war, I had many grave reasons for writing on the subject. For I saw prevailing throughout the Christian world a licence in making war of which even savage nations might be ashamed; recourse being had to arms for slight reasons or none; and when arms were taken up, all reverence for divine or human law being thrown away, as if men were thenceforth authorized to commit all crimes without restraint.

Gustavus, who had witnessed those crimes at first hand, is said to have remarked that " if Grotius found himself engaged in war, he would see that the fine lessons which he prescribes cannot always be put into practice."

VIII.

BY THE GRACE OF GOD, KING

When Philip II of Spain lay dying in 1598, in his little room in the gloomy Escorial, overlooking the palace chapel, another and very different king was ruling in France. Henry of Navarre, the ex-Huguenot, had that very year issued at Nantes his famous Edict of Toleration, according freedom of worship to French Calvinists. Where Philip II was passionately religious, somber, ascetic, quixotic, Henry IV of France, founder of the Bourbon dynasty, was smiling, skeptical, practical. Where Philip ruthlessly sacrificed his personal interests and the economic interests of the Spanish Empire for the Catholic faith, Henry IV exchanged his Calvinist faith for Catholicism in order to solidify his crown. In short, Henry IV reversed the medieval order and definitely placed politics above religion. Philip felt obligated to promote the spiritual welfare of his subjects, obligated to attend the autos-da-fé and watch the heretics burned. The ex-Calvinist Henry felt obligated to promote the material welfare of Frenchmen, while enforcing religious toleration in France.

The Valois kings who preceded this able Bourbon on the French throne had left the country in appalling shape. Francis I and Henry II had exhausted it in wars against the encircling Hapsburgs. Henry II's three sons, Francis II, Charles IX, and Henry III, had reigned

ingloriously in the midst of civil war between Catholic and Huguenot, war that had left the royal government financially prostrate,
large areas of the countryside uncultivated, roads and bridges in
ruins, town workers unemployed, highway robbery rife, and the
great nobles reasserting the rights they had lost to the Crown. Henry
IV and his prudent Huguenot minister, the Duke of Sully, rebuilt
the finances of the government and reformed the system of taxation.
They then set to work to increase production. Sully labored to promote agriculture. Henry fostered new industries, such as silk. He
introduced the silkworm into France, and the mulberry tree, which
provides the silkworm's food. He subsidized a merchant marine and
built a navy. The French began to threaten the commercial monopoly of Spain.

But the middle-class heaven which Henry and Sully were con-
structing for the French was rudely shaken in 1610. In that year a
Catholic fanatic assassinated the ex-Huguenot King; and his wife,
Marie de' Medici, took over the regency for her nine-year-old son,
Louis XIII. She rid herself of the parsimonious Sully and promptly
ran France on the rocks financially. At a loss for money, she called
the Estates-General, a medieval body that had once been roughly
equivalent to the English Parliament. But the three Estates, clergy,
nobility, and burghers, could not agree, and in three weeks they
were dismissed — for precisely a hundred and seventy-five years, as
it turned out!

The Regency was a failure because Marie de' Medici ignored or
misunderstood the very things which had created the French monarchy and which continued to nurture it. Monarchy had protected
the interests of the moneyed class against the feudal nobility, and
monarchy had been forced to learn to handle the money economy
itself. But Marie, besides running the government on the rocks financially, antagonized the middle class — as James I did in England
— by a pro-Spanish policy. Like James, she attempted to marry her
son to a Spanish princess. Unlike James, she succeeded. Both the
Huguenots and the great nobles revolted against her rule. Finally,
her son, Louis XIII, turned against her and took over the government.

Along with the government, Louis took over as minister one of
the most remarkable men in French history, Armand de Richelieu,

former Bishop of Luçon. Richelieu was a member of the petty nobility and had entered the service of the Church merely to find a political career. He was tremendously ambitious. His service to Marie de' Medici had secured him her intervention with the Pope, and the position of cardinal. He now set to work to free Louis XIII from the pressure of the Huguenots and the great nobles and to increase the power of France in Europe. Sickly in body, cold in his affections, interested in religion less than in Church administration, this thin-lipped, unpopular, inflexible statesman devoted his life to his program. Not even his master, the King, really liked him. But Louis recognized in him an absolutely loyal public servant who put the French crown above every other consideration, religious or political. For like Henry IV and his Huguenot minister, the duke of Sully, this Roman Catholic cardinal placed politics above religion.

This is why, although he subdued the rebellious Huguenots, he never dreamed of exterminating them. The most that Henry IV had been able to achieve was to end the civil wars between Catholic Frenchmen and Huguenot Frenchmen and to set up, through the Edict of Nantes, a sort of armed peace. As a guarantee that the religious minority would continue to receive toleration, certain fortified towns were turned over to the Huguenots. As a result, the Huguenots had in many cases come to regard themselves as a state within the state, not wholly unlike the Lutheran states within the Holy Roman Empire which contested the Emperor's power. They had their own assemblies, their own judges. They were in a position to fight for their rights, just as the great nobles did in the regency of Marie de' Medici. In fact, they sometimes combined with powerful nobles in contesting the power of the Crown. In 1625 the Huguenots rebelled and held La Rochelle against the King. Richelieu doggedly besieged them until the town fell. Then he had Louis issue the Edict of Alais, which reaffirmed the Huguenots' freedom of conscience and worship but took away their fortified towns. They might worship whatever God they chose, but there was but one King. Whatever rights the Huguenots enjoyed from now on, they enjoyed as a free gift from their King.

The same unconditional obedience must be exacted from the great nobles, to whom the monarchy still appeared a tyrannical and usurping power. The nobles were prepared to fight for liberty, the liberty to oppress others. Richelieu put an end to the liberty. His secret service worked tirelessly. Some of the nobles, even the most powerful, he executed, on a charge of treason to the King. He suppressed uprisings. He ordered that all the nobles' fortified castles, except those needed to protect the frontiers against foreign foes, should be destroyed; and he saw that the order was carried out. He forbade private war between nobles. He even forbade the social custom which for many decades preserved in miniature the right to make private war, the duel.

But supposing the Huguenots might never be able to defy the King again, and supposing that the nobles would never again dare rise in open, military rebellion, many of the nobles still had the means of thwarting the growing royal power, For the various provinces of the kingdom were administered by royal governors, and these were great nobles. Consequently, the King's orders were filtered through a class of officials to whose interest it was to weaken his authority. To counteract this local aristocratic power, the central, royal government had sent to some of the provinces officers known as " intendants," who took over some of the functions of the royal governors and who kept in touch with the central government. These intendants were drawn from the middle class, the very class the monarchy chiefly served. Richelieu developed this system and extended it to the whole of France. The nobles who held provincial governorships retained their honorable titles and their large salaries (they could not at this date have been deprived of these things too), but the King, acting through his intendants, took over many of the powers of taxation, police, and justice. The net effect was more order, more symmetry, more regularity, more reasonableness in the business of government, and a tremendous increase in the power, the prestige, and the responsibility of the King.

In foreign affairs, Richelieu subsidized the enemies of the Hapsburgs in the Thirty Years' War. That meant aiding the Dutch, who had ended their truce with the Hapsburg King of Spain, and were making their final fight for independence. It meant aiding the German Protestant princes in their struggle against their Catholic, Austrian, Hapsburg Emperor. It meant aiding the Protestant King of Sweden, Gustavus Adolphus, against the same Hapsburg. When the Peace of Prague threatened in 1635 to end the struggle before the Hapsburgs had been adequately weakened, Richelieu brought France herself into the struggle, and French armies fought the Spaniards and the "Imperials." They were still fighting them in 1642, when Richelieu died.

Richelieu's last great task, the destruction of Hapsburg supremacy in Europe, was shouldered after his death by a man whom he himself had trained, Cardinal Mazarin. Mazarin completed the triumph of France in the Thirty Years' War, by the fruits of the Peace of Westphalia and, eleven years later, by the Treaty of the Pyrenees. But in domestic affairs Mazarin was less successful than his master and predecessor. Compared with Richelieu, he labored under several disadvantages. Richelieu was a Frenchman; Mazarin never lost his Italian accent. Though Richelieu had fought the nobles, he himself was of noble birth: Mazarin was not. Richelieu had the backing, if not the love, of a king. But Louis XIII died the year after Richelieu; his successor, Louis XIV, was only five years old. Above all, Richelieu had one advantage that was decisive. He was the servant of a great idea, an idea which was growing during his lifetime. That idea was absolute monarchy. Richelieu's complete devotion to it made him unbending, ruthless, inexorable, even unlovable. But it also secured him the respect which singleness of purpose often secures. Doubtless he practised every guile that Machiavelli taught, but he did it for the King and he did it for France, not to feather his own nest. Mazarin's misappropriations of public funds not only exposed him to his enemies; it removed from him the support of those who, without loving Richelieu, had respected the idea he gave his life to: royal order, in exchange for feudal chaos.

The result was the Fronde, a series of spasmodic rebellions against Cardinal Mazarin and "the Cardinalists" — that is, against the government in power. The Fronde is thought to have gotten its name from a game the children of Paris played in the streets, a game often stopped by the police. And the Fronde that broke out in 1648, the year the Peace of Westphalia was signed, was the same sort of game. In that year the Parlement of Paris defied Mazarin. The Parlement, together with the twelve other parlements in the kingdom, was not comparable with the English Parliament. It was an upper court, a judicial body. But the Paris Parlement had in the course of time assumed the duty of formally registering the King's decrees as laws of the land. It now announced that it might refuse to register. Particularly, it declared that no tax was legal until approved by the Parlement; it ordered that the office of intendant be abolished; and it protected its rebellion by protesting against arbitrary arrest. The people of Paris, who disliked Mazarin, rose to defend the Parlement. So did the great nobles, who had suffered so much from both Richelieu and Mazarin. So long as Mazarin's army was at the front he was forced to give way. But like the policemen who broke up the " Fronde " which the Paris urchins played, Mazarin's army eventually returned and he resumed control. The Fronde had brought only confusion, for it was a coalition of contradictory forces, agreed only in opposing Mazarin. It served merely to demonstrate once more to the average Frenchman that in the King's power, and in the King's power alone, lay order. To nobody was it a more illuminating experience than to an impressionable little boy of ten, against whom in a sense the Fronde was directed. That little boy was Louis XIV, for the past five years King of France.

When Mazarin died, in 1661, Louis XIV was twenty-three years old. It was assumed that he would appoint another minister, as kings normally did, to carry on his government. He did nothing of the kind. He determined that he would carry on his government himself. When we look back on the work of Richelieu and Mazarin, we are tempted to feel that Louis had only to follow their lead, so well had they done their work. We are tempted to assume that the two cardinals constructed the absolute monarchy in France and that Louis had only to enjoy the fruits of their labors. But when Louis himself set down as an old man some account of his reign and its problems, he did not remember it that way. At ten, the Fronde had broken out. Could he know at twenty-three that he was safe from another rebellion of the nobility? The members of the Paris Parlement still longed to make that body the representative of the popular will against royal oppression. And Louis was not the only Frenchman who remembered the Huguenot rebellions and found those zealots an unreasonable and indigestible minority. We now know that never again, till the close of the eighteenth century, was the King's authority seriously challenged. But Louis could not know this, the year that Mazarin died. And we would do well to remem-

ber that it was largely Louis' judicious reign that placed his authority beyond challenge.

Richelieu enjoyed, as a Frenchman and a noble, advantages over
his successor, Mazarin, the naturalized Italian. Louis XIV enjoyed
enormous advantages over both. He was not a minister humoring a
king; he was the King himself. Of this advantage he was fully
aware. He was equally aware of the forces that supported monarchy.
He governed personally through a group of councils and through a
bureaucracy that was predominantly middle-class. For it was as the
champion of the middle class against the feudal nobility that the
modern European monarch had waxed strong. Louis wished his
servants to be drawn from the class whose interests he chiefly served.
Only princes, dukes, and marshals were exempted from addressing
Louis' middle-class secretaries of state as " Monseigneur."

Of the councils through which Louis governed, four were particularly important. The Council of State was a small body that met
with the King three times a week, and it was the pivotal organ of
government. Its members all enjoyed the right of free discussion, but
all decisions were the King's. Its meetings were secret and no min-
utes were kept. The so-called Council of Dispatches met with Louis
also, and dealt with domestic affairs. The Finance Council met in
his presence and was particularly concerned with taxation. The
Privy Council did not, as a rule, meet in his presence. It was composed of a large number of lawyers, and functioned as the supreme
court of France. But it was in no sense independent of Louis' personal authority. Louis' councils were merely his personal organs,
composed of his personal political servants. All important decisions
were his. He had therefore to be at his desk daily and to keep long
hours. Few modern businessmen have worked as hard as this seventeenth-century periwigged monarch. Was he not practicing what
he himself called " the trade of a king "?

He had the true leader's genius for utilizing the talents of others. Thus, it was from Mazarin that he inherited, along with other
able administrators, his famous finance minister, Colbert; but it was
Louis himself who entrusted Colbert successively with public works,
finance, the navy, commerce and agriculture, and the colonies.
When Colbert died in 1683, he had had a hand in every department
of the government except war. Louis had known how to use him.

Colbert's contribution to France was not the theory of " Mercantilism," the theory that a country should strive to accumulate through trade as much gold and silver as possible. Mercantilism, so often associated with Colbert's name, was the accepted economic theory of his age. But he assumed in addition that the total commerce of Europe was fairly well fixed and that if French commerce was to grow it must be at the expense of other nations. Where Louis' great minister of war, Louvois, wanted to destroy France's neighbors on the battlefield, Colbert would destroy them in the market place. That France was great, he said, was proven not only by her own growing wealth but by the poverty and wretchedness of her neighbors. It was as a vast business concern, in competition with other firms, that this son of a merchant wished to direct his country.

Colbert corrected some of the worst abuses of the tax system and made it more efficient, though he accomplished little in shifting the tax burden from the shoulders of the poor to those of the rich. Richelieu and Mazarin would have faced even more rebellions than they did, had they taken away not only the political power of the nobility but its financial privileges as well. In Colbert's day compromise was still imperative. Colbert encouraged Louis' war against Holland, because he wanted for his French shippers the business handled by the Dutch. He complained that of the world's shipping, the Dutch owned from fifteen to sixteen thousand vessels while France possessed only five or six hundred. He did all he could to foster industry and he regulated it in the interests of the nation as a whole. He protected it, through high tariffs, from foreign competition. For domestic trade he supplied good roads and canals and, since he was opposed to useless regulation, tried to abolish internal customs barriers between the various provinces. He encouraged exports, so as to bring France a gold surplus. He tried to free France from dependence on imports. When he found manufactured products entering France from England, or from Holland or Sweden or Venice or the Germanies, he imported workmen from those places, so as to produce the articles at home. By the same token he severely punished French artisans who tried to sell their skill to other nations. Though France remained overwhelmingly Catholic, the government discouraged men from entering monasteries, discouraged monasteries from extending charity to idlers, and closed the drinkshops during work hours. For neither contemplation nor idling nor drunkenness could help the growth of French industry.

But Louis was far more than a faithful and hard-working civil servant. He was a king, appointed by God to rule a people, and he incarnated God's majesty on earth. He had not been appointed by another man, as Colbert had been. He had not been elected, as the Estates-General had been, at their last inglorious meeting in 1614. He was born in the purple. Royalty was the station of life to which it had pleased God to call him. He was therefore answerable to no one but God, and the obedience of his subjects was his right. Did not the Church recognize that his power came from God when it anointed him with holy oil at his coronation? Conspiracy against the King thereby became blasphemy and sacrilege. He was the father of his people, and it was his heavy responsibility to provide for his children's welfare. If he abused his power, his subjects might still not refuse him obedience — as thinkers had held in the old free Middle Ages. They could only pray God to change the King's heart.

It was on theories like these, theories that were revolutionary and novel from the point of view of feudal society, that Louis based his actions. One cannot read his *Memoirs* without being aware of his stern sense of duty, of self-discipline, even of self-sacrifice. Modern democrats frequently think of Louis XIV and the other "divine-right, absolutist monarchs" of his day as vain, capricious, irresponsible. Capricious and irresponsible they were not, or they could never have brought Europe to believe in their divine right. At their best — and Louis was one of the best — they were the prudent inheritors of vast power, holding themselves morally obligated to use that power for the good of the state. The quality that gave Louis such genuine majesty was precisely that recognition, that self-restraint. He was in a position to tyrannize, and he tried to be just. He was in a position to idle his time in luxury, and he worked like a slave. Why? He gave the answer in his own words. They are worth reading closely. "One must work hard to reign, and it is ingratitude and presumption toward God, injustice and tyranny toward man, to wish to reign without hard work."

Having recognized that responsibility, and thereby won the respect and admiration of Europe, Louis could write with the greatest candor that the exercise of royal authority was "delightful." He did not need, like the modern office-holder, to pretend to hate power. If God took joy in His work, so did the King in his, and next to God's the King's power was greatest. Louis liked ruling, for he ruled creatively. He not only labored, with Colbert's aid, to provide the material needs of his subjects. He symbolized in his person and in his surroundings the typical aspirations of his age. That is why it is still called the Age of Louis XIV.

Some twelve miles outside Paris, in a flat, sandy, arid landscape, Louis converted what had once been his father's hunting-box into the most famous palace in Europe, the Palace of Versailles. Nothing short of a king's resources could have raised that stately building, with its severe baroque exterior, suggestive of the Italian Renaissance but less exuberant, more restrained. Only a king could have provided the luxurious apartments within, with their rococo decorations: cupids and cherubs and flowers everywhere. By a king's authority, great fountains threw their jets of water into the air; and in the midst of the waterless waste an artificial lake bore on its bosom pleasure-gondolas. Indeed, 30,000 soldiers had labored to divert the Eure River fifty miles, that it might pass Versailles. After a frightful loss of life from disease, the force had been withdrawn by the needs of war. The place had been dry, and the great fountains played pleasantly. It had been a wilderness, and huge parks stretched away, their walks geometrically arranged, their yew hedges decorously clipped, their groves adorned with statues. Those gardens spoke of the complete triumph of intelligence over Nature, of order over chaos — indeed, of royalty over feudalism.

To build Versailles, Louis collected the most famous artists he could find. To create there a life worthy of Europe's greatest monarch, writers read their productions, great nobles paid their compliments, great administrators carried on the affairs of Europe. Mansart, the architect, was called in to design the bulk of the palace, as well as the outlying Grand Trianon. Le Brun became official painter and directed a corps of workers in the task of supplying suitable murals. Girardon, the official sculptor, contributed statuary. Lenôtre did the gardens, planned the fountains, the labyrinths, the avenues and vistas, transporting trees from distant forests to achieve his effects.

A whole school of writers grew up under the constant influence of the court, some of them actually living at Versailles, many living on royal subsidy. Boileau was writing literary criticism in verse, and became the literary arbiter of Europe. Corneille's tragedies were being played. Molière presented his humane comedies before Louis, filled with wit and satire, deeply observant of human motive, in their language brilliantly just and precise. Racine offered his polished tragedies, modeled on the Greeks, compact dramas of crisis, pared down to the bare essentials of plot, so different from the exuberant English Shakespeare. Madame de Sévigné wrote her witty letters about court life. La Fontaine's fables in verse told sly tales of animals that behave so perilously like ourselves and our friends. Bishop Bossuet preached his great sermons, wrote history for Louis' son, whom he tutored, and stated philosophically the arguments for divine-right monarchy. Massillon preached his magnificent funeral orations. La Bruyère etched his character sketches, without rage, in quiet bitterness. And the great tradition of epigrams that the Duke of La Rochefoucauld had lately exemplified in his *Maxims* continued to flourish.

These are some of the greatest names in one of Europe's greatest literatures. What they represent in terms of human understanding, only lovers of French literature will recall. Louis XIV did not of course create these writers. He did not even patronize them all. Some he disliked. But in Versailles he furnished a social background for a group of writers eminently social. He provided an intelligent audience for a group of writers eminently intelligent. For in general these writers followed the classical doctrine which Boileau so brilliantly formulated. They avoided extravagance, eccentricity, violence, and sought self-restraint, dignity, urbanity. As a generation, they had inherited sufficient force to make self-restraint a virtue. They had built a political and social order that made men self-confident. And while contemporary architects were destroying some of the best Gothic in Paris to make way for their own baroque edifices, these writers turned away from both the crude beauties of medieval letters and the exuberance of the Renaissance, to the maturity and sureness of what the French still call their " Great Century," or the " Century of Louis XIV." Clarity and elegance they admired, simplicity and strength. Tact and good manners were at a premium, in art as in social intercourse. Art was aristocratic in its

restraints, though most of the artists were of middle-class origin.
They were worldly, as a group, and sure of their world. In 1687
Charles Perrault read a poem before the French Academy on *The
Century of Louis the Great,* in which he frankly rated the achievements of "the moderns" higher than those of the Greeks. Boileau
attacked him, and the dispute raged through Europe, eliciting in
England Jonathan Swift's *Battle of the Books.* But the same high
confidence in human powers that produced baroque architecture
produced the literature on which Versailles fed. Renaissance architects, to escape the outworn Gothic, had borrowed the style of the
Greeks and Romans. But their successors were going beyond classical imitation now. Renaissance humanists had escaped the Church's
scholastic Latin by imitating Cicero, but Charles Perrault was claiming that modern French writers excelled the Latins and the Greeks.
And where Latin had been the universal tongue of Christian Europe, French was becoming the universal tongue of civilized, secular
Europe.

What these writers had to say lacked certainly the scope of a St.
Thomas Aquinas, but their exploration was more detailed. They
lacked even some of the suggestiveness of a Shakespeare. They deliberately shut out the confusions of Shakespeare and made for themselves an island of intelligibility; and they tended to ignore what
they did not understand. They did to the complexities of human experience what Lenôtre had done to the Versailles countryside: reduced it to order.

They have been accused of flattering Louis, of a sickening adulation. But in praising Louis they were but praising their own French
culture, the powers of human reason, and their own seventeenth century. Scholastic writers had endlessly praised God; their descendants
praised His representative, the King. Perhaps many Europeans no
longer deeply believed in any higher power than the power of the
King. That accounts for their polite acceptance of the Church and
their rooted dislike of religious enthusiasm and ecstasy. It accounts
at the same time for the truly religious awe they felt in the presence
of the King and, to tell the truth, for the awe the King felt in his
own presence!

For Versailles was a sort of man-made heaven, a heaven very
much on earth. Its severe and mature architecture expressed the sev-

enteenth century's respect for human reason, as the Gothic cathedrals had expressed the soaring ecstasies of the medieval soul. To it, as to the cathedral, not only the architect, but all the other artists contributed, Le Brun with his painting, Girardon with his sculpture, Lenôtre with his landscaped terraces, Lully with his operas and ballets.

Jean-Baptiste Lully, who became Louis' court composer, was no genius of the first order, any more than Le Brun was, in the field of painting, or Girardon in the field of sculpture. But he and his pupils, who also received pensions from the King, contributed their share to heighten artistic communication in this human heaven, this highly civilized society. A Florentine by birth, though he was brought up in France, Lully took the " New Music " that had developed in his native Italy and adapted it to French needs. The music of the cathedral had been deeply religious and vocal. It had taken first the form of unison singing as in Gregorian plainsong; and had then developed the magnificent and complicated polyphony of Palestrina, of Vittoria, of Orlando Lassus, in which different voices weave together different but harmonizing melodies. Unhappily, the same mood that made the Renaissance blind to the beauties of " Gothic " painting and sculpture and architecture, made it deaf to " Gothic " music. And whereas stone and bronze and paint might await the understanding of later generations, disillusioned in turn with the secular art of the Renaissance, Gothic music died on the air of those early centuries, except where it was conserved by Church tradition. By 1600 the " New Music " was replacing it rapidly.

In that very year Peri and Caccini each produced a *Euridice* on the basis of Rinuccini's poem, and their compositions were to win fame as among the earliest operas. In 1600 also Cavaliere produced the first oratorio, his *Rappresentazione di anima e di corpo*. In each there is an instrumental accompaniment written for a definite combination of instruments. In each the music is dramatic, episodic, with solos — far indeed from the Gregorian chant, sung in unison, without accompaniment, without the strong time-beat of modern music, subservient to the holy words it was destined to make more significant. Even when that plainsong had given way to polyphony, to a complicated web of melodies, it had still been timeless, without episode. The secular New Music was replacing that ancient style, as the secular New Learning had replaced scholastic thought. By 1637, two years after Richelieu had thrown French armies into the German arena of the Thirty Years' War, in which the death agony of the old Christian unity was reducing Central Europe to chaos, the first opera house in Europe was built at Venice where people could listen to the work of the immensely popular Claudio Monteverdi, to his dialogues, his duets, his trios, his solos, his orchestral preludes.

But at Versailles French taste was exacting from Lully and his disciples less of the grandiose recitative that the Italians so much loved. They were requiring more instrumental embellishment, more sophistication, more intelligence. It is a music that, like the Italian New Music from which it was adapted, had departed from the Great Tradition. Nor did it possess the religious passion of the music which Heinrich Schütz was producing in Germany in the same century, work that foreshadowed the great German oratorios of the next century. Music did not achieve the position in French life that it did in Germany, where between 1550 and 1850 the Bach family produced some four hundred musicians known to us, a sort of family guild, so famous that in some parts of Germany the town musicians were called " the Bachs." But Lully and his school testify that the man-made heaven at Versailles required the service of every art to round out the unity which the monarch, the " mon-arch," the single ruler, typified.

Louis has been criticized for possessing mediocre taste in the arts, for pensioning the wrong artists, merely because they knew how to toady, for possessing himself a commonplace mind, for protecting the arts solely to increase his own prestige. These things are largely true. But not only did the artists he patronized bring prestige to the monarchy; Louis' patronage of the arts gave them the immense prestige of the Crown. By recognizing the arts as significant, Louis placed his government on the side of civilization, as against mere material well-being, such as the reforms of Colbert quite properly aimed to secure. His mind was indeed, in many respects, commonplace. But his judgment was remarkably sound; and the art of his period was an art that carried common sense and good judgment to the point of genius. It was an art that was highly communicative, carried on by artists who stimulated each other through their intercourse and their co-operation. Louis' government increased and ordered this co-operation. Perhaps his most typical act in relation to literature and art and science was his foundation or continued patronage of the great Academies. It was Richelieu who had officially organized a group of literary men into a "French Academy," charged among other things with compiling a dictionary of the French language. It was characteristic of seventeenth-century French civilization that it should feel the need of a clear and precise vocabulary with which to express the clear and precise ideas it lived by. But it was Louis who added, at Colbert's suggestion, the Academy of Sciences, drawing for its membership on a nucleus that had included Descartes, Gassendi, Pascal. The Academy of Sciences would include among its associates such foreign thinkers as Sir Isaac Newton. It was Louis who founded the Academy of Inscriptions and Belles-Lettres, the so-called "Little Academy," which was in fact an academy of archaeology and history. It was Louis who founded the Academy of Fine Arts — the "Beaux Arts" at Rome.

To Versailles, this center of European civilization, from all over France Louis collected the nobles. No longer should they be local kinglets, owing a grudging and intermittent obedience to the King. No longer would they remain rooted in the soil which had produced them, any more than would the trees that Lenôtre had transplanted to Versailles. They would become pleasure-loving courtiers, absentee landlords, and their political power would evaporate. If they wanted activity, they could follow their traditional calling of war, but only in the service of the King. Otherwise, they might share the delights and splendors of Versailles. What Louis wanted to deprive them of was their function of governing; let them give up that, and they might enjoy themselves as they pleased. But let neither noble nor Estates-General nor Parlement, neither individual nor organization, presume to represent the people, against their King.

So the sons of the nobles who had fought against Richelieu lived in the gorgeous chambers of Louis' resplendent palace; danced the stately minuet; heard the music of Lully; listened to the comedies of Molière; wandered in Lenôtre's pleasant avenues and watched the "Great Waters" jet from the bronze fountain statuary; cultivated the social graces; bowed low, and basked in the light of Louis' smiles. The King was generous in paying their gambling debts, but they must attend his presence if they would keep his favor. He had deliberately chosen as his device and as symbol of his power, the sun; because it was surrounded by planets and gave light and strength to all. He might have added, because it holds the planets firmly on their appointed courses. Around this Sun-King the nobles built up an elaborate daily ceremonial, as elaborate as any ritual ever practised in a cathedral. They attended Louis' waking in the morning; they handed him his articles of clothing; they served him his food; they tended his comfort and his glory as one tends an altar. The old Duke of Saint-Simon, with his solid traditions of aristocratic independence, might pillory these toadies, in his famous *Memoirs;* but he was forced to admit that Louis played his role with dignity and conviction.

With Bishop Bossuet insisting that the King ruled by divine right, with the substitution of Versailles, as symbol, for the medieval cathedral, and with the highly centralized state steadily absorbing power, it is not surprising that God's viceroy on earth, the King, should come into conflict with Christ's vicar on earth, the Pope. Between these two divinely ordained authorities, the ancient quarrel of investitures, that had raged centuries before between Pope and Holy Roman Empire, grew acute — the quarrel as to whether the Pope or the temporal head had the right to nominate appointees to wealthy bishoprics. In 1682 Louis XIV induced an assembly of French bishops to declare four "liberties of the Gallican Church": that the King holds his temporal powers independently of the Pope, that a general church council is above the Pope, that the ancient liberties of the Gallican, or French, Church are sacred; and that the principal authority of the Catholic Church is lodged not merely in the Pope but in the Pope and bishops jointly. The Gallican Church under Louis seemed on the way to achieving the independence from Rome that the Anglican Church had achieved under Henry VIII. But after a quarrel lasting eleven years, the King backed down.

The semi-divine monarchy collided not only with the Roman government of the Catholic Church. Henry VIII, while making himself the "only supreme head in earth of the Church of England," had beheaded Catholics who remained loyal to the Pope and had burned Protestants who denied Catholic doctrine. Now Louis, in the midst of his fight with the Pope over which of them should control the Catholic Church in France, persecuted those who contested points of Catholic dogma. This involved him with two important groups of his subjects. On the one hand, he joined the Pope in hounding the Jansenists, who were preaching from their center at Port Royal the puritan and pietist doctrines of Cornelius Jansen, a Catholic bishop in the Spanish Netherlands. On the other hand, he revoked the famous Edict of Toleration, which his grandfather Henry IV had issued at Nantes and which had accorded rights to the French Calvinists, or " Huguenots." In both cases he was greatly influenced by his Jesuit confessors, as well as by his passion for order and regularity in every sphere of life, even that of religious belief.

Loyola's Society of Jesus had grown greatly in strength and its members had shown particular skill in becoming the confessors and spiritual advisers of the politically mighty. In order to retain the loyalty of the great to the Roman Catholic Church, they were inclined to overlook irregular morals. Among their enemies they had the reputation of believing that in such matters the end justified the means. When the Jansenists, who sought true doctrine from the same source Luther had turned to, St. Augustine, began insisting that the ministrations of the Catholic Church were powerless unless the individual underwent his own inner " conversion," and when the famous French writer Blaise Pascal, whose sister was a nun at Port Royal, attacked the worldly teachings of the Jesuits, the Jesuit circles about the King, who regarded the Jansenists as little better than Huguenots in disguise, fought back. Louis secured from the Pope a condemnation of Jansenist doctrine, and Port Royal itself was first closed and then destroyed.

Louis was even more ruthless with the Huguenots. First he quartered dragoons in the houses of Huguenots — following the pattern of the " angel-makers " whom the Emperor Ferdinand had quartered on his defeated Bohemian subjects. When these " dragonnades," which included torturing the men and violating their wives and daughters, failed to win more than a fraction to the true faith, the Most Christian King revoked the Edict of Nantes, just three years after his assembly of French bishops had declared his independence from papal control; forbade freedom of public worship;

denied the Huguenots all civil rights; and forbade them to emigrate. Nevertheless, some 300,000 escaped from France to Prussia, Holland, England, and to England's American colonies. Since they had shown a characteristically Protestant skill for commerce and industry, their emigration inflicted heavy economic damage on France. Since they had suffered much at Louis' hands, they kept up in the Protestant countries to which they fled a lively propaganda against the Sun-King.

This propaganda fell on fertile soil. For Louis had fought two aggressive wars, he was about to fight two more, and he was regarded everywhere as the principal menace to European peace. This was not merely because he was eager for glory, though he was. The age he dominated, the country he ruled, the ideas he symbolized, all sought power. Christendom had built its cathedrals to the glory of one who said, " My kingdom is not of this earth." But Versailles had been built, and embellished with all the arts, to the glory of a Sun-King, whose kingdom was very much indeed of this earth. Louis symbolized a society which was rapidly increasing in wealth, a state that was steadily increasing its power, a culture that was overweeningly self-confident. And yet this growing Bourbon power was still flanked on the south, on the northeast, and on the east by territories belonging to its hereditary enemies, the Hapsburgs. Louis coveted the Spanish Netherlands and Franche-Comté (Free County of Burgundy), as Mazarin had taught him to do. Their acquisition would bring France nearer to her " natural frontiers," the ones God had obviously intended her to have: the Rhine, the Alps, the Pyrenees, and the ocean. It would likewise place Paris less dangerously near her most vulnerable frontier. Next, he wished in all other respects to preserve the provisions of the Peace of Westphalia, which effectually prevented the Austrian Hapsburg from consolidating the Holy Roman Empire into a national German state, on France's flank, as Wallenstein, that German Richelieu, had dreamed of doing for his master, the Emperor Ferdinand. He wished not only to keep the Hapsburg from effectually controlling the small German states of the Empire; he hoped to make himself, the King of France, their protector. Had not the French King Francis I actually bid for the Imperial crown itself? These were permanent matters of French foreign policy. They had been partially achieved by the Peace of

Westphalia. The Sun-King would try to achieve them completely and make all Europe revolve around Versailles.

Louis first laid claim to the Spanish Netherlands, on the grounds that according to the laws of inheritance in the Netherlands these provinces should " devolve " from Philip IV of Spain, who had just died, not on his successor, the weak-witted Charles II, but on Louis' wife, the daughter of Philip by a previous marriage. The war that resulted from this trumped-up claim was consequently known as the War of Devolution. Philip died in 1665. Within two years Louis had through clever diplomacy isolated Spain and seized the border fortresses of the Spanish Netherlands. But his triumphant conquest was interrupted by a shift in international affairs. England and Holland, who had been fighting a trade war, made peace with each other and formed with Sweden a Triple Alliance to force Louis to stop his advance, in order not to disturb the " balance of power " in Europe. Even so, Louis was allowed to retain a strip of the Spanish Netherlands.

Convinced that the Dutch would always block his advance into the neighboring Spanish Netherlands, Louis next determined to break Holland. He would thereby remove the chief obstacle to expansion, and at the same time smash the one commercial rival whom Colbert and the French middle class feared more than any other. In 1672, after buying off Sweden and Charles II of England, Louis hurled his magnificent armies against Amsterdam. The young Stadtholder, William III of Orange, promptly ordered the dykes cut, and the sea poured in on the French as it had poured in decades ago on the Spaniards. The Hapsburg Emperor Leopold, the Great Elector of Brandenburg, and several German states came to the rescue of Holland. Even Spain, alarmed at Louis' power, found it wise to help the country that had once revolted from her. Finally, Charles II of England was forced by Parliament to join the anti-French alliance, and Louis made peace. He had failed to crush Holland, but he secured from Spain several more fortresses in the Spanish Netherlands and all of Franche-Comté.

He now established special French courts of claims to investigate the territories France had gained in the Thirty Years' War and the recent Dutch War, territories ceded to her " with their dependencies," and by examining ancient feudal records to determine whether all these dependencies had been claimed and annexed. There were, indeed, little islands of foreign territory inside lands which France had annexed, which made Louis' eastern frontier a difficult one to defend. Louis' courts awarded some twenty important towns to France, including Luxembourg and Strasbourg. Louis promptly be-. gan to execute his own courts' decrees.

To protect the Empire from further French encroachments, the Emperor Leopold formed a league, known as the League of Augsburg, with Hapsburg Spain of course, with Sweden, and with several German princes. Nevertheless, in 1688 Louis advanced a claim to the Rhenish Palatinate and immediately invaded it. But in this crucial year, Louis' Catholic friend, James II of England, was deposed by Parliament, and replaced by his son-in-law, Louis's most bitter enemy, William III, Stadtholder of Holland. England thereupon joined the League of Augsburg. When peace came, nine years later, Louis for the first time had fought a war that brought him no new territory, except the city of Strasbourg.

Louis accepted this relatively unfavorable peace somewhat precipitately. He accepted it because he wanted his hands free for an even more serious problem than securing the Rhine boundary for France. Charles II of Spain was dying childless. The nearest heirs to the vast Spanish Empire were his two brothers-in-law, Louis XIV of France, and the Hapsburg Leopold I, Emperor of the Holy Roman Empire. If Leopold secured the succession to the Spanish crown, his new Hapsburg Empire would enclose France in the same vise as the Hapsburg Empire of Charles V a century and a half ago. It was Hapsburg encirclement that the Valois Kings of France had fought against throughout the sixteenth century. It was Hapsburg encirclement the Bourbons had constantly fought against — Henry IV, Louis XIII, and Louis XIV: grandfather, father, and son. How could the still unwon " natural frontiers " of France — Rhine, Alps, Pyrenees, and ocean — serve the French monarchy, if the vast empire of its hereditary enemy, the House of Hapsburg, hemmed the French monarchy in? To prevent just that catastrophe, Mazarin had married his young master Louis XIV to a Spanish princess, thereby establishing a claim on an inheritance that was now at last about to fall due.

For two reasons William III could not allow Louis XIV to secure the Spanish Empire. First, it would destroy that Continental balance of power which three European alliances in as many successive wars had fought to preserve, against the growing power of France. Secondly, both his Dutch and English traders found it hard enough already to secure trading concessions in Spanish or French colonial territories. If all those possessions were united under Europe's most powerful monarch, a huge trade monopoly would be erected against English and Dutch enterprise. Consequently, William attempted to patch up, with the two claimants, Louis and Leopold, various " partition treaties " that might solve peaceably the problem of the Spanish succession. In 1700, Charles II of Spain, determined to avoid the partition of his Empire, and convinced that no monarch but Louis could hope to keep it intact, bequeathed all his far-flung possessions to Louis' grandson, Philip of Anjou. A month later he died.

Louis, recognizing that his decision meant war, hailed his grandson Philip V, the first Bourbon King of Spain. " The Pyrenees," announced the Spanish ambassador to France, " no longer exist." It took Europe eleven years of warfare, on the Continent, in the colonies, and on the oceans of the world, to define precisely what that remark meant.

Louis opened hostilities by seizing the " barrier fortresses " in the Spanish Netherlands on behalf of the new King of Spain, fortresses which the Dutch by treaty occupied as a bulwark against French aggression. He recognized the deposed James II as the rightful King of England, in the place of Louis' bitter enemy, William III. He allied himself with Bavaria and Savoy. The French and Spanish armies prepared to defend the will of the dead King. On their side, William III and the Emperor Leopold organized a " Grand Alliance," which included England, Holland, Austria, Brandenburg-Prussia, Hanover, the Palatinate, Portugal, and which even drew Savoy from Louis' side. The Grand Alliance insisted that the Spanish crown should go to Leopold's second son, the Archduke Charles, and that the Spanish trade monopolies should be abolished. This plan would avoid uniting in the hands of one Hapsburg the possessions of Charles V, which would not only threaten France but would probably strengthen the colonial monopolies against English and Dutch traders.

Most of Louis' ablest generals had by now died, and those whom he had were outgeneraled by the English Duke of Marlborough and by Prince Eugene of Savoy. Defeat followed defeat: Blenheim, Gibraltar, Ramillies, Oudenarde, Malplaquet. The armies of the Grand Alliance entered France itself. The French and Spanish peoples rose to Louis' defense. Disagreements developed among the Allies. Finally, the Archduke Charles, the Alliance's candidate for the disputed Spanish crown, unexpectedly succeeded his brother on the throne of the Holy Roman Empire, thereby rendering him no longer suitable to William III. In the circumstances, a formula for peace was found.

By the Treaty of Utrecht, which ended the War of the Spanish Succession, Philip V was left on the Spanish throne with the proviso that the crowns of Spain and France should never be united. Moreover, Spain was compelled to cede to the Austrian Hapsburg, Naples, Sardinia, Milan, and the Spanish Netherlands, which now became known as the Austrian Netherlands. England secured Newfoundland, Acadia, and Hudson's Bay from France, and Gibraltar and Minorca from Spain, as well as tariff and trade concessions from the Spanish. The Dutch got back their "barrier fortresses" and secured a trade monopoly of the River Scheldt. The Elector of Brandenburg was allowed to assume the title "King of Prussia," and Savoy likewise became a kingdom.

Two years later Louis XIV died, after a reign of seventy-two years and after personally governing France for fifty-four. He had outlived his enormous popularity in France. His War of Devolution had indeed strengthened France's vulnerable northeastern frontier. His Dutch War had weakened the most dangerous competitors the French trading classes apparently faced, and the trading classes had ever provided the real support of absolute monarchy. But the War of the Palatinate was a costly and, on the whole, profitless venture; and the terrific War of the Spanish Succession exhausted France financially, cost her some of her most valuable colonies, and accomplished nothing except to keep the Spanish crown on the head of Louis' grandson, Philip V. True, this freed the French from the nightmare of Hapsburg encirclement. But even so, the average Frenchman gained less in security than Louis and the House of Bourbon gained in prestige; and for what they did gain, the price appeared too high. Louis had died, then, unpopular; but Versailles had not.

The Spanish dream of a reunited Catholic Europe had given way to the French dream of an orderly, wealthy, and civilized France, controlling and commanding Europe. For, though Louis in his later years was Catholic to the point of bigotry, and though he believed with most of his subjects that diversity of religious faith weakened the state, yet he freely followed Richelieu's policy of subsidizing Protestants like the Swedes against the Catholic Hapsburgs. His foreign policy was brutal, but it was the accepted foreign policy of every European state. Did he, with Colbert's help, attempt to smash the Dutch, in war as in commerce? So did England, though England was not under the thumb of a " vain despot." What made Louis more aggressive than his neighbors was that Louis had more power than they had. In 1688 he ruled perhaps twenty million subjects, at a time when the Dutch numbered some two and a half millions and the English perhaps five and a half. And while Holland was torn with dissension between its republican States-General and its increasingly monarchical Stadtholder, while England was still weakened by the cross-purposes of King and Parliament, Louis had at his disposal the political machinery which Richelieu and Mazarin, supported by the French middle classes, had toilsomely constructed.

His four wars kept Europe in turmoil. Yet the devastation they caused cannot compare with the destruction of the Thirty Years' War. In that dreadful struggle armies of freebooters, dressed in motley costumes, half disciplined and trailing thousands of camp followers behind them, lived on pillage and violence. Louis' great war minister Louvois organized disciplined troops, commanded by professional soldiers, and supplied with their own commissariat. They were carefully drilled, like modern soldiers; and they were the first soldiers of modern times to wear a regular uniform, and to fight with the bayonet instead of the time-honored pike. When they devastated the Palatinate, it was for strategical reasons, not from the habit of indiscipline. In most cases war touched the ordinary subject only through increased taxes.

The various states of Europe had to live together somehow. The old dreams of Catholic unity under a Pope, or of feudal unity under a Holy Roman Empire, had perished in the flames and tumult of the Thirty Years' War, and their epitaph had been written in the various clauses of the Peace of Westphalia. Europe therefore turned to international conferences, conducted on the basis of such ideas as Grotius had expressed in his treatise, *On the Law of War and Peace.* From Westphalia in 1648 to Utrecht in 1714 nine great international conferences attempted to fix the " public law " of Europe, and debated the issue of the sovereign state fighting for its " natural frontiers " or some other equally natural rights, and the " balance of power " which the weak were determined to preserve against the strong.

It should be clear that, in his wars of conquest, Louis XIV was considerably more than a vainglorious despot driving twenty million people to their doom. The French nation in the age of Louis XIV was conscious of its numbers, its power, its intelligence, its high level of civilization. By all these things, and not merely by armed force, it led Europe. The same necessity had driven it to support Richelieu, Mazarin, and Louis XIV, that was driving Denmark and Sweden toward " despotism ": the middle class, the men of money, the capitalists, saw in monarchy the escape from decadent feudalism and oppression by the nobility into an orderly, rational, centralized, middle-class paradise. In this paradise, a Colbert promoted prosperity, and a Louvois destroyed one's Dutch competitors. If wars were frequent, they were at least foreign and not civil, and with luck they could be fought on foreign soil. It was this vision of order and rationality that created the cultural outburst which focused at Versailles, which made the seventeenth century what Frenchmen still call the Great Century, and which permitted France to claim just tribute from neighboring nations as the most highly civilized state in Europe. German philosophers like Leibnitz followed in the footsteps of René Descartes. English writers like Pope and Addison followed in those of Boileau. French painting, French architecture, French dress, and French manners spread all over Europe. Where Spanish had in the days of the great Philip succeeded Latin as the language of royal courts, French now succeeded Spanish. Nor was it only the universal tongue of polite intercourse. A Descartes could deliberately turn from Latin to this powerful and precise new instrument to blaze a path for modern European philosophy. Human reason appeared able to create a paradise of power and well-being. Nowhere in Europe was reason more honored than in France. And of this France Louis XIV was, by the grace of God, King.

IX.

THE KILLING OF THE KING

In 1603 James VI, son of Mary Stuart, Queen of Scots, was riding through England to accept the English throne. For his remote cousin, the great Elizabeth, last of the Tudors, had finally died. James VI of Scotland had thereby become James I of England, the first monarch to unite the English and the Scottish crowns.

James I approached his task under severe handicaps. Although an intelligent and even a learned man, he knew next to nothing of English customs and English political institutions. He knew of course that he must deal with a Parliament, but he did not know the peculiar and complex relation that had grown up in the course of centuries between King and Parliament in England. Once an advisory council of the King's chief vassals; later, like the Estates-General of France, a body of representatives from clergy, nobility, and commoners; the English Parliament had developed into a bicameral body, a House of Lords, including both nobles and higher clergy, and a House of Commons, including both knights and burgesses. By the fifteenth century Parliament was initiating legislation, with the consent, of course, of the King, and as the feudal system gave way to a money economy, Parliament attempted irregularly to control royal policy by controlling the levying of taxes.

The Tudors, Henry VII, Henry VIII, and Henry VIII's three

children and successors, Edward VI, Mary, and Elizabeth, had avoided clashing with Parliament by avoiding as far as possible the crucial question of taxation. The Crown drew considerable revenues from its own properties: to that extent the executive was supported by endowment. This endowment Henry VIII tremendously increased by his confiscation of monastic property when the Anglican Church broke off from Rome, and when Henry replaced the Pope as its official head. Elizabeth backed business enterprises, including piratical raids on Spanish commerce, with the understanding that she was to get her share: the Crown thereby became a business partner of the moneyed class. But by the time James I came to the throne, several things had happened. Much of the Crown property had been dispersed by gift to, or through encroachments by, the great landowners: the Crown's endowment had by so much been decreased. Secondly, with the growth of a modern state, government expenses were increasing. Obviously, taxation was the proper solution. Given the Parliamentary tradition in England, that would necessitate cooperation between King and Parliament.

For such co-operation James I was peculiarly ill-fitted. James was sincerely convinced of the doctrine of the divine right of kings; he had indeed written a book on the subject. Yet the England of his day had outgrown that doctrine without wholly realizing the fact. The theory of the divine right of kings had had in Europe a very practical application. The King had been the champion of the middle class against a decadent feudal nobility. He inevitably appeared to have been divinely appointed to put down private warfare and make the world safe for the commoner. And he defended the kingdom against outside aggression. Richelieu would shortly consolidate divine right by overcoming internal disorder and by attacking France's foreign enemies. But the internal disorder which Richelieu later put an end to was raging in France at the very time that Tudor monarchs were at their strongest, and England had known no great internal disorder since the Wars of the Roses in the fifteenth century. Moreover, England, protected by the sea from foreign armies, had broken her strongest naval antagonist when she defeated the Spanish Armada. Briefly, England no longer needed a powerful monarch with a standing army and absolute power because she feared neither attack from abroad nor a turbulent nobility at home, while France feared both. In England, more than in most Continental countries, the nobleman had turned landlord, and he valued his holdings not for the men-at-arms they could produce but for the crops they would grow for market. The nobility was not a strict caste: it frequently intermarried with commoners. The antagonism between noble and merchant which stimulated absolute monarchy in France was lacking here. Commerce was growing, landlord and tradesman were getting rich, and what both wanted was a monarch who promoted their business interests.

James, arriving freshly from the more primitive economy of Scotland, was unaware of these new economic forces. He was likewise unable to gauge the power of the religious expression of them, Puritanism. Although England had outgrown the need for absolute monarchy sooner than any neighboring kingdom, the Protestant Reformation there had taken a form that was tardy and ambiguous. Under Henry VIII she had indeed officially turned her back on the Papacy; but in theory she retained Catholic doctrine. Under his son, Edward VI, Continental Protestantism had made substantial inroads. Then came the Catholic reaction under " Bloody Mary." Finally, under Elizabeth a sort of equilibrium had been reached, by which the Anglican Church had become mildly Protestant. During Elizabeth's reign Protestant doctrine had continued to spread, and the Anglican Church which James I must, as King, officially head, contained numerous " Puritan " reformers, anxious to purify the Church of what Catholic practices were left. Some of them wished to transform the Anglican Church into a Presbyterian Establishment; others were leaving the Church to form separate and independent congregations of their own and were therefore known as Separatists, or Congregationalists, or Independents. Such groups were naturally strongest in the commercial centers of the East and South of England, and particularly strong in London. Unfortunately for James I, the same men who opposed the Anglican Church he had been called to rule were those who would elect Parliament.

Before James ever reached London he was met by the " Millenary Petition," called millenary because it claimed to represent a thousand Puritan clergymen of the Anglican Church. This petition begged the King to Protestantize the Church still further. But James smelled Calvinism, and his experience in Scotland had convinced him that Calvinism was opposed to the spirit of a properly ordered monarchy, that it tended to give the Presbyterian clergy the right to supervise a mere king. In this judgment, the experience of the Continent bore him out. Calvin's Geneva theocracy had been a republic. Calvinist Holland had revolted against its Spanish monarch. Bohemian Calvinists were about to revolt against their Catholic Emperor. The Huguenots had proven a thorn in the side of the King of France. James rejected the Millenary Petition and read to its authors a pedantic lecture on monarchy, bishops, and constituted authority. Those clergy who refused to submit, he got rid of. Soon Puritans were fleeing to Holland, and from there some of them emigrated to North America.

Puritan dislike of the King was fed by the fact that his mother, Mary Queen of Scots, had been Catholic, though he was not; that his wife, Anne of Denmark, though brought up by a Protestant, had Catholic leanings; that James himself desired more tolerance for Catholics. His failure to aid his son-in-law, the Calvinist Winter King of the Bohemian Revolt, in the latter's struggle against the Catholic Hapsburg Emperor, was held against him. His peace with Spain and his attempt to marry his son Charles to a Spanish princess were held against him. For Spain was the great persecutor of Protestantism; besides, warfare with her was lucrative to Puritan shipowners, whose privateers battened on Spanish treasure ships. They feared a return of Catholicism to England: were not unknown thousands of Englishmen still practising popery in private? Were not Jesuit priests known to be conspiring everywhere? Had not a Catholic conspiracy to blow up the Houses of Parliament while in session — the famous "Gunpowder Plot" of Guy Fawkes — well-nigh succeeded? Moreover, their Puritan consciences were irked by the luxury of the court, maintained with their own good money, and by the debauchery they were sure went on there. Given all these considerations, Parliament wrangled with James I over the taxes his government needed if it were to operate successfully. Monarchy and Parliament were approaching a deadlock, when James died and his son Charles I came to the thrones of England and Scotland.

He was twenty-four years old, handsome, well liked. He had come to England as a little boy; and where James I spoke with a broad Scottish accent, Charles' accent was slight. He was quiet, melan-

choly, with a high sense of duty. In religion, he was a loyal Anglican; in politics, a firm believer in the rights and duties of kings.
Ever since he and his favorite, the Duke of Buckingham, had made
an unsuccessful voyage to Madrid to woo a Spanish princess, he had
joined Parliament in favoring war with Spain. True, he married the
fifteen-year-old Henrietta Maria, sister of Louis XIII, and therefore
a Catholic, but he publicly declared he would grant no concessions
to English Catholics.

Charles' failures began immediately. Parliament was eager to
help the Protestant side in the Thirty Years' War. The Bohemian
Revolt had failed, but Christian of Denmark was marching against
the Emperor and Catholicism. Unfortunately, following twenty years
of peace, both the English army and the English navy were in
wretched condition, and Parliament, partly out of distrust of
Charles' minister, Buckingham, persistently refused to vote adequate funds. An English army landed in Holland, intent on recovering the Palatinate for the Winter King, and failed for lack of provisions and equipment. An English fleet, composed partly of rotten
ships, fitted with tackle that had been used against the Spanish Armada nearly half a century earlier, and manned by half-starved
crews, attacked the Spanish port of Cadiz and failed utterly. Two
years later an expedition to relieve the Huguenots of La Rochelle,
besieged there by Richelieu, failed too. A second Parliament demanded the impeachment of Buckingham, and Charles dissolved it;
but the need for adequate funds forced him to call his third Parliament. This time Parliament granted subsidies, but not till it had
forced Charles to sign a " Petition of Right," by which he promised
not to levy taxes without consent of Parliament, not to quarter soldiers in private houses, not to establish martial law in time of peace,
not to imprison persons arbitrarily.

With the Petition of Right the issue was clear-cut. Charles had
admitted, under pressure it is true, that he could not levy taxes in
his own kingdom without the consent of Parliament, and Parliament was elected by the great landlords and the commercial interests. The House of Commons, where money bills traditionally originated, was in effect a committee of the great taxpayers. Evidently,
unless Charles could lay his hands on money from other sources than
taxation, the King must bow to the will of a special class in his king-

dom. Parliament even refused to make the customary grant of " Tonnage and Poundage " (the customs revenue) for more than one year, and the customs revenue was the Crown's most important source of dependable income.

Faced with these problems, Charles reached the ill-considered decision that he would govern without Parliament. He therefore revived old and forgotten laws, and imposed fines in their name. He sold to commercial companies monopolies of salt, soap, wine, and other commodities, and the monopolies of course raised prices. In so doing, he kept within the law, but he further decreased his popularity. The most hated of these indirect taxes was " ship-money." Since seaboard towns had previously had to build ships for national defense, Charles now levied on such towns a money tax for naval purposes. The next year, 1635, he extended the tax to inland towns, on the ground that the navy protected all alike. When the third annual writ for ship-money was issued, John Hampden, one of the richest landowners in England, refused to pay, in order to make a test case. A majority of the royal judges decided against him, but Hampden became the national hero of the Puritans.

It was through his religious policy that James I had aroused the opposition of Parliament. And the Parliament which had threatened to starve Charles I's government into submission was particularly loud in demanding greater toleration for Puritans. But Charles, who was legally head of the Anglican Church and a loyal Anglican besides, determined to rid it of the Protestantism which had crept in during the reign of Elizabeth. With the aid of William Laud, whom he had appointed Archbishop of Canterbury, Charles set himself to restore the traditional Catholic ritual of the Anglican Church. Although he was not head of the Scottish Presbyterian " Kirk," yet he and Laud set to work to reform that too and to bring it more in line with the Anglican establishment. It was in his native Scotland that he came to grief. The Presbyterian Scots banded themselves together in a solemn Covenant to protect their religion from " popish " contamination, and, incidentally, these Covenanters were officered by veteran fighters who had fought for Protestantism in the Thirty Years' War.

All his efforts had been for unity. The Royal Navy had been greatly improved, as one of the results of the hated ship-money. With

Archbishop Laud, he was attempting to secure an orderly and unified religious life for England. The unlucky Duke of Buckingham had been assassinated, but his successor as royal adviser, Thomas Wentworth, Earl of Strafford, had subdued an Irish rebellion for Charles, and would gladly have played the Richelieu in establishing for Charles a strong central government in England. But there was no room for a Richelieu, for there was no strong royal army to stamp out opposition to the central government. Moreover, none could be raised, for there was no money to raise it. The various indirect taxes were inadequate, Charles was pledged not to levy direct taxes without the consent of Parliament, and Parliament was opposed to his policies, political as well as religious. Finally, the government of England was administered largely through justices of the peace, chosen by the King from the very class of country squires who opposed his policies. There was no bureaucracy to replace them, no royal intendants, as in France, to see that the King's will was carried out. Nor was there popular support, as in France, for a strong central government to use such tools, had they existed. In such circumstances Charles tried in vain to suppress the Scottish rebellion without the aid of his English Parliament. In desperation he summoned it, but after the usual wrangling, Charles dissolved it in three weeks, so soon indeed that it came to be called the " Short Parliament." Still unable to cope with the Scottish rebellion, Charles bowed to the inevitable and summoned another Parliament. This one outlasted Charles himself: it is known as the " Long Parliament."

The Long Parliament promptly took steps to end what it regarded as royal tyranny. It sent Archbishop Laud and the Earl of Strafford to the Tower and by illegal procedure it eventually beheaded both. It abolished certain special tribunals of the King, where political and ecclesiastical offenders had been punished. By putting a stop to such indirect taxation as ship-money, it made the King more completely dependent on Parliament. It forbade the King to dissolve Parliament and by the Triennial Act provided that Parliament should meet every three years whether summoned by the King or not. But Charles, shorn of power as he appeared to be, did not despair of recovering what he felt was his inherited right to govern his own people. He had raised enough money to drive back the invading Scots. With Strafford gone, Ireland had risen again, and that would necessitate a royal army. With an army, more problems than Ireland might be solved. It was at this point that Parliament's actions led him to attempt the arrest of five of its leaders. Feeling itself threatened, Parliament began to raise a militia. Next, it seized the important port of Hull on the east coast, and secured control of the Royal Navy. Charles fled north and issued at Nottingham a call to his subjects to rally to the side of their King and suppress rebellion.

That was in March, 1642. The Civil War had started. When Charles fled, a Puritan member of Parliament, Oliver Cromwell, moved that England be put in a state of defense against the King. He and his party were determined to render the King impotent, and to abolish the office of bishop in the Anglican Church which Laud had reorganized and centralized. Now Cromwell went home and raised a troop of sixty light horse to fight for what he felt was religious and political liberty.

Oliver Cromwell was born in 1599, one year before his King. He was the first cousin of the wealthy John Hampden, who had risen to national fame by refusing to pay ship-money. He was a passionate, mystical, deeply religious man, a shrewd and prosperous country squire, a justice of the peace, and an Independent. He had served in the Parliament of 1628, which passed the Petition of Right. When he took his seat in the Long Parliament in 1640, he could see about him the faces of seventeen kinsmen, including Hampden. He backed the Triennial Act the following year. He was now proposing to serve in the field.

Charles was not wrong in supposing that many Englishmen would defend their legitimate King against a rebellious Parliament. To his standard flocked the high-church Anglicans, the Catholics, many squires, in short those groups which for one reason or another disliked the Puritan middle classes. Against him were a few great nobles, and the Puritans — chiefly small landholders, merchants, tradesmen, manufacturers, especially from London and the towns of the South and East, the richest and most " progressive " parts of England. Because these God-fearing Puritans cut their hair short in protest against the fashionable long curls of the " Cavaliers " who supported Charles, they were nicknamed " Roundheads."

Except for the Scots, whom the Presbyterian majority in the English Parliament now induced to fight again against the King, both

Cavaliers and Roundheads were largely civilian armies without experience or discipline. If the war dragged, Parliament would have the advantage, for Parliament had seized the machinery of taxation. Moreover, since Parliament controlled the sea, the commerce of the eastern ports would continue to provide taxable wealth. The same control cut off Charles' hopes of help from the Continent against the rebels. But while, in a long struggle where money counted, the Roundheads had the upper hand, Charles possessed the immediate advantage of a superior cavalry, since the elegant gentlemen who rallied to him were more accustomed to life in the saddle than many of the Puritans who must face them. Oliver Cromwell observed this fact at the battle of Edgehill, in the first year of the struggle, and drew the moral. The Roundheads must have more cavalry and cavalry with such high morale that it could face the impetuous charges of Charles' cousin, Prince Rupert of the Palatinate. Cromwell knew also where such morale was to be found: the dash and gallantry of the Cavaliers could not be overcome by men who were merely opposed to Charles' politics; it must come from the grim religious faith of the Puritan, fighting against popery for his God. Cromwell accordingly went home and raised a cavalry regiment of 1,100 "honest sober Christians," who sang psalms, smashed the statues of saints, prayed to the Lord, and killed Cavaliers with the same grim determination. Where the Cavalier horsemen dashed in madly, Cromwell's "Ironsides" approached the enemy at a steady, brisk trot, disciplined not to use their pistols until the opportune moment. The spirit of ascetic discipline had made the Puritan formidable in the business of buying and selling; it now made him formidable in the business of killing and being killed. Cromwell's Ironsides played a decisive part in defeating the King at Marston Moor in 1644. A large part of the Presbyterian Parliament's forces were now formed on the Cromwellian basis into a "New Model"; and the New Model next year defeated Charles decisively at Naseby. A year later Charles surrendered.

Parliament now exercised the sovereignty which Charles had tried in vain to assert. But the problems that Charles had failed to solve posed themselves in slightly different form for Parliament. As heads of the Church of England, Charles and Laud had run into the stubborn opposition of Presbyterian and Independent. But Parliament, which would have gladly made peace on a Presbyterian basis after Marston Moor, now ran into the stubborn opposition of the Independents, who no more desired their religious worship supervised by Presbyterian elders and ministers than by Archbishop Laud and his Anglican bishops. Charles had striven in vain to find the money with which alone sovereignty could be effectively exercised. Parliament, after the long-drawn-out struggle with the King, was at its wits' end for money, and the pay of the disgruntled New Model was heavily in arrears. Charles' troubles had been precipitated by disagreement with the Scots, and now Parliament could not persuade their Scottish allies to go home until they had been paid their agreed hire, £400,000. Yet the nation was being already taxed about double what Charles had exacted.

But the New Model army that threatened to overthrow the sovereignty of Parliament enjoyed one advantage over the Parliament when it was still but threatening the King. In 1642 Parliament had more means than the King of raising money, and with that money an inexperienced army. But in 1648 the Independents already possessed an army, and the superb New Model army at that, the finest army in Europe. What followed was inevitable. One of Cromwell's officers, Colonel Pride, took a body of musketeers to the House of Commons and "purged" it of 143 Presbyterian members. "Pride's Purge" ushered in a military dictatorship. The King's traditional sovereignty had been usurped by Parliament, which had raised troops against him. Parliament's traditional sovereignty, plus the sovereignty it had usurped from the monarch, was now in its turn usurped by the New Model.

What was left of the Long Parliament, the "Rump" which still sat, then tried the King, by quite illegal methods, for treason. For Cromwell, though he was not ambitious for power, had nevertheless concluded that Charles must go. Royalist feeling was still strong throughout England, though Charles' lack of political tact had rendered it impotent; and a restoration of Charles' power was more than a possibility. If the authority of Parliament and the religious policy of the Independents were to be preserved, there must be no turning back. On January 30, 1649, Charles I mounted the scaffold, courteous and cheerful. He declared to the end that he died a martyr to the liberties of the English people. If Parliament could illegally prosecute a King, which of the King's subjects was secure? Before a London crowd, horrified at what they could only consider sacrilege, the executioner held up the severed head of Charles Stuart.

Cromwell, the commander-in-chief of the army, was now by force of circumstance the actual ruler of England. For Catholic Ireland was in full revolt against this English Parliament of radical Protestants. The Presbyterian Scots were rallying to the dead King's young son, Charles II, and were preparing to march with him against these murderous Independents. The New Model alone stood between the Rump Parliament and destruction. Cromwell and his Puritan soldiers crossed to Catholic Ireland and savagely put down the rebellion. Next they met the Scottish forces at Worcester and crushed them utterly.

The corruption and mismanagement of the Rump grew intolerable, and Cromwell unceremoniously turned it out of doors. Cromwell next assembled a Parliament by selecting 140 men on the recommendation of Independent ministers. Surely this would at least unite Parliament and Army on a common religious basis. But the radical economic legislation of "Barebone's Parliament," so nicknamed from one of its members, who bore the typical Puritan name of Praisegod Barebone, disgusted Cromwell, and he sent a detachment of troops to evict this Parliament too. When one of his colonels asked its members what they were doing there, he received the very Puritan answer that they were seeking the Lord. "Come out of this place, then," he replied, "for to my certain knowledge the Lord has not been here these twelve years past." It is an interesting statement, if we remember that it was twelve years since the Long Parliament had raised troops against the King.

The Army leaders now prepared the "Instrument of Government," the first written constitution of modern times, providing that Oliver Cromwell should be Lord Protector for life, that the House of Lords was abolished, that Parliament should meet at least every three years to make laws and levy taxes, that the Protector might delay but not veto legislation, and that Congregationalism should be the state religion.

Under the Instrument of Government a new Parliament was elected. Royalists were of course excluded from the polls. But the Presbyterians, not Cromwell's Independents, managed to secure the

majority of seats. The new Parliament promptly began to quote
the law against Cromwell, as in the old days Cromwell and his revolutionary friends had quoted it against the King. But Cromwell now,
like Charles then, was discovering that meanwhile a state must be
run. " If," remarked the Lord Protector bitterly, " nothing should
ever be done but what is according to law, the throat of the nation
may be cut while we send for someone to invoke a law." Again he
dismissed Parliament, and this time he set to work to govern England through major generals, backed by armed force and responsible
to the central power alone. He had discovered the formula of Richelieu and his intendants, a formula the dead Earl of Strafford would
have been happy to use in behalf of the King's authority. But he
did not rule by force alone, any more than had Richelieu. His rule
rested in generous measure on the support of those same commercial classes whom Charles had failed to satisfy. He made advantageous commercial treaties with Holland and France. He permitted
industrious Jews to enter England. He punished the Barbary pirates
who preyed on English commerce. He attacked the Spanish in the
West Indies and took Jamaica.

But despite these brilliant foreign successes his domestic position
was a troubled one. As early as 1652, before he had chased the Rump
from their seats, he was beginning to see what was lacking. The executive needed not only to come to terms with the Puritan commercial element; it needed also the prestige of the Crown, a symbol the
vast majority of the English people identified with true authority.
Parliaments lacked this mystical prestige. So did armies. When one
of his lawyer friends discussed his problems with him, Cromwell
suddenly demanded: " What if a man should take upon him to be
King? " But his friend was horrified, and even when in 1657 he had
called one last Parliament together, and when this Parliament, eager
to put an end to military rule, begged him to accept the crown, he
declined. Moreover, with this last Parliament too he quarreled, and
he dissolved it next year. The same year he died.

Oliver Cromwell was not a theorist; his had been the practical
task of restoring sovereignty and order to a state torn by religious
dissension and economic contradictions. But in 1651, while the Rump
was still sitting, another man, a theorist of a high order, Thomas
Hobbes, published a treatise on the state and gave it the title, *Levia-*

than. Hobbes had been born in 1588, the year of the Spanish Armada. He had therefore witnessed the last fifteen years of Elizabeth's reign, had lived through the days of James I, Charles I, and now the kingless Commonwealth. According to Hobbes, a man's natural state is one of war, " of every man, against every man." And to the generation which had just lived through the horrors of the Civil War, he wrote of man's natural state:

In such condition, there is no place for Industry; because the fruit thereof is uncertain: and consequently no Culture of the Earth; no Navigation, nor use of the commodities that may be imported by Sea; no commodious Building; no Instruments of moving, and removing such things as require much force; no Knowledge of the face of the Earth; no account of Time; no Arts; no Letters; no Society; and which is worst of all, continuall feare, and danger of violent death; And all the life of man, solitary, poore, nasty, brutish, and short.

Doubtless, this description of a savage society applied more accurately to the Germanies, which had just emerged from the Thirty Years' War, than to England; but in England, too, men had known "continuall feare." Hobbes pointed out the escape from such conditions. All men covenant together to surrender their power to a "Soveraign," who will protect them against foreign and civil war. Thus comes into being

a COMMON-WEALTH, in latine CIVITAS. This is the Generation [that is, the origin] of that great LEVIATHAN, or rather (to speake more reverently) of that *Mortall God,* to which wee owe under the *Immortall God,* our peace and defence.

To that monster Leviathan, or " to speake more reverently," to that Mortal God, the modern state, we owe, Hobbes insists, complete obedience in all matters, political, economic, religious. For it is the Sovereignty, it is Authority. This Authority, whether Monarchy or Assembly — and Hobbes holds it may be either — owes nothing to its subjects. It has made no agreement with them. The agreement that generated Leviathan is between the various subjects, not between them and the Sovereign. On sovereignty there are no restrictions. No revolt against it is justifiable. " Tyrant " is but the name given a monarch by men who do not like him, just as those who dislike an aristocracy call it an oligarchy, and those who dislike de-

mocracy call it anarchy. Hobbes declared he had written *Leviathan*
"without other designe than to set before mens' eyes the mutuall
Relation between Protection and Obedience " — a relation that must
exist in any ordered society.

Such was Hobbes's theory of the state, and it earned him few
thanks. Those who had opposed Charles saw in it a denunciation of
their successful revolution. Those who disliked the new Commonwealth saw in it a defense against its overthrow. But it was specifi-
cally none of these things: it was merely a statement that nothing
can dissolve " the Mortall God," that is, the state, except its failure
to protect its subjects against foreign or civil war. So long as it does
that, its powers are unrestricted. This was Cromwell's true power,
as Hobbes saw it, and this was Richelieu's. For indeed, from the
medieval point of view, Britain and France had become just such
Leviathans, just such Mortal Gods, as Hobbes had described. They
were impersonal and non-moral monsters.

At Cromwell's death, the Mortal God threatened to die too. His
son Richard succeeded him in the office of Lord Protector, but Richard proved completely unequal to the task. The various army leaders
were quarreling among themselves, setting up the Rump of the
Long Parliament again, dissolving it, recalling it, wrangling with it.
A new civil war threatened, when one General Monk called a new
and freely elected " Convention Parliament," which restored the
monarchy and recalled the dead King's son, Charles II, from Continental exile.

" The Restoration " was brought about by the universal fear of
anarchy; but when Charles II had landed at Dover and taken possession of his throne, England seems to have suddenly realized how
glad it was to see the end, not only of the rule of the sword, but of
the rule of " the saints." The restless and divided people whom neither James I nor Charles I had been able to govern, had emerged
from Puritanism and military rule a disciplined nation; but, for the
moment, that nation was chiefly concerned with enjoying its new
freedom. The joy of living seemed to have come again to Merry
England; and Charles II, " the Merry Monarch," reigned over a gay
and brilliant court. Where his grandfather, James, had been physically awkward and intellectually pompous and pedantic, Charles II
was handsome, gracious, witty. Where his father, Charles I, had

been grave, inflexible, politically tactless, and deeply religious, the son was gay, flexible, skeptical. The new King, fresh from nearly two decades of exile and poverty, set about enjoying his inheritance and making his court the center of pleasure and of art. Under the harsh rule of the saints, the arts had been neglected. As early as the reign of James I the theater of Stratford-on-Avon had been closed by a Puritan town government, while William Shakespeare was still alive and actually living at Stratford. Now, under Charles II, a group of urbane and witty dramatists, Wycherley, Congreve, Vanbrugh, and Farquhar, produced their comedies of manners; and where the Elizabethans had indulged a hearty Rabelaisian humor, the dramatists of the Restoration pictured an elegant and sophisticated debauchery. The grave poetry of John Milton, loyal servant of the Puritan Commonwealth, gave way to the civilized verses of Dryden; and where John Bunyan, in *Pilgrim's Progress,* had painted the Puritan's steadfast faith, now Samuel Butler scoffed at his sanctimoniousness in sparkling satirical verse. The ostentatious barrenness of the Puritan conventicle gave place to the harmonious church buildings of Sir Christopher Wren. Court painters like Sir Peter Lely produced their portraits in the classical French manner. The severe and somber costume of the Puritan disappeared, in favor of the gay and ornate styles of the French court.

In music, even more than in the other arts, the Restoration meant, not an actual restoration of English things, but importation from the Continent. Under the Tudors England was a musical center. Henry VIII loved music, and was no mean musician himself. Elizabeth's organist of the Royal Chapel had been the great composer William Byrd; and James I's had been Orlando Gibbons. But the Puritans had abolished the traditional church music, as they had abolished the other arts which had for centuries adorned religion; and although they developed a severer music of their own for their worship, a great tradition had been lost. As for the secular music of the popular " masques " — a sort of primitive opera — such vanities were out of the question. The Restoration therefore, despite some great native composers like Henry Purcell, turned largely to the Continent for its music, as it did indeed for most of its cultural expressions. Unfortunately there was little kinship between this new and sophisticated music and the folk tunes the English poorer classes still remembered and loved; and the English were destined to become a relatively unmusical people.

But if Merry England had again come into its own, who now controlled the state, and in whose favor? Not Charles II, at least in the Continental sense. The Crown, as everybody, including the popular and intelligent Charles, well knew, was dependent directly on Parliament. Charles supplied to the government the symbol of traditional authority, which the great and powerful Cromwell had never been; but the true " Soveraign " of this new Leviathan was Parliament. There was to be no standing army with which a king might himself become sovereign. In the religious sphere, too, Parliament was to be supreme. The Anglican Church was again recognized as the state church, and was made subservient to Parliament rather than to the King, although the King remained technically its supreme head on earth. It was Parliament, and therefore the landlords of England, whether nobles or squires, together with the commercial interests with which they were financially involved, that ruled; naturally they ruled in their own interests.

With this arrangement Charles was by no means in sympathy, but he was determined not to " embark again upon his travels." Where his father had obstinately defended his rights against Parliament, Charles followed the easier method of corrupting Parliament through bribes. To get money for his extravagant court, he used openly only those methods which Parliament would approve, while he secretly accepted a far larger sum from Louis XIV for promising to help Louis in his Dutch War. He would have liked a standing army, but he was too tactful to stake his crown on the effort to raise one.

With Parliament's religious policy he was particularly out of sympathy. Secretly preferring the faith of his French Catholic mother, Henrietta Maria, whose exile from England he had shared, he loathed intolerance and bigotry and hoped to ease the lot of English Catholics. But while Parliament gladly tightened the laws against Puritan " Dissenters " from Anglicanism, they were as determined as their Elizabethan ancestors not to permit popery. Decades of Jesuit conspiracy to overthrow England's Protestant government equated Catholicism in their minds with treason. Louis XIV's government equated it with royalist tyranny and absolutism. And for the economic backwardness of Catholic lands like France, where peasants wore wooden shoes, they felt the true Protestant scorn. " Popery and wooden shoes " was a cant phrase of the time.

It was therefore a crucial matter that, although Charles had numerous illegitimate children by Nell Gwynn, the actress, and by his other mistresses, yet his Portuguese wife, Catherine of Braganza, had given him no legitimate heir. That meant he would be succeeded by his brother James, Duke of York, who was a Roman Catholic and an earnest bigot at that. Rather than see a Catholic mount the throne, one group of the governing aristocracy managed to put through the House of Commons an " Exclusion Bill," debarring James from the throne; but the bill was defeated in the House of Lords. Those who favored exclusion were nicknamed " Whigs," a slang term applied to rebellious Protestants. Those who preferred James to the risk of another civil war were labeled " Tories," a word applied to Catholic outlaws in Ireland. Thus were born two opposing parties in the governing class of England. The Whigs drew their support from the commercial interests as well as the landlords, while the Tories depended on the squire and the Anglican parson and in general upon all those who disliked what was left of Puritanism.

In 1685 Charles died — confessing on his deathbed the Catholic faith which he loved; and James II came to the throne. By appointing Catholics to civil office and by choosing them as officers in the army, by issuing a " Declaration of Indulgence " which suspended the oppressive laws against Catholics and Dissenters alike, James infuriated the Tories who had supported him, as well as the Whigs who had opposed his succession. Short of another revolution, what could the governing class do, except starve the royal government financially and hope for James' early death? His heirs were his two daughters, Mary and Anne, and fortunately both were Protestant.

The failure of Charles II's wife to produce an heir had proven crucial, for it placed the Catholic James on the throne. The fact that James' daughters were Protestant offered an ultimate way out. At this point another accident of family history removed hope. James' second wife, like him a Catholic, gave him a son and heir, who would of course perpetuate a Catholic dynasty in England. Yet during these very years Huguenot refugees streamed into England —

the Edict of Nantes had just been revoked — with lurid tales of how a Catholic king persecuted his Protestant subjects. Some of the Tories now combined with the Whigs and turned to James' Anglican daughter, Mary, whose husband — and first cousin — was William of Orange, Stadtholder of the Netherlands. At their invitation William and Mary crossed to England. The army deserted James, James fled to France, and the " Glorious Revolution " of 1688 — " glorious " because it was bloodless — was over.

William and Mary were seated on the English throne, but only when they had recognized a " Bill of Rights," in which Parliament laid down the rules for English monarchy. The King, or Queen, of England must be Anglican: that debarred James II's Catholic son. The King might not suspend laws or dispense his subjects from obeying them, as James II had attempted to do, in his Declaration of Indulgence. The King could not interfere with the election, or the freedom of speech, of his Parliaments. He could not levy taxes, or maintain an army, without Parliament's consent. The provisions of the Bill of Rights of 1689 were not unlike those of the Petition of Right of 1628. But whereas Charles I had indeed signed the " petition," in order to secure subsidies, William and Mary signed a " bill," or law, in order to secure from Parliament the right to reign. Moreover, Parliament now began granting taxes and making appropriations for the army for one year only. Finally, the religious problem was met by a Toleration Act, permitting Protestant Dissenters to worship in public. This right was not granted to Catholics.

In foreign affairs, the Glorious Revolution was crucial. Charles II and James II had been pro-French. But " Dutch William," Stadtholder of Holland and King of England, Scotland, and Ireland, led his willing English subjects into the War of the Palatinate to protect the European balance of power against the growing might of Louis XIV. His successor, Queen Anne, fought with Louis the even more successful War of the Spanish Succession. And in both wars England gained valuable colonies and commercial concessions.

William quickly learned that, in order to get the full support of the English against Louis, he needed to choose his ministers from whichever party, Whig or Tory, could muster a majority in the House of Commons when military supply bills came up. In Anne's reign it was arranged beforehand that if she died without heir the

English crown should pass to Sophia of Hanover, Protestant grand-daughter of James I and daughter of the unfortunate Winter King of Bohemia, or to Sophia's heirs. It was thus that George I, a German who could not speak English, and his son George II, who spoke it badly, followed, on the throne of England, Queen Anne, last of the Stuarts. In the circumstances, not only were the King's ministers chosen from the Parliamentary party in power: the King did not even attend meetings of his "cabinet." And it was this cabinet of ministers which, subject to the approval and support of Parliament, ruled England.

A series of accidents had shifted the sovereignty of England from King to Parliament. The death of Elizabeth without a direct heir, had brought a Scottish king to the throne. His pedantry and his tactlessness had helped to lose him the confidence of Parliament. His dislike of Calvinism and his ignorance of English political customs had led him into a breach with his Puritan Parliament. That breach, his son Charles I wanted the tact to heal. The execution of Charles and the inexperience of Parliament threatened to dissolve the state, and it was held together only by the heroic medicine of Cromwell's military dictatorship. At Cromwell's death chaos threatened again; and an army general placed on the restored throne the heir of the executed King, but upon the condition that this second Charles should bow to the will of Parliament. By chance, Charles II's wife was childless, and his Catholic brother succeeded him as James II. The English were convinced that Catholicism meant royal tyranny and religious persecution; and the accident that James's Catholic wife gave birth to a son brought on the Glorious Revolution, which called James' Protestant daughter and her Dutch husband to the throne. The accident that James' second daughter, Anne, left no children, placed the crown on the head of a German who could speak no English and who therefore left affairs, even more completely than had Dutch William, in the hands of his Cabinet and hence in the hands of a Parliamentary party majority.

Through those historical accidents there of course operated constant historical factors: the hatred and fear which the bulk of Englishmen felt for Catholicism; the passionate religious zeal of the Puritan which would bow to no authority but God but which in His name subjected the nation to a stern discipline; the greed of the landlord and financial magnate which, thanks to psalm-singing Puritan troopers, emerged triumphant over both King and Church.

Like the Thirty Years' War on the Continent, the contemporary struggle in England began in the name of religion and ended with economic and political motives uppermost. The landlords who now ruled England through Parliament had tumbled on a scheme for retaining the sovereignty of the state. There was still a real live King, whom Englishmen, particularly poor Englishmen, could revere, but he took his orders from a landlord Parliament. There was still an Anglican Church with traditional forms of worship; but the parson was now likely to be an easy-going, fox-hunting fellow, and there was no danger of his challenging the authority of the squire, as he had in the days of Archbishop Laud. For those humbler folk who craved a fuller religious life than the State Church generally afforded, there were various sects of Dissenters. Dissent must be tolerated, if only because some Dissenters were wealthy merchants and financiers. And the National Bank and the National Debt, which had been organized under Queen Anne and which financed the War of the Spanish Succession, were forces with which Parliament must reckon in any religious settlement. Tory landlords disliked the Whig financial interest, and in 1711 passed a law that none but large landowners should sit in Parliament. But this did not shake the moneyed interest. Even a landlord Parliament would have to listen to finance or it could not float loans. Anyhow, wealthy Dissenters habitually bought land in order to become respectable — and often became Anglicans for the same reason. Landlords were themselves capitalists: they farmed for profits, and English agriculture took the lead in scientific method, rotation of crops, and the selective breeding of cattle. Finally, the enclosure movement, which Thomas More was already lamenting under Henry VIII, and which monarchy had in vain attempted to arrest, now speeded up. Act after act of the landlord Parliaments permitted landlords to enclose, or hedge in, land that had been common, open to the use of a whole manor. The poor were pushed aside, became day laborers, or wandered to town, to increase there the supply of cheap labor. The small farmers, the yeomen, of England, who had formed the rank and file of Cavalier and Roundhead army alike, largely disappeared. The rich, both in town and open countryside, took charge.

But the rich governing class of England developed a marvelous political genius. It knew what it wanted: trade and colonies. And in war after war, it got both. It had developed a machinery of representative government, with a " constitutional " monarch for figurehead, that was flexible and sensitive to opinion. When the executive, which was now not the King but the King's Cabinet of Ministers, fell to cross-purposes with the legislative, there was a quick way out of deadlock. It was not necessary to behead the executive, as Charles I had been beheaded. It was not necessary to call in an executive from abroad, as Dutch William had been called in. It was not necessary to turn over the state to a wrangling, bungling legislative, as it had been turned over to the Long Parliament. Either the Cabinet resigned, and a new Cabinet was formed, which could command the support of a majority in the legislative; or if a Whig legislative lost the support of the governing class throughout the country, a Tory legislative was elected to replace it. Whig and Tory bid against each other, like rival sovereigns, for public support; and there were always means of cutting off the head of the sovereign — quite bloodlessly — or deposing him, in favor of a new sovereign. This was party government.

It was an instinctive and untheoretical solution. But just as Cromwell's instinctive solution of sovereignty had been rationalized by the political theorist, Thomas Hobbes, in *Leviathan,* so this Whig-Tory solution was rationalized by another political philosopher, John Locke. His *Two Treatises of Government* appeared in 1689, the very year the governing class of England placed William on the throne. In the first of these treatises Locke disposes of the absolutist arguments of Sir Robert Filmer, whose *Patriarcha* had appeared in 1681, before the death of Charles II. Filmer had claimed in his book that monarchy was the " natural " form of sovereignty, ordained by God; and that when the King was called " father of his people," the term was no mere metaphor. But Locke countered with the " natural " rights of the subject! And in his second *Treatise* Locke insisted that states arose, not, as Hobbes had said, when men in fear of each other and of anarchy deeded over all authority to an irresponsible monarch or assembly, but when they formed a compact with a sovereign to protect their " lives, liberties, and estates." " The great and chief end, therefore, of men's uniting into commonwealths, and put-

ting themselves under government, is the preservation of their property." If the sovereign encroached on the liberties of the people or
illegally taxed away their property, the state dissolved into a tyranny
and sovereignty reverted to the people.

But in Locke's day "the people," so far as the preservation of
property was concerned, were chiefly the landlords, the merchants,
and the bankers of England. At the beginning of Charles II's reign
a landlord Parliament had abolished certain feudal dues which landlords paid the King. These had long since been commuted to money
payment, but they were the last remnant of a system which recognized that land was "held," in return for social services, not
"owned." From now on, the landlord "owned" his acres. The
feudal dues the serf paid the landlord had also long ago taken the
form of a money rent paid by a tenant. Needless to say, such rent
was not abolished.

Yet the real " people " had gained something too. In the first place,
Parliament's victory over monarchy had made it clear in Acts of
Parliament that no man should be arbitrarily imprisoned and that
every man had the right to trial by jury. The landlords' "lives, liberties, and estates " had been made safe. The lives and liberties of the
poor, though not perhaps their property rights, had been made safe
also.

To secure an estate, it was but necessary, after all, to get rich. And
while not many of the poor could do that, a few consistently did.
Opportunity was legally, if not actually, open. In that sense, England was "free." But to get rich, one must embrace the Puritan
asceticism of work, if not the Puritan vice of close dealing as well.
When Archbishop Laud attempted to rebuild a decent system of
poor relief, the Puritan cry had been: "Giving alms is no charity! "
The Puritan loathed the medieval ideal of Christlike poverty, and
he loathed lazy beggars. Landlord and merchant and banker now
heartily agreed with him, and by the eighteenth century a system of
workhouses was set up, to make paupers earn their keep, and perhaps to make them realize that in a nation dedicated to economic
gain poverty was a disgrace and a mark of the Lord's disfavor. If
so, a convenient new form of penance had been devised, one highly
appropriate to the capitalistic society which evolved it.

X.

BRITAIN TRAVELS LIGHT

THE papal arbitration of 1493, which divided the extra-European world between Portugal and Spain, was an effort on the part of the chief moral authority of a united Christendom to avert a clash between those two Christian powers over the rich spoils that lay outside Christendom. To the east of the line grew up the commercial empire of the Portuguese, on the African coast, in India, in the Spice Islands; and their colonial empire of Brazil. To the west there developed a Spanish colonial empire in North, Central, and South America, and in the distant Philippine Islands which Magellan had discovered and claimed for Philip II. But would the other states of Europe respect these territorial claims? We have already seen that the growing commercial classes of many European states were looking around for money profit. Much of that profit they found in the stream of gold and silver that flowed into Christendom from Spanish mines in Mexico and Peru and from Portuguese mines in Brazil. The Spanish people, still largely medieval in their economic habits and institutions, allowed these precious metals to slip through their hands to the bankers and merchants of the Rhine valley and of Antwerp. The enormous purchasing power of the Spanish enriched these merchants, flooded Spain with their goods, and largely destroyed the trade and industry at home. And since the Spanish state, with its heavy military expenses in Europe, depended on those American mines to keep it going, everything depended on retaining safe communications with America. This was the medieval " government by endowment " rather than by taxes, with a vengeance. Even Portugal, though her practical monopoly of the trade from Asia around Africa gave her a genuine economic basis, suffered disorganization too from the flow of precious metals from Brazil.

It was certain that the other seaboard states of Christendom would share in this booty if they could. As Spain's power declined, her riches grew more tempting. For Spain, as Henry IV's great finance minister Sully observed, was " one of those states whose legs and arms are strong and powerful, but the heart infinitely weak and feeble." The mines of Mexico were rich, but the government at Madrid was weak. Yet, of the seaboard states that might have preyed on Spanish treasure, some could do very little. The Italian city-states, which had first taught Europeans to seek the wealth of the Indies, had been ruined by the competition of Portugal's cheap water route around Africa. The North German towns, which had once ruled the Baltic through their Hanseatic League, had grown weak; and there was no centralized monarch to back their enterprise, for the Holy Roman Emperor was at the mercy of his great vassals. The seafaring Dutch belonged to Spain until their war of independence against Philip II. Denmark, small and surrounded by powerful neighbors, accomplished little except to exploit the cod and whale of Greenland and Iceland and take possession of a few West Indian islands on the fringe of the great Spanish Empire. Sweden was not too exhausted by her participation in the Thirty Years' War to plant a small colony on the Delaware River, but it was captured by the Dutch, and European affairs kept Sweden busy after that.

There remained the important seaboard kingdoms of England and France. Five years after Columbus' first voyage, another Genoese, John Cabot, who had settled in Bristol, was commissioned by Henry VII, England's first Tudor king, to " seek out, discover, and find whatsoever isles, countries, regions, or provinces of the heathen and infidels, which before this time have been unknown to all Christians." Cabot reached Cape Breton Island in the mouth of the St. Lawrence and, like his fellow-townsman, reported that he had discovered the country of the Great Khan. Another Italian sailor, in the service of Francis I of France, explored in 1524 the coasts of Nova Scotia and New England; and ten years later a French sailor, Jacques Cartier, went there to find a northwest passage around this land mass to Asia and riches. Though he did not get to Asia, he did explore the St. Lawrence as far as the site of Montreal. But although Walter Raleigh under Elizabeth planted a colony on the coast of "Virginia" in what is now North Carolina, and although the Huguenot admiral, Coligny, planted colonies farther south, these and similar attempts, by French and English alike, all failed.

Elizabethan sailors like Hawkins, Drake, Cavendish, Gilbert, and Frobisher grew wealthy from preying on Spanish treasure fleets, pillaging Spanish settlements, freebooting on the Spanish Main, and transporting Negro slaves from the west coast of Africa to the Spanish colonies. Frenchmen like Coligny likewise profited from attacks on Spain. But it was not until the seventeenth century that permanent settlements of Englishmen and Frenchmen were established in the New World. In 1607 an expedition sent out by the London Company reached Virginia, sailed up a river which was named the James in honor of the reigning king, James I, and founded Jamestown. In the very next year, far to the north, a French explorer, Samuel Champlain, explored the valley of the St. Lawrence and founded Quebec. Other settlements rapidly followed. An English settlement was established in Bermuda in 1612. A band of Puritans, which had fled to Calvinist Holland to escape the persecutions of James I, ventured in 1620 a settlement at Plymouth, on the coast of what came to be called "New England." Other Englishmen followed, to Virginia and to New England, and the settlements grew in number and size. Englishmen likewise occupied a number of West Indian islands, on the fringe of the Spanish Empire. And the French were colonizing Canada and Acadia — now known as Nova Scotia. Moreover, an English East India Company was using the Portuguese route around Africa, and colliding with the Portuguese in India. Here too went the agents of a French East India Company. And both French and English were slave-trading on the west coast of Africa.

But in the new scramble for overseas wealth it was neither the English nor French who seemed likeliest to succeed; it was the Dutch. With a small and none too fertile country, the Dutch had taken to the sea earlier than either English or French. In the fisheries they had built up a seafaring tradition and a shipping industry. Already, by the time of the Emperor Charles V, the Netherlands were supplanting the Italian city-states as the banking center of Europe. In their revolt against Philip II their seaborne commerce not only enabled the Northern Netherlands to win their political independence, but to grow rich doing it. They preyed on the colonial dominions of Philip; and when the crown of Portugal was inherited by Philip and the vast Spanish and Portuguese empires were united, the Dutch had a good excuse to seize the colonies of Portugal in the East. The Dutch East India Company, organized in 1602, drove the Portuguese from Ceylon, Java, Sumatra, and from the Moluccas, or "Spice Islands." By the time that Jan Coen, governor of the Company, founded the city of Batavia in Java, in 1619, it was the capital of a vast commercial empire. In China, Japan, and India, the Dutch shouldered other European competitors aside. They discovered Australia, New Zealand, the Fiji Islands; and established a Dutch colony at the Cape of Good Hope.

By 1648, when the Peace of Westphalia ended the Thirty Years' War and conceded the independence of Holland, the Dutch were far ahead of both English and French. Although the bulk of their empire lay in the East, they had seized Tobago and Curaçao from the Spanish West Indies, and planted "New Netherland" in the Hudson Valley, pushing out the little Swedish colony on the Delaware and threatening the interests of the English in New England and the French in Canada. They had seized the best part of the Portuguese commercial empire; and though their possessions were less extensive than those of Spain, Spain was visibly declining, while the Dutch were thriving. Where Spain exploited her colonies chiefly for the precious metals she could get out of them, the Dutch exploited theirs as only shrewd merchants and bankers and shippers could. They dominated the carrying trade of Europe with their ships. They were, in a contemporary phrase, "the wagoners of all seas." They owned approximately half the shipping of Europe. And the wealth this shipping brought them allowed them to build and operate the best navy in Europe.

Now came the golden age of Dutch culture. Their language and literature never captured Europe as did those of the French. But their liberal government made Holland the refuge of persecuted thinkers, and the lack of government censorship made it the center of Europe's publishing business. Moreover, in at least one of the arts the Dutch excelled. Under the impulse of this new prosperity the ancient tradition of Flemish painting revived. But whereas early Flemish painting had been religious (as indeed what painting was not?) Dutch painting in the golden age of the seventeenth century was almost entirely secular. Nor was it classical in inspiration, as it had been in France ever since the Renaissance. The Dutch artists were realistic and homely. They painted the portraits of wealthy merchants and burgomasters, well-cultivated landscapes, and the piles of good things to eat, fish, meat, fowls, vegetables, fruit, that wealth was bringing to the Dutchman's table. If the Dutchman bought a religious painting, his good Protestant soul was likely to demand a scene from the Old Testament. But at its best this Dutch art is magnificent. In the early seventeenth century Van Dyck was painting the portraits of James I of England, of his son Charles I, and their families. There followed Rembrandt, with his rich and somber canvases, Frans Hals, Jordaens, David Teniers, Jan Vermeer of Delft, Jacob van Ruysdael.

But the Dutch colonial monopoly was proving even more oppressive than the Spanish, if only because it was more efficiently guarded. It was particularly oppressive to the English. Wherever English traders might go, there the Dutch seemed to be too. They collided over the fisheries in the North Atlantic, over commercial posts in India, over slave-trading in Africa and the West Indies, over settlements in North America. In 1651 the government of Cromwell, determined to foster English shipping at the expense of the ubiquitous Dutch, enacted a "Navigation Act," restricting English trade to English ships. The result was the first Anglo-Dutch War. It was a war which Cromwell personally opposed, for Cromwell dreamed, like his contemporary Grotius, of a union of Protestant nations. But the English merchants were for breaking their Dutch competitors. Although the English navy suffered some severe defeats, the English secured the valuable concession of a trading post in the Spice Islands. In the reign of Charles II a second Dutch War caught the English navy in a wretched condition, and a Dutch admiral, De Ruyter, entered the Thames, burned English shipping, and terrorized London. But again the English were ultimately successful, and the Dutch were forced to cede New Amsterdam, their colony at the mouth of the Hudson River in America. New Amsterdam, rechristened New York in honor of the Duke of York, the future James II, now joined the northern colonies of England to the southern, in an unbroken line. In 1672, Charles II, who was secretly in the pay of Louis XIV, helped the Sun-King to attack Holland in a war which Colbert, jealous like England of Dutch seapower and Dutch commerce, approved. But the English Parliament was opposed to Charles' pro-French and pro-Catholic leanings, and in 1674 it forced England's withdrawal from the Third Dutch War. The merchants of England recognized that their previous wars had done their work: Holland's power was declining. Meanwhile, under Colbert's careful management, the commercial and naval power of Louis XIV appeared likely to prove the real menace. It is worth noting that Protestant England fought Protestant Holland three times in a quarter of a century; and that the first of these wars was fought by the Puritan Commonwealth when the Peace of Westphalia had only four years before put an end to Christendom's last great religious war.

England withdrew from the Third Anglo-Dutch War in 1674, but Louis XIV continued to press Holland till 1678. Holland was exhausted by the French invasion, but the economic system which Colbert had fostered in France was seriously weakened too. By comparison with both, England was the gainer. When England withdrew, the carrying trade of Holland fell largely into English hands: French privateers were preying on Dutch shipping, and customers found English bottoms safer. This shift in the carrying trade was a body blow at Dutch wealth; for it was Dutch shipping and commerce, not Holland's meager internal resources, which had supported the Dutch navy and guaranteed Dutch domination on the seas. But curiously enough, it was the Anglo-Dutch alliance against Louis, which followed when the Glorious Revolution called Dutch William to the English throne, that finally guaranteed English naval superiority over the Dutch. For the purposes of that alliance it was agreed that if Holland would put in the field against Louis an army of 102,000 men to England's 40,000, England would supply five-eighths of the joint naval forces to Holland's three-eighths. Thus, the War of the Palatinate tended to stimulate the British navy and to turn Holland's resources from her navy to her army. This shift in naval power was confirmed by the Treaty of Utrecht. By that treaty the Dutch recovered the "barrier fortresses" against Louis, and were allowed to close the River Scheldt and thereby strangle the competing commerce of Antwerp. But the English got Newfoundland, Acadia, and Hudson's Bay from France; the strategic naval bases, Gibraltar and Minorca, from Spain; and valuable commercial privileges in Spanish America. In terms of Anglo-Dutch naval rivalry, the Treaty of Utrecht records the fact that Holland was handicapped by being smaller than England and more exposed to attack from Louis. Holland had therefore to watch her more powerful ally accumulate those very assets, colonies and naval bases, on which seapower must ultimately rest.

By the time William III crossed from Holland to take possession of James II's vacant throne, it was becoming evident to English traders that three Anglo-Dutch wars and a French invasion had destroyed Dutch dominance. Like Portugal, Holland had been handicapped by its lack of size. The mother country, peculiarly open to attack by land, could not withstand the expense in men and money that would alone have protected her. Like Portugal, Holland had shown more capacity for establishing trading posts than for founding populous colonies. Moreover, Holland was dominated by her commercial classes, and her foreign policy was sometimes better suited to a business firm gaining profits than to a nation gaining strategic power. Generally speaking, she shrank from war, because war was bad for business. But her love of profits led her to shut out the trading classes of her big neighbors, and war — disastrous war — was thrust upon her. Now, in 1689, with Holland pushed aside to the same unaggressive position as Spain and Portugal, the only expanding colonial empires were the English and the French.

The English faced the French in North America, in the West Indies, on the west coast of Africa, and in India. The English held a strip of the Atlantic seaboard of North America, from what is now Maine to Carolina, and a settlement in Newfoundland. Moreover, an English chartered company was trading for furs in the region of Hudson's Bay. From Maine to Carolina the population was estimated at nearly 300,000. In the South, with the help of Negro slave labor, the colonists raised tobacco and would later turn to rice and cotton. In New England, which was less adapted to agriculture, they were fishermen, whalers, shippers, rum-makers. As against this slender strip of territory, the French claimed the valley of the St. Lawrence, the region of the Great Lakes and the Ohio, and the Mississippi Valley, which French explorers like La Salle had traversed and which was named Louisiana in honor of Louis XIV. It was a vast region, but it probably contained not more than 20,000 Frenchmen, supported chiefly by the trade in furs. Nevertheless, French forts were springing up, and if the rapidly growing English population along the seacoast ever expanded beyond the Appalachian Mountains, there would be trouble. Moreover, most of the English colonies held royal charters granting them lands " from sea to sea " — that is, to the Pacific. In Newfoundland there were both French settlers and English; and in the Hudson's Bay territory both races competed for furs.

In the West Indies, the French held Martinique and Guadeloupe; the English, Jamaica, Barbadoes, the Bahamas, and a number of smaller islands. What both French and English were after here was chiefly sugar, and bases for trade with Spanish America.

In Africa, the English were at Gambia and on the Gold Coast, while the French had taken Madagascar, Gorée, and the mouth of the Senegal. The climate was unsuitable for European settlement. These were trading stations. There were ivory and gold dust and wax. Particularly, there were Negro slaves, and Negro slaves were in great demand in the Americas, wherever the climate would permit their use, for labor was scarce.

In India, the English had made a better start than the French. Like the Dutch, the English had been at war with Philip II, in the days of the Armada, when Philip ruled both the Spanish and Portuguese empires. Like the Dutch, the English had preyed on the Portuguese. They now held Calcutta, Madras, and Bombay — Bombay was the dowry the Portuguese princess, Catherine of Braganza, had brought Charles II. The French had posts at Chandarnagar and Pondicherry. The coast of India, like Africa, had a climate unfavorable to colonization by Europeans. But, more important still, although India was only half the size of Europe, it already contained probably two hundred million people. Unlike Africa, also, India possessed a central government: it had been organized into a vast empire by Mohammedan invaders in the sixteenth century. Fortunately for greedy Europeans, the Emperor, or " Great Mogul," held but a loose control over the Hindu population, and the Hindu local rulers, or " rajahs," were frequently at odds. This situation permitted European trading companies to wring trade concessions from local rulers.

In 1689, when the colonial struggle between England and France began, France enjoyed conspicuous advantages. France was a larger and much more populous country. Her government appeared more stable than that of England: England had come through two revolutions while Richelieu, Mazarin, and Louis XIV were centralizing the French government, and Louis' absolute monarchy was generally considered the most efficient form of government Europeans had yet devised. In America, New France was a homogeneous colony. It had one religion, the Catholic, in the name of which Louis had only four years previously revoked the Edict of Toleration which permitted freedom of public worship to Huguenots; and Louis had seen to it that such heretics should not settle in " New France," to corrupt the faith of the French settlers, and the faith of the Indians whom the Jesuits and other religious orders were busy Christianizing. New France was governed as provinces in old France were governed: by royal edict, administered through a royal governor, supervised by a royal intendant. As in old France, the local Parlement merely registered royal decrees. The English colonies in North America, on the contrary, developed local assemblies, which like the English Parliament at home, bickered with the executive; and the various colonies were jealous of one another's rights and separated by religious differences. The French army was admittedly the best, as well as the largest, army in Europe; and it was just now at the height of its prestige. In America, the military tradition was far stronger in New France than in the English colonies. Since communications between the home country and its colonies would necessarily play a decisive part in a colonial war, it is worth noting that Louis possessed a navy that bid fair to match his army. Richelieu had more or less founded that navy; and although, under the pressure of the Thirty Years' War, Mazarin had allowed it to deteriorate, Colbert had reorganized it, and what is more important, had provided a complete and sound basis for French seapower. He had stimulated production and commerce. He had developed merchant shipping. He had fostered colonies and markets. The French navy, therefore, rested on a strong foundation: foreign commerce brought France the means to support it, as foreign commerce had enabled the Dutch to support their navy; and the value of that commerce justified naval expenditure, as it had in the case of the Dutch. When Louis had taken over the government of his kingdom from the hands of the dying Mazarin, in 1661, France possessed 30 armed ships. In ten years Colbert had increased the navy to 196 armed ships. The next year Louis attacked the Dutch. To that Dutch War the commercial and colonial interests which Colbert had so carefully nurtured were sacrificed, and with the decline of French commerce came a decline in French naval power. Nevertheless, when the War of the Palatinate broke out in 1689, Louis controlled the seas sufficiently to place a French army in Ireland at the disposal of England's deposed Catholic King, James II, an army which William defeated the next year at the Battle of the Boyne. Moreover, in the very year that William successfully defended his new throne at the Boyne, the French navy beat the combined squadrons of Dutch and English off Beachy Head.

In addition to superior population, a better army, an apparently more stable government, a more homogeneous and loyal colonial population, than the English, and a navy that was successfully holding its own, the French possessed one more signal advantage. Although there were perhaps fifteen Englishmen to every one Frenchman in North America, the French could hope to draw more successfully than the English on native manpower, and native manpower of excellent fighting qualities. Both in India and in North America the French appeared more adept at winning the friendship of the natives. In Canada the French colonial was interested primarily in furs and therefore wanted to do business with the Indian trapper. But in the English colonies the European population was more interested as a whole in opening new land than in securing pelts, and they therefore constantly pushed the Indian out. Where the French in large measure supplemented the Indian economy, the English competed with it. The struggle between French and English had scarcely started when it became apparent that the French could count on more help from the Indians than the English could.

The War of the Palatinate soon put these apparent advantages to the test. It will be recalled that Louis faced, not only Dutch William, with the combined resources of his native Holland and his new British dominions. He faced likewise the League of Augsburg, including the Holy Roman Empire, Spain, Sweden, Bavaria, Saxony, and the Palatinate. In America, "King William's War," as the American colonists called it, resulted in the capture of the French fortress of Port Royal in Acadia, and an unsuccessful attack on Quebec — as well as the burning of New England villages by the Indian allies of France. Although the Treaty of Ryswick, which ended the war, restored the status quo in the colonies, something very definite had nevertheless happened. The French navy, which started the war so auspiciously, had by its end lamentably declined. Louis' unsuccessful efforts to obtain the Rhine frontier had forced him to apply his resources to his armies, to the neglect of his navy. Besides, the commercial interests on which Colbert had, a quarter of a century before, so successfully built up a powerful navy, were now languishing.

Five years after the Treaty of Ryswick, the War of the Spanish Succession broke out, a war which the British colonists called "Queen Anne's War." While Queen Anne's great general, the Duke of Marlborough, and Prince Eugene of Savoy, were pressing Louis hard in Europe, in America the British again captured Port Royal, again made an unsuccessful assault on Quebec, and attempted vainly to take Montreal. On the high seas English naval superiority, buttressed with Dutch aid, began to tell decisively. The French were defeated in the Mediterranean, Gibraltar was captured, and French privateers were driven from the seas. Moreover, since Spain, whose throne Louis had accepted for his grandson, was an ally of France, the British had rich Spanish treasure ships to attack, which they did successfully. We have already seen that the Treaty of Utrecht accurately registered the triumph of the British at sea and in the colonies. Although the Bourbon Philip V was allowed to remain on the Spanish throne, thereby placing the vast empires of Spain and of France in the hands of one royal family, Great Britain retained Acadia, which she rechristened Nova Scotia (that is, "New Scotland "), Newfoundland, Hudson's Bay, and the island of St. Kitts in the West Indies. Moreover, to secure her Mediterranean commerce, she now held the valuable naval base of Minorca, and the Rock of

Gibraltar, key to the inland sea. In addition, she got a trade concession, or " Asiento," from Spain, legalizing her trade with Spain's
American colonies, and granting her the exclusive right to supply
them with Negro slaves — thereby squeezing Spain's French allies
out of a lucrative commerce.

During the three decades of Anglo-French peace that followed the
Treaty of Utrecht, France took steps to protect her colonial empire
from further depredations. She built a fort at Louisburg, on Cape
Breton Island, to guard the mouth of the St. Lawrence against the
now dominant British navy. She strung a line of fortresses from
Crown Point, on Lake Champlain, through Fort Niagara, Fort De-
troit, Sault Sainte Marie, on to Lake Winnipeg and beyond, and
others on the Wabash and Illinois rivers, and down the Mississippi
to the Gulf. By 1750 there were over sixty French forts between
Montreal and New Orleans. She has been criticized for having
chosen the long outer crescent of the St. Lawrence, the Great Lakes,
and the Mississippi, rather than following from the start the Ohio
River, thereby tightening the vise on the expanding British colonies
on the Atlantic coast and shortening her own lines of defense. But
what she did do was quite enough to frighten the British colonies: it
looked as if their coast-to-coast charters would run up against a well-
fortified New France, including Canada and " Louisiana " — that is,
the Mississippi Valley.

In India the English East India Company was troubled by the
restless expansion of the French East India Company, and particularly by the latter's able governor-general, Dupleix. Dupleix was not
content to further French trade; he was interfering in Indian native
politics, recruiting native troops, or " sepoys," and fortifying his capital, Pondicherry.

Meanwhile, the Asiento, which Great Britain had wrung from
Spain in the Peace of Utrecht, had led to disagreements, and in 1739
a trade war broke out between the two countries. A year later Frederick the Great of Prussia seized the Austrian province of Silesia,
and the War of the Austrian Succession began on the Continent, a
war in which France, Spain, and Bavaria backed Prussia, and in
which Great Britain backed Austria. Saxony and Sardinia at first
helped Prussia, but later shifted sides. From this war France hoped
to secure the Austrian Netherlands, thereby winning her longed-

for Rhine frontier; the Elector of Bavaria wished to replace Maria Theresa of Austria on the throne of the Holy Roman Empire; and Spain hoped to recover the Italian provinces which Austria had taken from her by the Treaty of Utrecht. On the other hand, Austria was determined to recover Silesia from Prussia; and Great Britain subsidized Austria as a means of protecting Hanover, of which Britain's King George was Elector, against an aggressive Prussia. During the first part of the war France and Great Britain were not officially enemies, though French armies were helping Prussia and British subsidies were backing Austria against Prussia. But by 1744 French and British had come to blows in India and in America, where the struggle was known as " King George's War." In India the French captured Madras from the British, and in America the British captured Louisburg from the French; but the Peace of Aix-la-Chapelle, which concluded the War of the Austrian Succession, provided that all colonial conquests were to be restored. Despite this indecisive peace, it had become apparent during the war that the British navy, though it had been allowed to deteriorate greatly during the thirty years' peace, was nevertheless superior to the French. Peace came because both countries were exhausted. France's chief military effort had as usual been on the Continent; and the effort to protect King George's beloved Hanover had cost Britain heavily, in money if not in men. The problems of who should dominate India and of who should dominate North America remained unsolved.

The very year after the peace, the British organized the Ohio Company, to colonize the rich Ohio Valley; and that step was bound to produce a collision. The French began to tighten the circle around the British seacoast, by running a line of forts through western Pennsylvania, and by 1754 Virginia troops under a young officer, George Washington, moving against the French at Fort Duquesne, at the juncture of the Monongahela and the Allegheny rivers, were defeated at their own Fort Necessity. The " French and Indian War " had begun.

In India likewise the British and the French were at grips again. Dupleix, the brilliant agent of the French East India Company, having fortified Pondicherry, and having made alliances with half the neighboring Indian princes, had overthrown the ruler of the Carnatic and put a creature of his own on the throne. But at this point a young Englishman who had come out to India at the age of eighteen to serve the English East India Company as a clerk at Madras conceived the idea of overthrowing Dupleix's puppet ruler. Robert Clive, with some two hundred European soldiers and three hundred sepoys, marched on Arcot, the capital of the Carnatic, seized it, and then defeated the pretender. By 1754 the French reluctantly withdrew their support from their favorite, and Dupleix was recalled to France in disgrace. Two years later the ruler of Bengal seized the English fort at Calcutta and imprisoned 146 Englishmen in the stifling " Black Hole of Calcutta," from which only 23 came out alive next day. Clive promptly defeated the culprit and recovered Calcutta for the English East India Company.

Since 1754, although England and France were nominally at peace, their respective East India Companies had been at grapples again, and their nationals had been fighting on the common border of their American empires. Moreover, the British navy, which now decisively outweighed the French, had captured 300 French merchant vessels; and 6,000 French seamen lay in English prisons. Meanwhile, on the Continent of Europe there occurred a fantastic realignment of great powers. In the recent War of the Austrian Succession, Great Britain had subsidized Austria against Frederick the Great of Prussia in an effort to protect King George's Electorate of Hanover; while France had lined up with Prussia against her ancient Hapsburg enemy, now ruler of the Austrian Netherlands which the French so much coveted. But the Austrians proved too greedy of subsidies, and the British government shifted its support to the abler military power, Prussia, her recent enemy. In January, 1756, she signed with Prussia the Convention of Westminster, guaranteeing each other's German possessions. France was outraged, and in May she finally heeded the Austrian ambassador Kaunitz, whose dream for years had been to convert France to friendship for Austria. France and Austria now made an alliance, an alliance which reflected Austria's determination to recover Silesia from Frederick the Great, and the French King's disgust with Frederick the Great's desertion of his late French ally. The "Reversal of Alliances," or "Diplomatic Revolution," had occurred: France and England had swapped partners.

The French and Indian War in America and the struggle between the French and English Companies in India now became parts of a vast conflict that raged on the Continent as the Seven Years' War and that was fought on the high seas of the world as well. For England it began inauspiciously. Washington's defeat at Fort Necessity in 1754 was followed the next year by the defeat, near the same place, of British regular troops under General Braddock. And in 1756, when the struggle on the Continent began, not only was Britain's new ally, Frederick the Great, temporarily worsted, but the Marquis of Montcalm, whom France had sent to America, seized the strategic British fortress of Oswego, on Lake Ontario, throwing open the Ohio Valley to the movement of French troops from the St. Lawrence. A French squadron seized the valuable Mediterranean island of Minorca, which had been ceded to Great Britain by the Treaty of Utrecht over forty years before. Fortunately for England, at this point George II reluctantly chose as war minister William Pitt (the Elder).

William Pitt was a perfect embodiment of the commercial aristocracy whom the Glorious Revolution had placed in control of England. His grandfather, Thomas Pitt, had risen to wealth in the service of the East India Company, and as a wealthy landowner, enjoyed considerable influence in Parliament. William himself served as an officer in the army, but resigned to go into politics. Elected to Parliament in 1735, William Pitt joined the Opposition against the great prime minister, Sir Robert Walpole. Walpole's policy was to protect Hanover, of which his master, George II, was Elector, and preserve the peace with France which the Treaty of Utrecht had created. Pitt, on the other hand, stood for the interests of Parliament and the great landowners whom Parliament represented, and for the naval and colonial power which the moneyed class demanded. He therefore looked for a showdown with Britain's last great colonial rival, France. Against Walpole's peaceful Hanoverian policy Pitt flung the full force of his magnificent oratory; and when the newly begun Seven Years' War threatened in 1756 to turn against England, it was because Pitt enjoyed the confidence of governing class and people alike that he was called on by the unwilling King to take charge of the war and foreign affairs. It was Pitt now who wrote the King's "Speeches from the Throne," and they rang with a new note. Pitt covered the King's precious Hanover with a small "army of observation" and sent necessary money subsidies to Frederick the Great, Britain's Continental ally against France; but he refused to deplete British naval strength to protect Frederick's Baltic coastline and he threw his real strength into America and India. America, he declared, was "the fountain of our wealth, the nerve of our strength, the nursery of our naval power," and he meant to win it at no matter what cost. He knew the value of colonies and commerce, and he knew the power of financial credit. Between 1757 and 1761 the National Debt soared from £70,000,000 to £150,000,000. Conservative Englishmen were horrified; but the capitalist class on whose behalf Pitt was ousting French competitors from India and America continued to support the government. As for the Continental war, Pitt wished by subsidies to Frederick to divert French energies to fighting Prussia while he cleared Frenchmen from the colonies and from the sea. To those who objected to sending gold to Prussia, he declared that he would conquer America in Germany. Finally, his aggressive colonial policy made him the hero of British America, and colonial volunteers rallied eagerly to a war which was so much their own.

Strengthened by these colonial volunteers, a British army some 50,000 strong moved against the vital French fortresses of Ticonderoga, Niagara, Duquesne, and Louisburg. With the support of a strong British squadron, Louisburg was taken in 1758 and the St. Lawrence opened to British ships. In the same year the British captured Fort Duquesne and renamed it Fort Pitt — the future site of the city of Pittsburgh. The next year Niagara and Ticonderoga fell. A British army now marched up the Hudson Valley, intent on capturing Montreal; while an army of 7,000 under General Wolfe ascended the St. Lawrence River to take Quebec. That city was defended by one of France's ablest generals, Montcalm; and, high on its bluffs above the broad river, it appeared well-nigh impregnable. But by a ruse Wolfe ferried 3,600 of his troops up the river past the city by night and seized the Plains of Abraham, the high plateau which commands Quebec. At daybreak Quebec knew its danger, and Montcalm attacked; but the French forces were defeated, and a few days later the city fell to the British. The next year, 1760, the British secured Montreal and the rest of New France.

Meanwhile, Robert Clive was continuing his brilliant military career in India. Clive faced a very different military problem from Wolfe. America was a half-empty continent, whose warlike savages the French and British used against each other as auxiliaries. But India was rich, populous, and theoretically a centralized empire. From Dupleix, who had now been recalled to France in disgrace, Clive had learned the art of dabbling in Indian politics and raising sepoy armies to do the East India Company's fighting. In 1757 Clive led an army of 1,100 Europeans and 2,100 sepoys against the French-supported ruler of Bengal, who had perpetrated the atrocity of the Black Hole of Calcutta. At Plassey he met an army of 68,000 native troops, supported by fifty-three French cannon, with French artillerymen, as against nine cannon in Clive's little force. Against such odds, Clive amazingly won a complete victory. He promptly placed his own candidate on the throne of Bengal, collected from him £1,500,000 for the Company, and enriched himself personally. The British now controlled Bengal. By 1761 they had recaptured Masulipatam, defeated the French at Wandiwash, and taken Pondicherry. The east coast of India was theirs.

In that year, 1761, with England triumphant in America, in India, and on the sea, Pitt learned that the Bourbon monarch of France was forming a " Family Compact " with the Bourbons of Spain and of Naples. Pitt promptly demanded war on Spain, but his Cabinet would not support such a step and he resigned. But his task was done, and the entry of Spain into the war in 1762 came too late to save the French Empire.

The next year France, Spain, and Great Britain signed the Peace of Paris. In America France saved only two little islands on the coast of Newfoundland to serve its fishermen, several valuable " sugar " islands in the West Indies, and the unimportant territory of Guiana in South America. To Great Britain she surrendered the St. Lawrence valley, all French territory east of the Mississippi, and the island of Grenada in the West Indies. To Spain she ceded all French territory west of the Mississippi; while the Spanish surrendered Florida to the British. In India France got back her original trading posts, with the important condition that she should not fortify them nor maintain troops. The triumph of Great Britain over France, in the colonies and on the seas, was complete. Although the British had preyed on Spanish galleons, had infringed Spanish colonial monopoly, and had seized a few colonies like Jamaica, yet the bulk of the vast Spanish Empire still flew the Spanish flag. Although the British had smashed the seapower and carrying trade of Holland in the three Anglo-Dutch Wars of Cromwell and Charles II, and had even robbed Holland of such colonies as New Amsterdam, the Dutch still exploited a rich commercial empire in the East Indies and in the West Indies. But in the colossal struggle of the Seven Years' War the British had almost eliminated France as a colonial empire.

Almost, but not quite. She had lost nearly all her territory; her navy had been decisively beaten; but she still held important commercial and naval bases. For this reason William Pitt, and with Pitt a large fraction of commercial England, condemned the Peace of Paris as too easy. " France," remarked Pitt, " is chiefly, if not exclusively, formidable to us as a maritime and commercial power. What we gain in this respect is valuable to us, above all, through the injury to her which results from it. You have left France the possibility of reviving her navy."

That remark throws a flood of light on the Seven Years' War and on why Great Britain won it. For the war which the tireless Pitt waged against the French monarchy was a war for colonies and seapower. In such a war the advantages which France appeared in 1689 to possess turned out largely illusory. It was true that at the time of the Seven Years' War France had a population of nearly twenty millions while England had barely eight. It is true that the prestige of French arms was so great, and that the fortresses they constructed in the early 1750's appeared so formidable, that many Frenchmen were saying, and many Englishmen were believing, that the French would ultimately push the British-Americans into the Atlantic. But the French " Leviathan " was more old-fashioned in its organization than the British Leviathan. French society was still, in spite of its growing commercial class, largely traditional in its social organization. The businessman and financier dominated the British Parliament; and Parliament, not the King, guided British foreign policy. In France the Catholic priesthood still guided the religious policy of the state in the interests of religion, not of commerce. The remains of feudal economics were still strong in France: feudal agriculture, industrial guilds, a commerce laboring under provincial customs barriers. In England the Enclosure Acts had concentrated land in the hands of the great landlords, and improved agricultural methods were making these landlords capitalists, along with the bankers and shipowners. As for internal customs barriers, in 1707 the union of Scotland and England under one Parliament, which James I had desired in vain, and which had briefly existed under Cromwell, finally took place under Anne: the resultant " Kingdom of Great Britain " was the largest free-trade area in Europe.

The English, like the Dutch, were a trading people. When a French merchant purchased a title of nobility — and in the seventeenth and eighteenth centuries many did — he retired from commerce, for the love of gain still failed in France to command the esteem of the nation. But in England, as in Holland, even nobles engaged in big commercial enterprises: only petty commerce degraded socially. The dominant classes in England and Holland had therefore a stake in the seapower that protects commerce, which the dominant classes in France conspicuously lacked. But whereas the Dutch commercial aristocracy had exhibited some of the timidity of the small businessman, the British Parliament was a body of landed aristocrats, which not only reflected the commercial interest, but which possessed a powerful political tradition. This class did not hesitate to promote to an admiralty men of humble birth; while as late as 1789 French naval commissions were practically reserved to the nobility.

In such circumstances the British governing class showed an almost unerring instinct for seapower. And Great Britain's superiority at sea proved the deciding factor in the struggle. For American ports were weeks away from either France or England; distant forts in the interior of America were months away; and in India the very seaports themselves were six months or a year away. By dominating the sea the British effectually prevented the French from reinforcing adequately their distant colonial forts and armies. Had Britain been accessible by land, French military superiority would of course have told. But when in 1759 a French fleet was preparing to land an army of invasion, Admiral Hawke fell upon it in Quiberon Bay and destroyed it; and in that very year other units of the British fleet made it possible for Wolfe to capture Quebec. This naval advantage was by no means complete. It is estimated that in 1761 French warships and privateers captured three times as many British merchantmen as the British did French merchantmen. But that was partly because there were so many British merchantmen to capture: British commerce was steadily increasing during the war, as Dutch commerce had increased during Holland's war of independence against Spain. Moreover, one reason French privateers were so numerous was because French shipowners could not earn money on their investments by engaging in ordinary trade: the British made ordinary French trade unsafe. French privateers therefore made prizes — while British shipowners grew rich on a commerce which the British navy protected remarkably well, at least well enough for that commerce to flourish. British naval supremacy enabled the British to profit even by apparent disasters: when the Spanish came to the rescue of the French in 1762, one of the important net results was that the British had a reasonable excuse for seizing Spanish treasure fleets and growing still richer.

The highly centralized French monarchy, potentially a means of mobilizing national resources, could not function effectually in distant countries, communications with which the British constantly threatened. But even had the British not interrupted communications, distance alone was against governing from Versailles. When Burke some years later addressed Parliament on conciliation with the American colonies, he declared that " Seas roll and months pass between the order and the execution." In such circumstances, strong central control was fatal; what was wanted was a general supervision and plenty of local initiative. But in the matter of initiative, the British colonies in America with their traditions of local self-government enjoyed an immense advantage over New France, accustomed to turn always to Versailles, both for orders and for help. In distant India, the English East India Company pursued its own interests; when it needed help from the government it counted on getting it through directors of the Company who were also members of Parliament. But the French East India Company was practically a department of Louis XV's government; and when Louis' government was exhausted by the Continental struggle with Prussia the initiative of the French company was sapped at the source. From 1751 on, the business of the French Company declined, despite Dupleix's sensational and heroic achievements; but English business was thriving throughout the war. And in general the servants of the English

Company were encouraged to show more initiative than servants of the French.

On the sea, too, this willingness to take the initiative without definite orders characterized the British rather than the French. When the British Admiral Byng failed through too much caution to save Minorca, he was tried by court-martial and shot. Another admiral aroused indignation by not attacking sixteen French ships when he himself had fifteen. But similar caution on the part of French admirals of the same period went unpunished. In fact, French admirals were taught not to risk their ships, since French finances would not permit rebuilding the navy. The result was occasionally humorous: the French appeared to avoid naval battle in order that they might preserve their seapower! The British method of achieving seapower was to destroy as many enemy ships as possible. If British ships were lost, British commerce made it both possible and imperative to build new ones. For though the French monarchy never thoroughly understood the conditions of seapower — a complex of warships, of a reserve of merchantmen, of a profitable sea-borne commerce, of colonies with which to trade, and of naval bases for refitting and revictualing — the British Parliament understood seapower well enough. And at a period when wind and canvas determined naval strategy, when orders could not be issued except at long intervals, and when communications reached only as far as the human eye, aided by a telescope, the guerrilla-like initiative of British admirals was bound to excel the centralized bureaucratic control of the French navy.

William Pitt saw clearly enough that except for the " despicable Electorate " of Hanover, which because of King George one must somehow defend, England enjoyed the enormous advantage of being outside Continental Europe, and of therefore having no land frontier to defend. But France had. Even if the French frontier were not being threatened, French concern with the problem of where that frontier could best be drawn in the interests of national safety controlled French foreign policy and prevented any single-minded attention to seapower. France was therefore forced to support an expensive army; England was not. And the same navy that protected the island of Great Britain from invasion protected her communications with her colonies, and threatened France's communications with hers. From Pitt's point of view England's most important land frontier was not the borders of Hanover but the frontier of British civilization in North America. This, frontier French fortresses threatened, from the St. Lawrence to the Gulf of Mexico; but in so far as the British navy controlled the seas, it was a frontier which the reinforcements from Great Britain could get at and reinforcements from France could not. All too frequently adequate reinforcements would never have reached these distant colonial frontiers of France, even had the British not controlled the sea, for France had a land frontier in Europe that interested her far more and a diplomatic tradition based on the desire to extend and defend that frontier.

It is obvious that Great Britain's triumph over France was directly due to seapower and that British policy placed the nation's resources behind seapower, whereas French policy did so only half-heartedly. To explain this difference by saying that Great Britain is an island and that the British have always been a seafaring race is the baldest nonsense. Not until the reign of Elizabeth did Englishmen really turn to the sea; and the fishermen of Normandy and Brittany had a magnificent seafaring tradition. But the economic and political organization of Pitt's England concentrated the country's wealth in the hands of a commercial aristocracy, while the Glorious Revolution of 1688 had placed the control of national policy in their hands too.

It is also superficial to say that the British succeeded in doing something which the French tried but failed to do, or that the British had sounder political instincts than the French and avoided the over-regulation of French colonial policy. It is true that the French monarchy, like the Spanish, forbade Protestants to emigrate to the colonies, and it is true that in France as in most European countries Protestantism tended to be the religion of the very class of capitalist enterprisers, merchants, and sea captains, who would most rapidly develop a colony economically. It was the Huguenot Admiral Coligny, for example, who tried in the sixteenth century to plant French colonies on the Carolina coast. Louis XIV's Revocation of the Edict of Nantes in 1685 had caused this enterprising Huguenot element to flee France, and to add their commercial and industrial skills to his heretical enemies, England, Holland, and Prussia. Three years after the Revocation, when William of Orange crossed from

French to the task of colonization. The success of the British system increased its prestige in Europe, and that prestige acted as a dissolvent on the traditional concepts of Catholic Christianity and absolute monarchy to which many Continental countries still adhered.

In the seventeenth century, Versailles had dominated the cultural ideals of Christendom; as the eighteenth century wore on, the way of life followed by the British governing class exerted a steadily increasing influence. Even in France, Voltaire's *Letters on the English* and Montesquieu's *The Spirit of the Laws* were advertising British civilization. What was this civilization?

It was a civilization based on the " Principles of 1688," which John Locke had so brilliantly enunciated. For Locke became, as it were, the Bible of the eighteenth century. Your true upper-class Englishman was a landowner, with important financial investments. Perhaps he had a seat in Parliament. If not, he had a cousin or a friend in Parliament; and in any case the men who sat there had interests identical with his own. Authority exerted by any agency other than his own class, he resented and despised. Absolute monarchs were tyrants. And he would have no popery. In religion he was tolerant, if not indifferent. He was likely to be a Deist, who recognized the existence of God and but little more. Religious " enthusiasm " he thought vulgar, and he left it to John Wesley and his Methodists. For him God was a valuable symbol of authority, like the British King; and neither of them should be allowed to interfere too much with practical affairs. If he had philosophical interests, he could read the skeptical David Hume. If he liked history, he could read Mr. Edward Gibbon's latest volume of *The Decline and Fall of the Roman Empire*. For poetry he had the elegant and reasonable verses of Alexander Pope; and for tart worldly wisdom, Dr. Samuel Johnson.

He had no deep respect for the fine arts. He liked, of course, the graceful essays of Addison and Steele, just as he liked good talk in a London coffeehouse. In the novels of Henry Fielding and in the plays of Richard Sheridan he could recognize the contemporary scene which he dominated and loved. He was less musical than his Elizabethan ancestors; the leading composer of England was not even a native: he was the German, Handel, whom George I had brought over to his court. But our English gentleman would pay a painter, like Reynolds, or Gainsborough, or Romney, or Raeburn, or Beechey, to execute his portrait or the portraits of members of his family. And when these portraits were hung on the walls of his Queen Anne, or Georgian, mansion, they looked down on people who sat in exquisite Chippendale or Sheraton chairs and drank their tea from Wedgwood china or Chinese porcelain. Above all, this gentleman loved his estate. He was intent on improving his land, on breeding superior stock, on laying out lovely grounds and intricate gardens, on planting stately avenues of trees. From this estate his boys went forth to Eton or Harrow with other boys of their class, and later to Oxford or Cambridge. There, if they did not acquire a passion for learning, they at least learned to know men. They also would learn the give-and-take of outdoor sports, as a preparation for the give-and-take of a politically-minded aristocracy. By the law of primogeniture, the estate itself would descend to the eldest son. Like his father, he would most likely serve as justice of the peace. If he had numerous brothers a commission in the army could be secured for one of them, a commission in the navy for another. A fourth might become a fox-hunting country parson, with a good table and a meager store of theology. A fifth could enter the service of the East India Company, where he might grow rich enough some day to buy a country seat of his own and to found another county family. The sixth — for in those days of large families there might easily be a sixth — could try his luck in Virginia, where he would build an estate on the James River as much like the one he knew at home as tobacco and Negro slave labor could create.

Such were the men who in the eighteenth century elected their fellows to the British Parliament; and the Parliament they elected was undisputed " Soveraign " of a victorious Leviathan. Louis XV was sovereign of another Leviathan, but a much less effective one. For the absolute monarchy which Richelieu and Mazarin had prepared for Louis XIV, the monarchy which had created Versailles as the symbol and ideal of Christendom in the seventeenth century, was now in full decline; while the British Leviathan, a maritime and colonizing state governed by a landed aristocracy and commercial interests, was growing in political power and in economic goods. In England as in France, the middle class had rallied long ago around a monarch intent on destroying a decadent feudal system and making his kingdom safe for business; but in England, when the monarch had served his turn, the middle class had taken over the reins. It quarreled with James I, beheaded Charles I, gathered economic impetus under Oliver Cromwell and Charles II, ousted James II, and set up the constitutional monarchy of William III. In foreign affairs it was equally successful. Under Elizabeth, it destroyed Spanish seapower and preyed on Spanish treasure ships. Under Cromwell and Charles II, it smashed Dutch monopoly. In the reigns of William and of Anne, through alliance itself it weakened Dutch seapower. Under George I, George II, and George III, it swept the French from the seas and robbed them of a colonial empire. Its phenomenal success was not merely the success of one race over another but of the English country estate and the English countinghouse over Versailles itself, of the ideal English gentleman over the ideal King. Here was a new symbol of the good life for Christendom to follow.

XI.

THE HINTERLAND

By the Peace of Westphalia, in 1648, which closed the Thirty Years' War, Catholic Christendom and Protestant Christendom agreed to disagree. For a century and a half the provisions of that treaty remained the "public law" of an essentially lawless and anarchical system of highly competitive sovereign states, whose quest for security, wealth, and power was conducted necessarily at one another's expense. Clearly, the two quickest routes to wealth lay, one around Africa, to the storied wealth of India and the rich Spice Islands, and one across the Atlantic, to the gold and silver of South America, the sugar of the West Indies, the tobacco and furs of North America. We have watched the seaboard states of Europe struggling for that wealth. Their struggles were the colonial wars of the late seventeenth and of the eighteenth centuries. They were struggles, not for "markets" — machine production of goods inside Europe will convert them into that — but for the goods of the Orient and of the Americas that Europeans desired, and for the lucrative carrying trade that fetched them, and for the naval power that could protect such trade.

But many of these colonial wars, and others that were not colonial at all, were dynastic. Europe was governed almost entirely by kings, whose power approached the absolute in varying degrees, depending on how completely the King had been able to rob his nobility of its ancient governing function and to prevent the meddling of the new moneyed middle class which had made his own rise possible. The King's power was also inherited, as great financial fortunes often are today. Like those fortunes, royal power was subject to sudden increase by discreet shopping in the marriage mart. Some of Europe's leading states had been constructed largely by a shrewd choice of wives. Royal families therefore acquired long-term and traditional " interests," quite independently of the whims or fancies of the particular member of the family who happened for the moment to occupy the throne. The Bourbons of France, the Hapsburgs of Austria, the Hohenzollerns of Prussia were such dynasties. Their rivalries were by no means the mere result of royal vanity: they were based even more on a life-and-death struggle for security. This is why Europe's wars took dynastic form. The Battle of Blenheim helped decide the Spanish Succession: that a Bourbon, a grandson of Louis XIV of France, might sit on the throne of Spain, so long occupied by Hapsburgs, and rule the vast Spanish Empire, but only with the understanding that the Bourbon who ruled France and the Bourbon who ruled Spain should never be the same ruler. For that were to make Versailles, not merely the cultural capital of Europe, which it already was and which it long remained, but its political capital as well. And where would John Locke's " life, liberty, and property " be then?

Certainly during the eighteenth century Versailles showed itself less and less competent to direct the lives, liberties, and properties of Europeans. Nobody has ever done justice to the rise and fall of Versailles. It was of course an earthly paradise, an Olympus where earthly gods — the King, the nobles, and the fortunate of France, and even of Europe — might feast and divert themselves, and like the Homeric gods play with the destinies of those who dwelt below. But it was also a royal policy disguised as a palace and a park, a policy with two functions. It uprooted the nobles from their own little local seats of authority and made them either royal servants or, more often, decorative stage properties of the Crown: it thereby promoted the centralization of royal authority which had been Richelieu's dream. It also placed the King beyond the easy reach of those troublesome Parisians whom Louis had watched as a boy, revolting against Mazarin and his Cardinalists, and hence against the Crown. Louis XIV knew his park and palace were a policy: most of his nobles thought they were a palace and a park, and in them they learned idleness and love of pleasure. Unfortunately, Louis' great-grandson, who succeeded him on the throne as Louis XV, was himself the product of palace and park; and he too, like his nobles, learned idleness and pleasure. Versailles, which had robbed the nobles of their political function, robbed the King of his function too. If three generations will lead an American bourgeois from shirt-sleeves to shirtsleeves, three reigns will suffice to lead a king from Richelieu's triumph over noble and Huguenot to Louis XVI's death on the guillotine.

Long after the French monarchy was rotten with administrative paralysis, fiscal confusion, favoritism, interfering royal mistresses, and debt, Versailles dazzled the imagination of Europe, as the great cathedrals of the Middle Ages had once dazzled that imagination. The countless impecunious princelings of the Holy Roman Empire aped it longingly, as did Voltaire's fictitious Baron Thunder-ten-tronckh, in whose castle the naïve Candide tremblingly kissed the lovely Cunégonde. Yet its foreign prestige could not save the Versailles system from its nearer observers, the French bourgeois who paid for it, or from their spokesmen, the new school of French, and other European, writers who called themselves " the Philosophers." Few of them could be called that by a competent philosopher: they were rather journalists, publicists, economists, political theorists, sociologists, or all these things at once. They undertook an enormous work of intellectual demolition. They used such tools as the irony of Voltaire or Gibbon, the skepticism of Hume, the pathos and indignation of Rousseau, the statistical analysis of Quesnay and his free-trade Physiocrats with their hatred and scorn of the economic mercantilism of Colbert and his successors, the penetrating observation of Adam Smith. They attacked Christianity, absolute monarchy, superstition, political interference with trade, economic monopoly, the artificialities of social life in Europe.

But they did not merely demolish or attack. In the *Great Encyclopedia,* which Diderot started publishing in 1751, they attempted the most ambitious summary of their culture that had been attempted since the great *summas* of the Middle Ages. And although the *Great Encyclopedia,* unlike the *summas,* tried to furnish factual information from the accumulated store of the new natural sciences and elsewhere, its writing was slanted to the proclamation of a new cultural synthesis, a new account of the universe, and in effect a new and universal religion, based not on the revelations of God, which the Encyclopedists doubted, but on the reasonings of men, in which they had a burning, infinite faith. Diderot, as editor, was right therefore to invoke the memory of Francis Bacon. Knowledge is Power; and " the progress of enlightenment " would give, the Encyclopedists were quite certain, the power to raise all men from the ignorance and poverty and misery in which politician and priest conspired to keep them.

For the God of the Christians, in whose name Christians so joyfully burned each other at the stake, or tore each other asunder on the rack, or slaughtered each other on the battlefields of Europe, they substituted a somewhat abstract Deity, a Supreme Being, an Author of the Universe, a Great Contriver, a Prime Mover, a First Cause. Men could learn of him, not in Holy Writ, which was a fraud of priestcraft; certainly not in the " miracle " of the Mass, since there were no miracles; but in the Book of Nature. For the Great Contriver had cunningly contrived a vast machine called the Universe, which operated by mechanical laws; and these Laws of Nature had been discovered to mankind by such investigators as Voltaire's beloved Isaac Newton. It is our business to understand these natural laws, whether in the field of mechanics or politics or economics, to find out what is "natural" and do it. That is the whole duty of man. By discharging it, he can steadily progress; and what he will progress to is not the heaven of the Christian but the perfection of life on earth, which Posterity, though not the Encyclopedists, will some day witness.

Finally, the Newtonian machine which is the Universe operates automatically, whether a Great Contriver contrived it in the first place or not. So nothing prevented the Deist, who accepted Mohammedanism or Buddhism or the totems of the " noble savage " of America as exemplifying, quite as ably as Christianity, the " natural religion " of mankind, from substituting for this eclectic natural religion the Religion of Nature, minus any God at all. The Encyclopedists included, therefore, not only lukewarm Deists like Voltaire, but zealous atheists like d'Alembert and Holbach.

But in this perfectible new world, contrived or uncontrived, Frederick the Great of Prussia could apparently grab Silesia by force of arms as " naturally " as Maria Theresa could resent the theft. It had seemed unnatural for Jehovah to allow Lucifer to roam unmolested through the Book of Job. Now that Jehovah was banished, the problem of evil appeared to remain anyhow, even under what should have been the more beneficent reign of Nature. So the Encyclopedists more and more turned from the speculative to the practical, to reforming the human world which Nature ruled. And though they had started out to be " reasonable " and to eschew the " enthusiasm " of the tiresome early Christians whom Gibbon so disliked or the recent English Methodists who made themselves so ridiculous with their irrational fervor; nevertheless, as the century wore on, the Philosophers wept too, not for love of Christ, but for love of liberty, of justice, of truth, of humanity, for the poor, and even for the out-of-door beauties of Nature. Rousseau, most of all, wept copiously.

Since the Reformation the Catholics had persecuted the Protestants and had been attacked in turn. The counterattack was often led by that militant Society of Jesus which the Spanish soldier, Loyola, had founded. Now the Jesuits led the assault against the Philosophers, and at least for a while met their defeat. In 1759 they were banished from Portugal; in 1764, from France; in 1767, from the Spanish Empire; and in the same year, from the Bourbon Kingdom of Naples. Finally, in 1773, the Pope suppressed the Society of Jesus outright, and it was not fully and officially reconstituted till the political reaction of 1814, forty-one years later. The Philosophers had contributed largely to its overthrow.

Meanwhile, painting and sculpture reflected the return to Nature. At Versailles, Watteau painted his elegant, decorous picnics of ladies and gentlemen under the trees; Boucher portrayed fashionable shepherdesses; Greuze pictured his mildly suggestive and urbanely sensual young women; and Fragonard, his delicious and titillating scenes from bedroom or boudoir. For sex is no longer the terrible subject of a Shakespeare or a Racine: Madame de Pompadour and Madame du Barry taught people to be knowing about sex, to be sensible, to enjoy emotions without allowing them to destroy one's security or ease. Yet these emotions are so short-lived, that we must drop a tear, too, in the midst of our pleasure. And our pleasures must be urbane, delicate, intelligent, and witty. For there are intelligence and wit in the paintings and drawings of Perroneau and La Tour, in the sculpture of Houdon. There is indeed a witty, conversational quality about most of the painting and sculpture that the courtiers of Versailles admired, such as one might find in the plays they loved, by Beaumarchais or Marivaux.

Yet, far from Versailles, the life of the poorer classes of France was being painted by Chardin, directly, honestly, lovingly; and, in distant Spain, there was nothing trivial about the paintings of Goya. Far away, also, from the elegance, the gentle depravities, the petty blasphemies, and the delicious and melancholy decadence of Versailles, the great German musical tradition continued strongly. Haydn was developing the sonata, composing for the string quartet as if it were one great instrument, and becoming a master, like Handel, of the oratorio. Mozart, an infant prodigy, a child of the "Enlightenment," with its love of the natural and its love of the free, was adapting and deepening Italy's new art-form, the opera; and with his extraordinary sense of melody, was introducing that melody into instrumental music, to the delight of all Europe.

It was from the Hinterland of Europe that this great music came, from a Hinterland that was politically and economically a backward, stagnant area. Change, progress, science, invention, ideas, and the growth of wealth and population were on the western seaboard. Indeed, they were on the northwestern seaboard; for Portugal and Spain, having pioneered the sea routes, were sinking into apathy. Britain was the fountain of political liberty, admired and described by Voltaire and Montesquieu alike. Britain was the land of technology and invention. France remained the land of general ideas, of military power, of boundless resources, of tremendous population: by 1750 she had twenty million inhabitants; and by the outbreak of the Great Revolution in 1789 she would have added another six million. Her language was still the language of cultivated minds throughout Europe: in the arts of civilized living she was supreme. The Netherlands were Europe's money mart and Europe's printing press. Thrust aside by the British in India and America alike, Holland still retained a rich commercial empire in the East Indies. Britain, France, and Holland were the vanguard of Europe's expanding civilization.

Back of them lay the Hinterland, and first of all the Holy Roman Empire, composed predominantly of German-speaking peoples. But the Peace of Westphalia had been shrewdly devised by Richelieu to prevent the Empire from becoming a centralized monarchy on France's flank. It now contained more than two hundred states politically competent to make war and peace. It was a political crazy-quilt, except that in most crazy-quilts the differently colored squares at least do not overlap, as the feudal claims of the Imperial states persistently did. The Hapsburgs of Austria systematically managed to bribe or bludgeon the nine Electors into placing the crown of Charlemagne on the Hapsburg's head. But the same Hapsburg still ruled many lands outside the Empire, such as Hungary, Croatia, the Milanese, or the Austrian Netherlands — now Belgium. Three of the Electors wore the crowns of countries also outside the Empire. The Elector of Hanover was now King of England. The Elector of Brandenburg was also King of Prussia. The Elector of Saxony was elected to the crown of Poland, and hoped to make that royal crown hereditary. In addition, Pomerania was ruled by the King of Sweden, and Schleswig by the King of Denmark.

Scattered across North Central Europe, in unconnected pieces of various sizes, lay the Kingdom of Prussia and the other possessions of its king. Because of feudal jurisdictional conflicts, the boundaries of many of his possessions were in dispute. For generations their Hohenzollern rulers had been picking up a piece here, a piece there, by war, by marriage, by diplomatic barter. Frederick William, the Great Elector, encouraged immigration to his forbidding land of sandy wastes and pine barrens, with its harsh climate, and he also reformed administration. Above all, he built a hard-fighting army. For, from the start, the Hohenzollerns recognized that, if their domains were to survive at all, they would survive by human will and armed force. The poverty of these domains was against them. Their scattered distribution was against them. Their separatist traditions were against them. If they were to become a state, it would be by harder work, on the part of both ruler and ruled, than more fortunate rulers or peoples would submit to. It was the Great Elector's successor, Frederick I, who first wore the title, "King of Prussia."

King Frederick William I, who followed him, was a famous eccentric, but an able man. By harsh but careful taxation, economical administration, and plenty of bullying, he provided Prussia with a larger and better army than could normally have been raised. His one extravagance was a regiment of gigantically tall men, coaxed, bought, or kidnapped from all over Europe. It was this army of his that permitted his son Frederick II to win from his generation the title, "the Great." When the father died, in 1740, his subjects numbered around two and a half million, of whom a fourth were either immigrants or the descendants of immigrants. For he had brought in Huguenots from the persecution of Louis XIV, other Calvinist victims from other Catholic lands, craftsmen, and industrious folk of all descriptions, and he saw to it that his Lutheran majority made a place for his Calvinist minority. What God asked, through the King, of all Prussian subjects was hard work under conditions of religious toleration. The capital of this military kingdom, Berlin, had but 98,000 inhabitants. But it was, as Frederick the Great later said of it, the Sparta of North Europe.

Prussia was a state unique in Europe, a sort of caricature of the modern state that Christendom had at last evolved. It was a *tour de force,* a tension, a task. It was built on the hard human will, on naked force, and on cunning. Richelieu had used these things too in his work of fashioning France into a centralized, absolute monarchy. But he had used them on different cultural material — on the French people, with their ancient and complex traditions, Latin traditions, Christian traditions, esthetic traditions. If Richelieu violated these traditions, he had also to incorporate them. In large part, those traditions did not exist in the Northern Hinterland that was Prussia. It had never undergone the long discipline of the Roman Empire. It came relatively late to Christianity. It came early to Protestantism. Its core, Brandenburg, had been a Mark, a March, a frontier against the Slavic hordes from the East. Its outpost, East Prussia, had been hammered into accepting Christ by the mailed fist of the Teutonic Knights. It was a wolf pack that obeyed its leader. It lived dangerously, with ill-defined frontiers, an armed camp amid enemies, blindly obedient, where obedience was the price of survival. Whatever it had, whatever it was, had been planned for, schemed for, worked for, or bled for. Prussia was effort. It not only stood with weapons in its hands: it was itself a weapon, and its cutting edge was its monarchy.

We have watched Britain, in her colonial race with France, traveling light, as it were, and winning first prize. For she had been less concerned than France to transfer the culture of Christian Europe in its entirety to new lands. Her colonial effort had been more purely economic. The duel that Prussia would fight against Austria, the duel that would make Frederick II "Frederick the Great," offers us an analogy. Maria Theresa's Austria fought to conserve; Prussia fought to found, to initiate. Maria Theresa was Empress of the Holy Roman Empire, the superannuated embodiment and living symbol of a feudal, Catholic Europe that was passing away, but that Maria Theresa thought of as Christian civilization itself. All this, she fought her duel to save. Frederick's Prussian machine fought to win. Prussia was so much newer, so much more raw, so much poorer and harsher, that in a sense it was not worth conserving — except as one conserves a weapon, to win with it more pleasant things. The times fought for Britain, and they fought for Frederick; and eternity could wait.

Austria's possessions were rich, though her treasury was ill-run and ill-fitted to mobilize her wealth. Prussia was poor; but what money there was, followed well-worn grooves to the government's coffers. She was an artist at mobilizing wealth, as she was an artist at mobilizing men. Austria depended on old traditions and old loyalties. Prussia modernized. But what she borrowed from the older, more civilized, seaboard states of Christendom was not their intellectual tradition, or their questing spirit of inquiry, or their plastic arts. What she borrowed, and improved on, was their agricultural and industrial techniques, methods of central administration, and — above all — military organization. Although Frederick's grandfather had made some efforts to develop Berlin as a cultural center, his rough old father had preferred to collect soldiers for his regiment of giants. Thus it was that the great German tradition of music turned, not to Berlin, but to mellow Vienna. Handel, the Saxon; Gluck, the Franconian; Haydn, the Austrian; Mozart, the Salzburger, would all migrate to Vienna — as, indeed, Beethoven, the Rhinelander, would do after them. Madame de Staël, who loved and admired the Germans, complained of the raw newness of Berlin and Prussia.

Vienna had grown through the slow centuries, had had time to think and feel. Berlin had been imposed on the dreary Prussian countryside, as Versailles had been imposed. But Versailles brought the ancient and humane culture of France to a focus, where Prussia's culture was neither ancient nor humane. Prussia was a weapon.

Beyond the weapon lay Poland, where the feudal nobility had decisively won out over the monarchy, had kept Poland weak, exposed, the laughing-stock of European governments. Beyond that, lay the vast, sprawling, strange, and barbarous Empire of the Russian Czars. This was the land beyond the Hinterland. It was part of this story, only as Turkey was, and perhaps less than Turkey. At the court of Henry IV of France, men had discussed a European crusade to drive both the Turks and " the Muscovites" from the soil of Europe.

Historians of European civilization have allowed themselves to be fooled by the geography they studied as children, and have thought that Russian history was a part of the history of Europe. But Russia is part of another story, and one she has no cause to be ashamed of. Her roots are in Constantinople, not Rome: in the Hellenic, eastern portion of the Roman Empire, not in the Latin, western portion; the very letters of her alphabet came from Greek, where those of Western Christendom came from Latin; her theological tradition remained Platonic, where that of the West became Aristotelian. History treated her very differently from the West. At a time when Mohammedan closure of the Mediterranean dried up commerce in Western Europe and laid the economic basis for an agrarian, feudal culture, Russia was engaged in a thriving trade with Constantinople. But the Turks cut off Constantinople, whereas the Italians opened and policed the Mediterranean: feudalism and serfdom began their long decline in the West, while serfdom arose in Russia. By the eighteenth century, Western trading companies carried on trade with Russia, as indeed they carried on trade with India and America, but it was trade with a foreign culture. By the end of the eighteenth century, Russia was a military and diplomatic fact in Western Europe; but so was Turkey in the sixteenth, and so would Japan be in the twentieth.

In 1697 neither the Dutch nor the English nor the Austrians were under any illusion that the Russian diplomatic mission that sought to promote a crusade against the Turks was European. Among that diplomatic mission was the new Czar, a giant of nearly eight feet, a barbarian in his habits, a man of driving energy, determined not only to get help against the Turks, who still cut Russia off from the Mediterranean and the civilized world, but to learn from that world the techniques that made it rich and powerful. That young Czar, who traveled incognito, would be known to history as Peter the Great. In Holland, he worked as a common shipwright: Russia would need lots of ships as soon as the Turks could be pushed off the Black Sea and the Swedes off the Baltic. He visited factories: Russia must have those, too. He engaged nearly a thousand experts to teach his backward subjects the arts of Europe. He rushed to London to study their ships too. He went to Vienna. He headed for Venice, that ancient center of shipping; but he was called home by a military revolt. On his return he helped torture and execute the rebels with his own hands, and then set to work to Europeanize his country. He forced men to shave their beards; he forced the women to come out of their semi-Oriental seclusion and to mingle socially with the men. He forced both to wear European costumes. He visited Prussia, Denmark, and France, to learn from them too. He hated Moscow: like the men's beards, like the women's veils, it symbolized Holy Russia. So, when he had driven back the Swedes from the Baltic, he built St. Petersburg, on an unhealthy marsh, with a German name, and access to the sea he had been determined to reach. He brought in not only European technicians, but European officers to train the army he conscripted, and to teach his idle gentry to become officers too. He sent Russians to Europe to study. He demanded respect for the trading class that Russia must develop if she would be powerful. He started a canal system. He founded new industries. He reorganized the Russian Church. He personally simplified the Russian alphabet, and personally edited Russia's first newspaper. And he did all this in frantic haste, bullying and bludgeoning his backward, grumbling subjects into helping.

He helped attack the young Charles XII of Sweden; and when that military genius swept like a berserk into the Great Northern War, it was chiefly Peter who, by patient work, defeated him and put an end to Sweden as a great power, monopolizing the Baltic as a Swedish lake since the days of Gustavus Adolphus. He died at last, leaving his subjects breathless and exhausted. Many of them declared he was anti-Christ. But, by his defeat of Sweden, he had opened his window to the sea in the north; and though he had failed to open his southern window on the Black Sea, Catherine the Great would soon do that too. He had, before he died, by violent, backbreaking labor, introduced Europe to Russia and started an intercourse that would steadily broaden European influence after his death.

But the historic fact in the eighteenth century, not only for the Hinterland but for all Christendom, was neither the meteoric career of Charles XII, which left Sweden exhausted; nor the apparition of the uncouth giant from Muscovy with his hunger to know and to adapt; it was Frederick the Great of Prussia. He had spent his youth under a rigorous regime of study, learning the facts his brutal drill-sergeant of a father thought were alone important, shut off from the classics, loving the Great Century of Louis XIV's Versailles, loving and speaking the French tongue, despising German as barbaric, bootlegging the books he was not allowed, loving music and his flute, longing to write. His father's bullying became so intolerable that he tried to desert the army, Prussia, and his dreadful tormentor. He was caught, imprisoned, and forced to watch the execution of his beloved Lieutenant Katte, whom he had with difficulty persuaded to help him desert. When Katte's head fell, Frederick fell unconscious. After a profound struggle, he emerged from the ordeal what his father had labored to make him: a Prussian. He set to work to learn the operation of the relentless, mechanical Prussian state which he would one day have to direct.

His father had broken his will, as one might break the will of a domestic animal — or of a Prussian soldier. What Prussia could not use, he learned to live without. He retained his love of music and literature, but he acquired a capacity and even a taste for hard work and for requiring hard work of his subordinates. He had shown signs of a loving heart: he became egotistical, cynical, closed in. At his father's orders he married a woman he did not love, and he made her pay for his disappointment by almost ignoring her existence.

When he was twenty-eight his father died, bequeathing him the well-trained Prussian army. He had scarcely mounted the throne when he struck. Without warning, he led his army swiftly into the rich Hapsburg province of Silesia. By surprise, speed, superior military training and equipment, and cynical diplomacy, a combination of weapons that were to make him and Prussia famous and successful, he occupied Silesia; persuaded France, Bavaria, Spain, and Savoy to challenge Maria Theresa's right of succession; forced Maria Theresa to cede him most of Silesia; backed out of his alliance with her enemies; and left them to continue what was known as the War of the Austrian Succession. Later, when she seemed to be winning and when Frederick feared she might force him to surrender Silesia, he re-entered the war against her. The Peace of Aix-la-Chapelle, in 1748, left Frederick master of Silesia.

But Maria Theresa was determined to win back her lost possession. The reader will recall from the preceding chapter the " Diplomatic Revolution " that followed: how England decided to back Prussia; how the French and Indian War, which had broken out between Britain and France, spread to Europe as a Seven Years' War, with Britain helping Prussia and with France, Russia, and Saxony helping Austria. As usual, Frederick struck first — at Saxony; defeated a Saxon army; and forced it to serve with his own. After brilliant victories, crushing and apparently decisive defeats, the occupation of Berlin, the most dogged patience, and the good fortune of Russia's desertion of her allies, Frederick secured peace — and the continued and permanent retention of Silesia.

Nobody applauded Frederick the Great more loudly or more faithfully than the Philosophers; and this is an apparent paradox. In between his two great wars, Voltaire, who had already corresponded with him and even visited him, spent three years with him in his little palace of Sans Souci at Potsdam, with the title of Chamberlain. Their "friendship" was the mutual exploitation of two eccentric celebrities. Frederick fancied himself as a poet and needed Voltaire to criticize his verse; Voltaire, who had been persecuted in his native France, enjoyed being lionized by a king. The relation lasted stormily for three years, despite the fact that their two tongues were perhaps as sharp as any in Europe. Then it broke up. The fact remains that he had harbored Voltaire and that he harbored many other Philosophers, some of whom fled to him for safety. Certainly his aggressive wars did not fit too well into the Heavenly City the Philosophers were building for posterity, a city where Nature and Reason would rule. Neither did his Prussian bureaucracy. Where they preached liberty, Frederick ran Prussia as a peasant runs his farm, with a jealous eye to the health and number of his human livestock. Where they preached civil equality, Frederick distinguished sharply between noble blood and peasant blood. Where they believed in the perfectibility of mankind, Frederick called it that " damned race," " riff-raff," and other abusive names. Where they clamored for free trade, Frederick was a stricter Mercantilist than old Colbert himself. Where they savagely attacked Christianity, Frederick merely ignored it and let his subjects worship however they pleased.

But the King did enforce religious toleration. He did simplify and rationalize government. Though he claimed his barren soil produced only " iron and soldiers," he did form a literary court and did collect paintings. He did blaspheme obscenely in private conversation, in letters, even sometimes in his literary productions. He did love facts, as his dreadful old father had loved them. And from one end of Europe to the other the Philosophers sang his praises. They were mostly Frenchmen, with a scattering of Englishmen; and they praised him because he flouted traditions that oppressed them in their own country. Had they really known what kind of thing this Prussia was that Frederick labored to extend, they would have been aghast. Had d'Alembert really understood the distance between himself and Frederick, he never would have begged him to order a bust of Voltaire placed in the Catholic Church at Berlin, an act that would have struck Frederick as being as foolish as crossing himself. That the Philosophers were shocked to find him inviting the Jesuits in to help him educate his subjects shows how far they missed grasping his purpose. He was bored by their war on religion, if only because theirs was essentially a religious war; and Frederick was a skeptic — what the Jesuits thought the Philosophers were. He died at seventy-four at his beloved Sans Souci; but not before he had carved off a good big slice of Poland — West Prussia; and let Russia and Austria carve their slices too. It was done cynically, methodically, as part of a Prussian day's work. He loved power, despised men, served Prussia; and he died without hope of heaven or fear of hell. By a kind of cruel caricature this hero from the Hinterland showed Western Christendom whither it was bound. Christendom was so busy expanding, it failed to get the point.

XII.

EUROPE OVERSEAS

THE triumph of Clive in India or even of Wolfe in Canada could not excite Europeans as much as the triumphs of Frederick in the eastern Hinterland of Christendom. Yet Frederick's longest duel, the Seven Years' War, was partly a development of the French and Indian War that had broken out two years earlier in North America. For indeed the Western European culture, whose techniques and institutions Peter was trying to import into Russia and impose upon his unwilling subjects, had long ago leaped the sea. Historically, though not geographically, " Europe " now included New France, on the banks of the St. Lawrence; New England and the other British colonies on the Atlantic seaboard of North America; New Spain, in Mexico and Central America, and the other Spanish settlements in South America: Portuguese Brazil; the Dutch Cape Colony in South Africa; and in a few decades New Europe would even enter Australia and New Zealand. It included islands in many seas. And its forts, garrisons, and trading " factories " formed little cultural outposts in the populous Orient. But to the ordinary European, Frederick's new province of Silesia must have seemed more real than these strange and remote places. Europe had not caught up with its own history. In the European Legend of the eighteenth century the seas were wide indeed.

In the American Legend of the twentieth the seas are, if anything, wider. In that Legend the Pilgrim Fathers shake the dust of Europe from their feet and found our country at Plymouth Rock in 1620. Forgotten are the Negroes who reached Jamestown before the Pilgrims ever sailed. Forgotten is the settlement of Jamestown thirteen years before the Pilgrims landed. The Pilgrims dissented: they thereby qualified as Founders in the American Legend. Paul Revere hangs his lantern; the Redcoats are coming; and there is not time for Americans to remember the four colonial wars they fought for Britain against the encircling French. It is hard, too, to remember that the American Revolution was a civil war, fought in England with words between Whig and Tory, fought in America with words and weapons between Whig and Tory. It is hard, if only because Chatham and Burke had no British regiments helping Washington's raw levies against the Redcoats their King was sending overseas. Their thunderous words, defending the colonies against royal abuse of power, carried indeed even beyond the sea, but they were finally drowned out by the clash of weapons. The civil war became, in the Legend, a nationalist war. The English Whig became an enemy and the American Tory a traitor. Secession from the Empire became the birth of a new nation. When the nineteenth century brought a vast flood of Europeans to join those who had already opened a continent, it inevitably brought for the most part, not the governing class of Europe, but the governed, the underprivileged, the exploited, the starving, the oppressed, the rebellious; and the theme of secession, which had already run through the Legend, deepened. A patronizing scorn for this cultural dustbin caused a certain condescension among foreigners; and the American retorted by picturing all emigrants from Europe as daring pioneers and everybody who stayed behind as a coward or a stick-in-the-mud.

The Legend grew, and "American civilization" became un-European if not anti-European, differing from European civilization not as French civilization differs from English but as European differs from Asiatic. Was America not the New World? Were not Americans therefore a new nation, a young people? Were they not therefore comparable with Europeans, when Europe was young, when it was building its cathedrals, fighting its crusades, singing its *Song of Roland*? But were Americans indeed young, in that sense?

Or were they rather the most modern — and therefore the " oldest "
— representatives of the culture men call Western Civilization? Was
not their energy, their drive, their optimism due, not to a youthful
culture, but to the profound challenge of a new physical environment
in which they were able to do the things an eighteenth-century European longed in vain to do. It was an environment in which the
economic prizes were huge, in which the constraining debris of the
medieval past was absent, in which the vested interests of a decadent nobility, and at last of a decadent monarchy, could not block
the progress to power, not of a civilization that was young, but of a
class. That new class was the class that Jacob Fugger had done so
much to found, the class the monarchs of Europe had done so much
to foster, the class of which a decaying nobility had been so jealous,
and the class of which an obstinate peasantry had been so afraid. In
America that class would come into its own.

Unless we can temporarily forget the American Legend, and indeed the correlative European Legend about America, we can
scarcely hope to move with ease or understanding among the essentially European inhabitants of eighteenth-century Quebec or Bos-
ton; of Williamsburg or Charleston; of Havana or Caracas or Rio
or Buenos Aires. Unless we turn from the Legend, we cannot re-
discover in distant Batavia, among millions of Javanese, the busy
dockyards of another Amsterdam, the crowded wharves, the shaded
Dutch canals, the long quays, the great warehouses, the mountains
of coffee for Addison, Steele, and the other Europeans to drink. We
will not know at Cape Town that we are in Holland again — a
funny, constricted Holland, oppressed by the monopolistic management of a Dutch trading company. We will not recognize the Portuguese churches at ancient Goa, on the Indian coast.

We might be excused for overlooking such Asiatic outposts of
Europe's centuries-old culture. But our Legend will indeed blind us
if we cannot recognize on the banks of the St. Lawrence a whole province of that civilization, a province in which the French monarchy
even succeeded in re-creating in some degree the ancient feudal system it had done so much to destroy in Europe — a system with its
seigneurs and their land grants and their habitant tenants, with their
strips of land running down to the St. Lawrence, the great river that
tied them to Normandy and those other provinces of the King, so

much nearer Versailles, and yet still so far. But the habitant, in his tight little wooden house, comfortably dressed in his woolens and in winter in his furs, was no serf. If his life was rugged, its ruggedness was due to the long Canadian winter, not to his seigneur. The valley of the St. Lawrence did not invite the use of forced labor. New France sent chiefly furs to Old France, and lumber, and a little wheat.

On the banks of the Hudson, in this eighteenth century, the old Dutch houses are giving way to the homes of the English who took New Amsterdam from the Dutch; and the knickerbockers of the Dutch have become the knee breeches that prosperous Europeans wear everywhere, whether in New York or London or Paris. But the holdings of the Dutch patroons who had settled the valley lie, like the farms of the lowlier habitants, on a navigable river.

The role of the navigable river is decisive. The reason Virginia had become the wealthiest and most populous colony on the coast lies plain on the map to read. With the railroad yet to be invented, there were but two means of transportation: ship or horse. Even in England, it was only in the late eighteenth century that men like McAdam at last built roads superior to the roads the ancient Romans had built there some fifteen centuries earlier. Saddle or stagecoach or horse-drawn wagon or oxcart, transportation by land was a major problem in the colonies. The river, the bay, the ocean were the answer. That is why it was the seaboard states of Europe — Portugal, Spain, France, Holland, and England — that seized the leadership of European civilization and projected it across the face of the Globe. That was why the rivers of Virginia put her in easy touch with London — in cheaper touch than was many an inland European province with its royal capital. The Potomac, the Rappahannock, the York, the James were tidal estuaries that opened Tidewater Virginia to the world of commerce. On their banks, therefore, sprang up the spacious brick homes of plantation owners, with their private wharves where tobacco and other produce might be loaded for London. French St. Lawrence, Dutch Hudson, English James — they were all highways, with " frontage " for the producer; seigneur, patroon, and Virginia squire prospered because of that frontage. Theirs was a riverain culture.

But Virginia, in addition to thousands of miles of frontage, pos-

sessed a soil and climate uniquely fitted to produce the tobacco
which Europe had learned to smoke. Even the habitant of the St.
Lawrence grew tobacco — for his own use. But it was Virginia tobacco that London wanted. With two natural monopolies, soil suited
to tobacco and easy access to the rest of the world, only cheap labor
was lacking to make high profits flow; and the New England and
European sea captain rectified that lack with a new kind of serf for
a new kind of feudalism — Negro slaves from Africa. The same
kind of serf was dumped into the rich sugar plantations of the West
Indies, into Brazil and into many other parts of Latin America. In
addition, the native Indians proved reducible to forced labor. In
Latin America, too, therefore, as in the southernmost British colonies of North America, a new kind of manorial system grew up —
the plantation. African slave and Indian peon between them supplied
the exploitable labor that John Locke had failed to supply when he
tried to furnish Carolina with a feudal constitution. But slavery and
peonage would be under heavy pressure, not merely from the rising
humanitarianism that characterized Christendom in the "Age of
Enlightenment," but from the pressure of cheap or free land. It was
hard to exploit " labor " when labor could move West, exploit itself,
and pocket the profit.

A New Europe had arisen in the Americas, made in the image of
the Old. Its peoples were either of the same stock or, as in parts of
Latin America, largely the same; they spoke the same languages as
Old Europe, read the same books, discussed the same ideas. They
lived in similar houses and, wherever they amassed sufficient wealth,
wore similar costumes. They sang the same old songs, and told the
same old stories, played the same old games. In short they were Europeans. But their political status was peculiar.

They lived in some new province or other of a nation that also
governed older provinces on the Continent of Europe. But intimate
as were their cultural ties, they lived across an ocean from their respective capitals. Moreover, every colony had been founded by, or under the auspices of, a government in Old Europe; and the dominant
motive of those governments in founding colonies was the desire
to enrich the mother country. Their policy was therefore the mercantilist policy of Louis XIV's famous minister, Colbert: they tried
to monopolize trade so as to bring into the mother country as much

gold and silver as possible; and they tried to break the monopoly of competing governments. The colony was forbidden to buy what it needed from Europe except from the mother country, even if it could buy cheaper elsewhere. It was forbidden to sell its own goods except to the mother country, even if it could sell dearer elsewhere. It was forbidden to produce certain goods that the mother country preferred to supply at a profit. These rules, or modifications of them written in the same spirit, subjected the colony to constant monopolistic exploitation. The mother country was likewise apt to monopolize political offices for Europeans. The population of New Europe came to exist, therefore, for the benefit of Old Europe — or at least for the benefit of those private economic interests in Old Europe which succeeded in getting the ear of their governments. It is true that the inhabitants of Old Europe were the victims of similar monopolies; but, at least in England, they had more to say about government policy than the colonial. Nor did a whole ocean flow between profiteer and victim in England, to isolate, identify, and dramatize those who suffered together. Though the rules of the mercantilist game injured Old Europeans and New Europeans alike, for the benefit of special groups of Old Europeans — and sometimes of New Europeans — yet those rules were made in old Europe.

It was well-nigh inevitable that the ties that connected New Europe to Old should have snapped first in the English-speaking world. The idea that the people are sovereign had been more nearly put into practice in Britain than in any other European state. The colonies of Britain came nearer to governing themselves than the colonies of any other European state. Finally, Britain's triumph over France in the Seven Years' War was followed, as so many military victories are, by a period of political corruption and mismanagement; and the expense of that formidable struggle made the British government anxious to collect from its American colonies some of the cost of defending them. At the same moment, by an evil fate, George III was determined to have more say in his government than either George I or George II had ever tried to have. The elaborate restrictions of the mercantilist system were for the first time enforced, new taxes were introduced, and a king was exhibiting for the first time some of the stubbornness that had cost Charles I his head. The British colonies revolted and won their independence. Thirty-five years later Spanish America would revolt against Spain. The two men who best symbolize these two revolts are George Washington, the Virginian, and Simon Bolivar, the Venezuelan.

George Washington was born in 1732 on the bank of the Potomac, a member of the governing class of Virginia. His father and his two older brothers, like so many of that class, were educated in England. His father had sat in the House of Burgesses, the oldest legislative assembly in the British colonies; and his son would some day sit there too. But George was one of a large family, he lost his father before he was twelve, and he had his own way to make, with the help of excellent connections. He went at it methodically. Without much schooling, he became a land-surveyor at sixteen. As soon as possible he bought land himself. When he was twenty-one he was a major in the Virginia militia, sent by the Governor into the wilderness beyond the mountains to reconnoiter the forts the French were building. Next year, as colonel commanding two companies of infantry, he entered the same wilderness and engaged in a scuffle with the French. That was in 1754. Next year he returned as aide-de-camp to the British General Braddock, to attack Fort Duquesne. They were routed; but the French and Indian War had now begun in earnest. Washington was appointed Commander-in-Chief of the Virginia forces. He fought under the British flag till the end of 1758; then, with the Ohio lands definitely safe from the French, he resigned for reasons of health.

He had become famous throughout the colonies. He now settled at Mount Vernon, set to work to make it pay, kept his accounts, married a well-to-do widow, mastered his love for the wife of a neighbor, and served in the House of Burgesses. He had made his career, and he had done it by being methodical, foresighted, honest, diligent, courageous. He was a member of a strong and self-reliant governing class; he thought their thoughts; acted in ways they considered honorable; obtained their votes; danced and followed the hounds with them. Six feet in height, hardened by life in the wilderness, a magnificent horseman, somewhat silent, dignified to the point of majesty, he was the kind of man the Virginia governing class would follow.

They had their chance to do so. As George III and his inept Tory ministers proceeded on their way, Virginia and the other colonies became more and more outraged and talked more and more of the

keep his accounts, to talk with his friends. In less than three years he died.

He epitomized the virtues of his eighteenth-century Virginia, which were the virtues of eighteenth-century England. He was clear-headed, practical rather than speculative, socially responsible, anxious to distinguish himself by service useful to his community, prudent with money, courteous but reserved, physically and morally courageous, in his tastes aristocratic, in his politics conservative. He led a revolution by force to restore the rights of Englishmen. He helped write a Constitution that he thought would conserve those rights. He died, not merely respected, but venerated by his fellow-countrymen — and also allegedly the wealthiest man in the colonies, chiefly by a prudent speculation in Western lands.

Simon Bolivar, "the Liberator," was the Washington of Spanish America, and his career was Spanish where Washington's was English. He was born on a plantation, as Washington was, in 1783, the year in which the Treaty of Versailles recognized the independence for which Washington's ragged armies had fought. He owned Negro slaves, as Washington did. He, too, was bred to the saddle. But he was born rich, with the title of Marquis, where Washington was born in moderate circumstances, a member of a natural, but untitled, aristocracy of the land. His family, like Washington's, had moved from Old Europe to New Europe generations before. Washington had lost his father before he was twelve; Bolivar lost both parents by the time he was nine. Washington went to school to an Anglican parson in Fredericksburg, and remained all his life a staunch if theologically vague Anglican; Bolivar went to school to the inevitable Catholic priests; but a few years later he was a Freemason like Washington, and a freethinker. For Bolivar passed early to an amazing young tutor, Manuel Rodriguez, a revolutionary, an ardent disciple of Rousseau. Washington served in the Virginia militia, under the flag of his British King; Bolivar in the Venezuelan militia under the flag of his Spanish King. By fifteen, when Bolivar went to Madrid, he was better read than Washington, with a great deal less experience of life. Then or soon afterward he read Locke, Condillac, Raynal, Buffon, d'Alembert, Helvetius, Montesquieu, Mably, Rousseau, Voltaire: in short, the eighteenth-century Philosophers and their forerunners. At Madrid he discovered that he was not quite what he thought he was — a Spaniard. In Venezuela he must have known that the principal places in both Church and State were reserved for "Peninsular Spaniards." The Creoles — American-born Spaniards — formed the top social layer, with that restriction. Then came the mestizos, of mixed Spanish and Indian blood, then the Indians, and last the Negroes. Did Bolivar know Madrid's term for even titled nobility in Spanish America — "Cocoa Grandees"? If Washington had made the trip he wanted to make to England, where his father and brothers had returned for their education, he might have discovered how much less a Virginian planter was regarded by the English landed gentry than by the yeoman farmers whom he led at home or the Negroes whom he owned there.

At Madrid the young Marquis fell violently in love with a cousin, born in Madrid of a Venezuelan family; and after a visit to Paris, where Napoleon Bonaparte governed as First Consul, Bolivar married, took his bride home to Caracas, and was in nine months a widower. He returned to Paris and lived the life of a dandy. He was there when Napoleon, his revolutionary hero, disgusted him by taking the crown. He met a married cousin and made her his mistress, an act which for many reasons Major Washington, at approximately the same age, would have condemned. He was rich, idle, dissipated, restless, but without purpose, and unhappy. At this point a chance meeting with the German scientist, Baron von Humboldt, put it into his head that America should be freed from Spanish misrule. Bolivar had shortly before rediscovered his revolutionary tutor Rodriguez, and now they tramped through Italy together. He saw Napoleon crown himself at Milan with the iron crown of the Lombards. In 1805, on the sacred Aventine Mount overlooking Rome, Bolivar, with his beloved Rodriguez as witness, took a dramatic oath to liberate America from her Spanish oppressors. There had been no such dramatic moment in Washington's life: Major, Colonel, or General, he held formal commissions with stated objectives, whether from the Virginia House of Burgesses or the Continental Congress.

In 1806 Bolivar returned to his home in Caracas, but he significantly made a detour to visit the new United States of America. At Caracas he found a revolutionary junta which, like so many other juntas in both Spain and America, was declaring against Napoleon's

invited all the countries in both Americas to a great Congress at Panama to form a league of nations. He proposed permanent neutrality between league members; the Monroe Doctrine to be supported by all; international law to be adopted in the national codes; the abolition of slavery; democratic organization within member states; sanctions against members infringing agreements; a league army to keep the peace. Few countries even sent delegates to the Congress.

Indeed, the last years of the Liberator, the dictator of Colombia, were filled with bitterness. Many men of influence urged him to take the crown. He refused. He always remained faithful to the liberal and republican ideas of his beloved Rousseau; yet brutal events forced him to assume enormous personal power. He wanted to resign. He wanted to leave, perhaps to return to Old Europe, now that he had severed her political ties with so much of New Europe. His years of guerrilla fighting, of life in the saddle, of wrangling politically, of shooting the treasonous, of trying to create order, of making love to countless women and of loving greatly one woman, who left her English husband to follow him, of escaping assassins, of launching proclamations to his soldiers that exceed in power and eloquence even those of Napoleon, had worn him out. In 1830, after years of threatening to resign, he really did, and prepared to leave South America once more. He wrote his lifelong friend, Lopez Mendez: "I am old, ill, disappointed, slandered, and ill-paid....I have never approved revolution, and in the end I even regretted our revolution against Spain." And to a neighbor: "In twenty years of government, I have arrived at some few certainties. (1) America is ungovernable for us. (2) To serve a revolution is to plow the sea. (3) The only thing a man can do in America is to emigrate...." A few days before he died, he summed up, as he saw it, the life of Bolivar, the Liberator: "There have been three great fools in history: Jesus, Don Quixote, and I." A few months later, Colombia fell apart.

XIII.

LIBERTY, EQUALITY, FRATERNITY, MONEY

LESS than eight years after a British military band at Yorktown had played "The World Upside Down," Western Christendom throbbed to the news of the French Revolution. Three years more, and Christendom entered on the cycle of wars that would last almost without interruption for twenty-three years. That great convulsion would surpass in fury and destruction any ordeal it had undergone since the Protestant Revolution; and it would far surpass even that in the weight of arms employed, in the area of Europe and the world that would be fought over, in its visible effects on human institutions, laws, and property rights. It would send French troops to the pyramids of Egypt, an army of 600,000 Europeans to Moscow, the Pope to a prison in Savona, British troops to burn the Capitol in Washington, Nelson to Trafalgar, Bolivar across the Andes, the ships of seven seas to Davy Jones' locker, and Napoleon Bonaparte to St. Helena. Contemporaries would call it justifiably the "War of the Nations" or even the "World War." Its beginnings would make men hope that war could be abolished, and its end would be the greatest blood bath in which Europe had ever yet been plunged. It would inspire the poetry of Chénier and Wordsworth; the declama-

varieties. The early Revolutionary Wars were a mammoth and fanatical crusade, unlike previous European wars in their quality as in their size. In addition, the whole symbolical paraphernalia of the Revolution eloquently portrays a new religion. To wave aside that paraphernalia as hysteria or crowd psychology is to lose the principal key to the fervor of the armies that swept Europe. For, in 1793, the Year I of the French Republic, it was a seductive dream that led an ill-equipped and half-trained army against the Prussian troops which the Great Frederick had made legendary, against the Austrian troops of the Emperor of the Holy Roman Empire. It was a dream of what, not the City of God, but the City of Man might be, were it once rid of superstition, obscurantism, meaningless economic monopoly, and functionless social privilege, the whole pinned crazily together by the hireling bayonets of Europe's Christian tyrant-kings. The ragged French Republicans fought for themselves, for their fellow-revolutionaries at home, for Europeans everywhere, for all mankind, and for the happiness of that posterity so dear to the great Philosophers who blazed this trail to Freedom.

By the brilliant light of that revolutionary dream we should discern a symbol in the nationalization of Church lands that the Constituent Assembly could scarcely be expected to see. The Constituent was primarily interested in raising money; the Church possessed enormous holdings in real property; this property was held, they argued, for the good of the nation; and the government was the logical agent for administering it. Meanwhile, the financial crisis of the government, which had called the Estates-General together in the first instance, continued; and the inevitable disorders of the first months of revolution were cutting down tax receipts. But the interesting thing is the basic assumption of the Revolutionary government that they were as well qualified as the Church to administer the slow accumulation, through the ages, of the gifts of the faithful. Those gifts, at least in theory, had been made to promote the interests of the City of God; by government decree they would now promote the interests of the City of Man. And there seemed to be no difference. Were the gifts supporting the expenses of public worship? The government would undertake that expense. Did they succor the poor? The government declared itself responsible for seeing that every citizen had either work or government aid. The sick? The government would care for them. But gifts had been made by count-less Christians that these things might be done in Christ's name and for love of Him. Well, they would be done henceforth in the name of the government. And, whether the Constituent realized it or not, the economic underwriting of the old faith had been placed at the disposal of the new. That shift took place in 1789, the first year of the Revolution.

What the new faith was, became a little clearer when, the next year, all monks and nuns were formally released from their vows and invited to quit their monasteries and convents. A great many did so: monastic life had decayed sadly during the Century of Enlightenment. To the inhabitants of the City of Man, the function of perpetual prayer cannot have seemed very real; and the state of monastic life in France was hardly such as to enlighten them. Besides, the City of Man already faced another problem, the problem of the secular clergy, the bishops and parish priests. The nationalization of Church lands necessarily threw that problem in their laps, because the government had made itself responsible for the expenses of public worship. Feeling its way as it went, now appealing to the principles of the Revolution, now to the practices of the primitive Church, the Constituent cut down the number of bishops, rearranged the dioceses so that there would be one to each of the eighty-three new Departments into which the ancient provinces of France had been divided, lowered the princely incomes of the bishops and forced them to live in their dioceses, raised the income of the half-starved curates, lessened the authority of the bishop over his clergy. This was the famous "Civil Constitution of the Clergy"; and it was ostensibly on this act of the Constituent, not on the earlier confiscation of the French Church's property, that the Revolution collided with the Papacy. The Pope forbade the French clergy to take the oath to the Civil Constitution. The Constituent proceeded to install in office those clergy who would take that oath, and to secure the orderly consecration of its new bishops. There were now two Churches in France. One was legal but schismatic; the other was illegal but recognized by the Pope.

The problem was extraordinarily complex. The cleavage was not a conveniently neat rift between a Church of devout Christians and an outside world of nonbelievers. There were nonbelievers both inside and outside the Church, both inside and outside the clergy. There were Deists in both camps who wanted to worship God but considered ecclesiastical practice a clutter of irrelevant superstitions. A large part of the lower clergy had long urged the nationalization of Church property and the suppression of the religious orders. Many of them warmly endorsed the Civil Constitution of the Clergy and gladly took the oath. Intelligent persons everywhere regarded the Church as a dying institution, even when as good Deists they admitted the existence of God. Given these facts, it is not too surprising that the Constituent should have assumed, even, that the same electorate that chose its civil government should choose its clergy, and this although the electorate included Protestants, Jews, and atheists. For " The Church," as one member of the Constituent, a Catholic, put it, " is in the State, the State is not in the Church." When Martin Luther, after the debate with Eck, had exclaimed "We are all Hussites without knowing it," there is a sense of discovery in his remark. But although the Constituent, like Luther, came only step by step to its final position, its surprise is not at that position but at the violence of its collision with an institution it had assumed was dying. Many of the clergy shared the Constituent's rude awakening. During the early months of the Revolution, the elaborate public celebrations had expressed in their ritual a sort of blend, a syncretism, of the two religions, Christianity and the new faith, the religion of the Fatherland and of Humanity. Now there was rupture, if not between the two religions, at least between their respective governments, the Papacy and the Constituent. Back of that clash, indeed, lay a clash between the universe depicted in the *Great Encyclopedia* and the universe depicted in the medieval *summas.*

As the danger of foreign invasion increased, and as the National Convention hardened into dictatorship by guillotine, royalist and Catholic combined in the insurrection in the provinces; the " nonjuring " Church went underground and suffered its martyrdoms; and the dreaded " representatives on mission," those commissars of the Convention who were sent out to compel local administrators or dubious generals at the front, cried out bitterly against the " fanaticism " of the " men in black " and the " superstitious orgies " of the " sabbaths " they celebrated. Even the " constitutional clergy " came under suspicion, and by the end of 1793 the strange mixture of Catholicism and the new patriotic faith had collapsed and the field was open to the cult of patriotism. The traditions of that cult, its rites, its symbols, its songs were already familiar: the altar of the Fatherland, the Liberty tree, the tricolor cockade, the Liberty cap, the fasces of Unity, the level and the scales of Equality, the two clasped hands signifying Fraternity, the symbolic eye of Vigilance. Then there were the tokens of respect paid to the heroes and martyrs of the Revolution, their busts, and the solemn processions to place their bodies in the Pantheon. With Catholicism out of the way, the Revolution took over its terms and could speak now of the "Holy Mountain"—"the Mountain" was the extreme revolutionary party in the Convention and was now supreme—of "Holy Equality," "Holy Liberty," the "Sacred Rights of Man." Marat became a kind of canonized saint; his heart was solemnly presented to the Convention; and people addressed his heart in their prayers as they had once addressed the Sacred Heart of Jesus. A revolutionary orator near Strasbourg compared him, indeed, with Jesus, since "like Jesus, Marat ardently loved the people and loved none but them." From all over France, in a kind of ecstasy of devotion, rose the strains of the new Revolutionary hymn and marching song, "The Marseillaise."

At Nevers, the representative on mission, Fouché, an ex-priest who would one day gain fame as Napoleon's inexorable Minister of Police, baptized his daughter on the altar of the Fatherland and presided in the cathedral over a ceremony in honor of Brutus. The revolutionary calendar was introduced, partly to "abolish Sunday." It was Fouché, again, who forbade Catholic worship in public and ecclesiastical costumes too, made funeral services purely civil affairs, and inscribed over the cemetery gate: "Death is an eternal sleep." In the Department of Charente-Inférieure, Catholics and Protestants met, first in "the temple of the Catholics" and next day in "the temple of the Protestants," embraced each other "like brothers," swore to have no other religion except the religion of Truth, abolished the titles of priest and minister, and substituted "the beautiful title of preacher of morals." They further determined that the Protestant preacher of morals would frequently preach morality in the temple of the Catholics; and the Catholic, in the Protestant temple. Church vessels were broken, images smashed. The peasants near

Paris notified the National Convention that henceforth they would worship only Liberty. Gobel, one of the first Catholic bishops to take the oath to the Civil Constitution of the Clergy, now resigned his bishopric; and the event was celebrated in Notre Dame Cathedral. A scene from a current opera, " Offering to Liberty," to music based on the " Marseillaise," was performed in the cathedral, as well as an unpublished hymn to Liberty by the poet Chénier. A " Mountain " was constructed in the choir of the cathedral, crowned with an ancient temple, which bore the inscription, " To Philosophy." Two lines of ballet dancers from the opera, dressed in white, climbed the Mountain; and Liberty, also a young girl, emerged, took her seat on a throne of greenery, and received the homage of the citizens. Notre Dame Cathedral was rechristened the " Temple of Reason," and the performance was repeated for the special benefit of the Convention. Similar ceremonies took place on the same day in a number of French cities; and at Lyons the people dressed a donkey in bishop's robes, swung a censer before him, led him to the tomb of a Revolutionary martyr, smashed church vessels there and sent them to the foundry. But these orgies represented no permanent force, and Deism triumphed over atheism when the Convention decreed the honors of the Pantheon to Jean-Jacques Rousseau, who in the *Social Contract* had championed not only Nature but God, immortality, and a " civil religion " for the state. The Convention decreed that " the French people recognizes the existence of God and the immortality of the soul," and instituted a " Feast of the Supreme Being and of Nature." Over the door of Notre Dame this new confession of faith replaced the inscription, " Temple of Reason."

The Feast of the Supreme Being, like many another Revolutionary ceremony, is well known to us through pictures and descriptions. Robespierre, " the Incorruptible," that faithful believer in Rousseau and relentless executioner of the faithless, was elected President of the Convention that he might preside at the ceremony. An elaborate synthetic ritual took place at the Garden of the Tuileries: men bearing swords and oak branches, women carrying baskets of flowers; a salvo of artillery introducing the members of the National Convention; music; Robespierre, as President, pronouncing an invocation; the people singing a hymn, composed for the occasion, and carefully rehearsed in each ward the night before, a hymn to "Father of the Universe, supreme intelligence." Robespierre then burned in effigy Atheism, surrounded by Egotism, Ambition, and Discord; and from the ashes sprang, a little too automatically, a statue of Wisdom. There followed a solemn procession to the "Field of Union" at the Champ de Mars and to an "immense Mountain" crowned with a Liberty tree. The Feast was held in the provinces too. Atheism had been exorcised, the Convention had meanwhile abandoned its efforts either to assimilate the Church or to regulate it or even to forbid it, the temporary saturnalia of blasphemy had passed, Rousseauian Deism appeared triumphant. But the "immense Mountain" was not built of very durable substances, and except for a brief experiment with another synthetic cult, "Theophilanthropy," the stage was set for the future First Consul, the agnostic but realistic Bonaparte, to propose to the Pope a Concordat. By that device, the peasants would be able to hear the Church bells ring again, and the lovely music of those bells would not be marred by fears that the Church would claim its lands from them. As for Bonaparte, the Church would be of immense aid to him in teaching his new subjects the joys of obedience. The Church, torn loose from its roots in feudalism, would strike new roots in modern capitalism.

Because Bonaparte's Concordat endured for a century, it is easy to smile now at the Revolution's agonized efforts to find its metaphysical basis, its operable symbols, its moral sanctions. The scenes just recounted bring now only a faint smile at the vagaries of mass hysteria, and we turn away from them to the enduring political and economic reforms of the Revolution. But we should not turn away. For it was this Revolutionary "religion," which was to live on in dilute form as nineteenth-century liberalism, that launched the fanatical armies of the Revolution across the face of Europe and furnished them a vision for which men gladly gave their lives. It was the vision of a City of Man, more reasonable, more decent, more kind, more neighborly, more responsible, than the kingdoms of this earth had been. And, like the City of God that had preceded it, it was open not only to Frenchmen but to all men everywhere. Could that vision furnish some basis for a European unity that feudalism had lost — or never found; that lay in no El Dorado beyond the seas; that Spanish Philip II could not recapture or enforce; that Versailles could suggest but not create; that all the fleets of a free British Parliament could not, or would not, establish?

The Catholic Church got the bells; the peasant — and, even more often, the real-estate speculator or solid investor — got the Church's lands; and the autocratic First Consul of the Republic got the Church's support. That was the settlement of Napoleon's Concordat, a settlement to which the Revolutionary religion of Patriotism and Humanity had stumbled through, amid the harsh dialectic of events. Through the same harsh dialectic, the effort of the Revolution to open the City of Man to all mankind, not merely to Frenchmen, ended in the Napoleonic Empire with Fouché as Minister of Police. Or, later still, in a War of Liberation fought by the nations of Europe against their French liberators, in the growth of nationalism, and in a number of Cities of Man destined to destroy, or all but destroy, the civilization of Europe. This is a meteoric career for a vision, the great vision of all mankind living under law of its own making, of all mankind living free and at peace.

Just as the vision of self-government, of liberty under law, had been beheld by Rousseau and the Encyclopedists before the Estates-General were called to face the bankruptcy of absolute monarchy, so too the vision of peace had been beheld by Rousseau, by Kant, by Goethe. The two visions were actually, and by rights, one. Liberty meant the substitution of reason for brute force: so did peace. And basically, what the City of Man staked its future on, was human reason. Those who longed to build it included Catholics, Protestants, Jews, Deists, atheists. They therefore disagreed on whether man owed to God the reason he possessed; they did not disagree on whether man possessed it, or whether he ought to use it now to build a fairer City than had yet been built. Arguments about the precise relation of that City to God seemed no excuse for delaying construction.

In May, 1790, war threatened between Britain and Spain, over fishing rights off Vancouver. But the Bourbons of Spain and the Bourbons of France were united by a "Family Compact." Would the Constituent honor the Compact? It emphatically would not. "We must declare," suggested Robespierre in the debate, "that France renounces all ambitious projects, all conquests, and that she

considers her frontiers as having been fixed by eternal destiny...."
Volney went further: "You are going to deliberate for the world
and in the world; I dare to say you are going to convoke an assembly
of the nations." Mirabeau, the ablest statesman in the Constituent,
objected: France could not alone, by her self-abnegations, change the
face of European diplomacy. But the enthusiasts shouted him down:
the nation would naturally fight only wars that were national, that
is, defensive, and consequently, just. "Let every nation be free like
us," cried the curate Rollet, "and there will be no more war." The
argument is easy to follow, if unreal in the historic context. Kings
have ruled Europe. Kings have controlled the issue of war and
peace. Wars have therefore been dynastic. Remove the issue from
the control of kings, and no motive for war (which is a dynastic
phenomenon) remains. But, objected Mirabeau, history offered ample proof that free peoples made the fiercest wars. Into the new Constitution, nevertheless, the Constituent wrote: "The French nation
renounces the undertaking of any war for the purpose of conquest,
and will never employ its forces against the liberty of any people."
Within three years many of the same men would help impose a military dictatorship on France, and would conduct a popular, nationalist, revolutionary war against the thrones of Europe — the first of
Europe's great, modern, nationalist wars. That war would begin, indeed, as a war of defense, against intervention and counterrevolution, a war of independence, against military invasion. It would become a war of propaganda and liberation. It would end as a war of
territorial expansion.

But now the Constituent thought of the Fatherland and Humanity as one, just as it had a year before thought of the Revolutionary
religion and Catholicism as one. A good many foreigners agreed. A
month after the renunciation of war, representatives of many countries appeared before the Constituent, appropriately dressed in their
national costumes. Among the self-appointed delegates from the human race to France — Englishmen, Spaniards, Germans, Netherlanders, Italians, even Persians and Turks — no one stood out like
the Prussian Anacharsis Cloots, known as "the spokesman of the human race." "When I lift my eyes to a map of the world," he cried,
"it seems to me that all the other countries have disappeared, and I
see only France, regenerator of peoples." There is no longer any in-

ternational law in Europe, exulted the Revolutionary journalist Desmoulins, who was destined to die under the guillotine with the great
Danton. For the maze of treaties and bargains between the tyrants
who ruled Europe, Desmoulins substituted popular consent, without
noting that whole peoples, like tyrants, might disagree — and might
fight much harder for their own interests than they had ever fought
for their king's. A case of the new, popular public law promptly
arose: the people of Avignon, a town in France governed by the
Pope, voted to become part of the French nation. The Constituent
voted annexation, and waved aside the objection that it had recently
renounced all conquests. Three days after Danton and the Paris
Commune had overthrown the monarchy, with foreign armies advancing on French soil, the Paris Commune declared: " While re-
nouncing all plans of conquest, the Nation has not renounced furnishing aid to neighboring powers which may wish to escape from
slavery." Two weeks later the Legislative Assembly voted French
citizenship to George Washington, to Thomas Paine, to the English
democrat Joseph Priestley (who also was prophesying an end of
war), to the abolitionist William Wilberforce, to the German poets
Klopstock and Schiller, and of course to Anacharsis Cloots. For, indeed, all of them, and not merely Cloots, were spokesmen of mankind, and the eternal rights which the Revolution had declared, were
the rights, not merely of Frenchmen, but of all men everywhere.

But when the armies of the French Republic drove the invaders
out and themselves entered the Austrian Netherlands (Belgium),
what was to be done with this liberated country? Some of the German districts bordering France were applying for rescue and annexation. Netherlanders were demanding at least rescue from their
Stadtholder, the Prince of Orange. By November, 1792, the National
Convention decreed: " In the name of the French nation, that it
would accord fraternity and succor to all peoples who might wish to
recover their liberty." It was not that simple. The rescued Belgians
were refusing the generous French Republic's paper money. They
were made to take it. Deputies from Savoy came to request the Convention to annex their territory. One of the Constitutional bishops
was presiding, and waxed eloquent: " A new century is going to
open.... Liberty, hovering over all Europe, will visit her domains,
and this part of the globe will contain no more fortresses, nor fron-

tiers, nor foreign peoples." In any case, monetary inflation was hovering wherever the sons of Liberty abolished tyrants. The remedy was drastic: the French sequestrated state and religious property in the lands their armies entered, and requisitioned against Republican money. Everything has to be paid for, even Liberty. The slogan of annexation and requisition was: "War on the castle, peace to the cottage!" Not all the cottagers felt it covered the problem, but the slogan 'worked well enough. A contemporary declared its invention ranked with the invention of gunpowder.

The war that had started to protect the reforms of the Revolution from armed intervention now took two forms: a war for the "natural" frontiers of France, which the Convention decided were the Rhine, the Alps, and the Pyrenees; and a war to set up a ring of satellite sister republics protecting the flanks of "the Great Nation," the French Republic, which in turn would protect them. It was a program that outdid Richelieu, that outdid Louis XIV, and that guaranteed nearly a quarter-century of war against four successive European coalitions and, in the process, placed France in the power of Napoleon Bonaparte. Under Napoleon, the war slowly changed from a crusade of liberation against monarchical misgovernment and the economic disorder of a residual feudalism, and became a war of conquest and military glory and profitable rapine. Yet it was the crusade that made it possible for the young Napoleon to win his first great victories abroad and to seize power at home. It enabled him to root most of the reforms of the Revolution in the soil of France and many of them in the soil of near-by countries. By a familiar process of war, it forced even countries like Prussia to adopt some of those reforms in order to defeat France with her own weapons — just as the French had accepted military dictatorship to fight off the foreigners with their own weapons, monarchy and the sword.

For liberty, equality, and fraternity had had diverse careers. Equality fared best: the whole tumble-down edifice of social and legal privilege was destroyed over much of Europe. Beaumarchais, in his famous *Marriage of Figaro,* had made his pert hero lash out at the nobles, who "had taken the trouble to be born"; from now on, to a degree incredible to contemporaries, the prizes would go to those who had taken real trouble, and the fat jobs would not be monopolized by the wellborn. In that sense Europe became irrevocably and increasingly "democratic." But liberty fared less well than equality. It is true that arbitrary arrest became rarer; freedom of worship was secure; trial by jury took the place of a secret and inquisitorial system; but Napoleon left only the façade of self-government, and his censorship was strict and omnipresent. As to the third member of the trinity of aims, fraternity, that was hammered, in the crucible of war, into nationalism — nationalism, both in France and in other countries, of an intensity of which Europe had never dreamed. Before that mystical, tribal sense of community, the universalism of the early Revolution gave way.

While Napoleon brooded at St. Helena on his incredible career of world conquest, Europe relived memories too. They were memories of ruthless and basic reform, more efficient administration, needed public works, exciting and useful careers for the able and intelligent. Everything had been simplified. In 1803 Napoleon had reduced the German principalities from 250 to 39; and in 1806 he had abruptly declared the Holy Roman Empire at an end and had replaced it with the Confederation of the Rhine under French protection. Temporarily, at least, he had cleared Italy of its traditional rubble too: he had broken the foreign dynasties that held large sections of it; he had broken the Papacy as a temporal power; he had aroused a sense of national unity in place of the ferocious spirit of locality. But the Germans, the Italians, and the other Europeans remembered also the petty tyranny of a French bureaucracy, the pillage of French armies, the cutting-off of their trade with Britain, and above all the rigors of military conscription and of war taxation.

The insoluble problem had been Great Britain, "perfidious Albion." At St. Helena, surrounded by his British captors, Napoleon placed most of the guilt for aborting the new Revolutionary era squarely on the British. For decades, Bonapartists would echo his interpretation of events. He had almost united Europe, and could have brought it prosperity and peace, but for the British. The British had smashed Philip's Invincible Armada in the sixteenth century; they had wrecked Louis XIV's fleets in the seventeenth, and helped, under Marlborough, to wreck his armies; they had confiscated Louis XV's colonial empire and supported Frederick of Prussia against him with financial subsidies. They had subsidized from their vast new commercial and industrial wealth coalition after coalition against Napoleon's efforts to bring Europe the unity it so sorely needed. Having led all Europe in setting up parliamentary institutions, they had brazenly objected to the drive of the French Revolutionary armies to "liberate" neighboring peoples on the Continent. Having beheaded Charles I, they expressed pious horror when the Convention beheaded Louis XVI. To Napoleon's Berlin Decree in 1806, setting up his "Continental System" and a paper blockade against British goods, they had replied with their "Orders in Council," imposing a real blockade on France and on every country under her control. With Trafalgar safely in the past, and the British supreme on the seas, the last word went to the British.

Without the British, the Bonapartists cried, Napoleon could have brought all Europe under a common law, could have ended European warfare, could have eventually applied the measures of self-government and federation about which he so often and so eloquently talked. In short, he could have realized the City of Man, of which poor Anacharsis Cloots and the members of the Convention whom he praised, could only talk.

But the British would not have it. They could see in him only a dangerous adventurer, an able and insatiable military conqueror, and a tyrant who had quickly put an end to France's feeble efforts at self-government. They did not forget the summer of 1803, when he had assembled flatboats at Boulogne for a conquest of "the islanders." They saw in his success the end of what every Englishman meant by Freedom. And they made trouble for him however and wherever they could, until he fell. As for his dreams of European unity, they had selfishly less reason than any nation in Europe to gauge the horrors of a system of sovereign states, because their Channel gave them almost complete protection from the international anarchy of that system. They were inclined with Burke to be impatient of plans to free "Humanity." Freedom was a thing hard to come by, as they knew by experience, and best reached by trial and error, by killing a stubborn King here, by importing a Dutch King there, by remembering that you were English and that Englishmen know how to manage such things. They had sympathized with the French for objecting to Bourbon tyranny, were impatient when they grew declamatory about the Rights of Man, were not too painfully surprised when the French lost their new-won liberties. They objected

violently to the enlargement of France, particularly to an enlargement that included the Low Countries, and most particularly to one
that made Antwerp the port of a great power, able to compete with
London. It was therefore easy for them to think less about French
reforms in Central Europe than about French oppression there.
They were not impressed by Napoleon's propaganda in Europe —
though he was the first modern master of propaganda. They knew
that French goods went to satellite states duty-free, and that satellite
goods paid a stiff duty to enter France. They knew Napoleon's much
discussed plans for the unification of Europe were for the purpose of
leading Europe against Asia and the Americas. Fortunately for British plans, the Revolutionary reforms which remained Napoleon's
propaganda weapon long after the war had turned from liberation
to conquest and privilege, meant next to nothing to the Spanish people, and Napoleon's kidnapping the Pope proved to that fanatically
Catholic nation that the French were still the incorrigible atheists
who had just finished pillaging churches in France. To prove it, the
French armies unwisely pillaged Spanish churches, though doubtless
from other motives than atheism. So the ferocious guerrilla war went
on and on, bleeding Napoleon white. And at this unhappy moment
he shouted down his best advisers, attacked Russia, lost an army —
and the War of German Liberation began.

He had had nothing to offer Russia either, and there too he and
his Frenchmen were considered atheists. Holy Russia rose against
him — not so much her armies, which were successfully driven back,
but her Cossacks, her peasants, her distances, and her ghastly, destructive cold. He had forgotten how much he owed his successes,
not only to his consummate military genius, but to the fact that History had fought on the side of the French against reactionaries who
were fighting against History. Russia was not part of that History.
Spain had never really become part of it. In many ways, Spain was
Africa; and certainly, in many ways, Russia was Asia. Britain was
Britain, ruled the waves, loved freedom and a divided Continent.

The long epic was over. The French middle class had triumphed
against both the nobility that had long outlived its function, and
the monarchy that was hoist with its own petar, the system of
Versailles. There would be efforts to go back, but they would regularly precipitate fresh revolt. France ended her terrible struggle

fundamentally strong. Her population, despite the long conscription, had increased. She was wealthier: her productive economic forces had been released by the reforms and Napoleon had made his victims pay for the war. She had her Church, but no longer the powerful Church that Voltaire had feared and hated. She had the monarchy, but one that would assimilate itself more and more to the constitutional monarchy of Britain. She had money, and was making more money, with that powerful bourgeois urge toward prosperity that Balzac would paint so vividly in his novels. She had a clear code of laws, an orderly system of education, and Paris remained the center of Europe's intellectual and artistic life. Along with these solid advantages, she could tell the beads of her great victories: Valmy, Fleurus, Rivoli, the Pyramids, Marengo, Ulm, Austerlitz, Jena, Friedland, Wagram, Borodino — and the black bead of her great defeat at Waterloo.

At Waterloo, after fearful carnage, the Old Guard broke. The first news of Wellington's decisive victory to reach London, the first news that the Century of the Middle Class had now indeed begun, was brought by a homing pigeon to a French speculator on the London Stock Exchange.

XIV.

ENTER THE MACHINE

The dove of peace from Waterloo brought news of death. Not the death of the British infantrymen who stood firm when Napoleon's columns charged: infantrymen could have been replaced; but the death of War, the Purchaser. "On the day on which peace was signed, this great customer of the producer died." The coroner who spoke those words was the famous industrialist Robert Owen. For nearly a quarter of a century England had financed and equipped the armies of Europe. There were even soldiers in the tyrant Napoleon's armies who marched in British boots; for special licenses provided many chinks in Napoleon's Continental System. The British, Napoleon snorted, "were a nation of shopkeepers." They were, retorted the British proudly, "the workshop of the world." With the Great Customer, who had undone so many, now himself undone, Britain entered a postwar depression of a sort no country she had rescued would have to face.

For Britain had undergone during the "World War," a profound economic change. While Europeans gazed, with admiration or with fear, at Paris, heard the Rights of Man proclaimed, watched the liquidation of feudal privilege, beheld the fall of the most famous throne in Christendom, were astounded when the Revolutionary conscripts of the French Republic hurled back the professional armies of Austria and Prussia, hailed or cursed the liberators from France, succumbed to the lightning thrusts of the young Emperor, and rose at last against his tyranny, a less dramatic but more inexorable series of events was taking place in Britain. Britain was harnessing the Machine; or perhaps, the Machine was harnessing Britain. Already, machines were getting more powerful, more dexterous, and more prolific every year. The process was to continue, from then till now. In 1837 a French revolutionary named Blanqui would find a name for the whole complex process, a name that would stick, the "Industrial Revolution." Blanqui himself could not have guessed, of our machines today, how powerful they would be to act, how lightning-swift to think, how fertile to breed other machines, stronger, swifter, more fertile than themselves.

Why did this magical process begin in England, before spreading to Belgium, France, New England, and at last to every continent in the world? England was the first modern state to rid itself of serfdom, the first to abandon the feudal warfare of nobles, the first to check royal absolutism, the first in which the guilds declined, the first to open up, by the Act of Union with Scotland in 1707, a really vast free market for goods, the first to discover that losing political control of colonies is an excellent way to increase trade with them. Now she was the first to adopt the Machine. The acquisition and the increase of wealth had achieved a respectability which, on the Continent, had perhaps been achieved by Holland alone: even the English nobility joined in. The Puritan virtues of thrift and hard work became national ideals. It was the desire to acquire faster that called the machines into being; but the machines, by vastly increasing the rewards of commercial virtue, rendered that virtue even more praiseworthy. Neither the Church nor the Army could compete with the growing passion for business. The Church of England was, indeed, if anything more dormant than the Catholic Church in France, and like the French Church was packed with Deists; while the military virtues could not compete with business in a country without a land frontier. So long as the Navy held the seas, England was safe; and so long as England's merchant fleet carried her trade to seven seas, she could well afford a navy. Meanwhile, England's lively tradition of scientific experimentation supported her technical development, as Francis Bacon had dreamed it might. " Knowledge," Bacon had written, " is power "; and England found that Bacon was right.

Napoleon, unable because of the Channel to get at England with his vast armies, and chased from the seas by Nelson's victory off Trafalgar, tried to break the nation of shopkeepers with his Continental System, a blockade to cut off England from her European customers, and tried to develop a Continental industry that would keep the British broken. But smuggling was rampant, special import licenses had to be granted, the Continental System always leaked, and England had other customers, beyond the seas which she patrolled. Napoleon could not master the economic forces that were loose. England had the goods. The customers wanted the goods. The wars Napoleon himself fought all over Europe made Europe a bad place in which to start new industrial enterprises. Behind the Channel, protected securely by its fleet, lay the workshop of the world, and the voracious demands of war put its forges under forced draft. The workshop called England was not only the arsenal of every Continental people that fought against French tyranny; the profits of the workshop furnished the subsidies that raised coalition after coalition against the French. The workshop was also a bank.

There was, indeed, a dramatic hour when Robert Fulton, the American developer of the steamboat, demonstrated his invention on the Seine, and urged Napoleon to equip his navy with steam. That would have been to harness the Industrial Revolution in his plan to throw an army into England. But Napoleon rejected the project of steaming across the Channel; and the treacherous Channel tides rendered impracticable the thousands of flatboats he had assembled for his army at Boulogne. The hour passed, and he struck at Austria instead.

The French Revolution is a well-ordered French tragedy with a beginning, middle, and end. In some sense, the curtain rises when an absolute Bourbon monarch convokes the Estates-General in 1789; and, in some sense, the curtain falls when Napoleon goes into second exile, and the Bourbon dynasty is a second time restored, in 1815. But the Industrial Revolution has no tidy dates. It sprang from a series of technical devices that began early in the eighteenth century, that followed each other with increasing speed in the 1770's, that increased England's powers of production in geometrical progression, and that still continues throughout Christendom and throughout the world. It is no doubt an exciting dramatic symbol that James Watt took out his first patent for a steam engine in 1769, the year in which that human steam engine, Napoleon Bonaparte, was born. But faulty construction kept the former of these two engines from working. It is a more eloquent symbol that, in 1776, Watt's engine really worked, the American Declaration of Independence was signed, and Adam Smith published *The Wealth of Nations.*

For Adam Smith argued the freedom of the market place for all mankind; the Declaration had been provoked in no small part by barriers to that market place; and the steam engine would go far toward enabling man — or, at least, men who owned steam engines — to establish such a market place. The Declaration vindicated the " natural " rights of man, the political animal. Adam Smith defended his natural rights as a buying and selling animal. " The propensity to truck, barter, and exchange," says Adam Smith, " is common to all men, and to be found in no other race of animals, which seem to know neither this nor any other species of contract."

Fourteen years before these words were published, Rousseau's *Social Contract* had appeared and would become the handbook of the French Revolution. But the *Social Contract* is a political treatise, which rarely touches the production and distribution of material goods. True, in a footnote to the *Social Contract* Rousseau observes drily that " laws are always of use to those who possess and harmful to those who have nothing: from which it follows that the social state is advantageous to men only when all have something and none too much." There is no such heresy in Smith. Smith is a Briton, and John Locke had already, nearly a century ago, vindicated for the Britons the right of self-government that Rousseau was now urging. Smith assumes that right, but he is not writing a treatise on politics; he is writing a treatise on political economy, the first great treatise written on that subject; and the object of political economy, he asserts, is " to enrich both the people and the sovereign." Smith's central thesis is that economic nationalism, the mercantilism that Colbert had made famous in the reign of Louis XIV, and that even Britain practiced, is self-defeating. The whole machinery of monopolies, tariffs, bounties, and embargoes, ostensibly set up to bring gold and silver into a country and therefore to enrich it, Smith found a dangerous fraud. Gold and silver are not wealth, but the medium by which wealth circulates, and they will flow naturally to wherever business thrives and therefore can employ them. Government ought to let business alone, ought to let its citizens buy wherever they can buy cheapest and sell wherever they can sell dearest, ought to let men follow their own economic self-interest. Freed of government interference, the individual, with his natural propensity to truck, barter, and exchange, is "led by an invisible hand to promote an end which was no part of his intention. By pursuing his own interest he frequently promotes that of the society more effectually than when he really intends to promote it. I have never known much good done by those who affected to trade for the public good. It is an affectation, indeed, not very common among merchants, and very few words need be employed in dissuading them from it."

This doctrine of "let alone," of laissez-faire, had already been preached in France by a group known as "the Economists." But, precisely because it was nearer being practised in England than in France or anywhere else in Europe, Smith was able to observe what an economic heaven on earth laissez-faire in purer form might bring. His book therefore became the Bible of the new class of manufacturers that the new machines would bring into being. He agrees with the medieval schoolman that what gives objects their economic value is the human labor expended on them, but he substitutes for the medieval just price the price the traffic will bear, and this he thinks will be determined by the law of supply and demand. For the vision of the City of God, in which all men pray, for the vision of the City of Man in which all men vote, he substitutes the vision of "the great mercantile republic," the world market, composed of all men everywhere who follow their natural propensity to truck, barter, and exchange — and thereby to help each other. For commerce, he holds, "ought naturally to be, among nations, as among individuals, a bond of union and friendship...." For each buyer and seller to follow his own interest seems to him the only intelligent and self-respecting way of achieving the common good of the economic community. Observing dispassionately both himself and his neighbors, he notes that " man has almost constant occasion for the help of his brethren, and it is in vain for him to expect it from their benevolence only....It is not from the benevolence of the butcher, the brewer, or the baker that we expect our dinner, but from their regard to their own interest....Nobody but a beggar chooses to depend chiefly upon the benevolence of his fellow-citizens."

If " an invisible hand," however, is to guide us self-seeking buyers and sellers to a common good, there must not only be no interference from government; there must be none from private monopoly. Smith defends what the modern businessman calls " free enterprise." But his most acid comments are reserved for the way in which businessmen normally try to abuse their economic freedom, principally by establishing monopoly, " a monopoly against their countrymen." A tariff on imports, for example, is simply " a monopoly of the home market." Monopolies keep the invisible hand from conducting us to the common good.

Certainly, if any hand conducted England toward the common good, in the early stages of the Industrial Revolution, it remained modestly invisible, as well as shockingly inept. Adam Smith might properly retort that neither in England nor anywhere else have his principles really been applied. But his faith in economic self-interest was eagerly seized on by those who built England's first factories. And that self-interest wrote some of the darkest pages of human history. The medieval industrial guilds had long ago been twisted by the self-interest of the masters into monopolies to exploit apprentice and journeyman alike. The so-called domestic system that replaced the guild enabled men with capital to buy raw material, such for example as wool, and " put it out " to spinners or weavers in their own cottages, on a piecework basis. Pay was often bad, but the cottager and his family could supplement that pay by garden plots. Then the Machine came. In the early stages it was often driven by animal power, sometimes by actual " horsepower." But more and more, it was installed in increasingly large buildings, the new factories, at points where water power was available. Frequently the need for water power established factories where labor was scarce, and the countryside was scoured for any human riffraff that could be coaxed there and roughly housed. Moreover, this power fluctuated with the condition of the rivers: when it was available, all hands were pushed for long hours to take advantage of the available power. This would have been bad enough with men workers. But the new machines could often be tended as well by women and children as by men. Some of them could be better tended by them: children could get into positions that men workers could not or would not assume. For textiles, their fingers were conveniently small. And children were flowing to the new " mills." For the factory owners were quick to discover a new source of labor. The system of poor relief placed upon each Church parish responsibility for caring for its own poor. Parishes discovered that they could " apprentice " even very small children to the new factories and get rid of the cost of caring for them. If their parents were on relief, the children were taken from them and carted off to the factories. Parishes sometimes stipulated the proportion of idiot children the manufacturer would accept. Children four, five, or six years old often worked in the factories twelve hours or more a day, and might in rush periods work eighteen. The lash had to be used, if only to keep these tots awake. At the end of the day the smaller ones might be collected from the corners where they had fallen exhausted. Accidents were under these conditions frequent. At night the children were locked in workhouses to keep them from escaping from this hell. Cotton mills had to be kept moist and the day's work often left the mill hands soaked with sweat so that their clothes would freeze to their backs on the way home to their sleeping quarters. Frequently they were forced to take the midday meal while working, and frequently they had to clean the machines while in motion. Understandably, such work killed many of them, or deformed them, or left them tubercular wrecks.

But once these mills got going, they could produce cloth that would undersell anything a weaver could make in his cottage, and still leave an exciting profit that goaded the owner to lengthen hours and to speed up machinery. The invention of the steam engine put a new and more trustworthy form of power in the owner's hands: factories now tended to be located where coal could be had cheap. The hand weaver, driven to the wall, had to seek work in the new and hated factories. He could not always find work there, but his children generally could. There was no use paying a man a wage that would allow him to bring up a family, if each child, on a far smaller wage, could earn his own way. So the invisible hand guided more and more small children into the new and smoking hells of the Industrial Revolution. By a cruel irony, the very fact that children could earn their way gave rise to larger families, and a new class came into being, the servants of the Machine. Men, women, and children, herded into foul and unsanitary slums, old before their time, victims of alcohol or drugs, sexually promiscuous, stupid from overwork, a horror and a rebuke to the society around them, the new class served the Machine.

As the new industrial population grew, there appeared a vast new home market for agriculture. To take advantage of that market landowners improved their methods and sought to enlarge their holdings. Parliament was under constant pressure to push faster the Land Enclosure Acts which had begun in the sixteenth century with the shift from crops to sheep; and Parliament responded heartily to that pressure. Land that had been held manorially and in common was fenced off and farmed intensively. Agricultural production soared, while the cottagers who were squeezed out by the shift drifted to the towns to increase the supply of human labor power available to the new machines.

Slowly but inexorably the Machine harnessed England. There were, of course, protests. Among the governing class and landed gentry there were men who were horrified by the gross brutality of the factory system and who despised the upstart factory owners whose greed was the apparent cause of that brutality. Among the factory owners themselves there were men who were revolted by this new state of affairs but who, early in the game, felt themselves crowded by business competition into practices they abhorred. Above all, there were protests from the new class of slaves to the Machine. For the Machine was not only devouring workers and destroying the family life of the poor; it was competing with workers, throwing them out of work, leaving them to starve. In 1811 and 1812 occurred the famous Luddite Riots, in the woolen industry in Yorkshire, in hosiery knitting in Nottinghamshire, amid the new power looms for cotton goods in Lancashire. Bands of workers visited the factories and smashed the new machines.

The House of Lords was determined there should be no violence against the sacred rights of property. An act was proposed that a man should pay for the machine he destroyed with his life. The poet Byron attacked the act: it was his maiden speech in the Lords. But the act passed. That was the year that Napoleon, master of all Western Europe, marched on Moscow, partly to force Russia to observe the Continental System excluding British goods from market. It was not a time to tolerate assaults by workers on the source of England's new wealth.

Indeed, the economic and military competition between the national states lent a patriotic air to the mercantilism Adam Smith so hated. With England fighting for her existence against a tyrant striving for world conquest, it made sense to prohibit men legally from taking a machine out of England. It made sense too that those who knew how to make them should be forbidden to emigrate. As early as 1719 the efforts of Peter the Great to secure English workmen to start an iron industry in Russia led to an Act of Parliament "to prevent the Inconveniencies arising from seducing Artificers in the Manufactures of Great Britain into foreign Parts." In 1775 this same Russia offered James Watt £1,000 a year, a salary he had never dreamed of earning, to come to Russia and build steam engines. The emigration of skilled mechanics was forbidden until 1824. Particularly during the Napoleonic War the common good of all required Parliament to protect England's monopoly of machine production. That is, the common good of all His Majesty's subjects, which was the only common good Parliament felt responsible for. It felt in no position to protect the common good of Smith's "great mercantile republic," the buying and selling community of all mankind. This nationalism was to accompany the Industrial Revolution permanently. In 1833 a bill to limit factory labor to ten hours was under debate: the bill's opponents, observed Cobbett, had discovered that England's manufacturing supremacy depended on 30,000 little girls. No doubt there was some hypocrisy in this reasoning; but there seems little doubt either that many Englishmen did fear what the Machine might do if children were not fed to it. It might really emigrate to less moral lands, leaving the tall new smokestacks standing as a memorial of its passage under a frighteningly smokeless sky. Meanwhile, so many investors had acquired an equity in the factory system as operated that property rights had to be looked to. The same argument had been used about the abolition of the African slave trade, of which Britain had acquired a larger share than any other nation. In the decade beginning with 1783 Liverpool slaving ships carried over 300,000 Negro slaves to the West Indies; and a Liverpool Member of Parliament declared that while nobody would now introduce such a trade, yet so many interests and so much property now depended upon it that no equitable person would abolish it. The factory system too was a vested interest.

If Parliament betrayed Smith's doctrine of laissez-faire when it came to the export of machines or the emigration of skilled mechanics, it remained faithful to his doctrine of the invisible hand on the domestic scene. Let the manufacturer and the factory hand each look to his own self-interest. Let them strike a free bargain. For decades any combination of workmen for collective bargaining was forbidden by law. This would be a monopoly, and would do violence to free competition. True, Adam Smith had pointed out that the "masters" — the business enterprisers — will always secretly combine to keep wages down. But Adam Smith believed that a "thriving" or expanding economy, in which labor was in increasing demand, was the only real hope for the wage-earner. The Reverend Thomas Malthus was less hopeful: population would always press on subsistence. The poor must either stop breeding, or else their number would be cut by famine, war, or pestilence. The economist David Ricardo announced "the iron law of wages," which made it utterly impossible for the laboring class to earn more than bare subsistence. The economic process was viewed as mechanical and inexorable, like the Machine itself. The Machine was making England richer and richer. It would keep on doing so, if no bungling humanitarianism caused men to disobey the economic laws it laid down.

Against this do-nothing acceptance of the social anarchy the Industrial Revolution had brought to Britain, arose protesting voices, and of those voices the most interesting was that of Robert Owen. Owen was born, the son of a saddler and ironmonger, in a small Welsh town that wore the auspicious name, Newtown. He was born in 1771, in the period when Hargreaves' spinning jenny, Crompton's mule, Cartwright's power loom, and Watt's steam engine were also being born. His schoolmaster, Mr. Thickness, lived up to his name; but Owen learned to read, write, and reckon, and became his teacher's assistant at seven. At nine he went to work in a draper's shop, and at ten he was allowed to leave for London and his brother's, with forty shillings in his pocket. He worked for a draper in Lincolnshire, and for a bigger draper on Old London Bridge; and at eighteen, with an all-around knowledge of fabrics, and with little interest in the French Revolution that had just broken out, Owen borrowed a hundred pounds from his brother and was employing forty men, in a little factory in Manchester, to manufacture the new cotton-spinning "mules." At twenty he was manager of a cotton mill in Manchester and in charge of five hundred workers. In 1800 he was the manager and one of the owners of a cotton mill that would become world famous, at New Lanark, near Glasgow. Visitors from all over the world made pilgrimages to New Lanark, to witness a new kind of factory management. Owen took a typical industrial hell-hole and turned it into a decent place to live and work. He found between four and five hundred of the little parish apprentices, aged from five to ten, among his work force. He engaged no more of them.

Firmly and early convinced that environment and education can produce any kind of character desired, unmoved by the contention that the poor preferred drunkenness and filth, Owen built and operated for the children of his employees a school that became famous. During the years to come, he demonstrated that he could make manufacturing pay without degrading his workers, but he did not succeed in convincing his partners that he could treat his workmen decently and still make the mammoth profits of the early Industrial Revolution. He bought his partners out and formed a new partnership. But eventually the new partners too objected to his labor policy. They insisted on an auction of the mills, circulated reports that the mills were doing badly, planned to buy them in cheap. Owen meanwhile collected a group of new partners, this time men who shared his interest in conducting a model factory, a group that included several Quakers and the famous Utilitarian, Jeremy Bentham. The new partnership outbid the scheming ex-partners at the auction in Glasgow, bought in the mills, and set out shortly for New Lanark. Near Lanark a great shout arose and a multitude came running toward them, to the great alarm of Owen's peaceable new

Quaker partners. They made the postilions untrace the horses and themselves dragged the carriage into Lanark. Then the triumphal procession went to the mill town of New Lanark, paraded through the streets, and joyfully deposited Owen and his new partners at his home. They were only mill hands and this was only a public post they dragged. Bolivar was drawn into his native Caracas in a Roman chariot by twelve young girls. But this too was the triumph of a " Liberator."

Owen appealed to the governing class and Parliament to better factory conditions. When the war ended in 1815 and factory unemployment assumed frightening proportions, Owen urged England to face the new problems the Machine had set it and proposed a solution. Instead of meeting unemployment with poor relief, leaving the displaced workers idle and unproductive, Parliament or private initiative or both should set up co-operative villages, where some 1,200 persons could produce for their own use, selling what surplus they could. Owen had reversed the laissez-faire policy of letting the Machine dictate the shape of society. He proposed to plan a humane society that could use the Machine as its servant; and his highly successful management of the New Lanark mills convinced him and many others besides him that the solution was practicable. But it did not convince enough persons; and once Owen became persuaded that the governing class would do nothing, he turned to the laboring class itself, and became, not merely the founder of British Socialism, but the pioneer of the Trades Union movement and the pioneer of the Co-operative movement.

The rest of his life he devoted increasingly to his efforts to reform the new society which the Machine had brought into being. He dreamed of a Co-operative Commonwealth that would eliminate the rivalries of class, creed, and country. Efforts to reform Parliament and extend the suffrage did not interest him much. The problem was one of machine production, and one of universal education. It could be solved if men quit their defeatism. He attacked the " natural " law of supply and demand, as being essentially artificial. He attacked Malthus' statement that population must always press on subsistence. He knew from years of practical experience what a cornucopia of abundance the Machine could be. Production was not the problem: distribution was. The Radical Cobbett could scream his mockery at his Co-operative Villages, at "Mr. Owen's parallelograms of paupers." He went to America, and tried to establish one of his Villages, at New Harmony, Indiana, and lost four-fifths of his considerable fortune in the attempt. He founded innumerable societies to promulgate his views, published and lectured in England and America. "Owenite" societies sprang up all over England. He saw in organized religion only obfuscation and mutual recrimination; and, in a speech at London in 1817, he suddenly declared: " I am not of your religion, nor of any religion yet taught in the world."

This was not wholly true. He had a kind of religion, a vaguely deistic religion of Humanitarianism, that had already flowered, unobserved by Owen, in the French Revolution. One of his associates would later recognize that Owen's " Communities " were " a religion of industry." Lessons from one of his writings, " The Book of the New Moral World," were read in Owenite " Halls " and Owenite "Institutes." The Owenites even called their brotherhood the "Rational Society " and established " Rational Churches." When he was eighty-two he turned to Spiritualism and conversed familiarly with Jefferson, Franklin, Shakespeare, Shelley, Napoleon, the Duke of Wellington, the prophet Daniel, and most often with his old friend and earlier colleague in reform, the Duke of Kent. This, say his admirers, was merely dotage. No doubt; but not everybody who attains to dotage turns to Spiritualism. And it is deeply characteristic of Owen's childlike, loving heart, that not even Death himself could cut off the other members of his Co-operative Commonwealth, a Commonwealth to be built on the rock of mutual help, where the " great mercantile republic " of Smith was built on the shifting sands of enlightened self-interest.

Karl Marx was a humanitarian too, though not a Deist. During the years of Owen's decline, Marx was toiling in the Library of the British Museum, where the records of Parliamentary inquiries into factory conditions were slowly falling into place in his heavily documented, deeply Germanic, brilliant, and angry book, *Capital*. Owen had tried, in vain, to persuade the governing class to guide the Industrial Revolution into serving the whole community. Marx devotes none of his massive eloquence to what he considers a hopeless task. Society, he observes, is finally divided into only two classes, the rich and the poor, those who own the means of production and those who own nothing but their "labor power." Individuals like Owen may act disinterestedly: classes never do. In the French Revolution, the middle class — the moneyed class, the townsmen, the burghers, the bourgeois — rose and overthrew by force the feudal nobility that had oppressed them. This bourgeoisie now controls modern society, and faces with deep antagonism a rapidly growing class of propertyless laborers, the proletariat. Between them there is class war, as there was class war between nobility and bourgeoisie. The system of production, which at every point in history determines all human institutions, legal, cultural, and even religious, is now no longer the feudal system but the capitalist system. And capital is not money, or even what Adam Smith calls "stock." Capital is "a social relation between persons, and a relation determined by things," a relation of economic exploiter and exploited. Wealth becomes capital only when it is used to multiply itself.

The Machine, Marx holds, has vastly increased this power of multiplication. It destroys the free craftsman, who sells the fruit of his labor and skill, and creates a proletariat, a class of unskilled "hands," whose job is the simple and specialized one of tending some portion of the machine. Because the capitalist class pockets most of the value created by the labor of the proletariat, in the name of profit, the laboring class cannot as a class buy back the commodities its labor creates. This leads to the constant threat of "overproduction," which, as Owen had already seen, does not mean that society has too many commodities, or even enough, but that those who need them cannot pay for them. This fundamental contradiction in the system, Marx contends, leads to recurrent crises and depressions, ever more violent as society becomes more and more highly industrialized, and as capital concentrates in fewer and fewer hands. In the end, these crises will become intolerable; and the proletariat, a class brought into being by the Machine and partly recruited from those of the capitalist exploiters who have been squeezed out by bigger capitalists, will inevitably expropriate for the benefit of the workers the means of production. Marx shows with documentation in what sense the present capitalists have previously expropriated the free peasant and the free worker.

This revolution of the proletariat against the bourgeoisie, Marx holds, will inevitably occur. All the workers can do about it is to speed up their deliverance. To do this, they cannot depend on capitalists like Owen, no matter how well-intentioned; any more than the bourgeoisie had been able to count on nobles like Lafayette or Mirabeau in the French Revolution. They must become class-conscious, they must unite their forces in order to make up by their numbers for the meagerness of their individual resources, they must form a new party, to create a new world, a world of economic as well as political freedom, whose foreordained citizens will be all men everywhere who earn their bread in the sweat of their face. The whole of existing civilization is a creation of the bourgeoisie, and must be replaced. Existing national states, with their capitalistic governments, their " liberal " policies, and their necessary and merciless fight for markets, are bourgeois creations too. Hence national patriotism is bourgeois. The proletarian's loyalty must be, not to the bourgeois state, but to the international society of the future. Where Owen pled for understanding between classes, Marx taught the duty of the proletariat to hate its oppressors, and to plan ceaselessly for the day of revolt and freedom. That final triumph will be unlike the triumph of the bourgeoisie in the French Revolution. Then the bourgeoisie, aided by an embryonic proletariat, had overthrown the feudal nobility; but there still remained two classes, bourgeoisie and proletariat, to continue history's persistent war of classes. When the bourgeoisie is destroyed, only one class, for the first time in history, will be left: the class of workers, the proletariat.

The French Revolution was an open, heroic assault on intolerable social ills. It called on men everywhere to risk their lives in a revolt for the liberty of all men against a decaying system of absolute monarchy, for the equality of all men against a decaying system of feudal privilege, for the fraternity of all men against dynastic war. It sacrificed some of its liberty to the autocratic government of Napoleon in an effort to guarantee its newly won equality against counterrevolution. And its spirit of fraternity was hammered on the anvil of war into the spirit of nationalism, in France and in the countries she had " liberated." But the Revolution was a socially responsible attack on social irresponsibility.

The Industrial Revolution, by contrast, was in its essence socially irresponsible. It was subterranean, impersonal, anonymous, self-seeking, ambiguous, hypocritical. Robert Owen and many others tried to give it social purpose, tried to make it socially responsible. They failed. The story of that failure was repeated, wherever the Industrial Revolution spread: to Belgium, France, Germany, New England, the world. Owen called frantically on England and all Christendom to use the Machine and not be used by it. Too few heeded. The Machine had taken those who failed to heed into an exceeding high mountain and had showed them all the kingdoms of the world. They fell down and worshiped. Many heroic men and women in England strove heroically to persuade Parliament that the working class should be protected against the economic anarchy that the early manufacturers demanded in the name of freedom. To some extent they succeeded in alleviating the miseries of those whose lives the Machine devoured.

Marx grimly welcomed the chaos: it would concentrate capital, it would teach the workers the discipline of social production, it would torment them into the revolt without which history could not achieve a classless society. The self-interest of the capitalist, which Smith had accepted as inevitable and even defended, Marx considered inevitable too. But he trusted to the self-interest of a growing new proletariat to smash the capitalist when he had performed his historic function.

The surrender of the human will to the will of the Machine produced some curious and unlovely results. For was it not fundamentally this surrender that made the Victorian era reek of a new moral hypocrisy, a false sentimentality, an esthetic vulgarity? May not smug respectability, a reverence for money, and a genius for passing by on the other side and for looking the other way have been the well-nigh inevitable results of accepting (with what a sigh of regret!) the tyranny of the Machine and the doctrine that man, or at least a poor man, is a commodity in the market place, a thing to be bought and sold, a means and not an end?

Paradoxically, the Industrial Revolution came upon England too rapidly for men to understand its threat and too slowly and gradually and furtively to shock them into a full recognition. So much of it was private. So much of it took place in the factory, in what Marx would call " the hidden abode of production, on whose threshold

there stares us in the face 'No admittance except on business.' "
Adam Smith wrote too early to get a look into that hidden abode,
and what went on there never received its due share of publicity. It
is only fair to say that most people did not understand the Machine.
But Robert Owen did.

XV.

NEW NATION-STATES

THE French Revolution and the Industrial Revolution, between them, ushered in the tempestuous and tormented Age of Isms, an age in which our own generation flounders still: Industrialism, Capitalism, Socialism, Communism, Liberalism, Clericalism, Romanticism, Humanitarianism, Nationalism, Militarism, Imperialism. And these Ideas, or Ideals, or Ideologies (it was the French Revolution that invented the word ideology) wrangle with one another as the Greek gods wrangled on Mount Olympus and incite men against one another, as the gods incited the armies that fought on the plains of Troy. It is these godlike Isms that give the history of our age a certain dryness and make it oscillate between the sentimental and the brutal. It is these Isms that have made so many of its men and women into Ists.

The nineteenth century is an explosive and feverish century. If we make it begin at Waterloo in 1815, with the roar of the artillery which Napoleon was the first to mass heavily; if we make it end with 1914, with the crash and din of the German march through Belgium; its great punctuation marks are the Revolution of 1830, the Revolution of 1848, and the Franco-Prussian War of 1870 that unified modern Germany and delivered to modern Italy its capital,

Rome, at last. The Revolution of 1830 first broke out in Paris, before it swept through Europe. So did the Revolution of 1848. And the Prussian Bismarck saw to it that it would be Paris that declared war in 1870. The chronology of the period, 1815–1870, organizes itself most conveniently around the history of France and France's capital, which was still the cultural capital of Christendom itself. After 1870, Europe revolves around Berlin.

With the defeat and abdication of the great Napoleon, the victorious Allies produced another Bourbon king for France, the brother of the guillotined Louis XVI. The Republic, which had lasted from 1792 to 1804, was ignored. So was the reign of the Emperor Napoleon, from 1804 to 1814, when Napoleon was exiled to Elba. The Dauphin, the son of Louis XVI, who had died without reigning, was considered to have been Louis XVII; so the Bourbon brother was placed on the throne as Louis XVIII. He was succeeded in 1824 by a second and more foolish brother, Charles X. Under the Bourbon Restoration, the tricolor flag that had been carried across Europe by the Republican and Napoleonic armies, was abolished, and the white banner of the Bourbons was imposed as the flag of France. The Revolution had changed the royal title from "King of France," a feudal title based on the assumption that all the land in France was held ultimately from the king, to "King of the French," a title based on the Revolutionary assumption that the King was the leader of those who actually owned France. The Restoration restored the title "King of France." In place of the Constitution of 1791, written by the National Constituent Assembly; in place of the Constitution of 1795, written by the National Convention; in place of the Constitutions, confirmed by national plebiscites, that set up the Consulate and then the Empire; the King now granted a "Charter." For he did not admit that he ruled by the will of the people. He ruled, like his ancestors, by the grace of God, and because — to use the word that Talleyrand persuaded the victorious Allies to erect into a principle for restoring order throughout Europe — he was the "legitimate" ruler of France. All over Europe, the "legitimate" monarchs returned to their thrones, from which they had been chased by the Revolution or by Napoleon. And all over Europe they too concerned themselves with symbols that would turn the clock back to the good old days of the eighteenth century.

Against the stupidity and stubbornness of Charles X, in July, 1830, Paris rose; and the " July Revolution " chased him into second exile. On his throne it placed Louis Philippe, his cousin of the House of Orleans, whose father, under the name, " Philip Equality," had fought in the Revolutionary armies under the tricolor flag; and that flag was now restored. Now the son ruled, but as " King of the French " and by virtue of a Charter which he did not grant but which he accepted. The " July Monarchy " was a liberal, bourgeois monarchy. Those who set it up were the propertied class, but not merely the large landowners favored by Charles X. Freedom of the press, abolished by Charles X, was restored. The growing economic power of the Church was checked; and its influence over education was diminished. France withdrew from the " Conservative Alliance," under which she had joined Russia, Austria, Prussia, and Great Britain in maintaining order in Europe, and under which the Restored Bourbon monarchy had even put down a revolution in Spain. But when the July Revolution spread to various states in Italy and in Germany, to Belgium, and to Poland, the new French government made it clear that there would be no new crusade like that of the French Republic, to " liberate " the oppressed. It was too anxious to avoid intervention by the great powers in France itself.

The July Monarchy of Louis Philippe set out to conserve the gains of the Great Revolution, with its " liberal " political institutions. To conserve those gains, the French had turned to Napoleon, as First Consul. But the military crusade he inherited and deliberately expanded, first furnished Napoleon with justifications for suppressing civil and political liberties, and finally brought the defeat of France and the Restoration of the Bourbon dynasty. Louis XVIII governed wisely; but Charles X fought liberalism, fought constitutional government ("I would rather saw wood than be a king like the King of England "), compensated the émigré nobility that had now returned to France after aiding her enemies throughout Europe, and strengthened the Church, with its traditional hatred of the Revolution. The July Revolution was France's answer. Louis Philippe carefully refrained from the ideological extravagances of the Republic, from the military ambitions of Napoleon, and guaranteed the liberties Napoleon had suppressed. The Great Revolution had been saved.

But Louis Philippe also exploited the Industrial Revolution, which had spread to France under the Bourbon Restoration. Factories rapidly multiplied. And since the French Revolution had swept away internal tariffs, and since the population of France was still greater than Britain's, though growing more slowly, the new factories, protected by national tariffs, operated in the largest free market in the world. Wealth grew fast. Yet it was largely the Industrial Revolution that undid the "Bourgeois King." The city proletariat of wage-earners which it promptly created suffered the same horrors from which Reform was now rescuing the same class in Britain. They would find leaders in the intellectual classes that could not meet the high property qualification of the July Monarchy. These latter complained to the minister, Guizot, that only the rich could vote. "Then, get rich," was his reply — and it was the reply of the July Monarchy to evil in general. In addition to these leaders, the proletariat would find at least temporary allies in the "clericals," the "ultramontanes," those who sought to increase the political power of the Church and who were accused of receiving their orders from "beyond the mountains," from the Pope. The clericals were particularly concerned to rescue public education from the Voltairian liberalism of the July Monarchy.

Meanwhile, the Industrial Revolution went on undermining the government that had promoted it. Wealth grew; misery grew. In 1842, six years before the explosion, Heinrich Heine wrote as Paris correspondent to an Augsburg paper:

Everything is as quiet as a winter's night after a new fall of snow. But in the silence you hear continually dripping, dripping, the profits of the capitalist, as they steadily increase. You can actually hear them piling up — the riches of the rich. Sometimes there is the smothered sob of poverty, and often, too, a scraping sound, like a knife being sharpened.

And, again, less metaphorically:

Today, when I visited some of the factories in the Faubourg Saint-Marceau and discovered there what kind of reading matter was being spread among the workingmen, who are the most powerful element among the lower classes, I thought of Sancho's proverb, "Tell me what you have sown today, and I will predict to you what you will reap tomorrow." For here in the workshops I found several new editions of speeches by old Robespierre, Marat's pamphlets at two sous a copy, Cabet's *History of the Revolution,* Cormenin's poisonous little works, and Buonarotti's *Babeuf's Doctrine and Conspiracy* — all writings which smell of blood. The songs which I heard them singing seemed to have been composed in hell and had a chorus of the wildest excitement. Really, people in our gentle walks of life can form no idea of the demonic note which runs through these songs. One must hear them with one's own ears, for example, in those enormous workshops where the metals are worked and where the half-naked, defiant figures keep time to their songs with the mighty blows which their great iron hammers strike upon the ringing anvil. ... Sooner or later the harvest which will come from this sowing in France threatens to be a republican outbreak.

In 1848 the republican outbreak came. Students and workingmen clashed with government troops in Paris, barricades were thrown up, the July Monarchy crashed, and the Second Republic emerged. It emerged self-consciously and according to the book. Historians like Michelet had recently told the detailed story of the Great Revolution; and in 1848 the terminology and even the leading events are repeated as if the actors were real actors with real script to follow. After all, by now Frenchmen had a Great Tradition to follow in the matter of revolutions. But, although there was the same concern with symbols, including flags, the argument this time was not between the white banner of the Bourbons and the tricolor of the Republic: it was between the tricolor and the red flag of the Paris workingmen. It was the spread of this new revolution to Germany that brought Marx and Engels hurrying back from England to issue their *Communist Manifesto*. For this revolution was socialistic at the barricades, and partly socialistic even in the Provisional Government that would set up the Second Republic. The first and " Great " French Revolution, confronted with the extremist proposals of the Paris proletariat led by Babeuf, had stamped out his movement and triumphed over " the conspiracy of Babeuf " — about which Heine's factory hands had been reading. Even in 1830, when the July Revolution had spread to Belgium, whence the new British steam machines had spread earlier than to France, there were not many machines for the workingmen to smash. And a bourgeois National Guard could organize to defend Brussels from the common enemy, the Dutch, and ambidextrously " defend property " against their

272   THE PILGRIMAGE OF WESTERN MAN

overenthusiastic fellow-revolutionaries. The leader of the machine-wreckers was hurriedly sentenced to twenty years, without seriously interrupting the march of Liberty and national independence.

But by 1848, in Paris, the proletarians were both more numerous than the Belgian workers had been and more class-conscious. Their leaders, like Louis Blanc, were determined that the bourgeois liberals should not use them for the dirty work at the barricades and then shove them and their new problems aside when the drafting of a constitution should begin. The right to work, which had indeed been recognized by the Great Revolution, now had teeth put in it: Blanc saw to it that "national workshops" should be planned to care for unemployment. But the teeth turned out to be false teeth: the antisocialist ministers saw to it that the workshops would be sabotaged, and 100,000 workmen were set to work digging up, for no purpose whatever, the Champ de Mars — the Champ de Mars, that "Field of Union" to which their hero, "old Robespierre," had marched in procession more than half a century before.

The Revolution had produced an economic crisis; taxes were rising, and the peasants were horrified by an army of paid workers digging in the ground with no purpose except their wage. The antisocialists in the Provisional Government had seen to it that government work would be useless work. When the new National Constituent Assembly met, it was thoroughly antisocialist. The workingmen, recognizing that they had been tricked, revolted, threw up barricades again, and some 70,000 defended them to the cry of "Liberty or Death." From the troops which the government called out, several thousand got death and several thousand got deportation. From then on, the socialists hated the Second Republic, and the antisocialists wondered if it would be strong enough to govern without a military dictatorship.

Although no foreign foes threatened the new government as when Napoleon rose to power, the fear of domestic disorder that had helped him rise, again gripped France. And a "Napoleon" stepped forward. He was Louis Napoleon, son of the great Napoleon's brother Louis, who had reigned briefly as King of Holland in the great days of the Emperor. He had published a book on *Napoleonic Ideas*. He had led an insurrection against Louis Philippe, been deported to America, led another one, been condemned to life imprisonment, and had escaped to England. With the fall of Louis Philippe, he hurried to Paris, and within less than a year had been elected the first president of the Second Republic. It took the new President three years of manipulation to secure control of the government; to shoot, exile, or intern his opponents; and to win, by an overwhelming plebiscite, the title of Emperor. Just as Louis XVIII in 1814 ignored the First Republic and the Emperor Napoleon I, and pretended the Dauphin had reigned as Louis XVII, so now Louis Napoleon ignored the Bourbons of the Restoration and Louis Philippe alike, pretended that Napoleon's son had reigned as Napoleon II, and himself took the title Napoleon III. The "Second Empire" had succeeded to the Second Republic. It would endure until Bismarck and the Franco-Prussian War would destroy it, and would be succeeded in 1871 by the Third Republic. That, in turn, would endure until Hitler's Reich would overwhelm it.

"The Empire means peace, my conquests must be of an economic nature," President Bonaparte had promised. But the forces that Napoleon III shortly faced, made that promise hard to redeem. He had inherited from the Great Revolution a religion of Liberty in which he had genuinely believed, and that belief was confirmed by the chilly reception the Second Empire received from the conservative monarchs of Europe. But French liberals, like Victor Hugo, who had gone into exile, could not forgive the Emperor's assassination of the Second Republic. The socialists hated him too. The clericals, strengthened now by the fright of a part of the middle class who turned to a restoration of Church power as a bulwark against socialism, knew the Emperor was no clerical. To strengthen his dubious claims to power, he appealed to nationalism: he sought popularity and prestige in successful military ventures. It was basically that need for prestige that released the violence of war in Christendom again.

Ever since the Congress of Vienna in 1815 Christendom had enjoyed a relative peace after the frightful wars of the Revolution and Napoleon. At that Congress the Emperor of Austria and the King of Prussia had joined the Czar in a "Holy Alliance" to keep down revolution in the name of the Holy Trinity, and to intervene wherever revolution might show its head. Britain joined the three conservative powers in a Quadruple Alliance "for the peace of Europe"; and, after a period of probation, France joined too. Indeed, in 1822,

Of the four men, Cavour alone was successful, and more than successful, in reaching his goal. The risings throughout Italy that followed the February Revolution of 1848 had been crushed. Austria had reconquered Venetia and Lombardy and had overwhelmed the little army of Piedmont that had attempted to rescue them. The Pope, good Italian that he was, sent soldiers to help Lombardy; and then, good pope that he was, thought better of his attack on a Catholic power and precipitately withdrew. A rising in Rome caused him to flee to Naples, and the revolutionaries proclaimed the Roman Republic. Mazzini, who had lived in exile for seventeen years, conspiring and propagandizing, hurried to Rome, and was chosen a member of the " Triumvirate," the executive branch of the new government. Garibaldi was its general. But Catholics throughout Europe were scandalized. And President Bonaparte, of France's new Second Republic, was looking for French Catholic votes. He therefore sent French troops against Rome, and destroyed the sister republic. Both Mazzini the Triumvir, and Garibaldi the general, wanted the government and the army to take to the hills and fight a guerrilla war; but the legislative refused. On the eve of the French entry into the city, in the Piazza before St. Peter's, Garibaldi reviewed his little army. Seated on his horse, he cried: " Let those who wish to continue the war against the foreigner, come with me. I offer neither pay, nor quarters, nor provisions; I offer hunger, thirst, forced marches, battles, and death." Some four thousand followed. Order, of the Austrian variety, was soon restored throughout the peninsula. Piedmont was crushed; its king had abdicated; but his son, Victor Emmanuel II, steadfastly refused Austria's demand that he rescind the new and liberal constitution his father had recently granted. On that constitution, and on the new liberal state it symbolized, Cavour as prime minister would build the Kingdom of Italy.

When Great Britain and France in 1854 entered the Crimean War to protect Turkey against Russia, little Piedmont sent help, for no other reason than to get " the Italian question " aired at the Peace Conference and to place the liberal Western powers under obligations to Piedmont in her coming struggle with Austria. Mazzini, again in London exile, denounced these jackal tactics; but Cavour got his way. In 1859 Louis Napoleon helped Piedmont drive Austria out of Lombardy, although he made peace before Venetia too could be won. Tuscany, Modena, Parma, and the northern portion of the Papal States rose, and requested annexation to Piedmont. Napoleon III agreed to the annexations, in return for the cession to France of Savoy and Nice. Cavour secretly encouraged Garibaldi and his Thousand Redshirts to sail from Genoa and liberate Sicily and the South from their Bourbon tyrant. A plebiscite annexed these Bourbon lands to Piedmont. The Papal States were eager to join too; the Piedmontese drove out the weak army of the Pope, held a plebiscite, and annexed all but the Patrimony of St. Peter — Rome and a small territory around it. Venetia was also still missing. Shortly thereafter Cavour died. But in 1866, when Bismarck threw Prussia against the Austrian Empire, the new "Kingdom of Italy" sided with Prussia and, although badly defeated in the field, was rewarded with Venetia. Napoleon III, still with one eye on clerical support, guarded Rome; but when Bismarck's Prussia fell on France in 1870, the French troops in Rome were needed for more serious business. Italy thereupon seized Rome, left the Pope in the Vatican, and proclaimed Rome her capital.

The birth of Italy left Mazzini cold. He had wanted, not merely a politically united territory, but the moral and political regeneration of the Italian people through their own effort, without playing jackal to France and Prussia. He also wanted a democratic republic. In short, he wanted the triumph, not of cleverness, but of heroism. For Mazzini was looking beyond Italy to a decadent Europe that he believed a democratic Italian Republic could save for "God and the People." That was why, in his youth, as a hunted exile, he had founded "Young Italy," a society whose membership would be secret, as was the membership of the Carbonari to which he — and Louis Napoleon, long before — had belonged, but whose program was public. That was why, in Switzerland, he had persuaded other exiles to form Young Germany, Young Poland, and above all Young Europe. That was why he later formed the Peoples' International League, and the European Central Democratic Committee. He planned, too, a new Encyclopedia, that would teach the new, liberal, democratic nationalists of Europe the message of his book on *The Duties of Man,* where the *Great Encyclopedia* of the French Philosophers had taught only the Rights of Man, rights which the French Revolution had propagated through Europe. That was why, as late as 1866, he was busy founding the Universal Republican Alliance. He was fascinated by the thirteenth-century Italian monk, Joachim of Floris, who held that the Age of the Father had been succeeded by the Age of the Son and would be followed by the Age of the Holy Spirit. Mazzini looked on the Catholic Church as the instrument of the second Age; and foresaw an imminent Third Age at last, a democratic, liberal Age, in which the various nations, many of them, like Italy, in fragments and living under foreign tyrants, would co-operate freely together for the good of all. But, to achieve that unity, a new and Italian Rome was needed, the capital of a new and heroic Italian people. Once Rome had imposed political unity on the Western world. Again, Papal Rome had brought Catholic unity to medieval Europe. A new Rome would teach unity to the modern world, a world of democratic equality, of liberal institutions. But neither Mazzini's kind of Rome, nor his kind of Italian unity, nor his united Europe emerged; and he died a bitter and disappointed man.

Prussia was the weapon with which Bismarck built the German Empire. The unity of the German-speaking states, like the unity of the Italian-speaking states, was blocked by the ramshackle Austrian Empire. For though German-speaking Austria was the leading state of the Germanic Confederation which the Congress of Vienna had set up, Metternich's Austria also ruled Poles, Ruthenians, Slovaks, Czechs, Rumanians, Magyars, Serbs, Slovenes, and Croats. These groups felt the same kind of nationalist aspirations that Italians and Germans felt. Prussia, on the other hand, the only other great power in the Germanic Confederation, was, except for the Polish population she had annexed, overwhelmingly a German-speaking state. And, between 1818 and 1852, Prussia persuaded most of the other German states to enter a customs union with her. This union greatly promoted the interests of the liberal middle class, which in some states was introducing the factory and the machine. The Prussian monarchy was not liberal, but it was progressive and enterprising. During the years of the Conservative Reaction following Waterloo, Prussia stuck to her conservative commitments with Austria and Russia. Even when the Revolution of 1848 caused a liberal revolutionary Assembly at Frankfort to set up a German federal empire and to offer the imperial crown to Prussia, the Prussian monarch refused and still continued to co-operate with the Emperor of Austria. But when his successor appointed Bismarck "Minister-President," Prussian nationalist interest began to turn against the Austrian hegemony of the Germanies. Bismarck strengthened the army over the constitutional objections of the Prussian legislature; and prepared to solve the "German question" in traditional Prussian style.

In 1864 he persuaded Austria to join him in a war on Denmark, to rescue the partly German provinces of Schleswig and Holstein. He then picked a quarrel with Austria over those provinces; and in 1866 defeated her decisively in the Seven Weeks' War. Frederick the Great had advised that Prussia's wars should be "short and lively." This one was, partly because the Prussians had gotten practice in the Danish war in the new art of moving armies by railway transport, partly because of a new Prussian weapon, the needle gun, partly by lightning speed and superior strategy, and partly because Bismarck's genius for diplomacy neutralized other great powers. Bismarck made a quick and generous peace: he would shortly need at least the neutrality of Austria. In 1870 he provoked Napoleon III to declare war on Prussia, gained an overwhelming victory, imposed a crushing indemnity on the new Third Republic, annexed Alsace-Lorraine, and crowned his King "Emperor of Germany." The coronation took place in the palace that Louis XIV had built at Versailles, the palace so many little German princelings had aped, the palace that symbolized a powerful united France, with its traditional and successful policy of preventing the formation of a united German state on its flank. It was a catastrophic finale to France's second fling with a Bonaparte.

The new German Empire was a different state from the new Kingdom of Italy. Italy was a liberal constitutional monarchy, whose unity was based on plebiscites. The new German Empire, though its constitution was theoretically federal, had been built, in Bismarck's phrase, with "blood and iron." Although Prussia had persuaded the other German states to enter the customs union; although she had persuaded some of them to join a "federation" with her and later still the Empire, many of them had been conquered and annexed, and others entered because they could see no practicable alternative. It is fair to say, although it oversimplifies what happened, that Bismarck conquered the Prussian legislature, and that a military Prussia conquered Germany, after conquering Austria and France and forcing them not to meddle. The state that emerged was a hierarchical state and a Prussianized state, with a proof in its hands that "short and lively" wars get results, and that states rest on naked force. The Hinterland of Europe, after long travail, had brought forth a modern nation state that caricatured the modern states of the Atlantic seaboard. The Prussia of Frederick the Great had been a weapon: its enlarged version, the German Empire, would be a weapon too.

The ideas of the French Revolution made the Paris of Napoleon I the focus of political and military power in Europe. But those ideas underwent a profound shift when the focus became the Berlin of Bismarck. Liberty, Equality, Fraternity promised Christendom a New World, and one that neither monarchy nor Church had achieved. Liberty promised government by consent, not blind force. Equality promised justice at last, after the most shocking and palpable injustice. Fraternity promised co-operation between all men everywhere, with the nations of men living in peace and concord. Surely, these were high goals, worthy of a Christian civilization; and all over Europe men lifted their eyes in hope and exaltation.

But these three ideas collided with the vested interests of decaying monarchy and feudal privilege. And those who had lifted their eyes, now took up the sword to defend the three ideas. They were willing to die for them. They were also willing to kill for them. A passionate love of liberty became a passionate hatred of tyranny, and under the stress of concrete events, a passionate hatred of specific tyrants. Love of justice became a flaming hatred of privilege, and of the specific persons who enjoyed privilege. Love of humanity became, as the armies clashed and clashed again, a fierce nationalism, and at last a hatred of foreigners. For, as the century wore on, the danger of war steadily grew. Wars were more destructive now. Already Frederick the Great had substituted for the leisurely maneuvers and checkmate of royal mercenary armies, the modern objective of destroying the enemy. But, "short and lively" as Frederick wished Prussian wars to be, he could not foresee the furious tempo of Napoleon, or his vast conscript armies of citizen-soldiers fired with a passionate nationalist zeal, citizen-soldiers who were not cynical professionals but desperate fanatics. The Industrial Revolution came, and furnished men with deadlier and ever deadlier weapons. It created huge populations, that yielded huger conscript armies of fanatics. It created a complex economy, in which Continental Systems and naval blockades could spell both the ruin of industry and inevitable defeat, and also stark hunger for millions. It created, even in peacetime, a new colonial tension over the distant raw materials on which now hung, not merely the profits of a few merchants, but life itself; and a tension over distant markets without which the machines would grind to a standstill and the servants of the Machine would face idleness and hunger. It created the Marxian Socialist, who had been taught that the desperate and precarious existence of the national community was not his affair, and who might at the final hour side with the armed enemies of the nation-state, enemies who waited, poised, behind each frontier.

Under the ghastly new pressure of the system of sovereign nation-states, armed with ever more dangerous arms, every institution of Christendom underwent a profound perversion. Love of home became hatred of the foreigner. Protestant Christianity flirted with nationalism and sometimes appeared as mere religious tribalism. Catholic Christianity catered to oppressed groups of Catholic nationalists. Or else, to counter the charge that Catholics — along with Jews, socialists, and even sophisticated cosmopolites — might prove disloyal or only faintly loyal when the next inevitable day of violence came, Catholicism went nationalist too. Or, afraid of betraying the universality of Catholicism, Catholics became fanatical clericals, attacking anything that appeared to weaken the power of the Papacy. The nation-state became a kind of church itself: it had its flag, an elaborate ritual surrounding that flag, its anthem, its rabidly nationalist newspaper press, its national educational system under pressure to teach loyalty, its hysterical determination to impose the common national tongue, its mawkish patriotism that most men found ridiculous only in small and hence weak states. Local peculiarities were erected into important and admirable qualities: folkways, folksongs, folk legends were hysterically glorified. Nations made themselves into primitive tribes rather than modest portions of the human community; and the human race broke up into curious, new, and imaginary entities called "races." A bogus science of race flourished in Germany and throughout Europe. By 1855 a French nobleman, Gobineau, had developed the myth of the "Nordic" race, superior to any other. Serious scientists speculated on the possibility that the races of men did not stem from a single source, that they differed as species. The Englishman Houston Stewart Chamberlain, who had become a German citizen, advertised the superiority of German culture over other cultures. Kipling picked up " the white man's burden." The backward, primitive races of the Americas, of Asia, of Africa could be enslaved, legally or only in fact, because they were inferior. The dream of the early nineteenth-century liberal, that all men were free and equal brothers, was twisted and perverted into racism. In the midst of all this dangerous nonsense, men who retained their critical powers when faced with their personal defects, lost those powers when they thought of the " nation " they belonged to, as a fatuous father loses those powers when he looks at his son. They gave to their fellow-citizens a respect that can properly be given only to mankind; and sometimes they gave that mystical and misty abstraction, the " nation," a reverence due only to God.

Whence did this folly come to a highly civilized continent? Knowledge, particularly scientific knowledge, was growing rapidly. Modern techniques were giving man an undreamed-of mastery over Nature. Population was multiplying. In countless ways man's inhumanity to man was diminishing. As for mass hatred, as for the attempt to spread truth by violence, surely neither was new to Christendom. It was Christendom that launched the Crusades, the Spanish conquest of America, the Inquisition, the religious wars, the long persecution of the Jews, the African slave-trade. But, almost unobserved by many Europeans, the nineteenth century had brought this new poison of mystic tribalism into the common life of Europe.

Did it not come, quite simply, from Europe's too long postponed failure to organize itself politically? Feudalism had brought local disorder and warring barons. The King's Peace had brought local order and occasional " foreign " wars. The wars of religion threatened to destroy Christendom. But the national monarchies had learned to live together, peacefully enough, at least, to allow a magnificent culture to flourish. Now the absolute monarchs had given way to the sovereign peoples. The sense of common cause had developed into nationalist groups that threatened the very existence of polyglot states like Austria, and laid the basis for new states through new and popular wars. The Industrial Revolution provided newer and more powerful weapons; while quicker transportation and communication flung the nations of Europe into economic interdependence, economic competition, and dangerous proximity. Each nation became an armed camp, and civilization could not flourish in armed camps. As the danger increased, the sovereign state had to ask of its citizens more and more, if it proposed to survive. They must offer their bodies in war, if needed; but, in peace and in war, they must offer the blind devotion of their souls. Church and school must inculcate that devotion. Minorities were a menace.

It was an ugly and dangerous poison. But it was a poison intended as a desperate remedy. After all, the nation-states were the only existing sources of positive law: without that law, obviously, there would be anarchy. The " Concert of Europe," the diplomacy of the great powers, tried to keep the precarious peace; and for brief periods did keep it. But there were ominous signs that war, even as a last and occasional resort, was no longer tolerable. There were even more signs that fear of the Next War was destroying Western civilization. It had been the liberal dream to substitute reason for violence. But the political system of Europe, the system of sovereign nation states, each reserving the right to shoot it out with its neighbor, was based on the assumption of violence. This was what Prussia knew; it is what Prussian historians like Treitschke stated; and it was why Bismarck brushed the liberals easily aside. In safer states, notably in Britain, snug behind her Channel with her fleets on every sea, liberalism had easier sailing. But the Prussian knew that in these liberal states, even in Britain, there was a certain hypocrisy. They had, so to speak, already shot it out.

This violence was the poison that worked throughout the European system. It embittered the fight between capitalism and socialism. It embittered the fight between liberalism and clericalism. It incubated the realism of Flaubert, the naturalism of Zola, the sensuality of Baudelaire, the nihilism of Nietzsche, the cult of violence of Sorel, the sadism and activism of d'Annunzio. Despite the Holy Alliance, despite the Concert, despite the Peace Congresses, the Geneva Conventions, and the other efforts to coax peace out of international anarchy, the specter of the Next War steadily poisoned, steadily brutalized, the collection of armed camps called Christendom.

XVI.

MEN LIKE GODS

BETWEEN 1870 and 1914 the Pilgrim City suddenly, unexpectedly, and gloriously came, not to the Promised Land it thought it was seeking, but to a better Promised Land. It had dreamed, in its medieval childhood, of a mystical land of milk and honey, unlike this vale of tears: and suddenly it stood on a high plateau of plenty, where there was real milk and real honey, and nothing mystical about either. For the obedience and self-denial and impotence of childhood, it obtained limitless power and self-assertion. For the impossible medieval task of achieving "spiritual" perfection in the midst of squalor, famine, and pestilence, it faced the glad prospect of indefinite progress toward an earthly paradise. It had outgrown its wistful childhood and had come down to earth, and it was a good earth. It had exchanged the dubious delights of eternal bliss and final repose for fruitful and exciting effort in a Century of Progress. In the ancient Hebrew myth, when Adam had eaten of the tree of knowledge, had not God said that "the man is become as one of us"? The prophecy seemed to have been fulfilled. Man had indeed eaten of that tree, though perhaps not till he had left Eden, perhaps not until modern times, and the power of its fruit had indeed produced men like gods.

Looking backward across the centuries, the generation of 1870–

1914 might have assessed the successive visions that had guided the steps of Christendom; and some members of that generation did. Unhappily, however, most of those who did look backward, looked only backward. Too often, they mistook the accidents of the Great European Tradition for its essential principles. The majority, intoxicated by the new era of size and plenty and power, were not interested in the past, or wrote histories of it only to account for something the glorious present had at last broken with, had at last shaken off. Thus it was with the quarrel of the clericals and the liberals. The clericals, or at least some of them, were able to recognize that the liberal of the early nineteenth century and the more materialistic and "scientific" liberal of the later Prussian Hegemony had developed, not only free institutions or scientific laboratories, but what were in effect new theologies, and that these theologies, although they had some of their roots in Christian doctrine, were in large measure in sharp conflict and flat contradiction with Christianity. Faced with this fact, the clericals frequently and ardently supported corrupt and tyrannical governments that were less candid than the liberals and certainly no more Christian than they, but that were delighted to get the support of the Church. Thus arose the unholy alliance of "the throne and the alter" which the liberal so much hated and despised. The liberals, meanwhile, were in many cases driven to write off Christianity, or at least the Christianity the churches seemed to be talking about, as a congealed mass of unexamined mythology condemned by its own fruits, out of its own mouth. Europeans tended to divide into what, to use Emerson's phrase, were "a party of memory" and "a party of hope." And the two parties seemed determined not to learn from each other. As the century wore on, the tension between the Church and the religion of Liberty shifted somewhat to an equally confused struggle between Christian theology and the religion of Science — or, as men said simply, between science and religion. It was a struggle in which religion steadily lost ground.

The decisive factor in that defeat was almost certainly the Machine. The exploration of matter by means of hypothesis and experiment could never alone have drawn most men's allegiance. Indeed, most men remained basically ignorant of the processes of "pure" science. But the thing, precisely, that distinguished most strikingly the scientific thinking of modern man from that of the ancient Greek was that modern science did not remain merely "pure." It was borrowed by, and supported by, "applied" science, or technology. Scientific laws were incarnate in the Machine. And it was because those laws had taken on flesh that modern man believed and would apparently be saved. If "Science" became a modern God, if scientific theory replaced theology as the regulative and architectonic branch of all human knowledge, the Machine itself became the Mediator and the Redeemer. It mediated between the abstract laws of Science and the concrete needs of mortal men. It mediated precisely by becoming like man and dwelling among men: by pumping out mines as he had pumped out mines, by drawing his water, hewing his wood, spinning his thread and weaving his garments, by bearing his burdens faster than he could bear them, paddling his boats, plowing his fields, reaping his grain, and making his daily bread. The Machine redeemed man from toil. It entered into the hospital to heal him of sickness, or to protect him from pain. It transfigured itself into a telegraph and carried his messages by code; or into a telephone, and put him in communion with all those who truly turned to the telephone; or into a radio, and brought him knowledge and entertainment in his loneliness. It became a telescope, and let him gaze at stars no man had seen. It became a submarine, and carried him to depths that only the fish had known. It took on wings, and lifted him toward the heavens themselves.

It was because of this incarnation of the Machine that man believed in the "miracles" of Science — the Machine with its dual nature. For the Machine did all that man could do; or it would do all of it soon, when man's increasing faith permitted it to reveal its full powers; and yet, at bottom, it was Nature operating by the inexorable and mysterious laws of a partially known godhead. It would mediate between Nature, and Nature's creature, Man, whom Nature had "evolved" from the dust of the ground. But it would mediate only if man imitated his new Redeemer by achieving increased mechanical efficiency. And so man learned to imitate the Machine, by living intimately with it, by serving it faithfully and promptly. It was a severe discipline, but it promised him redemption from all the evils of this life. It promised him his lost "dominion over creation." It promised him power and proud citizenship in a new City, the City of Nature, whose name is Industrialism, whose inexorable rulers are Matter and Force, and whose missionaries are commanded to spread ceaselessly the use of the Machine. Like Augustine's City of God, this City too would be a Pilgrim City, moving through the desert of agrarian peasant society with its primitive techniques, its poverty, its ignorance, and its military impotence.

Many who still professed Christianity, many who still talked of humanism, of democracy, of liberalism, belonged to the new industrial City of Nature, and hymned its mounting victories. For perhaps no City in history ever expanded either its power or its extent more rapidly than this new City did. It had changed the whole face of Christendom. It had made men feel that the secret of the good life had at last been found, that mankind had progressed further in the nineteenth century than in all preceding centuries added together, that for the first time man was master of his fate. And the new power in which he rejoiced appeared to be increasing in geometrical proportion. Those who lived before the First World War will readily remember, with wistfulness or shame, the curious sense of elation, of millennial expectation, that pervaded the atmosphere of those years. It was not a quiet joy, but a restless optimism.

There were indeed doubters. But doubters could be referred triumphantly to the daily miracles of Science and the general amelioration of man's lot. It was indeed true that the universal progress applied chiefly to material things, but it promised redemption from those very things, a redemption that would surely permit man the leisure to realize his full excellence in every field. Meanwhile, the basis of human culture was being secured: a high standard of living, literacy approaching the universal, an expanding suffrage, widespread and increasing physical comfort, abundant food and shelter, relief from pain, new cures for disease, longer life, the fuller satisfaction of physical desires, even of desires newly created by the new power to satisfy.

If it was good to be alive on this earth, then it was certainly good that mankind should increase and multiply; and, under the new dispensation, man was multiplying beyond all dreams of the past. Between 1800 and 1914 the population of Europe tripled. Yet during that period Europe had poured millions upon millions of men and women into every continent on earth, and especially into the

THE PILGRIMAGE OF WESTERN MAN

United States. Paradoxically, it was because those millions left Europe, that Europe's population increased. For the emigrants fell on the rich new continents like locusts, quarried their virgin soil, rifled their mines; and back to Europe poured the booty — foodstuffs and raw materials, to feed the new industrial proletariat of Europe and to feed the mills in which they served the Machine. Out to the new lands there poured back a stream of finished goods. The seas had once borne the tiny, bobbing galleon with its slender cargo of luxuries for the rich; or had seen pass swiftly the sleek clipper, her sails bellying before a long-awaited wind. Now those same seas were a network of busy shipping lanes, where the great tramp-steamers wallowed their inexorable way in all weather with Kansas wheat for Liverpool or cheap Manchester cotton cloth for the teeming poor of India or heavy pig iron for the steel mill: commerce was now for the millions whom the Machine had haled into the new world market. Its products moved, therefore, in vast cargoes by sea, through the new canal that cut the sandy wastes of Suez, or the newer canal that cut at Panama the Continental Divide of the Americas. They hurried over the thousands of new miles of railway that crisscrossed Europe, that spread across the sprawling prairies of the United States, and that penetrated every continent. This was the "great mercantile republic" that Adam Smith had seen emerging, that he wanted to free from the petty bonds of mercantilist policy. Its commerce, he had held, "ought naturally to be, among nations, as among individuals, a bond of union and friendship...." And, to support this commerce, to furnish what Smith called "the great wheel of circulation," there sprang up, centered in London, an international financial and banking system whose operations dwarfed the achievements of Amsterdam in the primitive days of the great Jacob Fugger.

Invention supplied these vast markets; the hunger of the markets stimulated invention, and made it possible to build more laboratories and train a bigger army of scientific personnel. A new world came into being, a world of rayon, synthetic dyes, machine guns, submarines, telephones, radio transmission, dynamos, electric lights, streetcars, sewing machines, typewriters, bicycles, cameras, motion pictures, turbines, Diesels, automobiles, "flying machines," oil fields, rubber plantations, concrete roads, farm machinery. It was a world also of vast and towering new cities, sucking up population from the surrounding countryside, sucking up food from all over the world, spewing out industrial goods to every land. And these cities bred a new human type, highly specialized, news-hungry, hustling people, getting their food from cans, their information from the daily press, their fads from advertising, their fun from films. They were perhaps a type no stranger to the nearby farmer than the city guildsmen of the Middle Ages had been to the peasant. But that was because the modern farmer was partly urbanized himself. Even so, he was not modern man. Modern man lived in the great cities. He did not make what he needed; he made money, and with the money he bought what he needed. He knew, far better than the farmer, that his life itself depended on the Machine, on the empire of new markets that the Machine demanded the right to penetrate. The American skyscraper expressed his domination over others. He dominated the countryman, because he was better organized to create monopoly, whether in the field of finance by the control of credit or in the field of industrial production by tariff protection and limitation of production. Although the size of urban families shrank, he could count on the countryman to produce children, and he could count on the power and physical comfort which the skyscraper symbolized, to draw those children to the urban labor market.

The domination which his neomercantilism gave him at home, over the farmer that produced his food and the miner that produced his fuel or raw materials, extended to weaker nations: he was armed against them by cheaper products for trade in peace, and by more terrible weapons for imperialist wars. Even the religion of the City of God aided his domination of remote lands: never in the history of Christendom had missionary enterprise flourished on such a scale, though it was not always easy to tell whether it was Christian salvation that was being spread, or a newer salvation — salvation by standard of living. In any case, for the first time in the recorded history of the human race, a single civilization dominated the entire globe.

Inevitably, that domination was more superficial than it sometimes appeared. The machines themselves, born in England, spread to Belgium, France, Germany, more thinly to other countries in European or overseas Christendom, but especially to the United States. They

spread a little, even beyond Western Christendom, to Russia, to India, and even more to Japan. But the products of the Machine spread
almost everywhere. With them spread at least a veneer of European
customs, European costumes, European notions of political democracy, of humanitarian reform. Europe's earlier visions, divine-right
monarchy, Renaissance humanism, the medieval synthesis, from
which Christendom itself was turning away, spread little or not at all.
It was the City of Nature, ruled by invisible Science, redeemed by
the visible Machine, a City whose citizens were men like gods, ruling
the world in power and pride, that slowly bound all men together
in acquisition and enjoyment, in optimism and progress, in forget-
fulness and hope.

How great was that exultant hope can be seen from the series of
great International Exhibitions that started with the London Exhibition of 1851 and that still continues. Prince Albert, the royal consort of Queen Victoria, who originated this first great Exhibition,
expressed that hope, and Christendom's pride in having European-
ized the world:

Nobody who has paid any attention to the peculiar features of our
present era will doubt for a moment that we are living at a period of
most wonderful transition, which tends rapidly to accomplish that great
end to which indeed all history points — *the realisation of the unity of
mankind....* The distances which separated the different nations and
parts of the globe are rapidly vanishing before the achievements of modern invention, and we can traverse them with incredible ease; the languages of all nations are known, and their acquirements placed within
the reach of everybody; thought is communicated with the rapidity, and
even by the power, of lightning. On the other hand, the *great principle
of division of labour,* which may be called the moving power of civilisation, is being extended to all branches of science, industry, and art....
Gentlemen, the Exhibition of 1851 is to give us a true test and a living
picture of the point of development at which the whole of mankind
has arrived in this great task, and a new starting-point from which all
nations will be able to direct their further exertions.

And of this same first Exhibition Thackeray hymned:

> See the sumptuous banquet set,
> The brotherhood of nations met
> Around the feast.

The London *Times,* on the opening day, announced the "first morning since the creation that all peoples have assembled from all parts of the world and done a common act." They were to do the "common act" again in 1855 at Paris, in 1862 at London again, in 1867 at Paris again, in 1871 at London again, in 1873 at Vienna, in 1876 at Philadelphia, in 1878 at Paris again, in 1884 at New Orleans, in 1893 at Chicago, in 1900 at Paris again. These great International Exhibitions were, so to speak, the General Church Councils of the new religion of Progress, councils which millions of the faithful attended, to marvel and to report to their neighbors at home.

If what Prince Albert called "the moving power of civilization" — the same "great principle of division of labour" that excited and rejoiced Adam Smith — had created this "sumptuous banquet" of material Progress, it seemed logical to apply it throughout all man's labors. Indeed, Adam Smith himself had claimed its applicability to scholarly inquiry. Knowledge now began to divide and subdivide into specialties. And since practically nobody any longer found intelligible the medieval claim of theology to be the "queen of the sciences," the science of physics was enthroned to save the unity of knowledge. Not only did astronomy, chemistry, biology, and geology attempt to imitate its methods, its detachment, its proofs. So did physiology, psychology, philosophy, archaeology, anthropology, economics, political science, history, philology, and the new science of sociology. In almost every field of thought, statistics and fact-finding replaced the attempt to order principles. Everybody wanted at all costs to be scientific; although not all who wanted to be, were as aware as the great physicists were of the tentative and hypothetical nature of the laboratory sciences which other branches of knowledge now tried to imitate. The growth of popular, and even compulsory, education; the imaginative writing of men like Jules Verne and H. G. Wells; the "popular science" of the daily press; the great Exhibitions — all these factors were pressures toward assimilating every branch of knowledge to what went on in the physics laboratory. And in the popular mind, the daring and speculative hypotheses of the physical sciences became the absolute Truths of Modern Science, which furnished a new creed and a new set of dogmas for a new religion, with real, not Biblical and poetic, miracles.

Acceptance of the new theology of Science, and of Progress as the

Way of Life, no doubt produced its strains. The Machine-Universe in which modern man now dwelt offered its daily and gratifying surprises; but the Law of Progress itself decreed that they were pre-ordained and impersonal surprises. Modern man, sprung now, not from the hand of God but by fixed laws from some lower form of life or even, eventually, from inert matter, could feel little sense of being a free person. His new Universe felt suddenly tight, con-stricted despite its vastness, oppressive. His immediate environment, also, sometimes pressed in upon him. The Machine certainly did work that would have been fearfully heavy for man to do — assum-ing, indeed, that it had to be done — but it did not always appear to have brought the leisure it promised. It appeared instead to bring a sort of preoccupied idleness and a nervous waiting for the hour when it must again be tended. Even men who never touched a real machine felt as if they were tending the Machine itself, as if, so to speak, they were living in shifts. It was as if leisure could be found only in a sense of the eternal, the timeless; and the Machine oper-ated in time and on time. For much of mankind the dread of fam-ine had all but disappeared in a majestic world food market; mod-ern medicine had made pestilence unlikely, had improved the health of millions, had postponed Death himself, and might, so some men speculated, bring the death of Death. But new and nagging worries, a sense of waiting for something that never arrived, seemed to have replaced those dreads, now that man looked not to eternity and bliss for himself but for a future time of prosperity, either for himself or his descendants. And as creature comforts improved, there was a tantalizing tendency for earlier luxuries to become necessities, which quickened the pace and increased the tension of modern living. Sometimes it seemed that if technology would merely shift less fast, one could learn to love new objects and use them wisely before an-other technological revolution made them obsolete and snatched them away for shinier substitutes.

The artist was particularly dubious of the new dispensation. Men like John Ruskin and William Morris, writing in the Machine's na-tive land, shrank from the ugliness and bad taste that spread like a pall through Victorian England. An artist like Van Gogh might even go insane. The artist type had changed now from the full-liv-ing Renaissance creator to somebody a little peculiar, who probably

lived in an attic and who might, like Gauguin, retreat farther than
that, to the South Seas, or to some other primitive spot less full of
machine-made objects than Europe, less full of machine-made men.
Or he might see his world in fragments, like the impressionists, or in
naked and abstract forms like the cubists. The division of labor, that
"moving power of civilisation," reduced the factory worker, according to Karl Marx, to the fraction of a man, performing a fractional
and hence unintelligible process. Apparently it reduced the artist to
the fraction of an artist: in no case was the nineteenth century's
burst of hope for the future a fair exchange, for the artist, for that
century's loss of memory. The artist was finding the new world
hard to love, and therefore hard to paint or sculp. Often, he fell back
on reporting, as the new " social scientist " did, when he reported the
facts of existing social orders rather than ask himself what social order a man ought to achieve. In the same way a novelist might por-
tray photographically the life he saw about him, even its ugliness.
Or a poet like Baudelaire, faced with the lack of central intelligibility in the world about him, might write with bitter eloquence of
what such lack invariably produces in man, the horrible burden of
Boredom. Or like Anatole France, the writer might laugh ironically
at the whole business, with a skepticism more inclusive than Voltaire's.

It was perhaps partly because Christendom was becoming unintelligible to its own artists that it turned more to the art of other cultures, including primitive cultures, for some comprehension of human existence. It was in the nineteenth century, for example, that
it turned to Russia. Ever since Peter the Great, Russia had been considerably influenced by Western Christendom, particularly in the
field of technology. Now, for the first time, Christendom was influenced by Russia. Chekhov's psychological insights and Gorki's social problems already had counterparts in the literature of Western
Europe. But there were no counterparts to Dostoevski or Tolstoi,
either in greatness or in direction. For the rampant materialism and
individualism of the West, Tolstoi offered an almost Oriental simplicity and faith. And Dostoevski consciously turned away from
what he called " Europe " to the deep sense of community that he
found in Holy Russia.

While some few Europeans were turning away from Europe to

Russia, most of them were unconsciously turning in the opposite geographical direction toward that new Europe which they had themselves created, the United States of America. For here in North America, Europe had re-created its modern self and without much of the tradition that guided and hindered its original. In Europe, just as a man was waxing ecstatic over Prince Albert's vision of the future, a Gothic cathedral might meet his gaze, standing in some half-deserted square, or he might stumble upon a Renaissance château, or enter the resonant halls of a palace where once a king held absolute power. In America none of these things would summon old loyalties or re-create departed glories. All was new, all was driving energy, all was hope, not for the " future " life of a timeless spiritual world, but for a future in time, just around the corner, toward which America of all lands was moving fastest and with surest step. Once the Civil War had broken the Southern governing class, no class held in check the newly rich who ran the country. A steady stream of immigrants from the laboring class of Europe entered the country yearly to wedge in at the bottom of the economic and social scale and to thrust upward, like a great lever, every other social layer. Russia to the east of Europe, and Europe's own offspring to the west, were alike engaged in a vast folk movement. As the Russians streamed eastward to reach the Pacific at last, led by their frontier Cossacks, the Americans streamed westward toward the same Pacific, led by their frontier cowboys. But whereas the Russian advance was agricultural only, in America industry followed after. And it was largely European investment as well as European manual labor that enabled America to push with such energy and speed across the Great Plains, over the towering Rockies, and onward to that other coast.

What the river of immigrants contributed to America besides their muscle, their energy, and their skill depends in part on what was in their hearts when they left Europe. There are no statistics on that, and there can of course be none. But all the evidence suggests that they sought primarily economic opportunity, the nineteenth-century form of personal salvation. They sought, too, freedom from the burden of military conscription, that burden which the democratic era had brought Europe's system of sovereign nation-states. And in America, where even second-rate skills fetched rewards that first-rate skills in Europe could not guarantee, they learned better even than Europe the optimism of the Age of Progress. They learned that land can be not only a peasant's family heritage, but real estate, capable of bringing enormous unearned increment. They learned the joys of an anarchical economic system in an environment of apparently unlimited resources. They learned to reverse exactly the medieval hierarchy of economic pursuits; to respect, first the financier, whose backing would open a golden West; next, the businessman, whose commerce in all commodities brought quick profits; next, the industrialist, who supplied clothes and shelter; and last, the farmer, who produced only the food without which all would perish, but who was thrust aside in American esteem by the growing power of urban business. It is of course true that, in the midst of all this hurry and confidence, where religious faith so often gave place to financial credit, hundreds of thousands of men and women found means to live quiet and useful lives and to cherish the faith of their fathers; for not even the great migration across the Atlantic could wholly destroy human memory. But it was not those men or those women who gave direction to American civilization.

If the idea of Progress ruled America more completely, yet it effectively ruled Europe too. It had had indeed a long pedigree. Bacon had contributed to it. So had Descartes, the eighteenth-century Philosophers, the French Economists, Adam Smith in England. Even Gibbon, whose *Decline and Fall of the Roman Empire* would seem to suggest that civilizations not only are born but also die, thought we might " acquiesce in the pleasing conclusion that every age of the world has increased, and still increases, the real wealth, the happiness, the knowledge and perhaps the virtue of the human race." As for the danger of another Middle Ages, which Gibbon called " the triumph of barbarism and religion," he thought " it may safely be presumed that no people, unless the face of nature is changed, will relapse into their original barbarism." Priestley, whom the Constituent Assembly had made an honorary citizen of France, was more enthusiastic. He was confident that with increased division of labor,

. . . nature, including both its materials and its laws, will be more at our command; men will make their situation in this world abundantly more easy and comfortable; they will probably prolong their existence in it and will grow daily more happy. . . . Thus, whatever was the beginning of this world, the end will be glorious and paradisaical beyond what our imaginations can now conceive.

But it was Comte who really enthroned Progress in the current of European thought. Every branch of human knowledge, he held, passes through three stages: the theological or religious, in which man invents what he believes; the metaphysical or philosophic, in which he abstracts general principles; the scientific, or " positive," in which he appeals to observation and to " facts." Europe, he insisted, had passed through the first two stages, and must enter the third. Catholicism was now no more than " an imposing historical ruin." The critical philosophy of men like Hobbes had also done its work and run its course. It was time for scientific thinking to take over, and for society to be reorganized sociologically, and governed by scientific sociologists. He even invented in his later years a new religion, in which Humanity, not God, was the object of worship.

The poets of Europe joined in. Tennyson, in *Lockesley Hall,* found consolation for a private sorrow in the slow, sure Progress of Man. Victor Hugo in *The Legend of the Centuries,* saw man, the heroic rebel, thrusting aside a horrible past — " that world is dead " — and progressing to a golden future. But the final triumph of the idea of Progress was due perhaps to Darwin's *Origin of Species,* which was published in the same year, 1859, as Hugo's *Legend.* During the next two decades, Darwin's evolutionary hypothesis struggled against the traditional Christian view of man's origin, and won. If Galileo had convinced European man that his earth was not the center of a universe lighted for his comfort by the heavenly bodies, Darwin and those whom he influenced convinced Europe that Darwin was right in his prediction, on the last page of *The Origin of Species:*

As all the living forms of life are the lineal descendants of those which lived long before the Cambrian epoch, we may feel certain that the ordinary succession by generation has never once been broken, and that no cataclysm has desolated the whole world. Hence we may look with some confidence to a secure future of great length. And as natural selection works solely by and for the good of each being, all corporeal and mental endowments will tend to progress towards perfection.... There is grandeur in this view of life, with its several powers, having been originally breathed by the Creator into a few forms or into one....

In the popular opinion of the late nineteenth century, this was not mere interesting hypothesis: it was what Comte would have called "positive" knowledge; it was "the facts"; it was what "Science says." To Darwin's optimistic view of biological growth, Herbert Spencer added an application of Progress, of necessary Progress, to sociology: "The ultimate development of the ideal man is logically certain — as certain as any conclusion in which we place the most implicit faith; for instance, that all men will die." Even conflict produced "the survival of the fittest." By 1889, the Comtian Frederic Harrison, lecturing at Manchester on the "New Era," could speak with confidence of "the faith in human progress in lieu of celestial rewards of the separate soul" — with confidence that all over Europe men accepted the dogma of Progress and believed that prophecy of Priestley that "the end will be glorious and paradisaical beyond what our imaginations can now conceive."

By the opening years of the twentieth century, the citizens of Christendom proudly stood on a pinnacle of material power that exceeded every previous dream of man. Moreover, the pinnacle had been built by man's own efforts and hence invited an understandable pride. It had been built by human reason, by "the scientific method," by a rapidly growing technology. The rules were already known by which it could be built even higher. To the critic who scoffed that it was a purely material achievement, modern man could reply that not only were he and his fellow-citizens more comfortable physically than their fathers had been; but that liberalism was everywhere triumphant or about to triumph, that political privilege had been sharply curtailed, that economic privilege was under attack, that in short, social justice was a goal universally professed. If religion and art seemed often to be lagging, might not that be that they still lacked an adequate material base? Seek ye first a high standard of living, and all these things shall be added unto you. It was good to be alive in the years of man's unbelievable power and of man's increasing hope for the future. It was good to be alive in the opening years of the twentieth century, for they were in all truth wonderful, glittering years.

XVII.

WORLD WAR ONE

FROM this bourgeois, Baconian Eden modern man was ejected with a sudden violence unique in his experience. In a few days, millions of men were mobilized to kill and be killed. It was as if some terrible madness had seized on the citizens of the City that Matter and Force had so benignly ruled. Across the tranquil, smiling, midsummer countryside of Europe swept vast armies, bearing more deadly weapons than man had ever known. The earth rocked and the sky reeled. The great gray ships of the British Royal Navy hurried silently to their appointed posts. It was the summer of 1914.

What could have caused this frightful collapse of a civilization that ruled the world? For years that problem would be argued: whole forests would supply the paper for the controversy, rivers of ink would flow, bitter recrimination would rage, long after the heavy guns were silent again, and the casualties counted — more than eight and a half million dead, more than twenty-one million wounded, nearly eight million prisoners or missing. More men had died in battle than had died in all Europe's wars since 1790, including therefore the vast French Revolutionary and Napoleonic wars. For years the guilty world would stridently argue "war guilt." Without a scapegoat there would be so much blood to wash away, from so many hands. For between 1914 and 1918 most of the nations of Europe and many of those in overseas Christendom and the Orient had, in that stately Victorian phrase of the London *Times,* " done a common act." They had conscripted their able-bodied men, they had watched through their tears as those men marched off to " the front," they had indulged in a war of propaganda, of cathartic hatred, and of lies about " the enemy." They had prayed to God to injure the nations they were fighting. They had wallowed in the self-praise or self-pity of nationalism. And some of them had made a fortune out of the war boom, while doing all these things. At the front the able-bodied men did a common act also: they lay in the mud and filth of the trenches that zigzagged across Europe, tormented by vermin, by the stench of what was left of shattered comrades, and by the rats that fed on what had been human. Like rats, they hid in dugouts underground while hell rained from the skies. They watched for the pillar of poison gas by day and the pillar of Verey lights by night. They listened to the screams of the dying, impaled on the web of barbed wire in " no man's land," that thin, disputed strip between trench of friend and trench of foe. They waited, sweating, bayonet on rifle, for " zero hour," to " go over the top," to follow behind the advancing barrage of their own artillery, to plunge into an enemy trench to shoot and stab men like themselves. They returned for the too brief leave in London or Paris or Berlin, to their hysterical wartime gaiety and the civilian's wounding questions about life at the front, to their wives or to their women or just to Woman, counting the hours until their descent again into hell. They lay in mud again, wondering what had sent them to this hell; and sometimes they died wondering, with merciful suddenness or in an agony that seemed to have no end.

Many causes had sent them; but, above all, one chief cause. The postwar literature that would try to weigh the causes of the World War would deal with the many, but would rarely mention the one. That literature would speak of the suppressed nationalities that struggled for independence from the polyglot Austro-Hungarian Empire; or the secret treaties by which each sovereign state in Europe attempted to secure allies in the event a storm should break; or the spread from Prussianized Germany of universal military training and heavy armaments; or the clash of Austrian and Rus-

sian interests in the Balkans; or the French Republic's desire to recover Alsace-Lorraine; or the German Empire's desire for colonies
and its challenge to the naval supremacy of Britain; or the mistakes
of judgment which the diplomats of the great powers made at critical moments. But most of these causes, which were sins of commission, were themselves effects of one chief cause; and that chief cause
was not a sin of commission but of omission, not anything that anybody did but one thing that nobody tried to do, a thing which only
a few men knew had to be done. That missing "common act" was
the establishment of government for a new community that modern
technology had created.

In 1850 Prince Albert could assert without fear of challenge that
his era, an era of "most wonderful transition ... tends rapidly to accomplish that great end to which indeed all history points — *the realisation of the unity of mankind.*" But could he have guessed how
complete that unity would be by 1914, in the economic sphere; or
how incomplete, in the political? Near half a billion souls now dwelt
in Europe; and, at least in the West, where population was densest,
their economic ties were close and getting closer, they spoke each
other's language, they read each other's literature, they enjoyed each
other's paintings, listened to each other's music, traveled without
passport across each other's frontiers, discussed with each other the
latest hypothesis of modern science, used each other's inventions, and
sang the triumph of a common civilization. But politically they were
organized in a score of separate sovereign states, armed against each
other. Hobbes had pointed out, two and a half centuries before, why
such sovereign states, such "Leviathans," face each other, and must
face each other, "in the state and posture of Gladiators; having
their weapons pointing, and their eyes fixed on one another; that is,
their Forts, Garrisons, and Guns upon the Frontiers of their King-
domes; and continuall Spyes upon their neighbours; which is a
posture of War."

It is true that Europe had consisted for centuries of a group of
Leviathans facing each other in "a posture of War," and occasionally doing actual battle. And Europe had survived. But there were
some new factors that even intelligent Europeans for the most part
overlooked. It was by no means certain that Europe's civilization
could survive what war had now become. Democracy gave war

vaster armies, both absolutely and in proportion to the total population. It gave war a fanatical nationalism, that would make it more
ferocious than it had been since the old wars of religion. Industrialism gave war more destructive weapons. By knitting Europe tightly
together, it all but guaranteed that local war would quickly become world war. The comfort that Europeans drew, therefore, in
the early twentieth century, from the fact that Europe had always
had wars, was false comfort: Europe had never had wars such as
the war which threatened to break out. Finally, the suspicion that
this might be the dreadful case, made war not quite imaginable. A
universal schizophrenia prevailed. Governments armed for war,
while not really believing in war. Nobody could put this schizophrenia more clearly than Winston Churchill would put it, writing
in 1923 of his service in the British Cabinet of 1914.

The British Government and the Parliaments out of which it sprang,
did not believe in the approach of a great war, and were determined to
prevent it; but at the same time the sinister hypothesis was continually
present in their thoughts, and was repeatedly brought to the attention of
Ministers by disquieting incidents and tendencies.

During the whole of those ten years [1904–1914] this duality and dis-
cordance were the keynote of British politics; and those whose duty it
was to watch over the safety of the country lived simultaneously in two
different worlds of thought. There was the actual visible world with its
peaceful activities and cosmopolitan aims; and there was a hypothetical
world, a world "beneath the threshold," as it were, a world at one moment utterly fantastic, at the next seeming about to leap into reality — a
world of monstrous shadows moving in convulsive combinations through
vistas of fathomless catastrophe.

In the golden summer of 1914 Europe plunged in a few swift days,
and despite the frantic telegrams of tired and frightened statesmen,
from " the actual visible world with its peaceful activities and cosmopolitan aims " into the " world ... of fathomless catastrophe."
Increasing tensions compelled defensive measures until, again in
Churchill's words, " As the ill-fated nations approached the verge, the
sinister machines of war began to develop their own momentum and
even to take control themselves." For the train of powder had been
carefully laid, and all that was needed was a match. This was supplied on June 28, 1914, when a Serbian fanatic assassinated an Aus-

trian archduke. One month later Austria declared war on Serbia. Within one week alliances and understandings had dragged in Russia, Germany, France, and Great Britain. Before the War would end it would draw in Japan, Turkey, Italy, Bulgaria, Rumania, the United States, and other powers.

Germany first made a quick lunge into France, hoping to knock France out of the war and leave herself free to fight Russia. But her armies were forced back to a long front extending from neutral Switzerland, westward toward Paris and northward to the Belgian coast, and on this " Western Front " French armies in the south and British in the north fought Germans for four years. The Western Front bent backward and forward slowly and indecisively, and into its trenches were poured for destruction millions of men and machines of war. The Germans introduced poison gas; the British introduced tanks; and both sides made use of both weapons. The airplane was a new weapon too; but it was small, slow, built largely of wood and cloth, used chiefly for reconnaissance, for photography, for dropping small bombs on ammunition dumps or railway yards. Britain's fleets blockaded Germany in an attempt to starve her industrial plant and eventually her population. Germany retorted by trying to blockade Britain with submarines. But British and French seapower enabled the Allies to draw heavily on overseas foodstuffs and overseas manpower. On the other hand, Germany's " interior lines " enabled her to shuttle her troops from the Western Front to the Eastern Front, where she and Austria-Hungary confronted Russia in another line of trenches, and back again. This Eastern Front, too, tended to stabilize into a line of trenches. It ran north and south through Poland, a little east of Warsaw; and this Front also chewed up millions of men in a war of attrition more often than of movement. Eventually, Italy entered the War, and an Austro-Italian Front chewed also.

It was this Europe, bleeding to death through its three gaping wounds, the Western Front, the Eastern Front, and the Austro-Italian Front, that found a leader in a President of the United States, Woodrow Wilson, and received from him a statement of purpose for what was fast becoming the futile suicide of the older provinces of Christendom. It is of course not true that he was the first Ameri-

can to whom Europe had instinctively turned. On the eve of the
French Revolution a generation of Europeans who longed for political liberty and chafed under meddlesome, ineffectual tyranny had
found a hero in George Washington. The same generation had been
moved by the homely wisdom of Benjamin Franklin. Nor had they
failed to recognize in Lincoln, un-European though he was, something that stirred in their own hearts. But Washington and Franklin
were colonials, and even the great Lincoln was a frontiersman in a
still struggling, young republic. Wilson was the chief magistrate of
a fresh and vigorous ally, unscathed by the war that had all but
destroyed Europe, a powerful America, rich in money but even
richer in young manpower. For the cause of the Allied peoples who
fought Imperial Germany, he spoke with confidence, hope, vigor,
and eloquence.

Wilson was born in Virginia in 1856, of Scotch-Irish stock, the son
of a Presbyterian minister. He passed the impressionable years of his
youth in Georgia and the Carolinas amid the physical and spiritual
devastation that had followed a terrible civil war. After a year at
Davidson College in North Carolina he finished his undergraduate
training at Princeton, studied law at the University of Virginia, practised briefly and not too successfully in Atlanta, made up his mind
to teach, and took his graduate work at the Johns Hopkins, where
he wrote his doctor's thesis on " Congressional Government."

At the age of thirty he took his young Savannah wife to Bryn
Mawr, where he taught for three years. After teaching for two more
years at Wesleyan in Connecticut he accepted in 1890 a professorship
of jurisprudence and political economy at Princeton. Within two
years, when he was forty-four, he was chosen president of Princeton.
He knew that liberal education in America had collapsed. " You
know," he declared to a body of teachers, " that the pupils in the colleges in the last several decades have not been educated. You know
that with all of our teaching we train nobody. You know that with
all our instructing, we educate nobody." He went to war on the
wealthy clubs that dominated student life. " I have told the authorities I will not be the President of a Country Club. Princeton must either be an educational institution or I will not remain." The " side
shows," the student activities, were crowding education off the cam-

pus. And he was determined that there should be real learning, and that it should take place in the democratic atmosphere that had come to characterize the country at large.

He had stated the issues, but he had not yet won "the battle of Princeton," when his fame as a hard fighter against privilege brought him the offer of the Democratic Party in New Jersey to nominate him for Governor. He accepted, fought a hard campaign, and then to the horror of the political bosses who expected to control this professor, kept his pledges. He introduced many reforms, and he fought the "trusts," the big business monopolies that were the curse of New Jersey. Two years later, in 1912, the Democratic National Convention nominated him for President.

Wilson set out by attacking the alliance between the Republican Party and "privileged big business." He was convinced that economic greed threatened to convert the American democracy into a plutocracy. He wanted to clip the wings of monopoly, and he wanted more. His Presbyterian blood was up, and he rallied the American people to a moral regeneration of the country. America was ripe for his mild radicalism: "We need no revolution, we need no excited change; we need only a new point of view and a new method and spirit of counsel." The Republican Party was weakened by the secession of Theodore Roosevelt and his "Progressives." Wilson won.

On April 7, 1913, he delivered his first message to Congress. And he shattered precedent by delivering it in person, as Washington and John Adams had done, and as no President had done since. In the months that followed, Congress under his vigorous leadership lowered the protective tariff, introduced a Federal income tax, passed the Federal Reserve Act to wrest from Wall Street the monopoly of credit, set up a Federal Trade Commission, passed the Clayton Anti-Trust Act, forbade injunctions against strikes, surrendered toll exemptions for coastwise shipping which the United States had claimed with dubious right at the Panama Canal. The new President had none of the dash or bravado of the elder Roosevelt; he was dignified, reserved, a little shy; but he was clear-headed, incisive, purposeful, fearless, and he got things done.

In foreign affairs he did his best to discourage the "dollar diplomacy" that was rampant in Latin America, limited all he could American intervention in a Mexican revolution, insisted on the strictest neutrality toward the frightful war in Europe, defended the rights of American shipping against British and Germans alike. He made desperate efforts to mediate a peace in Europe. The neutrality problem became more and more difficult. Both Britain and Germany naturally pelted the American people with propaganda, but Britain did much the better job of it. On the other hand, a flood of European immigrants had entered America for decades, and 15 per cent of the population was foreign born. Most of the German-Americans sympathized with Germany; and the Irish-Americans carried on their centuries-old vendetta against the English. But many other " hyphenated Americans " took violent sides in the conflict. National unity was a real problem, whatever policy Wilson followed. As Germany grew more and more desperate in her efforts to starve Britain, her submarine attacks on shipping brought the loss of more and more American lives. The British, who dominated the surface of the seas, could stop neutral vessels and search and seize contraband. But the Germans, who had determined to make a quick effort to starve Britain by sinking all ships within the waters surrounding her, could often, for lack of space, not even rescue survivors. As the ships went down, note after note went from Wilson to the German government. The firebrands shouted for an end of note-writing and a prompt declaration of war.

But Wilson was back at his old job: he was teaching. He was teaching the American people, sinking by sinking, note by note, that they had no alternative to war. And on April 2, 1917, he asked Congress for a Declaration of War, a war "without rancor and without selfish object," for "the world must be made safe for democracy." The United States must fight "for the right of those who submit to authority to have a voice in their own governments, for the rights and liberties of small nations, for a universal dominion of right by such concert of free peoples as shall bring peace and safety to all nations and make the world itself at last free." Wilson insisted on Selective Service in a country that had never known conscription except during its Civil War; and got it. With Lloyd George, he fought for a unified command; and got it. He raised an army of some four million; he got more than two million overseas, and of these, nearly a million and a half were at the front when the Germans collapsed.

But he had not fought with men and munitions alone. He had fought with ideas, with ideas expressed in words that robbed the Germans of their purpose and their will to fight, and that heartened the peoples of Britain, and France, and Italy. On January 8, 1918, in a message to Congress, he laid down his "Fourteen Points" as the proper aims of a just peace, and it was on the basis of those fourteen points that the German government at last requested an Armistice. Point Fourteen called for a "general association of nations" to guarantee the peace and make it permanent.

On November 11, 1918, the universal massacre ceased. In that month the Republican party won both houses of Congress. On December 18 Wilson landed in France and thereby broke both a precedent and a record: no former President had ever left the United States while still in office; and no other human being ever won from the common people of Europe the ovation that Wilson won. During the nineteen months of American participation he had become their spokesman, and as their spokesman he demanded justice and freedom and an end of war for all men everywhere. The instrument for achieving those ends was to be a Treaty without greed or vengeance and, as an integral part of that Treaty, a League of Nations that could keep the new-won peace and keep it for good. To get the League, he sacrificed freedom of the seas to the British; he conceded a Saar plebiscite to the French; he let Japan keep Shantung; he surrendered the Trentino to the Italians. He did these things with a heavy heart, convinced that they were wrong, but counting hopefully on the League to right all in the end. He returned to America with at least the League, and the Republican Senate refused it. His health seriously impaired by his long fight at the Conference of Versailles, he nevertheless embarked on an arduous speaking tour across the United States, to get the backing of the American people for the Treaty he only half believed in and for the League that would justify the blood that had been spilt. He spoke his way to the Pacific coast and had started back again. On September 25, 1919, at Pueblo, Colorado, he cried: "There is one thing American people always rise to and extend their hand to, and that is the truth of justice and of liberty and of peace. We have accepted the truth and we are going to be led by it, and it is going to lead us, and through us the world, out into pastures of quietness and peace such as the world never dreamed of before." The speech suddenly broke off: Wilson had suffered a cerebral thrombosis; the rest of the tour was canceled; and he returned to Washington, where nine days later he suffered partial paralysis. He remained a semi-invalid for the rest of his term of office and thereafter. In 1920, he looked on the presidential election as a plebiscite, and his Democratic candidate lost. He never lost faith that the American people would eventually insist on joining the League of Nations. On February 3, 1924, he died, after winning a war and losing a peace.

Thirteen days before Wilson died, the head of another state died: Nicolai Lenin, Communist dictator of Russia. He had been born nearly fourteen years after Wilson in a little town on the great Volga River. When he was seventeen, and a month before he graduated with highest honors from the Simbirsk Gymnasium, his older brother, whom he adored, was hanged for complicity in a terrorist plot against the life of the Czar. Vladimir Ilich Ulianov — he assumed the name Lenin later, for revolutionary purposes — promised himself vengeance. He studied law at the University of Kazan, as Wilson had studied law. He practised a little, as Wilson did. He discovered Marx, as Wilson discovered Adam Smith. Where Wilson taught political economy in colleges, Lenin went to St. Petersburg and secretly taught Marxian revolution to factory hands. In 1895 he went to Switzerland for his health and had a chance to meet Russian socialists in exile there. He returned to St. Petersburg and organized a Union for the Liberation of the Working Class, was arrested, was imprisoned, and at the age of twenty-seven was sent to Siberia. There he was joined by Nadezhda Krupskaya, a revolutionary whom he had known at St. Petersburg, now also an exile. They were married; and they were to work together for the triumph of the proletariat till Lenin's death. Like so many revolutionaries sent by the Czarist regime to Siberia, he had leisure for study and plotting, and Lenin wrote his famous work on *The Development of Capitalism in Russia*. Released in 1900, he went again to Switzerland to found *The Spark*, a Marxist periodical secretly smuggled into Russia, with the motto, "From Spark to Flame." At a Congress in London of the All-Russian Social Democratic Labor Party, Lenin and his "Bolsheviks" (majority), with their program of arousing the industrial worker and peasant to revolt, won out over the "Mensheviks" (minority) and their program of worker support for the liberals who sought political democracy of the European brand.

When the Czarist government tottered under defeat by Japan in 1905, Lenin rushed back to St. Petersburg to fight, not the Czar, but the Mensheviks; and the Czarist secret police, more afraid of political democracy than of Lenin's dream of working-class revolt, gave the Bolsheviks a free hand against the liberals and Mensheviks. The outbreak of world war in 1914 found most socialists, including the Mensheviks, willing to participate, if only political democracy could be won; but Lenin and his Bolsheviks stood out against participation. This was a capitalist, imperialist war, declared Lenin; and it was the job of the Marxian to convert it into universal class war. Lenin issued a manifesto to that effect. He opposed equally the "reformists" who wanted to revise Marx's doctrine and secure the rights of the working class by an evolutionary process and he opposed the "anarchists" who wanted to use terrorist methods without a clear strategy. He wanted a rising of the propertyless against the propertied class; and he planned that in Russia the Bolsheviks should guide that rising and set up a dictatorship of the proletariat.

On April 4, 1917, two days after Wilson had asked Congress for a declaration of war against imperialist Germany, he and a small group of his Bolshevik lieutenants left their Swiss exile for Russia, where the Czar had been overthrown and where Kerensky was setting up a political democracy pledged to continue the war against Germany, the war that Wilson hoped would make the world safe for democracy. Lenin crossed Germany in a sealed train furnished by the German government, which wanted no Bolshevism in Germany but wanted plenty of Bolshevism in Russia. The evidence is strong that the Germans also furnished him with funds. While the revolutionary government of Kerensky looked on with growing distrust, Lenin launched a ruthless crusade in his newspaper, *Pravda,* for "peace and bread"; and the hungry, war-weary Russian workers listened. Once he was driven into hiding in Finland; but he stubbornly returned to his task: to stir up universal revolt against the new democratic government, make peace with the Germans, and strive for class war throughout Europe.

He got his revolt. He overthrew the government and set up a Bolshevik dictatorship. A Czechoslovak army, which had deserted their Austrian oppressors and was crossing Russia to Vladivostok to join the Western Allies, rose against the Bolsheviks on the Volga. The British, anxious to restore a Russian government willing to continue the war on the Eastern Front, intervened with American help at Archangel in the north, at Baku in the south. Armies of Russian " Whites " fought the Bolsheviks. Food was scarce. Lenin signed a peace with the Germans, ceding them an immense territory. But he would not read it before signing it. " What," he cried, " not only do you want me to sign this impudent peace treaty, but also to read it? No, no, never. I shall neither read it nor carry out its terms whenever there is a chance not to do so." The German general who laid down these harsh terms later admitted that they served merely to infect Germany's Eastern Front with Bolshevism.

At the invitation of the Bolsheviks, the peasants had seized their landlords' properties: now, finding that most of what they grew was collected by the new dictatorship for the factory workers, they began to plant less. Russia entered a period of frightful famine, during which some five million starved to death. In November, 1921, Lenin coolly recognized that he had gone too fast; and to the horror of his Bolshevik staff started paying the peasants for what they grew and encouraging the growth of small business. This was the " New Economic Policy ": three years before, he would have scorned it as a Menshevik weakness. Meanwhile, he ruled by terror and with a secret police that would have done the Czar credit. He worked furiously in his offices in the Kremlin, in Moscow, whither he had transferred the government from St. Petersburg, now given the equivalent Russian name of Petrograd, soon to be rechristened Leningrad. In December, 1922, he was paralyzed by cerebral sclerosis. He never fully recovered, and died on January 21, 1924, thirteen days before his great contemporary, Woodrow Wilson.

In the period of their supremacy the two men tower above their contemporaries, and each offered Christendom a solution to the problems the Age of Progress could not solve. Both men fought for justice, for freedom, and for peace. Their strategy differed profoundly, because their premises differed profoundly. Neither of them had a great or speculative mind. Both of them thought keenly. Lenin thought more quickly than Wilson, and should have. For Lenin was traveling lighter than Wilson.

Wilson, despite his characteristically American doubts about "tradition," faced the problems of the twentieth century in the light of many traditions. He was a devout Christian, of the active, Bible-reading, Protestant type, with more interest in morals than in doctrine. He had something of the Renaissance humanist about him, with a loving care for the right word. He respected abstract reason. He believed passionately in the ideals that the French Revolution had fought for, and in the Anglo-Saxon tradition of sturdy self-government. He was humanitarian. And he assumed that man was progressing toward a better civilization. Although his interest was politics rather than economics, he was far from unaware of the problems the Machine had created. And he could say in private to his brother-in-law, after five years in the White House: "The world is going to change radically, and I am satisfied that governments will have to do many things which are now left to individuals and corporations. I am satisfied for instance that the government will have to take over all the great natural resources. What does that mean? That means it will have to take over all the water power; all the coal mines; all the oil fields, etc. They will have to be government-owned.

"If I should say that outside, people would call me a socialist, but I am not a socialist." This, he held, was the only way to prevent Communism.

Had Lenin been able to tune in on that conversation from his office in the Kremlin, he would have given one of those Gargantuan laughs of his: this little bourgeois professor could not "say outside" that he favored even this milk-and-water, Menshevik program, when what was necessary was the destruction, root and branch, of the class the professor himself belonged to, of their precious democracy, their elections, their bought-up Parliaments and Congresses, and their imperialistic wars.

As for Wilson's Christian principles, Lenin had stopped believing in God when he was sixteen. Characteristically, he no sooner decided that God was a fraud than he tore off the cross he wore around his neck, spat on it, and threw it away. As for Wilson's humanism, Lenin was not insensitive to good literature, but he tended to read it for its Marxist content. For, what the Bible was to Wilson, Marx was to Lenin; and in dealing with his Marxian Bible, Lenin was a fundamentalist, who shouted excommunications at those who would interpret it too loosely. He distrusted abstract reason, unless he could see that it was headed for class revolt. The French Revolution was merely the triumph of the bourgeoisie over the nobility: what was now wanted was the triumph of the working class over the bourgeoisie. And it could come only by the same method: hatred and force. Nor could bourgeois shibboleths like liberty, fraternity, equality, help bring it off. Like Wilson, Lenin was in a sense a humanitarian, fighting the strong to rescue the weak. But where Wilson had to steel himself before he could send other men to death in battle, for no matter how righteous a cause, Lenin easily sent men to their death if it would promote the Revolution, and the happy triumph of all men, joined fraternally in productive labor. Helping that Revolution to happen was the surest route to Progress. To help it, he condoned lies, theft, and murder. Did Wilson's armed forces hesitate to deceive, plunder, or kill " the enemy "? Neither did the Bolsheviks. But "the enemy" were not poor German workers driven to the shambles by German capitalists; the enemy were precisely all capitalists, German or otherwise. The working class was in a state of war with them; all things are fair in war; and Lenin, their general, was directing the assault, in hiding when necessary, at the head of a government if possible. As for Communist " morality," " We say that our morality is entirely subordinated to the interest of the class struggle of the proletariat. . . . We say: ' Morality is that which serves to destroy the old exploiting society and to unite all the toilers around the proletariat, which is creating a new Communist society.' "

And beneath all these differences of premise, lay the metaphysical base. Wilson recognized that the substitution of Force and Matter for a God that created both had corrupted the civilization he sought to salvage. Lenin gladly accepted the substitution. He never tired of insisting on materialism. On his premises, Lenin was justified in the acts which so many men, including socialists, have condemned.

Both men failed of their goal. Wilson was fighting for democracy. A few weeks before he called for war on Germany, all his prospective allies were practising self-government, even Russia. For the bloody Czarist bureaucracy had been overthrown. Before he died, Mussolini had overthrown democracy in Italy; Hitler had started his long fight to destroy it; Lenin had strangled it at birth in Russia;

Bethlen had seized Hungary; Pilsudski would shortly seize Poland. Wilson had fought for the League, for a Covenant among nations, an end of war. He had challenged the statesmen of Europe to lay down their arms, to trust each other, to stake all on " collective security." But the League was no solution of the problem of war, even had the founder's own government consented to join it. The League had all the weaknesses of the old Articles of Confederation, which the thirteen sovereign states had to supplant with a common, federal government. The League was not a government. It could record agreements, which might or might not be kept, which might or might not be understood the same way by all parties, agreements between sovereign governments, retaining armed forces. And none of these governments could responsibly leave to anything other than a higher government the obligation to protect the lives and property of its citizens. It was because the federal government, provided by the Constitution of the United States, had taken over that very real obligation that the governments of the thirteen sovereign states could responsibly disarm.

The League did many useful things, but it could not hope to prevent war. It could not relieve member governments from the burden of defense. It could not therefore prevent the growth in armaments or the new skein of secret treaties. The European community, knit tightly by common economic necessity and by a rapidly growing technology, remained politically unorganized — that is, organized in separate armed camps, and camps that were obligated to remain armed. Incipient violence so permeated that community that it could be truthfully said to be organized for war. In 1920, with an exhausted world hoping against hope that the League, or something, could prevent another holocaust, a British colonel wrote a history of the recent war under the title, *The First World War*. Men were outraged by his cynicism. However, he had hit on the future title for the war just fought. Probably not even Woodrow Wilson, in the days when all Europe turned to him, could have persuaded the peoples of Europe to federate. But, by not federating, they came as near as men can come to guaranteeing another war, and the League could not invalidate that grim guarantee.

Lenin looked forward to federation, but he was convinced there would have to be world revolution first; for " the free federation of nations," as he and Zinoviev wrote in 1925, "is impossible without a more or less prolonged and stubborn struggle of the socialist republic against the backward capitalist-democratic states." On Lenin's premises the implicit violence that exists between two or more governments in the same community was more than matched by the implicit violence between the class of wage-earners living under all the governments and the class of exploiting capitalists living on the fruit of the wage-earners' labor, under the same governments — controlled, of course, by the capitalists. Lenin, like Wilson, wanted justice and freedom and peace. He wanted the justice that would come from giving each man the fruit of his own labor, the freedom that would come from not having that labor exploited by others, the peace that could not come so long as the daily violence of exploitation continued. Until then, he proposed to meet violence with violence, to desist only when strategic retreat was indicated, to fight with every weapon, "moral" or immoral.

But he did not reach his goal. He succeeded in establishing a Communist dictatorship that bore a remarkable resemblance to the Czarist dictatorship which the Mensheviks had begged him to help them fight. He doubtless succeeded in getting a juster distribution of goods in his Communist state. He was annoyed to find himself the object of a kind of Byzantine adulation — the same adulation the Czar had received. He could hope that in time, as Communism became the habit of a people, opposition and conspiracy would die away, government itself would "wither," and men would be truly free. He could hope that, when the working class in "the backward states" had destroyed their oppressors, as the Russian workers had done, then all men would be free; and, as his beloved Marx had predicted, pre-history would be over and true history would begin. These were hopes, based more on a pious reading of Marx than on the facts about him. Wilson had hopes, too, based on a pious reading of the Bible. But the secret police, under successive designations, ruled the Russian people; and Europe remained organized for war.

XVIII.

MEN LIKE BEASTS

THE Long Armistice that lay between World War One and World War Two lasted from November, 1918, to September, 1939 — nearly twenty-one years. It was an armistice and not what it claimed to be, a peace, because it left intact the system of sovereign nation states that had been hallowed by the Peace of Westphalia two and a half centuries earlier, that implicitly assumed periodic wars, that had nearly wrecked Christendom in World War One, that was powerless to bring either political justice or economic order to the new world community which modern technology had created. The Imperial German Government, with its close teamwork between big industry and big armies, had had wartime plans for imposing a reinforced Prussian Hegemony on all this anarchy. Frederick the Great had imposed order on Prussia and its conquests. Bismarck had used "blood and iron" to impose it on all the Germanies. The Empire he thereby founded had imposed it with some success from 1871 until the horrible catastrophe of 1914. For a while it seemed as if a victorious German Empire might impose an even more durable peace, by naked force, on the whole world. But the Prussian appeal to force only called forth the greater force of the French, British, and American democracies, and meanwhile Woodrow Wilson was beckoning the world to another road to a durable peace. In his Fourth of July speech at Mount Vernon, during the last, bloody summer of World War One, Wilson declared: " These great objects [of the peace] can be put in a single sentence. What we seek is the reign of law, based upon the consent of the governed, and sustained by the organized opinion of mankind." Four months later, on the Western Front, the Prussian Hegemony buckled and collapsed.

That collapse did not establish a reign of law, since no mere collapse could. It merely determined that, at least for the time being, it would not be established by the Prussian formula and by German armed might. It placed the responsibility for establishing it, squarely in the laps of the victorious Allies: France, Great Britain, Italy, and the United States. Their enthusiastic and ambiguous response was the League of Nations, " sustained by the organized opinion of mankind."

But the League did not provide law — except in terms of that most grandiose of modern metaphors, " international law." The League was a relationship between governments, not between the men and women who inhabited Europe, men and women whose myriad economic and other relations were governed solely by competing national governments. The League provided an Assembly whose members were delegates appointed by governments. It provided no Assembly in which the elected representatives of human beings could make law for those human beings. It provided no courts in which such laws could have been applied to such human beings. It provided no police to enforce such applications. It provided no direct protection for the life or property of any man. For it was not a government. Where a government for Christendom should have existed, there existed instead a power vacuum. In a phrase made popular during the Long Armistice, power was lying in the streets. The German Imperial Government had tried to pick it up. It had been knocked from Germany's mailed fist — and allowed to lie again.

In that power vacuum the sovereign nation-states of Europe praised " collective security " — and took military precautions. It was freely announced that a second World War would destroy civilization — and a growing mountain of armaments was prepared just in case. In 1931 President Hoover estimated that the world was spending 70 per cent more on armaments than in 1914, on the eve of the first World War. France, remembering two German invasions in a generation, flanked by a Germany more populous than herself, more prolific, with a more powerful tradition of war, with more industrial potential for making it, unravaged by invasion, at least in the West, smarting under defeat, under huge and indefinite claims for reparations, and under the loss of German population to the new " succession states " on her borders — France, faced with these facts, maintained a powerful army, multiplied her defensive alliances, and built her " Maginot Line " of communicating underground fortresses from Switzerland to Belgium. The Maginot Line might have been designed in a dream by some now dead *poilu,* as he lay in the mud and blood and vermin of some zigzag trench of World War One, resigned to war but modestly wishing it could be fought comfortably and efficiently. That it fatally stopped short of the North Sea suggested that the schizophrenia which Winston Churchill remembered from 1914 had again seized governments, or had never left them: a schizophrenia that juxtaposed " the actual visible world with its peaceful activities and cosmopolitan aims " (now called " collective security ") and the " hypothetical world . . . of monstrous shadows moving in convulsive combinations through vistas of fathomless catastrophe " (now a world of growing armaments).

As for the other great powers, they found other ways of hiding from the common task that faced them all. Britain, now in the infancy period of military aviation, still relatively safe behind the Maginot Line that Nature herself had built for Englishmen and that the British navy jealously watched, lamented that the French were such a high-strung race; struggled with the Irish problem, the Indian problem, the problem of unemployment; and favored the recovery of Germany and of German purchasing power for British goods. Italy was preoccupied with the danger of Communism in her industrial North; later, was submitting to Mussolini and a Fascist gangster government; was protesting the meagerness of her territorial gains from World War One; and, finally, was circumventing the League and trying to build an African Empire. Japan was digesting her easy gains in Asia and the Pacific and planning further expansion. The United States had withdrawn behind the Atlantic — so much broader than the Channel, so much deeper than the Maginot — disillusioned and cynical, refusing to join the League. As if the Atlantic felt too shallow, the United States, in 1922 and again in 1930, built tariff walls against imports, walls of the sort the Republican party normally built. The second of these walls created semi-panic in the world market, and within eighteen months twenty-five countries took countermeasures. The world market that had so largely contributed to the wealth of Christendom immediately before the war, was rapidly disappearing. The world's capitalist economy was undergoing strangulation. To the clutter of new tariff walls, erected by the new nation-states that Wilson's " self-determination " and " consent of the governed " had built from the debris of the Austro-Hungarian Empire, the Russian Empire, and bits of Germany — new states jealous of their new sovereignty and their precarious military future — was now added widespread manipulation of currency to gain temporary economic advantage.

Meanwhile, the United States was demanding payment of more than eleven billion dollars which she had advanced her recent allies against Germany. Those allies had little or no gold with which to pay these billions, and could obtain dollar credits only by exporting goods to the United States. But it was just those goods that American industry was determined, with the aid of the Republican party, to keep out of the hands of the American consumer. Industry was demanding a monopoly of American consumers, and was effectually getting it. So the War Debts dragged on, unpayable but unsettling. And America, no longer a debtor nation depending on European exports, European capital, European labor, was now a creditor nation trying from lack of statesmanship to squeeze blood from a turnip. The turnip retorted by changing Uncle Sam's name to Uncle Shylock. Americans felt hurt, remembered their war dead, remembered Europe's recurrent wars, remembered in many cases with what disgust they or their ancestors had shaken the dust of Europe from their shoes, conveniently forgot some of the less creditable episodes in their own national history, and announced that Europe could stew in its own juice. So it stewed; and a few years later it boiled over, and scalded America again.

Unable to pay their debts to the United States except in goods, and forbidden by the new Republican tariffs to send goods, Europeans might have somewhat readjusted world economy by sending themselves. But the United States wanted no more of that: in 1920, 430,000 immigrants arrived. In 1921 the figure almost doubled and Congress passed an immigration act. Three years later a more stringent act was passed. For decades Italy, for example, had exported much of her surplus population to the United States: in the first ten years of the twentieth century, 204,587. The Act of 1924 dropped Italy's yearly quota to 3,845. To judge by American legislation, Europe was a bankrupt ghetto, under embargo and waited on by an American sheriff.

According to Woodrow Wilson, " America was created to unite mankind." It was the last thing America wanted to do with its time. It wanted to make money. It was undergoing an incredible economic expansion. It was feverishly enjoying itself. It had entered the period of hot jazz, Chicago gangsters, Hollywood stars, bathtub gin, sexual promiscuity, debunking, paper profits, new millionaires. America was fully prepared to sign the Kellogg-Briand Pact " to outlaw war," and to ratify the Prohibition Amendment outlawing alcoholic beverages — so long as it had plenty to drink, and could let the anarchy of international relations breed a new war in peace. Perhaps, of all the Maginot Lines built in that period, to prevent war or to forget the last one — Maginot Lines of concrete, or salt water, or pieces of paper — the Kellogg Pact was the most ingenuous and characteristic.

In 1929 what Americans called the " New Economic Era " collided with reality. It was to have been, according to those who profited most from its fairy gold, an era that would transcend the business cycle and the economic depression and lead all mankind out of the valley of poverty for keeps. Now the era came to a sudden and surprising end in Wall Street, which had replaced London as the center of finance capitalism for Christendom and the world. How closely the world economy was integrated, even in the face of tariff walls and economic nationalism generally, was quickly demonstrated, as paralysis spread through the United States, through Europe, and the world. The revered captains of industry speedily dumped labor from their pay rolls, and the bread-lines grew. The United States, Europe's El Dorado for centuries, whose movie films had demonstrated to Europe's millions that its wealth and luxury were limitless, now burgeoned with shantytowns, with Hoovertowns; and debt-ridden farmers took to arms to defend their land from foreclosure. Nearly one-third of America's wage earners had no wage. Had capitalism collapsed, as the Communists had predicted it must? Had political democracy collapsed, as the new dictators like Mussolini had predicted it would?

In the United States both political democracy and the capitalist economy reasserted their vitality. The American people, in the elections of 1932, threw out Hoover and his Republican party, and put in Roosevelt and the Democrats. Roosevelt, who had served in the administration of Woodrow Wilson, now took up Wilson's crusade for domestic reform. Wilson's " New Freedom " was now Roosevelt's " New Deal." Roosevelt proceeded to lead Congress through a series of basic and long overdue reforms. He would not go so far as Wilson had thought, a decade before, America would have to go if it would avoid Communism: he would not propose " to take over all the water power; all the coal mines; all the oil fields, etc." But he did move toward further government intervention in the economic process, in the interests of the laboring class. He did recognize that assembly-line production rests on mass purchasing.

But he failed to bring the United States out of hiding in the field of international affairs. He failed to persuade the Senate that the United States should join the World Court. He failed to arouse the American people to the true gravity of the deterioration in international affairs in the late thirties. He succeeded only in persuading them to join the armaments race.

France, Great Britain, and the United States were all protected in varying degrees from the political and economic chaos of the Long Armistice by relatively strong economies and by long traditions of self-government. The German Republic was not; and on March 5, 1933, one day after Roosevelt's first inauguration, the German Reichstag turned Germany over to Adolf Hitler.

Hitler had been born nearly forty-three years earlier, on April 20, 1889, in the little city of Braunau-am-Inn, in Austria, just across the river Inn from Bavaria. He was the son of a petty government official. He spent an unhappy, quarrelsome, frustrated childhood; and by fifteen he was an orphan, dependent on relatives. He went to Vienna to study art, but failed the entrance examinations to the art academy. He became a laborer in the building trades. Later he painted picture postcards. He also developed a ferocious anti-Semitism. In 1912 he left his native Austria and settled in Munich as a second-rate commercial artist. From this dreary existence he was rescued by the outbreak of the First World War, and he joyfully enlisted in the Bavarian Army. He was wounded in 1916; won the iron cross; but never rose higher than corporal. When the German armies collapsed in 1918 he dedicated himself to rescuing his adopted land from the ignominy of defeat.

In 1919 he joined a political " party " that already contained six members, a party that he was to lead, to expand, and to rechristen the " National Socialist Party." From the start, it was a party of ruffians and rowdies, who carried side arms, who organized harangues, and ejected hecklers by force. Hitler, with his crude and guttural speech, his pasty face, his wild eyes, his unruly forelock, and his Charlie Chaplin mustache, discovered that he was a spellbinder. He organized his rowdies into a sort of private army, dressed them in brown shirts, adopted the mystical swastika as party emblem, introduced the ancient Roman salute which Mussolini had adopted for his Fascists in Italy, devised banners, posters, elaborate rituals. Encouraged by the discontent that followed a frightful postwar inflation, Hitler attempted in 1923, in Munich, to seize the government of Bavaria. This " Beer Hall Putsch " failed completely and landed him in jail, where he improved his leisure by writing *Mein Kampf*, a melodramatic and mendacious account of his " struggle." In the confused violence of those pages Hitler screamed denunciations of the Treaty of Versailles which now held defeated Germany down, at the Marxists who threatened to overthrow the German state, at finance capitalists, and above all at the Jews — who, he declared, were both the leaders of the international finance that now enslaved Germany and the leaders of the Communists who wanted to destroy all. Indeed, the whole of civilization was threatened, he insisted, by a world-wide Jewish conspiracy.

Charged with treason for his Putsch, he was inexcusably pardoned and released. Meanwhile, Anglo-American loans were rehabilitating Germany, and this rehabilitation spelled temporary ruin for the Nazis, whose strength was based on social and economic unrest. But when the United States had run through its boom-and-bust, when the Great Depression spread like a pestilence throughout the world, when American loans to Germany abruptly ceased, and bread-lines multiplied, the Nazi party grew alarmingly. And by January 30,

1933, Hitler was able to exact from the senile President of the German Republic, General Von Hindenburg, the Chancellorship of the Reich. By March Hitler and his Nazi party had destroyed representative government in Germany and were ruling by terror. By murder, theft, confiscation, brutal diplomacy, and an unexcelled use of propaganda he had within six years built a " totalitarian " state that made Mussolini's Fascist Italy, and even Stalin's Communist Russia, seem benign. And he was ready to resume the German expansion that the Long Armistice had cut short, twenty-one years before.

The Nazi " New Order " was perhaps the most obscene episode in the long history of Christendom. It was obscene, monumentally destructive, and basically empty, and that is why its history is hard to tell. The reason for this emptiness, this fundamental unintelligibility, is not far to seek. When beasts behave like men, as they do in Aesop's *Fables,* in La Fontaine, or in *Uncle Remus,* stories about them have meaning; but in proportion as men behave like beasts, their history is meaningless. History is concerned with that species of animal which acts in the light of ideas; but men like beasts act by a very dim light, and the acts themselves can be scarcely seen. The years of the Nazi are years of deliquescence and putrefaction and stench.

Goebbels, that master of the twisted word who served Hitler as Minister of Propaganda, christened the Nazi disorder " the Third Reich." The First Reich was the Holy Roman Empire, composed primarily of Germanic states, and it lasted from 962 until Napoleon declared it dissolved in 1806. The Second Reich, the German Empire which Bismarck built on " blood and iron " and Prussian will, was proclaimed defiantly in the Palace of Versailles in 1871 after France had been crushed in the Franco-Prussian War; and it was smashed by World War One in 1918. The Third Reich, declared Hitler, would last a thousand years. It lasted twelve.

It was built on negation and on hatred: hatred of the Jew, of the Communist, of the rich, of work, of foreigners, of reason, of political equality, of the weak. Its " philosophy " was a thing of shreds and patches, a witches' brew of contradictions — not fruitful paradoxes, but muddleheadedness. It was driven by its own desires and passions, its envy and greed and fear. Its opportunism was not the opportunism that the greatest statesman watchfully employs, but the

ering of the Prussian militarism that World War One was to have destroyed forever in favor of a peaceful, reasonable, and morally regenerated world.

Why did the rest of Christendom tolerate the growth of this hideous cancer? Alas, one must answer that the cancer was in them too. Nazi Germany was merely its point of greatest malignancy. Christendom made rough estimates of the cost of World War One, in terms of soldiers killed or wounded in action, of money or materials spent, of war debts and reparations owed; but no statistician computed, or could compute, the growth in the cult of violence, the deliberate wartime schooling in how to hate, the discovery of how few tales dead men tell, the sense of relief men had found in irrational violence. Had not force won the war, and was it not well won? Perhaps the " devastated regions " in Eastern France were more quickly repaired than the devastated regions in the human mind. Maybe some of the men who had died could have led their peoples out of the lethargy and skepticism that befogged them now in the Long Armistice: certainly, many fine minds and high hearts had been lost, along with many strong bodies. In any case, those who were left had jaded imaginations and exhausted nerves. A popular Marxism and a popular Freudianism supplied a design for living. Not the acute analysis or moral indignation of Marx, nor Freud's courageous attempt to apply human reason to the reading of the irrational passions of men; but a cheap acceptance of the view that the human belly and human sex are the only real sources of social action, and the rest is " rationalization." A love of sewage often paraded now as candor. There were loud protests over the horror of war; but when a book or a play or a movie, like the German *All Quiet on the Western Front* or the British *Journey's End* or the American *What Price Glory?* was to be read or seen, not all the posters advertising them as peace propaganda were wholly convincing. Certainly, many who had not lain in the trenches discovered vicarious means of engaging in war.

If the Ku Klux Klan in America, or the Croix de Feu in France, or Moseley's handful of Fascists in Britain, used violence, not everybody was outraged. The ravings of Huey Long or Father Coughlin were not without appeal. Skill in propaganda was admired, whether it was national advertising to frighten or cajole the public into buying, or the obscene ravings of a political demagogue. There was a cynicism about the uses of language that boded ill for representative government and its complete dependence on reason and the word. It was an era of double-talk. Arguments were more and more examined, not for their validity, but for the motive behind them and the identity of the person who must have paid to have them spread. Communication was degenerating into ventriloquism, supported by the mass media of radio and movie screen. The common processes of self-government were thought of primarily, if not exclusively, in terms of "salesmanship." Above all, "abstractions" like justice, right, wrong, had an increasingly hollow ring. Society was increasingly anti-intellectual, and increasingly victimized by mountebanks. The moral issues which Wilson had called on his generation to face now sounded unconvincing. Americans found it difficult to believe that Mussolini's brutal Fascism could be fundamentally wrong, if it was really true that at last in Italy "the trains ran on time." The French upper classes read Mussolini's writings — which really were more intelligible than Hitler's — with deep interest. Men felt a growing sense of relief that what their fathers called "morals" were really "mores" and could be studied disinterestedly in sociology, anthropology, and the other "social sciences," sciences that were descriptive and not properly normative at all, sciences that dealt with shifting "values." T. S. Eliot's poem *The Wasteland* was not an inaccurate picture of Christendom during the Long Armistice. In that Wasteland there was no power of the human spirit strong enough to stop Japan from seizing Manchuria, or Italy from raping Ethiopia, or Hitler from making one "last territorial demand" after another. There were a dislike of principles or ideas, a fascination with whatever seemed to succeed, a great deal of boredom, sensation-mongering, and fatalism. Hitler, who was neither genius nor statesman, was temperamentally enough like a good medium in a trance to sense the vacuum in the Wasteland.

Hitler discovered early two important facts. One was that the Wasteland that surrounded him was already hungry for lies, for rationalizations, that would justify its own torpor and moral insensitivity. What he told it, had to be only moderately plausible to be accepted, provided it was what cowards and sluggards and skeptics wanted to hear. The success of his propaganda demonstrates, there-

power in 1933. By 1944, late in World War Two, there were some 300 such camps, containing an estimated 1,200,000 inmates, and perhaps ten times that number had passed through them to their death. After the war the War Crimes Commission would amass the frightening legal evidence of what went on in the concentration camps: ingenious and unspeakable tortures, that Europeans had complacently assumed could not be used in Europe in modern times; the most degrading vice; a savage determination to break the human will. It was as if the Nazis were doing to millions what Frederick the Great's father had done to him, when he forced him to witness from his prison window the beheading of his best friend, Lieutenant Katte, in order to make a Prussian of him — and succeeded. The " SS Institute for Heredity " was turned loose to perform medical experiments on prisoners, experiments in atmospheric pressure or in the effects of immersion in ice water. Men were murdered so the Strassburg University Museum might enlarge its collection of skeletons. Extermination camps were set up for the systematic elimination of Jews and other " undesirable " racial stocks like Poles; and these were supplemented by gas vans, that could move quickly from village to village and save the expense of bringing the victims to the camps. The extermination camps yielded usable products: human fat for soap (really, this time), bones for fertilizer, garments for reprocessing, human hair for industrial yarn and felt. Above all, they yielded human labor, which was assigned for working to death. The whispered rumors of what went on in the camps meanwhile served to discourage opposition to the Nazis among the population outside. Finally, the camps were used to raise the stamina of the German race: 275,000 lunatics and cripples were done to death. There were ways of replenishing the German race numerically: Himmler offered financial support to all Dutch and Norwegian women who would bear children by German soldiers.

For the Nazi racists were determined that the future would belong to Germans, not by the mere annexation of soil from neighboring states — Imperial Germany had planned that in World War One — but by the extermination of Slavs that held the needed soil. " It is our task," declared Himmler, " not to Germanize the East in the old sense, i.e. to teach the people living there the German language and German laws, but to see to it that only people with Germanic blood should live in the East." Meanwhile, the Nazis were running their economy on slave labor from these undesirable European races — as Europeans had so often done through the centuries with non-Europeans, particularly Africans. When Nazi Germany fell, there were more than six million slaves on German soil, some at first coaxed there by pay or rations but droves of later ones dragged there by force. And in the Protectorate of Bohemia and Moravia Germans had legal exemptions far exceeding the " capitulations " that Europeans had wrung from weaker peoples in Egypt, China, or Morocco. Systematic steps were taken both to rob neighboring peoples of their leadership, as for example by shooting thousands of leading Poles, and to rob whole races of their biological vigor by starvation rations. War had done this often in Europe. Indeed World War One had done it, and that was one reason the Nazis could seize Europe. But now it was done " scientifically."

Europe had become a chamber of horrors, a chamber that would have staggered the imagination of those nineteenth-century philosophers who saw Western, scientific civilization on the threshold of an earthly paradise. But four years of organized violence, followed by a wasted and frittered and futile peace, had left Europe disillusioned, callous, and insensitive. Moreover, there was the risk of being taken in again by propaganda, and the Long Armistice loathed being taken in.

Was there also the frightful fascination of watching others give way freely to one's own repressed and inhibited passions? Were the Western democracies a little hypnotized by seeing their own racial bigotry, moral skepticism, intellectual and esthetic vulgarity, their own demagoguery and worship of success, their flight to irrationality, their hatreds, resentments, and petty blasphemies casting their huge, convulsive, and uncertain shadows on the screen that Hitler was holding up for the biggest shadow show of modern times? It was like witnessing the brutalities and blood lust of a bullfight, morally protected by a justifiable doubt as to whether the bullfight is real, or merely more Hollywood, done with mirrors.

If this is too cruel an interpretation to place on the tolerance the Western democracies showed toward the news of horror that filtered through Nazi censorship, perhaps we can at least surmise that Western man had become a Laodicean, who was neither cold nor

Czechoslovakia, seized Memel from Lithuania, and on September 1, 1939, flung his armies into Poland. The Second World War had begun. At each stage of his aggression he had assured the French and British that this would be his last territorial claim; and because they so longed to avoid war, they believed him. But the rape of Czechoslovakia convinced them they must risk war, and they guaranteed Poland. Now they made good that guarantee, not by defending Poland, which was beyond their power, but by declaring war on the aggressor.

Hitler planned to crush Poland, to avoid a western front, and to convince Britain and France it was not worth fighting over something already accomplished. The French army was unready, and lay waiting in its Maginot Line, demoralized by radio propaganda from Berlin. The British army was almost nonexistent, although the naval war with Hitler was in full progress. Thus, in the West, the German and French armies stood on their guard. " Twilight war," the British called it. " Phoney war," commented the American public. When the phoney war had lasted seven months, Hitler made undeclared war on Norway and Denmark and of course seized both. A month later Holland and Belgium were grabbed, and the weak Chamberlain government in Britain fell. All through the Long Armistice Winston Churchill had warned Britain and France of what was coming, but he had been thrust aside as a wailing Cassandra. Now he came to power.

Hitler's mechanized hordes swept from Belgium into France; the tiny British army was evacuated at Dunkirk; Italian armies invaded France from the southeast; and in a few weeks France had surrendered to Hitler. Since Britain refused to make peace, within six weeks the German air force went to work on British cities. Churchill's Britain, supported by her dominions and colonies, now stood alone. France was under occupation. Russia had signed a nonaggression pact with Hitler before Hitler struck at Poland; and, while he was busy seizing Europe, was herself busy annexing buffer states: a large slice of Poland, a piece of Finland, all of the Baltic " succession states " that Lenin had temporarily sacrificed at Brest-Litovsk in World War One: Lithuania, Latvia, Estonia. America had introduced peacetime conscription, had started " Lend-Lease " aid to Britain, but still hoped it could leave Europe to stew in its own juice, pretty deep juice now and boiling hard. In June, 1941, nearly two years after the rape of Poland, Hitler flung his armies into Russia. The Royal Air Force still disputed the air above the tiny Channel, the narrow moat that kept Hitler's huge armies out of stubborn Britain. Six months later Japan bombed an American fleet at Pearl Harbor; Britain declared war on Japan; Germany, on the United States. These events happened in December, 1941. It was May, 1945, before the Russians, driving back from the Caucasus into Germany, and the Anglo-Americans, driving through North Africa into Sicily and Italy, and in June, 1944, from Britain into Normandy and at last across the Rhine, finally forced Germany to surrender. It was another four months before the long drive of the American navy, army, and air forces, across the wide Pacific, had brought the Japanese to give up a hopeless struggle.

Christendom's second lesson in the cost of dispensing with a common government was somewhat severer than the first. World War One had cost more than eight and a half million lives and more than twenty-one million wounded. World War Two nearly tripled the dead and for the twenty-one million wounded substituted around thirty-four and a half. But these figures do not tell the story. Because of the emergence of modern airpower, many of the dead were now women and children; and the Nazi concentration camp, gas chamber, and slave gang failed, like the bomber, to distinguish between soldier and civilian. In World War One the young men had had to die to protect the lives and property of their families: in World War Two many young men came home to find their families killed and their property destroyed. It was becoming clear that national armies could no longer perform the basic defense function of government, and therefore that national governments could no longer serve the purpose for which they had been set up when the feudal system had failed. Now the nation-state system had failed too. As if to keep Christendom from forgetting its political system had failed, many of the loveliest cities of Europe lay in ruins, and many priceless art treasures that had reminded Europe of what man can be had disappeared from the face of the earth. Whole populations had been uprooted and deported; and the earth swarmed with "displaced persons " and " stateless persons," hungry, diseased, and helpless. Crawl-ing from bomb shelter and house cellar, Europeans were guessing that Man himself might be a displaced person.

It is certain that Man himself was now " stateless," for the simple reason that no existing state could any longer preserve him from what modern war, with its mass weapons of destruction, had be-come. World War Two had left modern man in search of a state, in search of a City in which he might claim again the precious human rights of citizen.

But there was no City anywhere. Where the City should have stood there stood instead two armed camps: the U. S. S. R. and the U. S. A. Must the City remain forever a mirage? The hungry, the cold, the orphaned, the weary, the ill, the dispossessed, and the hunted sought the City in vain, while the " cold war " between Rus-sia and America slowly took form. With cigarettes for money, with rubble for homes, men and women stood in their endless food queues and watched the hope of peace grow dim. The war to save democracy, the war to end war, had ended in 1918 with a League of Nations and a Long Armistice, but no peace. With a sense of despair they had entered the flaming furnace of World War Two, the Ger-mans had terrorized Europe again, the Americans had sent weapons again, had sent armies again, late again, the Germans had broken again, and now there was, not peace, but Armistice Two. They had seen all this before: this, in the American phrase, was where they had come in. There was neither true peace nor a City that could build peace. The nearest thing to a City was another league, this time christened " the United Nations."

The very name of the new league of sovereign states hopefully echoed the names of three governments, the three who drafted its Charter while World War Two was obviously drawing to a close: the United States, the United Kingdom of Great Britain, and the Union of Soviet Socialist Republics. The opening words of the Char-ter, "We, the peoples of the United Nations . . ." hopefully echoed the Preamble of the American Constitution, " We, the People of the United States. . . ." But the telltale Article 2, basing " the organiza-tion " on " the sovereign equality of all its members "— that is, on the sovereign governments to which the new league was responsible — echoed the constitution of no constituted state: instead, Article 2 echoed Article 2 of the Articles of Confederation which the thirteen British colonies had set up in 1777, and had found unworkable, precisely because in their own Article 2 "Each State retains its sovereignty, freedom, and independence...."

Franklin Roosevelt, the founder of the United Nations, died a few weeks before Germany collapsed and a few months before the United Nations Charter was signed at a Conference in San Francisco. He perfectly understood that a league of sovereign powers, as distinguished from a common government of all the men and women in all the component states, could not preserve peace. But he had served in the government of Woodrow Wilson and had watched the Senate reject the League of Nations; and now, twenty-five years later, he was determined that this time America should enter at least a league. Besides, had not the league of thirteen rebellious British colonies transformed itself after trial and error into a genuine government, and all under the title, "United States"? Might not the United Nations do as much? In any case, it seemed unlikely that the American government or people would go further now than a league, as for different reasons it seemed unlikely that the Soviet Union would. For the two world wars that had been such bitter lessons to Europe had reached America in attenuated form. In World War One her loss of life had been relatively slight; the theaters of war lay far from her shores; and the exigencies of war had vastly increased her industrial potential. World War Two cost her more heavily in lives, and much more heavily in treasure; but war orders and government subsidy expanded her industrial potential phenomenally and left her by all odds the most powerful nation on earth. Surely, backed by this enormous strength, her government could do for Americans what Europeans knew their governments could no longer do for them: protect their lives and homes from modern war and from the fury that rains from the sky by night and by day. True, the League of Nations which an American had founded had not been able to keep the peace. But a league which the American government had now joined might be different. This one called for a police force: it "had teeth in it." But as time wore on, there seemed no place in the new league to fit a good denture. The United States and Russia had both wanted to retain the right of veto in the great-power Security Council. And quite naturally. Since the United Nations was not a government capable of regulating the common affairs of men and women throughout the world community, but a league of governments, each retaining if worse came to worst the right to shoot it out, no member government could very well disarm and still meet its moral obligations to its people. The conclusive proof that each government did retain the right to shoot it out lay in the fact that nobody seriously contested the right of each government to retain its armed forces — for defense only, of course.

Meanwhile, there were signs that America and Russia, the two giants whose cold war kept peace precarious, were engaged in perhaps the vastest armament race in history. Only perhaps, for it was difficult to get precise figures. Little was known of Russia except that she had huge resources in manpower, a young but rapidly growing industry, and that she appeared to control a Communist " fifth column " in most foreign countries. America, as in 1941 when Hitler ruled Western Europe, was introducing peacetime conscription. American laboratories rather than munition factories were working full blast, both the laboratories of industry and the laboratories of universities. The whole direction of American scientific inquiry was being redirected toward weapons of war. But, above all, America had " the bomb."

During World War Two, President Roosevelt, learning that Hitler might discover how to apply current knowledge of the structure of the atom to the manufacture of superbombs that could overwhelm the democracies, authorized huge expenditures for secret work on atomic bombs. The work was successful, although too late to affect the war in Europe. After Roosevelt's death, when the war with Japan was drawing to its close, the Army Air Forces dropped two of the new atomic bombs on Japan. The first struck Hiroshima and obliterated 60 per cent of the city: between 70,000 and 80,000 men, women, and children were killed or missing. Two days later a second plane dropped a second atomic bomb on Nagasaki: between 35,000 and 40,000 persons were lost. The threat of further atomic bombs was followed by prompt surrender, and World War Two was over.

The press hailed the " Atomic Age." The people were told that much more destructive bombs than those used could be manufactured, and that there was no defense against them. They were also told that the newly discovered techniques for releasing atomic energy meant a source of power capable of bringing a golden age if it could but be directed to peaceful uses. For reasons of national security the engineering process of building the bombs was kept a deadly secret, and estimates were promptly made of how long it would take other governments, particularly the Russian government, to discover the process independently. A favorite estimate was five years — that is, till 1950.

There were military men who depreciated the deadliness of the bomb, who preferred incendiaries, or who guessed that biological warfare, the spreading of deadly diseases, some of them newly developed for that purpose, might kill more people more quickly and more cheaply than atomic bombs could. But those scientists who knew most about the bomb were convinced that it was quite capable of destroying civilization and they clamored for a final elimination of war.

Whatever the relative merits of the bomb as against biological warfare, for example, as the best means of quickly eliminating large populations, or indeed of rendering large areas incapable of supporting life, whether human, animal, or vegetable, to millions of people the "A-bomb" was the needed symbol. It convinced them that war, which had before appeared a brutal if regrettable necessity, was now a useless form of suicide. They believed the statement that in World War Three, a term now frequently employed, the conquered would be wiped out, while the "victor" would be only 90 per cent destroyed. And in larger and larger numbers they began to turn to a proposal which for decades they had brushed aside as "starry-eyed idealism." Unofficial opinion polls showed that even in unscarred, remote, and powerful America, a majority of the people wanted a federal world government capable of preventing war. Two world wars had not convinced them that war could ever be abolished; but two atomic bombs convinced them that war had to be abolished. Two world wars had not convinced them that world government was possible, whether it was desirable or not; but two atomic bombs convinced them that it was necessary.

But how could it be got? Lenin had offered world government: a world-wide federation of Communist republics. The nucleus of that world-wide federation already existed: the Union of Soviet Socialist Republics. Prerequisites: the destruction of the exploiting bourgeoisie, who held down the working class by force and chicanery; and the establishment, perhaps temporary, of the " dictatorship of the proletariat." In short, Communist revolution on the Russian model. But the peoples of Western Europe shrank from that solution. Even Lenin would have expected the " possessing " class to shrink; but the bulk of the proletariat shrank too. Lenin — or, now Stalin — was inviting them to give up something the Russians had never had: political freedom. And most men and women turned, not to Communism, but to democratic socialism. They hoped and believed that they could obtain the economic justice the Communists promised, without sacrificing the political freedom, the civil rights, the representative institutions and responsible government that were among the proudest achievements of Western Europe. As for overseas Christendom, as for the United States at least, Americans were chanting the praises of private enterprise, or, as businessmen preferred to call it, " free enterprise," and nobody clamored for free enterprise more loudly than those who had managed to erect a monopoly.

How could world government be got? Hitler had offered world government, a Prussianized version based on the " short and lively wars " of Frederick the Great, on the " blood and iron " of Bismarck, on a hierarchy of races, on a hierarchy of classes. It would offer little freedom and less equality, but it offered the proven German genius for enforcing political order and for organizing machine production. Undoubtedly, of those men and women in the countries Hitler had seized and occupied, many who were guilty of " collaborating " with Hitler's Nazis were swayed not only by fear, or greed, or hatred of Communism, but by recognition that the system of sovereign nation-states had broken down twice in a generation and should be scrapped. Europe certainly, and the whole world to a lesser extent, had been knit into one small and crowded community by Science and the Machine. Somebody had to govern it: the rapid conquests of Hitler suggested that maybe he could do it. At the beginning of the Long Armistice, had not Oswald Spengler pointed out, in his *Decline of the West,* that Western Christendom was growing old, as other civilizations before it had grown old; and that, just as those others had turned to the world conqueror to enforce peace, so the Western World was now inexorably entering the Age of the Caesars? When he had written, most people had brushed his book aside: they were still confident they could forget the horror of World War One, rebuild a genuine and durable peace, and re-capture the intoxicating optimism of the glittering and successful nineteenth century. But now, in the midst of World War Two, could they be so sure? Was the only alternative to Lenin's offer per-haps Hitler's offer? Might not his rule, if loyally accepted, eventu-ally discover the necessity for granting political liberty and a modi-cum of economic justice too?

The first World War had been " the war to end war." The second had been a war to end Hitler. Would the third be a war to end civili-zation? Men read Spengler again, and even more men read Arnold Toynbee's *Study of History* and *Civilization on Trial*. Even in America, armed with a stockpile of atomic bombs, and grimly wag-ing cold war on Russia, the only other Titan among the great pow-ers — even in rich and comfortable America, miraculously avoiding or postponing the expected postwar depression, men asked whether Western civilization would survive. And men knew now, what their ancestors had so often denied, that America was part of that civili-zation. After World War One, America had sullenly withdrawn and had refused to enter the League of Nations. After World War Two, she had somewhat grimly entered League Two, the United Nations. But even that did not suffice: trained by Roosevelt's " Lend-Lease " during the War, the Congress astonished itself and the world by voting billions as a free gift to rebuild the economy of Europe. It justified itself by reflecting that this handsome gesture of solidarity would save Western Europe from collapsing, going Communist, and falling into the hands of the Soviet Union. World War One had cost billions, and had left a trail of ten billions in debts owed Amer-ica, almost none of which could be paid. American investors then poured other billions into rehabilitating the German economy, and lost most of their money. World War Two cost more than one and one-tenth trillions of dollars, with property damage of nearly one-fourth of a trillion; but America's share was a paltry third of a tril-lion, followed by a still more paltry six billions of postwar aid — with more to come. Still, even in money value, Armistice Two had come high. And underneath those cold figures lay the memory of the

young men who had died in the American sector of that long Western Front in 1918; of the Tomb of the Unknown Soldier erected in
America, as in other lands; and of the brutal fact that in effect Americans had dug up the bodies of those young men in 1941, restyled
their uniforms and combat helmets, handed them more terrible
weapons, and sent them forth to suffer death a second time. Net result: Armistice Two. Could anything, men asked, short of world
government, end this bloody farce?

The answer of history appeared to be an emphatic No. But how
set one up? For centuries men had dimly or partially seen the problem. Dante had dreamed of a universal, Christian state, in place of
the little warring states that he saw about him, tearing the Italian
community to shreds. Henry IV of France backed old Sully's
" Great Design " of a European league. A stream of peace plans had
run through the centuries. Montesquieu and Rousseau, in the eighteenth century, saw the way in which a community cut up into sovereign states might secure common government: by federation. It
remained for the Founding Fathers of the American Union to apply
the principle of federation to a concrete historical situation. It was
repeatedly applied again. The federal principle was America's chief
contribution to world civilization.

During the Long Armistice of 1918–1939, men began to see that
a very old problem had appeared in new and terrible form. The
problem in general terms was how to replace anarchy with government, and Hobbes' seventeenth-century statement seemed still valid:
it must be done either by submitting to a conqueror like Hitler or
by common action and agreement, as had been done in the Founding Convention at Philadelphia. Alexander Hamilton, in the first of
the *Federalist* papers, recognized that at Philadelphia the second
method was on trial, and on trial for all mankind. But since then
modern technology had made the whole planet a much tighter community physically than the thirteen colonies had been. Radio had
made communication instantaneous. The airplane had made transportation feel almost instantaneous, whether the plane carried pas-
sengers, goods for commerce, or bombs for war. An intricate technology had made all countries dependent on each other; and sometimes
the dependence was a matter of life and death. A few weeks after
Japanese bombers had swarmed over Pearl Harbor and hurled

America into World War Two, Americans received a rude lesson
in the technological interdependence of countries. They had thought
of America as an exception or near-exception to the rule: surely the
American economy, enjoying the resources of a continent, was self-
sufficient. But it appeared that the very rubber in their tires, without
which their cars would apparently not run, came largely from Ma-
laysia. That discovery ranks not far behind the bombing of Hiroshima in convincing the American people that America might be in
a state of interdependence with the rest of mankind, and might have
to care what happened to that mighty neighborhood.

The problem which confronted the generation of Armistice Two,
the first generation of the Atomic Age, was clearly the oldest political problem of all: how to find government for a community that
lacked it, even if each fraction of the community already lived under a government of its own. It had been solved by tribes that had
merged to form a village, by villages that had merged to form city-
states like those of Renaissance Italy, by city-states that had merged
to form empires or to form sovereign nation-states. Now it was nation-states, not villages, that were the governed fractions of an un-
governed community. What was terribly new about the problem
was that this time the community was world-wide, bound together
for weal or woe by modern science, modern technology, and the
clamorous needs of modern industry. When twentieth-century man
confronted the old problem in this new form, his imagination reeled.
Even Woodrow Wilson, who held that "America was created to
unite mankind," had hoped that the armed fractions of the world
community, the sovereign nation-states, could govern the world in
peace, if united by solemn covenant in a league. Even this close student of the American Constitution, which the men of Philadelphia
set up when the "League of Friendship" was failing, as all previous
leagues in history had failed, could not apply the argument of Alexander Hamilton to a whole planet, could not grasp the force of
Hamilton's argument that the price of peace is justice, the price of
justice is law, that the price of law is government, and that government must apply law to men and women, not merely to subordinate
governments. Now Wilson's League One and Roosevelt's League
Two had vindicated Hamilton. They had authority only over sovereign governments and none over the men and women crowded to-

gether on a shrinking planet. The world community was crying for a government. Only its fractions, the nation-states, possessed governments, and no one of those governments could any longer protect its citizens, unless it conquered the other governments. Faced with this frightful danger, the various sovereign governments developed the schizophrenia that Churchill had already noted in the world of 1914: they made desperate efforts to co-operate for peace, they made equally desperate efforts to prepare for possible aggression, and these two desperate efforts canceled each other out — and thereby increased the desperation of each effort.

Small wonder that, with the atomic bomb to stimulate the sluggish imagination of man, more and more men recognized that the choice lay between world government and World War Three. The small number who had pleaded for it in the Long Armistice or during World War Two had been denounced as crackpots for their pains. The bomb destroyed that accusation, along with the women and children of Hiroshima. Many agreed with Toynbee that there would be world government soon in any case, either by war and conquest, establishing world despotism, or by the free and deliberate choice of the peoples of the world, who would set up a common government as the thirteen colonies had set up a common government. By 1949 there was widespread public discussion of how to set up a federal world republic.

The arguments that had been advanced against this heroic enterprise during the Long Armistice now sounded thin. In those days the French statesman Briand could not even persuade the sovereign states of Europe to federate. Differences of language, ancient traditions of mutual animosity, made such plans sound silly. There had always been wars in Europe, and there always would be. But World War Two taught people there had emphatically not always been wars like World War Two. What had seemed to be the chimerical dream of " idealists " now looked like the most urgent task of a generation. It was the belief that civilization could survive the next war, and the belief that a league like the United Nations could preserve peace, that began to appear idealistic and starry-eyed. Europeans looked eastward, and most of them shuddered at the approach of Russia and Communist dictatorship. They looked westward and shuddered scarcely less at what seemed to them the anachronistic and aggressive capitalism of America. They looked downward and saw the possible battlefield of these two forces. With their countries impoverished and their governments impotent to defend them, they turned to federation, at least of Western Europe if not of the whole world.

In the harsh light of Armistice Two, they were beginning to discern the real difficulties of the problem instead of the imaginary ones men used to talk about. Languages were no insurmountable obstacle, as witness the federated Swiss with their three tongues. It is true that the French and Germans had a long habit of intermittently shooting each other, but they were powerfully united too by a common desire to live. The bill for intermittent shootings was steadily mounting: heroic remedies were growing popular. Tariff wars and currency wars were growing less popular as their results grew more devastating. Common defense forces were beginning to look like the only defense forces worth paying good tax-money to maintain. These were not the real difficulties. It was not the kind of words people used when they talked; or the kind of paper money with which they bought, or tried to buy, food; or the wretched privilege of paying for ineffectual national armaments — it was not these things that stood in the way. It was the tug of war between four major ideologies and their subdivisions that made the problem tough, at the very moment that this same tug of war exacerbated international tensions and made a world government even more imperative. These ideologies can be briefly and inaccurately labeled Democracy, Communism, Fascism, and Christianity. They were respectively based on the writings or sayings of John Locke, Karl Marx, Adolf Hitler, and Jesus Christ. Their official living spokesmen appeared to be Truman, Stalin, Franco, and the Pope. All of them had supporters in nearly every country. Between them they disputed the soul of Western Man.

Anglo-American democracy was sired by Adam Smith out of John Locke. It stood for self-government, free elections, the secret ballot, a free press, freedom of assembly, guaranteed civil rights, freedom from arbitrary arrest and secret trial, free competition between political parties, a free market in which to buy and sell, freedom to worship according to one's individual conscience. It was the heir of the English revolutions of the seventeenth and eighteenth centuries and the French Revolution of the eighteenth. In America it fiercely declaimed Adam Smith's arguments against government intervention in business and Locke's arguments for the sanctity of private property. In Western Europe, though hardly at all in America, it shared Adam Smith's and Locke's provisos: that if government should not control business, it followed that government should not grant it subsidies, tariffs, and other monopolies; that businessmen make poor statesmen, because they are too concerned with their private advantage; that the individual's property is sacred only if genuine opportunity exists for those without property to acquire some of their own. In Western Europe, democracy was surer than in America that the Industrial Revolution had happened, that it encouraged dangerous monopoly, that the right to employment was a kind of "property" proper to every citizen. Both in Europe and America democracy condemned totalitarian government, dictatorship, secret police, concentration camps, the police state. In Europe it was steadily turning to socialism; in America it clung, often with an hysteria that baffled Europe, to private capitalism.

International Communism, with headquarters at Moscow, sought a world-wide revolution of the working class against those who exploited their labor for profit or interest, saw in the political and civil rights so precious to the Democrat only the hypocritical devices of a ruling and exploiting class; accepted violence and deceit as the necessary weapons of class war; accepted dictatorship and secret police as necessary also; viewed the collapse of capitalism as inevitable; held that Communism was the only genuine "democracy," since it and it alone governed in the interests of the working class, the overwhelming majority of the people; hated the heresy of West European democratic socialism even more than the heathenism of capitalist America, because the heretic is always more dangerous to the faithful than the heathen is; denounced religion as an opiate of the people; and, in Russia at least, obviously accepted Marxian materialism, not as a working political hypothesis but as a dogmatically held religious faith, organized on an authoritarian basis, with the obligation to evangelize by the word and by the sword.

Fascism was basically a reaction against Communism; accepted the political devices of Communism; had no carefully worked-out doctrine, as Communism had; was strongly nationalistic and traditionalist; was anti-Christian, like Communism, in spirit, but had proved skillful in making its peace with the Vatican, and even in defending the Vatican's interests against Communists. What universal applicability it possessed it derived from its opposition to the powerful internationalism of Communism. Now that Hitler and Mussolini were dead, and their Nazi and Fascist parties dispersed, only a few rulers like Franco, the head of a cruel but weak Spanish state, remained to exemplify its supremacy. It still looked to many men who openly professed Democracy to be perhaps the necessary device for coping with the destructive class war of the Communists. These democrats usually declined to distinguish between Communist totalitarianism and Fascist totalitarianism. Their methods were indeed similar, even though their theoretical aims were poles apart.

The claims of Christianity were most frequently and most vigorously asserted by the Pope. Neither the Protestant churches nor the Orthodox churches nor the Jewish community were organized monarchically to speak promptly and with a single voice. But the Roman Catholic Church was. Like the Communist Party, and like the Fascist national state, it was organized on authoritarian and hierarchical lines. Its creed was in flat contradiction with the materialist creed of Communism, and it ceaselessly denounced the Communist creed. Shorn of the last vestiges of temporal power in 1871, it still exercised enormous political influence in Western Christendom and possessed a longer political experience than any other institution. It had denounced Fascism too, wherever the Fascist incautiously assailed it; but liberal democrats charged it with finding means of coming to terms with Fascism, as in Spain, in their common attack on Communists. It attacked the evils of Western capitalism. It had never been enthusiastic about liberalism; and, wherever it was strong enough, it did not hesitate to cast aside freedom of religion, or at least the freedom of Protestants to worship in public. It issued periodic appeals to Protestants to return to their allegiance to Rome. It watched narrowly the recrudescence of the " schismatic " Russian Orthodox Church, well aware that a thrust of Orthodoxy into Western Europe would leave Rome in the apparent position of defending the evils of capitalism. To many Protestants and Jews it seemed inattentive to any appeal to unity in Christendom or the world which did not base itself on common allegiance to Rome.

Yet most of the men who now inhabited a shrinking, crowded planet were neither Catholic, Protestant, nor Jewish. Could they preserve a Pilgrim City that had now expanded to the ends of the earth and included, whether they liked it or not, liberal democrats, Communists, Fascists under new names, and men of many religious faiths? Arnold Toynbee suggested that they might. Examining the problem in 1948, he asked:

> What shall we do to be saved? In politics, establish a constitutional co-operative system of world government. In economics, find working compromises (varying according to the practical requirements of different places and times) between free enterprise and socialism. In the life of the spirit, put the secular super-structure back onto religious foundations. Efforts are being made in our Western world today to find our way towards each of these goals.... Of the three tasks, the religious one is, of course, in the long run by far the most important, but the other two are the more urgent.... The political task is the most urgent of all.... *

The leading statesmen of the Middle World, the world that lay either geographically or ideologically between America and Russia, publicly agreed with their peoples that it was imperative to " establish a constitutional co-operative system of world government." But how could this possibly be done without the leadership of the two states that dwarfed the power and resources of the others? How could this be done without America and Russia? And though public-opinion polls appeared to indicate that the American people were ready, their government apparently was not. And their government could always offer the excuse that the Russian government would turn down the invitation, even if this excuse required the gift of prophecy.

There were increasing signs that a beginning might be made by a common federal government for Western Europe. But some governments of Western Europe, forced by the wrack of war to become economic clients of America, feared that " Western Union " might precipitate invasion by Russia, intent on preventing the consolidation of an anti-Russian bloc. In such an invasion they would face Communist sabotage at home and a quick defeat before America could

* From *Civilization on Trial* by Arnold Toynbee, copyright 1948 by the Oxford University Press, Inc.

hope to protect them. That American atomic bombs might later wipe out Russia's cities seemed somehow to be inadequate compensation for that ordeal. The problem therefore seemed to remain on the laps of America and Russia. It was a horribly difficult problem. Could they afford not to attempt a solution? Some men suggested that constitutional governments, as distinguished from despotic ones, can be established only where there is already a sense of community, a sense of common belief and purpose, not merely physical proximity. But was that common sense of purpose likely to emerge from a cold war? These men retorted that Russia and America must stop the cold war and learn to co-operate peacefully without a common world government, with nothing nearer government than League Two, the United Nations. But Russia and America were both caught in a vicious circle. The absence of common government threw each back on its own measures of "defense"; and neither could take those measures without endangering the other and forcing the other's pace, and hence its own. This would have been true even if there had been no war of ideas: it would have been true if both had been capitalist, or both Communist, or both Fascist, or both indeed Catholic. The Russo-American armament race was not, after all, the first armament race in history. It was merely the first armament race that had not yet had time to produce intolerable strain, an insoluble clash of interests, an "incident," and war. And Toynbee had all the historical evidence on his side when he declared that war at this stage of the Pilgrim City's pilgrimage would spell despotic world government. This looked like the last chance to choose freedom by deliberately and bravely establishing justice, justice in the whole new world community, the mighty neighborhood.

Could any other course of political action commend itself to common sense? There were doubtless some democrats who dreamed that a victorious war might end dictatorships forever. But could democratic, liberal institutions survive the kind of war men had every right to expect? They were having a harder and harder time surviving the cold war of Armistice Two. There were doubtless men who dreamed that the destruction of Communist Russia would leave the world free to be saved by capitalism; but European capitalism had scarcely survived World War Two. Would capitalism anywhere survive World War Three? There were doubtless fanatical Fascists who would accept almost any catastrophe provided Communist Russia could be smashed; but was that dream more than fantasy? There were doubtless fanatical Catholics who would accept an atomic apocalypse as the just retribution of a civilization that had whored after strange gods and could learn only by universal catastrophe to submit again, or for the first time, to the authority of Mother Church. Can many Catholics have expected Providence to choose this way of chaos? As a matter of fact, could not the battle of ideologies be more fruitfully fought out under law than under arms? Would universal violence advance anybody's cause? Would it advance the cause of John Locke, or of Karl Marx, or of Adolf Hitler, or of Jesus Christ? It appeared most doubtful that it would. None of them, except Jesus Christ, could be supposed even by his followers to have foreseen the kind of military weapons man would build by the middle of the twentieth century.

Perhaps it was too late in the cold war for governments to take the risk of leading their peoples to a peaceful solution. Talk of peaceful solutions was a bad way to prepare civilian morale for what bade fair to be so much the most awful war in history that the ancient and terrible word, war, might not be fit to name it. Yet if government did not act, who could? The sword of Damocles hung, for the first time in recorded history, over a civilization that had knit together the whole of mankind. This challenge provoked responses in many lands. Among the more interesting was a proposal that came out of Britain, that land of political proposals.

A group of Members of Parliament, convinced that time was running out, became equally convinced that their own leaders, though they understood the disease and had pronounced the remedy, dared not in the then circumstances of the cold war issue the necessary call for a constitutional convention of all nations. They thereupon determined to rally opinion to a popular initiative. Remembering the unofficial Peace Ballot of 1935, in which eleven and a half million Britons had cast their ballots, these Members of Parliament determined in 1947 to organize a similar ballot to choose delegates to a People's World Constituent Assembly, to meet in 1950 and attempt to draw up a constitution under which mankind might govern itself. They immediately pledged influential Britons to campaign for places in the British delegation. They discussed with groups similar to theirs, in a dozen other countries, preparations for choosing delegates from those countries. They hoped to persuade even America to participate, and they extended invitations to all countries, including Russia. If a constitution could be agreed upon, it would be submitted to the various governments of the world for ratification by local constitutional process.

They were under no illusion that their effort was more than a forlorn hope in a period when all other hopes seemed more forlorn. They estimated they would have to raise a million pounds to finance their British campaign and enlist half a million volunteer workers. The task was appalling. But they were members of the Mother of Parliaments, with a deep faith in the common sense of the common man. They had ample evidence of the vast sense of fear and frustration that gripped their own constituencies and that gripped the peoples of the world. And there was a vicious circle, a deadlock, that had to be broken, a deadlock that they believed could not be broken until the imaginations of millions had been moved, and until governments could count on solid and informed support for the joint action they must take.

A banner had been raised, a banner to which all the millions of men and women could rally and under which they could act together in a common cause, the establishment of law in the world community. That a hundred members of the British Parliament endorsed that banner was a political phenomenon that would have left the nationalistic nineteenth century dazed and incredulous. It would daze many men of the twentieth century, who had begun to wonder whether democratic government could any longer cope even with local, national problems, much less with those of a world gone mad. For few had discovered that most national problems were no longer soluble by national governments in a world tottering and divided and terrified, and that therefore political action had become frustrated and futile. Now somebody was pointing a way out of the madhouse the world had become, out of frustration, futility, folly, and famine. The way was by no means foolproof, but at least it made sense. At least it substituted common action for individual paralysis and despair.

The way out could not bring heaven to earth. But the men of the twentieth century, except perhaps for Communists, did not expect to bring heaven to earth, as their fathers had expected to on the eve of World War One. World government was clearly not the sufficient cause of a good society; it was only the necessary condition for the survival of the present society, leaving it some time and some energy to think of more interesting things than mere survival. And while the British Parliamentary Committee sought to arouse a popular initiative, in one small part of the planet even the national governments began to perceive that the alternatives were to "federate or perish." In Western Europe, where modern civilization had been born and whence it had spread, with various degrees of dilution, over the whole globe, moves toward a "Western Union" began to occur. While Moscow fulminated against world government as a bourgeois conspiracy to stave off an inevitable proletarian revolt, while the American government evaded the issue with weasel words about "the reign of law," the statesmen of Western Europe began to plan.

Modern Russia and modern America alike had been called into being by Western Europe. Russia had been attacked by Europeans under Charles XII of Sweden, under Napoleon I of France, under Emperor William II of Germany, and under Adolf Hitler; but she had been attacked more successfully by the Western techniques which Peter the Great had brought back from the dangerous West, by the industrial revolution that had penetrated from the same West, by the Communist ideology of the German Karl Marx, and by all that the observant eyes of Lenin saw before his return from exile in that same dangerous West. In large measure Eastern Orthodox Christendom had been made over in the image of Western Europe. Meanwhile, in the West, Europe had called into being another giant, bone of her bone, flesh of her flesh, the United States of America, innocent or nearly innocent of some of her greatest traditions, fabulously rich in money and machines, half frightened of her own power and vast new responsibilities, at times movingly helpful, at times frighteningly insensitive.

Now these two giants appeared to be girding themselves for a struggle, and a struggle over Europe's already prostrate form. The prospect of a common and probably final catastrophe aroused a sort of common West European patriotism, and increasing pressure for a common government and a common economy. The American government was underwriting European economic recovery, and the pressure of the recovery program was toward a rehabilitation that would ignore national frontiers. The fear of Russian armed force was driving American opinion toward underwriting Western Europe militarily as well as financially. Political unity for Western Europe had become common talk. It would not of course solve the problem of a common government for the world-wide civilization that had sprung from Europe's womb. But it would be perhaps a step toward such government; and in any case it was in itself necessary if Europe was to revive. If Europe's colonies and former colonies could be included, it could be a considerable step indeed.

Underneath and behind the practical considerations that forced Europe to examine her common memories, lay those memories themselves. Memories of the cathedrals that had sprung from Europe's common soil, dedicated to saints revered in common, regardless of petty political frontiers; memories of the Crusades and of Levantine luxury; of a Genoese who had sailed west under a Spanish flag to find an El Dorado that was not Cathay but that would become an English-speaking melting-pot of the millions that would follow him for centuries to come. Memories of the great painters of the Renaissance who had called Europe away from the contemplation of the invisible to delight in what the eye beheld; of Luther and Calvin and the others, calling on her to turn back and search her soul; of Erasmus laughing at man's folly, of Shakespeare and Racine painting his glory and misery, of Galileo reaching for the stars; of the dark deeds of Christian slave-traders on the coasts of Africa; of the conquest of wealthy India, the opening up of the China trade, the settlement by Europeans of once unknown continents; of brutal injustices to primitive colored folk; of the little children worked to death at the new machines, and the raw French recruits of Napoleon surging across Europe, smashing the remains of an outworn feudal system; of new European nations coming to birth, of the hopeful, proud middle-class paradise of the nineteenth century, so rudely smashed by two World Wars; of the common resistance against the Nazi, the common torture of the concentration camps, and the common indignities of the postwar world. It was this Europe, with these memories, that bade fair now to be the Balkans of the future, petty states with *opéra-bouffe* politics, worked by strings from Washington or Moscow. Even those Europeans who prayed in no cathedral, who remembered no Crusade, who had scarce heard of Columbus or Luther, of Erasmus or Shakespeare or Galileo or Leonardo — even those Europeans sometimes dimly knew that Europe was the cradle of what men called civilization and that it was tottering to its ruin. Even they felt obscurely that this time neighbors must close ranks, must lend each other a helping hand, if the Pilgrim City was to resume its long and arduous pilgrimage.

BIBLIOGRAPHICAL NOTE

THE foregoing pages have traced briefly the course of a great human tradition, a body of ideas. Those ideas have been debated, have been applied, have been embodied in institutions, have guided the acts of men, have helped them to read events, and to support disaster. The reader who would explore this tradition further can do it by reading two types of books. There is, first, the vast literature of histories, biographies, and reference works catalogued in such bibliographical compilations as the *Guide to Historical Literature* (*1931*), edited under the auspices of the American Historical Association by Dutcher, Shipman, Fay, Shearer and Allison. In this direction one may seek the particular and the specific with which history by its nature deals: the date, the place, the act, the name.

But history sends us also in another direction, to the general ideas by which men have lived; and it is when men have seen the world clearly by the light of those ideas that they have acted greatly. To the reader who would see his own world and the world of his forebears by that light, I would recommend a quite different choice of books. I would recommend those books which clearly reflect that light. They will be his surest guides in deciding which dates, which places, which acts, and which names, of the millions recorded by historians, are most significant and relevant for him.

I therefore list below a few books of this sort, written during the period covered by the present work. I have listed only those that are presently available in English. Precisely because so many readers have found in these books the great ideas which have guided Western Civilization, most of them have been made available in inexpensive editions, in such series as Everyman (E. P. Dutton), World Classics (Oxford Press), or Modern Library (Random House). I have omitted contemporary books dealing with earlier periods, even where they exhibit greatness, as does R. H. Tawney, for example, in

Religion and the Rise of Capitalism (Harcourt, Brace). But I have included those that strongly reflect the author's own times, as do the works of Gibbon, Spengler, and Toynbee. Practically all of the books listed occur in the foregoing narrative. A few are now considered too difficult for people to read, unless they have previously taken a " course " in something or other. I urge the reader to ignore this myth.

Here is the suggested short list:

THOMAS AQUINAS, *Summa Theologica*
FRANCIS OF ASSISI, *Little Flowers*
THOMAS À KEMPIS, *Imitation of Christ*
DANTE, *The Divine Comedy*
CHAUCER, *Canterbury Tales*
MARCO POLO, *Travels*
MACHIAVELLI, *The Prince*
The Bible
The Book of Common Prayer
LUTHER, *Addresses*
CALVIN, *Institutes of the Christian Religion*
MORE, *Utopia*
BOCCACCIO, *The Decameron*
RABELAIS, *Gargantua*
ERASMUS, *The Praise of Folly*
LEONARDO DA VINCI, *Notebooks*
CELLINI, *Autobiography*
GALILEO, *Two New Sciences*
MONTAIGNE, *Essays*
CERVANTES, *Don Quixote*
MARLOWE, tragedies
SHAKESPEARE, plays and poems
BACON, *Novum Organum; New Atlantis*
GROTIUS, *On the Law of War and Peace*
MILTON, *Paradise Lost*
DESCARTES, *Discourse on Method*
PASCAL, *Pensées*
RACINE, tragedies
MOLIÈRE, comedies
HOBBES, *Leviathan*

LOCKE, *Second Treatise of Government*
SWIFT, *Gulliver's Travels*
VOLTAIRE, tales
GIBBON, *The Decline and Fall of the Roman Empire*
HUME, *Treatise of Human Nature*
BOSWELL, *The Life of Samuel Johnson*
ADAM SMITH, *The Wealth of Nations*
KANT, *Perpetual Peace*
GOETHE, *Faust*
HAMILTON, MADISON, JAY, *The Federalist*
ROUSSEAU, *The Social Contract*
MILL, *On Liberty*
THOREAU, *Walden; Civil Disobedience*
MARX, *Capital*
DARWIN, *The Origin of Species*
DOSTOIEVSKI, *The Brothers Karamazov; The Idiot*
TOLSTOI, *War and Peace*
FREUD, *The Interpretation of Dreams*
ELIOT, " The Wasteland " (in *Collected Poems*); *The Idea of a Christian Society*
SPENGLER, *The Decline of the West*
TOYNBEE, *A Study of History; Civilization on Trial*

   Books are, of course, not the only intelligible remains of a civilization. Amidst the wrack of two World Wars, some of Western Civilization's greatest architecture still speaks visibly. In its museums one can still see the glory of its painting, its sculpture, its handicraft. And, thanks to technological advances in recording, whoever can afford a private library of books can afford a private library of recordings; whoever can read the great words of Shakespeare can listen to the great harmonies of Bach.

INDEX

Acadia, Canada, 153, 180, 184, 188
Adages (Erasmus), 72–73
Addison, Joseph (1672–1719), English author, 155, 202, 221
Africa: Italian empire, 316; Moslems, 57; route around, 58, 63; slavery, 64, 223
Agriculture: Austria, 213; England, 158; France, 133, 138; Luther, 46; Middle Ages, 6, 19, 23, 29, 33; Northern Europe, 57
Airplanes, 302, 340
Alba, Duke of, Fernando Alvarez de Toledo (1508–1582), 95, 104, 105
Albert, Prince (1819–1861), Prince consort, 290, 291, 300
Albert of Brandenburg (1490–1545), archbishop, 42–43
Albigensians (sect), 31, 85
Alembert, Jean le Rond d' (1717?–1783), French philosopher, 209, 218, 228
Alsace-Lorraine, 123, 279, 300
America, 220–32; England, 288; immigration, 294–95; industrialism, 294; progress, idea of, 295
American Revolution, 220
Anabaptists (sect), 47, 50, 54, 89
Andes Mountains, 231, 233
Anglican Church. *See* Church of England
Anne (1665–1714), Queen of Great Britain and Ireland, 173–75, 188, 196, 204
Anti-semitism, 319, 320, 321, 326, 328
Antwerp, Belgium, 42, 104
Aquinas, Saint Thomas (1225?–1274), xi, 10, 13–16, 18, 30, 31, 69, 81; *Summas*, 17, 66
Architecture: baroque, 141, 142, 143; Byzantine, 57; Catholic countries, 126; England, 170, 203; France, 141, 142, 143–44, 155; Middle Ages, 24; Renaissance, 70, 77. *See also* Cathedrals
Aristotle (384–322 B.C.), Greek philosopher, 41, 69, 80

Armada, Spanish, 106, 109, 113, 157
Articles of Confederation, 312, 335
Artisans, 8, 12
Arts: Byzantine, 57; Calvinism, 126; England, 170, 202; ethical controls, 68; France, 141, 142, 144, 145, 146, 209–10; Gothic, 74; Greek, 68–69; machine age, 292–93; medieval, 14–16, 29, 57, 74; pope, 37; Renaissance, 41, 74–79; Roman, 68–69; Spain, 111
Aryan race, 326, 330
Asia: Christianization, 58–59
Atomic bombs, 336–37, 339, 342, 347
Augsburg, League of, 151, 188
Augsburg, Peace of (1555), 94, 118, 119, 123
Augustine, Saint (354–430), xi, 6, 15, 148
Austria: Bohemian revolt, 115–16; Conservative Alliance, 269; Croats, 278; Czechs, 278; Denmark, 279; Ferdinand, 96, 99; France, 191, 217, 244; Germany, 323; Grand Alliance, 152–53; Hitler's occupation, 331; Holy Alliance, 273; Italian states, 274–75; Lombardy, 275, 276–77; Magyars, 278; Napoleon I, 252; Poland, 218, 278; Prussia, 213, 277, 278; Quadruple Alliance, 273; Rumanians, 278; Ruthenians, 278; Russia, 217; Saxony, 217; Serbs, 278; Seven Weeks' War, 279; Seven Years' War, 217; Slovaks, 278; Slovenes, 278; Thirty Years' War, 122; Venetia, 275; Victor Emmanuel II, 276; World War I, 301–02; World War II, 331. *See also* Hapsburgs; Metternich, Prince
Austrian Succession War, 189–91
Auto-da-fé, 101, 132
Avignon, France, 37, 244

Bacon, Francis (1561–1626), English philosopher and writer, xi, xii, 208, 252, 295

357

NAPOLEON'S EMPIRE